RAILWAY
MODELLING

RAILWAY MODELLING

Norman Simmons

PSL

Patrick Stephens Limited

AN IMPRINT OF HAYNES PUBLISHING

First published in 1972
Second edition June 1975
Third edition January 1980
Fourth edition September 1981
Fifth edition October 1983
Sixth edition August 1988
Seventh edition 1993
Eighth edition 1998

British Library Cataloguing-in-Publication Data:
A catalogue record for this book
is available from the British Library.

ISBN 1 85260 596 0

The details in this book are to the best of the
author's knowledge and belief both accurately
described and safe. However, great care must
always be taken when assembling electrical
equipment, and neither the publishers nor the
author can accept responsibility for any
accidents which may occur.

All photographs by Len Weal unless
otherwise credited.

Patrick Stephens Limited is an imprint of
Haynes Publishing, Sparkford, Nr Yeovil,
Somerset, BA22 7JJ.
Tel: 01963 440635 Fax: 01963 440001
Int. tel: +44 1963 440635
Fax: +44 1963 440001

E-mail: sales@haynes-manuals.co.uk
Web site: http://www.haynes.com

Typeset by J. H. Haynes & Co. Ltd.

Printed in Great Britain by
J. H. Haynes & Co. Ltd.

Contents

Introduction

The continued unprecedented growth of interest in railway modelling, sustained by new ideas, new techniques, new scales and gauges, and an ever-increasing flow of new products from manufacturers and suppliers, has resulted in the hobby becoming more and more complex.

The variety and apparent intricacy of the hobby can be bewildering to a beginner. But he (or she!) need not be put off or make a false start if time is taken to digest the basics within this book. The amazing scope and variety of the hobby is fully examined, with detailed advice on not only how to recognise problems but also how to tackle or avoid them. Readers can then decide for themselves what type of model railway best suits their need, or their pocket, and how they can make a start.

In the years since this book was first published, it has gone to seven editions, thus exceeding even my best hopes and certainly those of my publisher, and I am more than proud to find that it has now established itself as a classic 'primer' on the hobby. This latest, eighth edition has been revised to take into account as many as possible of the changes which have occurred within the hobby since the previous edition.

The popular image of a model railway is a plaything for children. In many ways this is good since it ensures a steady flow of young recruits to the hobby. Many of today's adult railway modellers, myself included, started with a child's train set. But when you see the highest form of the art, as developed by the leading model railway personalities, you realise that there is more to it than at first meets the eye. Whilst it may not be possible for everyone to reach the same high standard of craftsmanship as set by the hobby's top exponents, the goal is there and is worthy of attainment. Anyone with the slightest glimmer of interest in railways or aptitude as a model maker can find a consuming and worthwhile challenge in railway modelling and is capable of leaving his mark.

Railway modellers are notorious for adapting materials and drawing inspiration from a number of different sources unconnected with the hobby, but to a much larger extent they rely on a healthy supporting trade—commercial manufacturers, suppliers and retailers alike—who provide the basic raw materials and necessary parts for the hobby. The trade is in turn sustained by the modellers. It follows, therefore, that the more railway modellers there are the better it will be for everyone concerned with the hobby. I hope this book will encourage others to take it up and expand the ranks still further.

There has rarely been a more interesting time to take up railway modelling when considering the developments taking place in the full-size railways throughout the world today. Eurostars, Bullet Trains, TGVs, tilting trains, are familiar names to wide sections of the public. As one of the most energy efficient methods of land transport, environmentally friendly and with the ability to obtain high speed point to point journey times unattainable by other means, railways are accepted as having an important role to play well into the foreseeable future. As a subject for modelling there can be few rivals offering such a diverse range of interests.

I would like to acknowledge the assistance of Len Weal, Peter Parfitt, the Railway Enthusiasts' Club, Andy Hart of the SNCF Society, Philip Reid of the Epsom and Ewell MRC, Geoff Helliwell and John Woodman who allowed me to share the pleasure of his layout on so many occasions. I am also indebted to Dr C. G. Sumner and Roger Amos for information incorporated in Chapters 4 and 6 and to Dave Smith of Cove Models who provided much appreciated help and support.

Finally, I must acknowledge all those railway modellers, who write articles for the monthly magazines and take the trouble to exhibit their models and layouts at exhibitons, for the inspiration and encouragement they have unwittingly given.

Norman Simmons
Fleet, Hampshire

CHAPTER 1
What is railway modelling?

Basically speaking, railway modelling is the art of creating in miniature a working replica of a full-size railway. It is perhaps significant that we refer to the subject as *railway* modelling, not train modelling or engine modelling. Herein lies the essence of the difference between railway modelling and most other forms of model making, since we concern ourselves with the railway as a whole. This means the sum of many things—locomotives, coaches, wagons, track, stations, signalling, civil engineering such as bridges, embankments, cuttings, viaducts and tunnels, and the landscape through which the railway passes. All these facets require space in which to set them out and space in which they can be operated. Unlike, say, aero or ship modelling, where a static model is considered as an entity in itself and occupies no more space than the overall dimension of the model or the glass case in which it is often kept, railway modelling has to have sufficient space for all the many individual items to be properly displayed and integrated. Also, all these individual parts take time and money to acquire. Whereas you can become an aeromodeller with quite a modest outlay on one kit and a few simple tools, it takes quite a deliberately conscious effort to decide if you want to take up railway modelling. It is natural, therefore, that you will want to give the subject some careful thought and consideration before you start and before you commit yourself.

Having decided to take up the hobby it might be helpful to consider three important points before you actually begin. Decide what you can afford in three things, namely space, time and money. These considerations will, in many ways, dictate the kind of model railway you will be able to create. If you have space, time and money in abundance then there need be no end to the size, shape, scale and extent of the layout you set out to build, but if any one of these factors is limited it will more than likely have a restricting effect on the model railway. Too little space to spare will cramp the size and possibly the scale of the layout. Too little spare time will limit the amount of equipment you will be able to build yourself and will increase your dependence on the trade or else affect the extent of the layout. Too little money to spare will obviously cut down the amount of ready-made proprietary equipment you will be able to buy and will mean that you will have to construct as many things as you can yourself with the cheapest basic raw materials.

As a model railway is a cumulative thing which builds up gradually over a period of time it is, in my view, vital to consider these three important points before you start so that you know what you are letting yourself in for at the beginning. There is no point in spending a lot of money on expensive equipment because it looks nice in the shops, only to find that there is not enough room at home in which to operate it. Also, it's no good thinking you are going to build the most elaborate layout when you haven't the space to put it in, or the time to spare to keep it properly maintained. Similarly, you cannot expect to build all your track, rolling stock and accessories if you never have time enough in which to do it. In the rush of enthusiasm at the start of a new hobby it is all too easy to gloss over and overlook these points.

I think it is very important not to be too ambitious and to risk over-reaching yourself at the beginning. A model railway is essentially a working model and a great deal of the satisfaction of creating one is, of course, to be able to operate it when it is built. If you are too ambitious to start with, the end may never appear in sight and the struggle against time and the drain on your financial resources may lead to disillusionment and the ultimate abandonment of the project. Learning the hard way like this might lead

you to wasteful scrapping of earlier efforts or, at worst, complete alienation with model railways and the search for another hobby. Although I consider it important to start with modest aspirations, you should always keep the future in sight. In choosing a site for the model railway, for instance, pick one that can be extended later on. A simple project can always be incorporated into a larger scheme at a later date, provided you have given thought to this at the start. Examples of this can be found in a branch line layout which can be incorporated into a larger main line scheme; the extension into the garden of a layout built in a garden shed; the continuation of a layout round the walls of a room or the extension of a track from one baseboard to another. It is very easy to be taken in by the large and complex layouts you see at exhibitions when you first become interested in model railways, but it

GWR pannier tank 5412 heads the daily goods to Winbury. Superb scenic modelling on the REC O gauge layout.

(Photo: Peter Parfitt)

Landscape modelling to perfection in 2mm scale.

is important not to aim too high to begin with and to start with more modest, more easily attainable aims.

Railway modelling is literally a hobby for all ages. It is also one that can be enjoyed by both sexes, although it must be admitted it is more often the pastime of men and boys. Some marvellous work has, however, been done by ladies, some of it self-inspired and self-created but more usually as a contribution to a husband's layout rather than a project that has been started and finished alone. There is more than one exception to this though, and some fine models have been made by ladies. I know of no examples of layouts built by brothers and sisters or mothers and sons (although I expect to be proved wrong) but of course one of the most common relationships in railway modelling is the joint efforts of a father and son. Model railways are an acknowledged favourite pastime for children and, if aided

and encouraged by parents can foster a unique and lasting father/son relationship. I know few other hobbies which can offer so much in bridging the generation gap, always provided that there is the germ of appreciation to begin with. A keen father forcing interest in railway modelling on to an uninterested son can, of course, have the opposite of a beneficial effect, but I fancy that these cases are in the minority. Even if the son later chooses other interests which he finds more absorbing and turns his back on a model railway, leaving the father to carry on alone, I feel sure the first combined efforts, the working side by side and the pooling of ideas, will have helped to create a bond between them.

Railway modelling is an ideal pastime to take up during retirement. The big bugbear of lack of time becomes less of a problem with no business affairs to attend to. Provided that your eyesight and manual dexterity remain reasonably intact the limitations of a fixed retirement income can be compensated for by the time factor, which will allow more opportunity for hand construction and a consequent saving In money. An older person with a store of memories can very often be the envy of younger people when it comes to building historical models. Recollections of day-to-day events are very often of things which were not thought important enough to be recorded at the time and so, therefore, cannot afterwards be found in books. It is often amazing how many details of such commonplace things that occurred as relatively recently as the 1930s can be clouded by time. The colours of GWR stations and the exact shade of green used by the Southern Railway in this period have been the subject of controversy, since precise details of these simple features, because they were so simple, escaped accurate documentation at the time. Anyone with accurate recollections of this period has been listened to with baited breath. We are, of course, all getting older and if we cannot find time now for building the model railway of our dreams it is near to the next best thing to do some quiet research and fact-storing during the odd quiet moments. This can perhaps be put into use when retirement comes along and at long last we can use the time between 9.00 am and 5.00 pm to do some actual modelling.

The hobby can also he very educational in that it develops many latent skills and encourages you to exercise your mind. Planning and building the railway develops the ability to draw, to paint and to create with the hands, as well as promoting craftsmanship, patience, and an understanding of basic handyman techniques. You need not be an artist to be a railway modeller, but in building a model railway you are in a sense creating a three dimensional picture and developing a means of expression and skill, much as an artist does. Attempting to copy faithfully the prototype (which is the expert's word for the original or real thing) develops your powers of observation and an appreciation of everyday things. A train journey to most people seems to be a tiresome thing which has to be endured in order to get from one place to another. A railway modeller, on the other hand, can find it very absorbing, studying things which he knows he is going to model. Subjects as mundane as fencing, hedges, trees, the layout of signals, station furniture, posters, trackwork, station platforms and the formation of trains can all be taken for granted until you have the joy of building them in miniature and then you realise how little you know and just how much detail has simply not been looked at before. The scenic side of railway modelling can help you to develop a tremendous sense of colour; you learn to appreciate the subtle shades that go to make up a grassy meadow or field, trees, foliage, brickwork, concrete, earth, ballast and the surfaces of roads and footpaths. In trying to create these subjects in model form you become aware of what these things are like in real life.

Also, in attempting to follow the full-size railway in depth, modellers need to undertake a degree of research into the prototype. To do other than this is merely playing trains, which is really only scratching the surface. There is currently a vast field of literature on railway and allied subjects, a great deal in public libraries and much more in bookshops up and down the country. Whilst I know some railway modellers have little knowledge of the prototype, and some surprisingly enough take little interest, I feel that to make the whole thing really worthwhile you cannot afford to remain too ignorant of the full-size original of any model you are creating.

There are umpteen railway and model railway clubs throughout Britain and in many other countries of the world. Some of the railway clubs specialise in specific branches of the hobby, for example a particular preservation project like the Bluebell Railway Preservation Society; a former railway company like the Great Western Society; a particular geographical or national location like the Irish Railway Record

Club night in the clubhouse of the Railway Enthusiasts' Club, Farnborough, Hampshire. The N gauge group's layout, Rechorough & Whittleton, receives attention whilst other members relax at the well appointed bar.
(Photo: Peter Parfitt)

Society, or a type of propulsion like the Electric Railway Society, to mention just a few categories and just one example in each. Clubs catering for the model railway hobby are usually organised nationally, or even internationally, and, although they may have their recognised centres or local groups (particularly true of the preservation societies of course), they rely on news sheets and club magazines for maintaining contact between members. There are some similarly organised model railway clubs but the aim of the majority is to provide a permanent meeting place where club members can co-operate in building one or more club layouts. By their very nature, therefore, most model railway clubs are geographically organised and are largely run

to serve the needs of individuals within a given district. Because there are so many, and changes occur so frequently, it is not practical to list them in these pages.

Most of these model railway clubs hold exhibitions from time to time and one way of finding out what railway modelling is all about and how you can go about it is to visit one or more of them. Just one word of warning though, you must remember that in the majority of club exhibitions the staging has been done in members' spare time and with limited resources. Most exhibitions are one or two-day affairs and the exhibitors, who often receive no more reward than the satisfaction of showing their models to others, may have devoted all their available spare time for weeks beforehand as well as during

Above *The Model Railway Club layout Tidmouth Junction specially built with the youngsters in mind, is proving popular at this exhibition.*

Left *A selection of model railway magazine covers.*

the show, with the added risk of damage and pilferage to their models. I take my hat off to the many exhibitors who do take the trouble to show off their work to the delight and pleasure of others. Perhaps because of the limited time available (either because the exhibitor's own time is restricted or, as is more often the case, because the hall where the show is being held can only be hired for a limited period and there is thus insufficient time in which to set up the exhibits), some model railway layouts on display seem to have more than their fair share of gremlins. The floor may not be level, resulting in the baseboards being distorted The power points may not be ideally placed, or some important piece of wiring or paintwork may have got damaged in transit. All of these things can cause trouble which may not reveal itself until the public audience is assembled. The visitor who sees rolling stock derailing or locomotive stalling on point-work may form the wrong impression. The sight of a soldering iron almost permanently plugged in might give the idea that this is always necessary with a model railway but it needn't be and more often than not it isn't. Also exhibitors have to eat on occasions and a break in operating sessions can sometimes only be avoided if the reins are handed over to other less experienced and maybe junior members, who are perhaps not familiar with the controls or the wiring circuit.

Whether by luck or design I don't know, but some exhibitions are better than others and I cannot over-emphasise the necessity of seeing as many as you can and forming your opinion over a period rather than making a snap, hasty judgement after one visit. Model railway exhibitions are in many ways unique in that I know of few other hobbies which give rise to so many. This perhaps demonstrates the attraction of railway modelling as much as anything, and the wide cross-section of people you see at these exhibitions is surely conclusive proof of the universal appeal of the hobby to both sexes of all ages. Perhaps one of the main attractions is that, all things being equal, railway models are *working* models.

At a model railway exhibition you can usually glean some idea of what the organising club is like and you can judge if it is the sort of club you wish to join and whether it is likely to cater for your main interests. Many other clubs nearby are usually invited to exhibit, and should you be thinking of joining one an exhibition is a good way of getting to know those in your district. As well as the local clubs which cater for local interests there are also national clubs which devote themselves to specialist model fields, such as the N Gauge Society or the Gauge O Guild. There are also many full-size railway clubs, preservation societies, etc, that embrace model railways as part of their interests and models are often used to promote the clubs' aims. I enjoy enormously visiting exhibitions. The amount of effort and enthusiasm that is in evidence is often quite staggering and everyone is co-opted into making the exhibition an entertaining affair for the public, from the local dignitary who is often invited to open the show, to the sisters, girl-friends, wives and mothers who run the refreshment counter.

Railway modelling is usually regarded as a highly individual form of modelling in that the modeller works unseen at home amidst his own family and home surroundings, but if you are in need of companionship, the local model railway club may provide just what you are looking for. As a means of acquiring information, hints and tips, ideas, encouragement and sometimes even assistance, there is no better advice I can give than to seek out and join your local club. If there isn't one nearby then I humbly suggest that an advertisement in the local paper or in one or more of the various hobby magazines is more than likely to find someone else of like mind who is willing to join forces with you in starting a club of your own. New clubs are being formed all the time, as you will discover from becoming a regular reader of the hobby magazines.

There is a very comprehensive selection of British magazines devoted entirely to the hobby of model railways. The longest running is *Railway Modeller* which started publication in 1949. Details of all current magazines can be found in Appendix 2. Whereas some magazines aim to be comprehensive which may result in an overlap in the type of content matter one with another, others set out to cover a clearly defined niche in the hobby. As it may not always be readily apparent from their titles you really need to see copies of them all and approach each one with an open mind before deciding the ones that best cover your particular interest. Many more magazines covering the model railway hobby are published overseas in languages appropriate to their country of origin. Devotees of overseas railways can have access to most of these through specialist magazine importers but more immediately available is the UK published magazine specialising in overseas railways, *Continental Modeller.*

I would regard a regular subscription to one if not all of these magazines as essential if you wish to find out more about the hobby and keep abreast of the many new developments which are forever taking place. The classified advertisements often provide opportunities to purchase second-hand equipment with which you can make a start in the hobby, and the advertisements of the many manufacturers and retailers keep you informed of the steady flow of new products, of which the hobby never seems short, The main feature articles showing the achievements of modellers are a constant source of inspiration and there is usually a wealth of prototype information, photographs and drawings on which you can base your own models. The regular receipt of each new magazine is an event to which I personally have always looked

The Railway Enthusiasts' Club's extensive N gauge layout 'Recborough and Whittleton' runs a mix of proprietary, kit and scratch built models. The Class 33 and DMU seen here are by Graham Farish.

(Photo: Peter Parfitt)

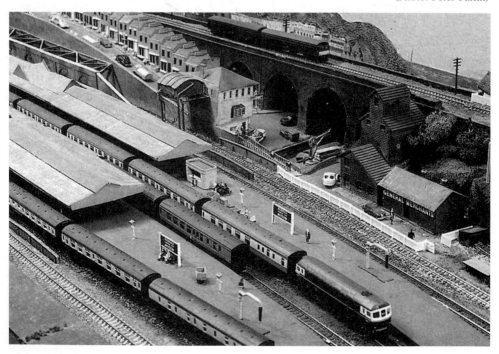

The LMS Lickey Banker 0-10-0 'Big Bertha' and the LNER Garratt 2-8-8-2T were both solitary members of their respective classes. Nevertheless 4mm scale kits have been produced as shown by these made up models of DJH kits.

forward for most of my life and still I can find something new and interesting in every new edition. I am sure much of the expansion in the model railway hobby in recent years has been due to the specialist press, and in return they rightly deserve the support of every modeller.

Reference has already been made to the trade, to both manufacturers and retailers, and the importance of a thriving model railway industry cannot be over-emphasised. However much you may aim to avoid the

use of commercially produced models and to construct your own model railway as far as possible, there are almost bound to be some items which will have to be bought. The super craftsman may stop at nothing, and even produce his own locomotives and rolling stock. Maybe a few even think nothing of casting and turning their own wheels and building an electric motor, but I am willing to bet that very few individuals have drawn their own rails! Most scratch-build modellers who work from basic raw

The inviting interior of Cove Models, Farnborough, Hants, typical of many model railway retailers throughout the country.

(Photo: Peter Parfitt)

materials, rather than using kits or adapting commercially produced models, incorporate ready-made parts such as wheels, motors, and ready-mixed paint and transfers in their finished models. Even the raw material itself would in some cases be difficult to obtain if it were not for the services of the model railway retailers who alone are prepared to supply the specialist sizes in the relatively small quantities that modellers need.

In the past the manufacturing side of the model railway industry in Britain tended to divide itself into two parts; on one side we had the large scale production firm that catered for the toy market where considerations of cost, robust construction and high production runs were uppermost, and on the other side we had the specialist model railway

firm which aimed to satisfy the enthusiast largely through kits and spare parts. Many of the smaller firms will be quite unknown to newcomers, but to enthusiasts these firms have become firmly established household names. A list is included in Appendix 3 and like most other Appendices in the book the list is growing with each edition. It is probably true to say that many more train sets are sold as toys than ever find their way into a purpose-built model railway, but it is also true to say that there has been a shift in emphasis in recent years and, with constant voice through the clubs, magazines and individual comment, the mass produced products sold as toys are now nearer to scale models than they have ever been This is particularly marked in the most popular British 4 mm

Above *Not all American locomotives are big and massive. Portrayed here is a compact 4–6–0 operating on the Racoon Valley Railroad, an HO layout is based on the American mid-west.*

Below *The realism and detail of Continental commercial models can be appreciated in the snow-covered setting of Wintertal, an HO layout based on German practice.*

scale 00 gauge where, as well as improving standards of scale and authenticity, all the main manufacturers have become aware of the need for compatibility in couplings, track and wheel standards. The scale-minded model railway enthusiast who opts for 00 gauge is able to choose—from the products of the large-scale manufacturers—a selection of authentic scale models that are ready to run straight from the box. Notwithstanding the higher standards now being achieved, prices are commendably low and allowing for inflation the latest products offer better value for money than ever before. Because the specialist side of the business aims at a more limited market production runs have to be smaller and the unit cost for each item is often higher than the mass-produced product. Some of the moulds, machine tools and materials used in commercial model making are very expensive and manufacturers have to consider this aspect carefully before embarking on a new item or range of products, Most of the smaller specialist firms avoid the higher costs by using less expensive techniques such as white metal castings, perhaps the most common, and by offering their products in kits. The other alternative to high tooling costs is to manufacture by hand, and of course today this is even more expensive, which accounts for some quite small but exquisitely detailed hand-built models costing tens and even hundreds of pounds.

The variety of products available today; ready-to-run models, kits, component parts, accessories, electronic control systems, etc, has never been surpassed and great credit is due to the industry for the way it has responded to, and in some cases even created, a demand for more and more new items. There is now, as a result, hardly any basic requirement in the material sense missing from the hobby and we are very fortunate in having such a firm base on which to develop.

However well the hobby may be organised, with clubs, magazines and manufacturers, it would be nowhere without the model railway retailers. I cannot emphasise too strongly how important it is when starting the hobby to pick a good model railway retailer, a shop which is managed and staffed by someone who is prepared to look after you and to guide you through the early unfami-liar days. Provided you do not choose the last Saturday afternoon before Christmas, or some other time when the shop is packed with customers, most retailers worth their salt are prepared to offer advice as well as service and to spend some time with their customers. A list of leading retailers who stock model railway items is included in Appendix 4, and reference to one of the magazines will keep you abreast of any new ones that open up within reasonable distance of your home town or those prepared to deal with you through the post. They are scattered far and wide and seemingly few towns or populated districts are without a model shop of some sort. As with most things in life, there are the good and not so good retailers and you are best advised to shop around, but when you have found a dealer with whom you get on well, stick by him and I am sure you will soon become firm friends. The META sign referring to the Model Engineering Trade Association was at one time a good indication that you would receive responsible salesmanship and good advice but alas this body has now ceased to exist.

The American market for model railroads is, of course, very much bigger than its British equivalent and this is reflected in the truly tremendous range of items available, particularly in the 'ready-to-run' field. Many of the well-known European manufacturers—such as Rivarossi and Liliput—make models specially for the American market and these are also sold in Britain and in other countries. A growing number of enthusiasts outside America are tempted to model American-style lines, probably due to the availability of the very colourful and well-finished American models in both HO and N scales. There are two major American railroad modelling magazines, *Model Railroader* and *Railroad Model Craftsman*, both journals of high repute, and these should be required reading for anyone wishing to model American railroads (or indeed wishing to see what such projects might offer).

In America the major organisation supporting and guiding the hobby is the National Model Railroad Association (NMRA), which caters for both the enthusiast and the trade and has some overseas branches including one in Britain.

The other major model railway market is the Continent of Europe, and the European manufacturers between them turn out a fantastically large range of models covering, principally, the systems of France, Germany, Italy, Switzerland and Austria (though other nations are catered for in a smaller way). Once again the 'ready-to-run' side of the market is very well looked after, with models available in all the common scales (except 00). Standards are high and the quality, again, tempts a lot of British modellers to turn to Europe for the basis of a layout. In both Britain and America there are a good number of hobby shops which now stock European models.

With model railways moving further and further away from the toy train set image there seems to have developed a greater dividing line between model shops staffed by model makers who are keen on their trade and toy shops which often rely on girl or lady assistants who are more informed about dolls and teddy bears than they are on the intricacies of an 00 gauge 12 volt DC electric train set. At one time most toy shops of any standing boasted a working train set circling an oval track in their shop window, but nowadays such a sight is rare and the salesmanship does not extend itself to anything more than the display of a few static boxed items in a corner of the window. This seems a pity as there is no doubt that many of us who are now adults, active in the model railway hobby today, started off with a toy train set which we were given every encouragement to possess. I think it is very important that we retain a steady flow of new recruits to the hobby by this time-honoured means and wherever possible I think we should try and make up for the apparent lack of drive on the part of some toy shops by encouraging wherever and whenever we can an interest in toy trains amongst our nephews and nieces as well as sons and daughters.

These then are some of the aspects of the model railway hobby as they appear on the surface today. But foremost are the thousands of individuals who like yourself had to start somewhere at some time and have found railway modelling a creative, absorbing and worthwhile hobby and pastime. With the help of the following chapters I hope it will not seem as bewildering as it may appear at first glance, and that you will not be put off joining in. If you do decide to enter the ranks I am sure you will find yourself very welcome.

CHAPTER 2
Finding room for a model railway

At one time it was commonplace for a toy tin-plate train set to be unpacked from its box, set up on the floor ready for an operating session and then packed away again afterwards, almost as a matter of course. Part of the fun perhaps was creating new methods of laying the rails and dodging the table and chair legs that got in their way. The dark cavernous spaces under armchairs and sofas became tunnels and the rise and fall of the tracks over carpets and rugs gave the locomotives a chance to show off their haulage powers. Any sense of realism that was aimed at leaned heavily on the imagination to bring it to fulfilment. I am sure those early manipulations of standard-length straight and curved rails points and crossings, gave one a good start over less fortunate children when it came to geometry lessons at school! Certainly much ingenuity and skill was required to ensure perfect geometrical form for the layout, and it was a point of honour not to strain the tracks together when perhaps we knew perfectly well that another ¼ straight rail was required. The rails in those days were fairly robust affairs, and they needed to be to withstand clumsy juvenile hands and the occasional misplaced foot of the operator–or even worse, a heavy footed parent! Such a layout was invariably clockwork and O gauge, or even something larger if one goes back still further in time.

It was with the coming of electric propulsion and the smaller 00 gauge (more about the various gauges in Chapter 4) that the floor lost favour and we came to talk of table-top layouts. For the first time the relatively small 00 gauge made it possible to consider a table top as a space on which to build a model railway and at the same time the small size of 00 gauge necessitated moving up from the floor because the rails could not be made so strong and play resistant and it also became difficult to handle the small models so low down. With track of any size, too much connecting and disconnecting of the rails weakens and distorts them in time. The rail joints can become a potential source of derailments and also a point at which the electrical conductivity can break down. There is a good reason why full-size railway lines are referred to as the permanent way, and this is how they should be on a model railway if perfect running is the aim. So I think we can say quite definitely that any idea of a temporary track system laid out on the floor or any other position where the rails have to be put down and taken up has to be ruled out. The establishment of this idea, basic though it may be, is to some extent the first important step in making progress from a toy train set to a model railway. There is, of course, a lot more besides!

If not the floor, then where can we go? The usually acceptable answer is somewhere about table-top height. This probably suits some people but I would advise studying your own physical build first before slavishly copying past accepted practices. I am 6 ft 2 in tall, which is generally accepted as being a bit above average, and I find something higher than a table top is more comfortable. This is particularly true if I am standing up at a table, and more often than not I find this position more appropriate when operating a model railway than sitting down, which somehow never seems to be entirely satisfactory. There always seems to be something out of reach when you are sitting down and the constant bobbing up and down can be more tiring than standing up all the time. Table-top height is usually around 2 ft 4 in or 2 ft 5 in, but I find something like a kitchen working top height of around 3 ft is the minimum convenient level and I am happier if the layout can be higher still, say something like 3 ft 6 in. I had a layout at one time which, to clear the furniture it was built on, had to be at a height of approximately 4 ft. I found no snags to this whatsoever, and many advantages, most of all the fact that I liked to get my eyes down to the level of the track on occasions to find a viewpoint more nearly matching that of the real thing. Also, there is far less back-aching stooping when the layout is reasonably high off the ground. To go too far can, of course, be a distinct disadvantage, since if the layout is too high the background becomes hidden by the foreground and visibility is reduced, which makes it rather difficult to check the setting of points to see whether a road is clear. Once again, to draw on full-size practice, remember that signal boxes are perched up high above rail level. To sum up I would say the ideal measurement is somewhere between 3 ft and 4 ft depending on your height.

The width of a layout is also a factor which can be determined by your own build and physical proportions,. At 6 ft 2 in I have a fairly long reach and I am perfectly comfortable stretching across to the centre of the table, but this might be beyond the reach of a smaller person. All these details are, of course, just a matter of common sense but often they do not occur to some people until the layout is well advanced, and then it may be too late to do anything about it. It saves a lot of trouble if these points are considered at the outset before any hard work is done.

Tables are instinctively thought of as being the ideal shape and size for a model railway baseboard. They are quite satisfactory on a number of occasions although they can be inhibiting in respect of the type of layout you can build. In my view there is a much better alternative, namely the layout built on a series of shelves of varying width around the walls of a room, as shown in Fig 1. A round the-wall layout is much more accessible and provides far more scope for an interesting layout. Also, in many cases, it is still possible to carry out the normal functions in the room, for example a bedroom or a bed-sitter with the layout *in situ* round the walls, whereas a table-top baseboard providing less amount of usable track space would dominate the centre of the room, as shown in Fig 2. Normally a baseboard 3 ft or more in width

Fig 1 *Much more model railway can be accommodated around the walls of a room, compared with a table in the centre (see Fig 2)*

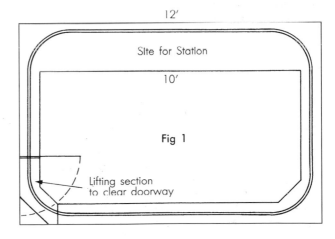

Fig 1

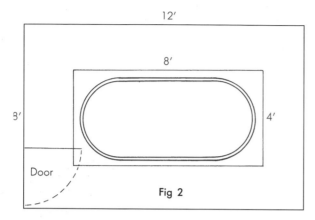

12'

8'

3'

4'

Door

Fig 2

Fig 2 Left *The same size room (12 ft x 8 ft) as in Fig 1, but with a table in the centre–which occupies all the available space–provides a much smaller working area.*

Fig 3 Below *A table against the corner of a room provides more usable space or, alternatively, permits the use of a larger table. However, access to the far corner of the layout becomes a problem.*

requires access on both sides. This would certainly be true of a continuous run layout built on a table where the running tracks have of necessity to be laid near the edge. If the table is pushed to a wall or into a corner to make more usable space in the room, this will make a large part of the model railway inaccessible.

A point worth noting comparing Fig 1 with Figs 2 and 3 is that the baseboard areas are roughly the same whereas the track footage in Fig 1 is double the length of the track footage in Fig 2 and 3. The prospects for developing the track layout on the station site in Fig 1 are also far greater yet there is much less dominance over the room. If the room is being used for other purposes and space is limited the site for the station need be no more than 2 ft in width. This would be ample for 00 gauge. The shelves round the remaining walls can be as little as 4 in wide for a single track in 00 gauge, 6 in for double track, although something wider would be preferable if the lineside is to be developed with scenery. An additional bonus is that the space under the station site can be used for storage as I will explain later.

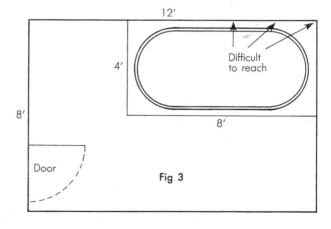

12'

4'

Difficult to reach

8'

8'

Door

Fig 3

Supports suitable for a round-the-wall layout can be of the simple metal bracket type for the narrow shelves or they can be made up from 2 x 2 in timber, such as shown in Fig 4. These would be 'Rawplugged' to the wall and in effect the wall adds strength and support to the layout. The gap across the entrance to the room can be bridged or by a removable section of baseboard which can be simply lifted out and put away when the layout is not in use.

I appreciate that in the case of rented homes, it may not always be possible to fix brackets directly to the wall. In such circumstances it will be necessary to provide some form of free-standing bracket or trestle.

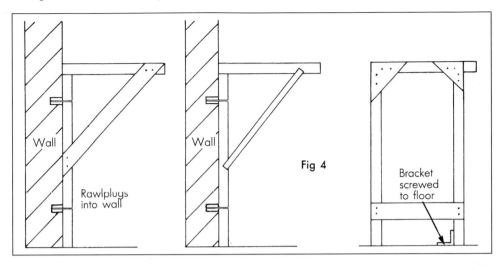

Fig 4 *Two types of wooden bracket and a trestle support for a 'round the wall' type layout. The trestle can be free-standing, thus avoiding the necessity of screwing into the wall.*

Alternatively, it may be possible to fix the free-standing type of bracket to the floor instead of to the wall, thus compensating for any lack of rigidity normally provided by fixing to the wall. Failing all this, a good stout piece of furniture such as a chest of drawers is an ideal base on which to fix the main baseboard for a model railway. As I will explain in Chapter 5 when talking about layout planning, with an end-to-end type of layout it is not essential that it should run completely round the room, and the chest of drawers can then form the base for the main terminal station with an extension to one side providing sufficient room over which to operate a service.

There is sometimes a temptation to give too little thought to the possibility of ever having to uproot the layout. If the time comes to make a move it may then be found that the layout cannot be removed from the room without dismantling, or else it has become so firmly fixed in position that it means the track becomes damaged when trying to dislodge and dismantle the baseboard. Unless you are absolutely sure you are not likely to move, or your circumstances are never going to change, it is as

well to make some provision for the easy removal of the layout if and when the time comes. This can be done by ensuring that the baseboard is divided into individual sections, each being reasonably portable. No hard and fast rules can be laid down for the size of these baseboard sections as the maximum dimensions will depend on the entrance to the room. A downstairs room with a pair of French windows opening out on to the lawn will probably have no restrictions at all, but an upstairs room reached up a winding staircase will obviously need some consideration. I mention this knowing that many, if not most, baseboards are assembled in the room in which they are to be used and I once had a devil of a job myself with a baseboard which measured 8 ft x 4 ft in an upstairs room which led off a narrow landing. In these circumstances something less than the height of the door frame, say about 6 ft, would have been better for the maximum length of the baseboard. This would have enabled it to have been turned on to its end and would have made the job of removal much easier.

A permanent layout fixed to the walls of a room can be removed when necessary

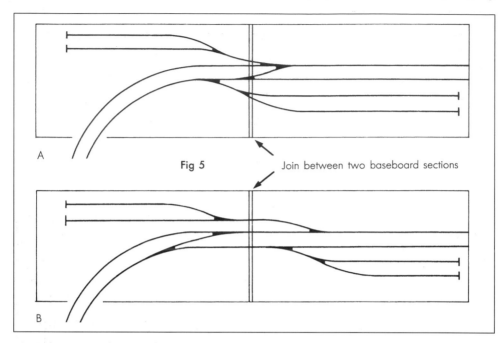

A

Fig 5

Join between two baseboard sections

B

Fig 5 *The position of points should be planned either side of the join between the two baseboard sections, as a 'B', and not straddling the join, as in 'A'.*

provided the baseboard is not so long that it becomes difficult to handle. Greasing the screws when they are fixed into place will prevent them rusting and will make them easier to remove; the holes they leave in the wall can simply be filled in with plaster. The layout itself, that is the baseboard containing the track, can, however, be a problem unless the individual baseboard units are made completely self-contained. This means stopping all rails short at the baseboard edge and making all wiring readily accessible where it crosses from one board to another. If this is done thoroughly it will facilitate rapid removal of the layout should you wish to exhibit it at any time, and it would be worthwhile keeping this idea in mind. The individual baseboard units should in this case be of a size that can be easily transported and you might like to check on the interior dimensions of your car before you make any decision. Something like 4 ft x 2 ft

is probably a maximum size for reasonably easy handling. Where you have no ideas of showing your handiwork at exhibitions, the baseboard units need not be entirely self-contained. The rails can be allowed to bridge the gaps between the baseboard units, providing the possibility of a disturbance at some later date is designed into the layout, and steps can be taken relatively simply to lift the rails. For example, make sure that there are no points or crossing straddling the gaps between the units and ensure that there are only straight rails which can, if necessary, be cut simply with a hacksaw blade as shown in Fig 5.

There are any number of materials you can use for constructing baseboards and their supports, but timber is generally favoured as being easy to work, durable and of sufficient strength for the purpose. There are many different ways of constructing baseboards too, but my own particular

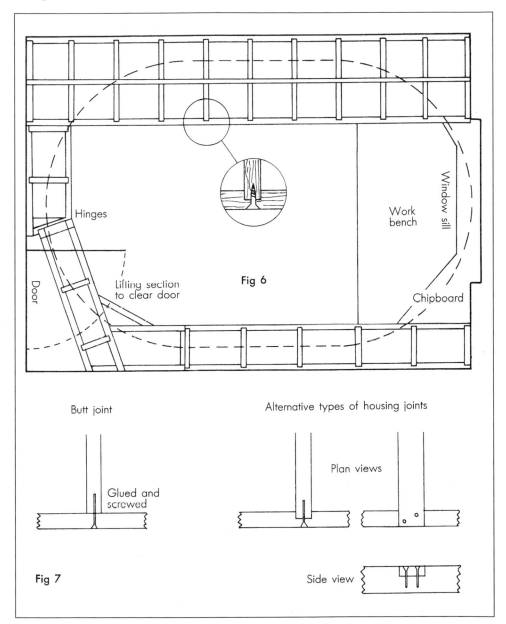

Hinges

Door

Lifting section
to clear door

Fig 6

Work
bench

Window sill

Chipboard

Butt joint

Alternative types of housing joints

Glued and
screwed

Plan views

Fig 7

Side view

Fig 6 *Suggested 2 in x 1 in open framework baseboard installed round the walls of a room 10 ft x 7 ft 6 in. The track is carried over the workbench by a piece of chipboard to provide greater clearance beneath. Note the use made of the window sill to provide valuable extra space.* **Fig 7** *Simple butt joints (left) are, in many cases, adequate for baseboard framework, but simple housing joints (right) make the frame that bit stronger and more professional-looking.*

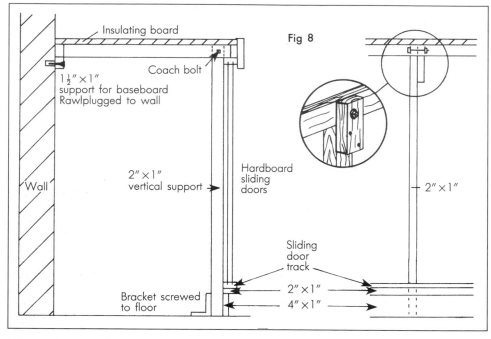

Fig 8 *Cross-section and part front view of a baseboard supported along its back edge by 1½ in x 1 in batten Rawl-plugged to the wall. The front edge is supported by vertical 2 in x 1 in timber, bracketed to the floor and bolted to the baseboard framework. The cupboard space formed beneath can be fronted by hardboard sliding doors, as shown.*

favourite, assuming a layout is built round the walls of a room, is the tried and trusted open framework made of 2 in x 1 in timber with a covering of ½ in insulation board. An example of such a framework built round the walls of a room 10 ft x 7 ft 6 in is shown in Fig 6. Here the main area of the layout, which incorporates all the important station, goods yard and engine servicing facilities, is built on a framework 10 ft x 2 ft along one long wall of the room, and narrower framework only 1 ft wide extends the layout along one end and along the other long side of the room. An opening section across the door allows access to the room, at the furthest end of which the layout is carried across the work bench by a piece of chipboard The chipboard was used at this point because it is more self-supporting than the soft insulating board and did not require supporting

underneath with the 2 in x 1 in framework. This gave a lot more clearance above the work bench. A number of modellers prefer to use chipboard rather than insulation board and I would suggest that, when a layout is likely to be moved more often, it is probably preferable since it is much more robust, harder and likely to retain screws and other fixing devices much longer and firmer. Its disadvantages are that it is heavier, more expensive and much more noisy if the rails are laid directly on it.

To make the framework using 2 in x 1 in timber can be very easy if you are content to have simple butt joints which in many cases are all that are necessary. Alternatively, the job can be made a little stronger and perhaps more professional by using housing joints as shown in Fig 7. Housing joints are easy to do with a tenon saw which has a depth gauge built on. The one I use has a metal bar bolted to the blade of the saw, the bolts passing through slots in the blade. The height of the bar can be adjusted by releasing the two wing nuts which hold it in place and, when released, allow the bar to slide up or down. The height of the bar above the teeth of the blade will determine the depth of the saw cut, thus ensuring that every cut is made exactly to the same depth. With a simple gauge such as this it is perfectly possible quickly and accurately to cut a whole row of housing joints along the baseboard frame side members, and to a constant depth. Provided that all the cross members are cut to exactly the same width, this will ensure that the baseboard is kept to an even width. Two 1¼ in no 8 screws are sufficient to hold each joint when using housing joints, but of course something longer will be required, say a 2 in or 2¼ in screw, if your are using ordinary butt joints.

The ½ in insulation board which forms the top of the baseboard should be supported at 1 ft intervals so, on a framework 2 ft wide, support should be provided lengthwise down the centre of the frame. This can be a length of 1 in x 1 in timber inserted in grooves cut in the cross members. I suggest supporting the back edge of the baseboard on a length of 1½ x 1 in timber screwed to the wall and if possible, depending on the location, with similar supports at each end. If a wall is not available to give support at one or both ends, vertical supports cut from 2 in x 1 in timber are sufficient to provide enough support to the front edge of the frame, as shown in Fig 8. The vertical supports can be screwed to the floor with brackets and at the top they can be bolted or screwed to the baseboard frame cross members. The result of such a construction is a perfectly rigid and robust assembly which will withstand any reasonable assembly which will withstand any reasonable weight or strain without distortion. The cost need not be all that expensive either. The space under a baseboard such as this can be very useful for storage, and sliding doors or a curtain can be fixed along the front of the

unit to make it a reasonably tidy piece of furniture. The sliding doors facing the cupboard under my own layout are simply sheets of hardboard sliding in specially provided track which can be obtained from almost any do-it-yourself store.

One does not need to be a carpenter to be a model railway enthusiast and there is no need to be put off by the idea of having to build a baseboard. The degree of skill required is only very basic and tools need consist of little more than a saw, set square, chisel, mallet, screwdriver and something to make the holes for the screws. Ideally use an electric drill but a hand drill will also do the job and is cheaper but a little slower.

In America there is a popular style of baseboard underframe which was evolved by the magazine *Model Railroader* and goes under the name of 'L-girder construction'. It is both simple and economical. The basis of this type of framing is the L-girders themselves which are made from 1 in x 4 in planks so forming the L-shape. The girders thus formed are used longitudinally like the long sides of the conventional type of underframe, and support legs are attached to these and cross-braced. Joists of 2 in x 1 in wood are then screwed at about 12 in intervals across between the girders, which are always used with the 'L' in an inverted position, presenting a flat edge to take the joists or anything else which needs to be attached. For station yards or flat areas generally, insulation board sheet is just screwed down to the joists in the usual way. Out in the 'country' risers can be screwed to the L-girders as required to take the track bed above or below datum level. To give a valley, for instance, you can attach the second run of L-girders below the first when you get to a corner, a chimney breast, or some other convenient point and the L-girders can be made up of lengths from 3 ft to 6 ft or more as required to suit your layout and any rise or fall in the terrain. For a very 'scenic' type of layout this system gives obvious advantages.

The choice of baseboard surface is a vexed one and there are champions for each different sort. One material that most people

L-girder construction. The L-girder forming the longitudinal part of the structure can be seen bolted to a 2 x 2 in leg at one end. Transverse 2 x 1 in timbers support the insulation board surface.

agree is not any good for a model railway is hardboard. It is too thin, too liable to warp, will not take pins or screws and is altogether an undesirable material for this job. I must admit, on a well-supported surface and in a position where the layout is rarely disturbed, I strongly favour ½ in thick wood fibre insulation board. One of its biggest virtues is that it lives up to its name and has a sound deadening property which is an important factor when running model trains, especially where noise might cause disturbance to other people. A model train running on rails laid directly on to a hard surface, such as deal or plywood, can make a deafening sound and, apart from the irritation, which can be particularly bad on a continuous layout where the train goes round and round, it can also take away much of the realism. As well as its sound-deadening

properties, insulation board is relatively light, very easy to work, cheap in comparison with other alternatives, takes pins for fixing trackwork etc, and can be gouged out easily to lay in point rodding or to cut out inspection pits or holes in the surface of the baseboard exactly where and when they are required. Should you find ½ inch insulation board difficult to obtain Sundeala is a desirable alternative. It is in fact the first choice of many people and a number of specialist model railway dealers stock the material in sizes convenient for railway modellers.

Sundeala is particularly suitable for portable layouts but if the layout is likely to be subjected to a lot of handling it may be preferable to consider using a harder surface such as chipboard. Rather than just sit on the timber framework chipboard is robust enough to add strength to the structure

9mm or similar thickness plywood is a popular and lighter alternative to softwood timbers for baseboard structures. As shown here, transverse members can be shaped to the finished contours of the layout. Careful pre-planning is essential in such cases. Besides reducing weight, the hole can be utilised for cable runs.

when screwed and glued in place. Blockboard, medium density fibreboard (MDF) and the thicker, coarser grained plywoods can also be used but you are moving up the scale both in cost and in weight and it is desirable to keep the weight down otherwise moving and storing the baseboard when not in use is going to be an aggravating business.

With the problems of weight in mind and also taking note of the dubious quality of some of the soft wood timber on offer today the search for alternative materials has led to the adoption of 6 mm or 9 mm external grade plywood as a medium for constructing model railway baseboards. When suitably braced along open edges and reinforced in the corners with stripwood glued and pinned into place plywood can be assembled into a very rigid yet lightweight structure. It lends itself particularly well to the 'open plan' type of baseboard where the transverse members of the supporting framework can be shaped to the finished contour of the model railway landscape and the baseboard surface consists simply of strips of plywood cut out to follow the line of the track. The spaces in between can then be filled in with lightwight scenic covering material. The problem of sound deadening which follow from laying track on to

plywood can be resolved if an insulating material such as foam ballast inlay, cork sheet or ⅜ inch pin board is placed between the track and the plywood. With this type of baseboard the track plan needs to be thoroughly thought out before construction begins as it may not be easy to re-route the track or lay in additional tracks should the need for this be realised only after the layout is up and running. For this reason the 'open plan' type of layout is best left until you have gained more experience. In the early experimental days it is preferable to have a broad flat even surface on which to spread your track, rolling stock and accessories so that you can move things around until you are satisfied with the result.

The baseboard framework shown in Fig 6 encircles most of the room, but the all-important bridging section across the door is something that needs to be given special attention. It is, of course, possible just to have a section of baseboard which can be dropped into place and lifted out when access to and from the room is required. However, it is much more convenient if this section is pivoted at one end and made to hinge upwards. The important point to remember in a situation such as this is to keep the fulcrum point of the hinge well above the level of the track.

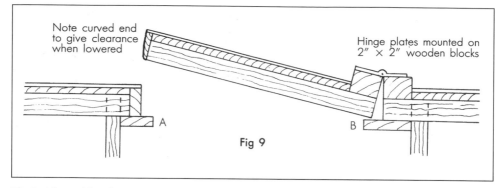

Note curved end
to give clearance
when lowered

Hinge plates mounted on
2″ × 2″ wooden blocks

A

B

Fig 9

Fig 9 *A hinged baseboard section to span a gap across a doorway. Note how the strain is taken off the hinges by the supports 'A' and 'B'.*

Other points to watch for are the ends of the rails. Make sure they are well anchored. (See Fig 10). Fig 9 shows an example of a type of hinged section which can be used and which is easy to make out of timber using techniques no more complex than the baseboard framework already described. The hinges, ordinary 2 in square ones known as backflaps, are screwed, or preferably bolted, right through 1 in thick spacing blocks and into or through the framework itself. The best way to fit the hinges is to place the hinged section into position and support it at both ends with suitable pieces of timber screwed to the underside of the baseboard framework. After the hinges have been screwed and/or bolted in place the support at the hinged end can then be removed. It is preferable to complete all work on the baseboard and the hinged section before laying the track.

Carrying the current across the gap left by the hinged section can be accomplished in a number of different ways. The simplest is to carry a lead down one leg of the baseboard

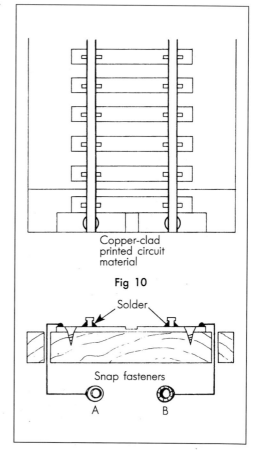

Copper-clad
printed circuit
material

Fig 10

Solder

Snap fasteners

A   B

Fig 10 *Contact wires are soldered to the copper strip on both sides of the track as shown using A dressmaker's snap fasteners socket and B dressmaker's snap fastener lug. Solder A to one wire and B to the other having first passed each wire through the folding section baseboard as shown.*

support, along the floor and up the other. The hinged section itself can be wired up to the adjacent baseboard with the wiring loose enough to take care of any movement when the section is raised. The snag with a system such as this it is very easy to make a mistake and drive a locomotive off the end of the rails when the hinged section is raised. Some form of rubbing contact can be arranged between the hinged section and the rest of the baseboard which can be made to carry the current across the bridge, but will cut the current off as soon as the bridge is raised. An alternative to the rubbing contact idea would be to have a snap fastener system to carry the current. Separating the snap fasteners to allow the bridge to be raised would break the circuit on one of the running rails which would prevent the locomotive from getting anywhere near the edge. (See Fig 11). This system is also suitable for portable/exhibition layouts needing a folding section which is not permanently attached to anything other than the baseboard. It is also useful for 0 gauge modellers for coach lighting links between carriages and for many other wiring uses.

I appreciate that not everyone is in the fortunate position of having a whole spare room in their house which can be devoted entirely to a hobby, whether it is railway modelling or anything else. But it must be emphasised that, however desirable it may be to have a model railway room, it is not absolutely essential and there are a number of different solutions to the space problem which can be considered as alternatives. I suppose the first obvious hunting ground if a normally habitable room cannot be spared is to find some other area within the house that is not usually lived in, such as the loft, basement or garage. A basement is probably the best of these three alternatives because it is often a place where there is an even temperature. It is cool in summer and not too cold in winter and, if the property is in a fit condition at all, it should not be damp. But I realise that less houses are built in Great Britain with basements these days and

the older houses that were built with them are becoming fewer in number. The next most practical location therefore is the loft.

The loft can be a very worthwhile area to investigate, as the pages of model railway magazines will testify, since a large number of very successful layouts have been constructed in this otherwise unused and neglected space. At first glance the average loft does not look very promising. To begin with it is probably difficult to get into. Once access has been gained it is awkward to move about inside since, in all probability, there are no floor boards and you have to move on tiptoe from joist to joist, at the same time dodging the roof-supporting beams. Most lofts are dark, cavernous, dirty and dusty places and the air smells anything but fresh and sweet. No wonder that many people, on making an investigation of their loft, feel that the odds are too great, and turn their back on the place, close the trap door and forget all about it. But if you are prepared to spend a few pounds on bringing the place up to scratch it is surprising what can be achieved. Make no mistake, it will cost a few pounds, but the outlay will depend on how much of a handyman you are and what tools and materials you have on hand. When making a case for spending a few pounds from the household budget, remember that there are a considerable number of side benefits to be derived from having the loft converted, apart from the obvious one of making a place fit for a model railway to live in. It will enhance the value of the property, assuming it is your own; it will give greater heat insulation to the whole house; and the improved access and habitable space created will be useful for storage and for other domestic purposes.

The first thing to do is to improve access to the loft. The generally accepted method is to install a form of loft ladder and there are a number of different proprietary designs available. When designing ladders for lofts, most of the specialist manufacturers seem to have made provision for nearly every contingency, and it seem that few situations are so difficult as to make the fitting of one

A simply constructed lift bridge providing access to a doorway. Just visible are the rail ends soldered to strips of copper-clad printed circuit material.

or the other of these ladders impossible. I can only speak from experience about one type of loft ladder–a wooden version manufactured by Benson's, Pontefract Avenue Works, Pontefract Lane, York Road, Leeds–which has proved thoroughly satisfactory since it was installed. I hasten to add that I have no connection with this firm other than being a very satisfied customer. When in use, the trap door leading to the loft can be opened and the ladder brought down into position within seconds, and all with the very minimum amount of effort.

Having improved the access to the loft the next step is to fix up some form of lighting, with a switch near the trap door entrance. Fluorescent tubes are recommended as the ideal lighting system, since they reduce the amount of shadows. A power source for the railway can also be considered at this stage.

Then the all-important floor can be laid. Articles appear from time to time in the various do-it-yourself journals and magazines about the subject and it is as well to look at some back numbers and study them thoroughly before embarking on the job, since a number of practical considerations need to be looked into. If in doubt, professional advice should be sought to ensure that the joists, which will form the base of the floor, are of sufficient strength to take the added weight of the floor and yourself when walking on it. With the access improved, the floor boarded and lighting installed, the loft already begins to take on a cosy, inviting atmosphere. Any further improvements such as insulation, heating,

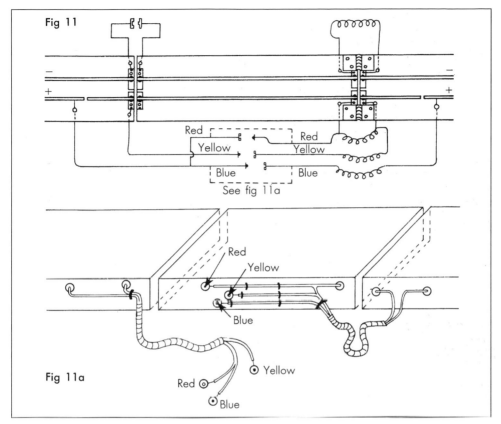

Fig 11

Red
Yellow
Blue

See fig 11a

Red
Yellow
Blue

Fig 11a

Red
Yellow
Blue

Red
Yellow
Blue

Figs 11, 11a *Care must be taken to ensure there is sufficient wire at the hinged side of the folding section before fixing so that it can be lifted easily. Different coloured wires are used so that the correct connections can be made (blue to blue etc). As this section is self-contained it can be used on both permanent and portable layouts.*

ventilation and decoration, can follow when time permits, Meanwhile a start can be made on the all-important model railway.

As an alternative to a basement or loft, the next likely place to be considered is the garage. Access is usually no problem, although the presence of a car will most likely limit the space available, but the difficulties of heating, combating dampness, extreme temperature variations, dirt and dust are usually greater. I am not much in favour of a garage as an all-the year-round location for a model railway, not only because of these difficulties but also because the average brick-built garage can be a pretty cheerless place in the winter. Speaking for my own garage it is very difficult to keep clean because of the dirt that falls from the car, the leaves that blow under the door, the shavings that fall from the work bench and the cobwebs produced by the countless spiders that choose to make it their home, to say nothing of the perpetual dust which rises from the concrete floor or falls from the unplastered walls. I don't doubt that these difficulties could be overcome, and the place knocked into shape made draught-proof and damp-proof, kept

David Jenkinson's O gauge garden layout shows how well the model railway can blend with a rock garden setting. (Photo: Brian Monaghan)

clean, heated and even decorated. However, I do not relish the idea of being separated from the rest of the household and banished to the garage every time I want to enjoy some work on my model railway. You may or may not feel the same.

Perhaps a better solution if you have to seek covered accommodation outside the house is to invest in a garden shed built specially for the purpose of installing a model railway. There are any number of different sizes and varieties available to suit almost any location. With a raised floor and with suitable insulation of the walls they can be made cosy, dry and comfortable inside, even during very cold winter weather and with adequate ventilation they need not get too hot in the summer. It is important to avoid the direct rays of the sun in a building such as this, especially when the sun is at its fiercest, since sunlight can have a very damaging effect on a model railway. The deterioration of plastic models in shop windows after exposure to the heat of the sun is known, but in addition to the heat effect which produces twisting and bending of the plastic the sun also fades the colours. This can be particularly bad with printed card parts used for lineside buildings, and can also play havoc with the colours in the various materials used for creating scenic effects, grass, bushes and trees, etc.

Extreme conditions such as high temperatures, the glare of the sun or undue exposure to dampness should be avoided wherever the layout is built, since there are limits to what many of the materials used in railway modelling can withstand. For one thing, it follows from the reduction in scale of the model that tolerances cannot be so great as they are with the real thing; so it only needs a slight displacement of the model to make it almost unworkable. If the wood used for a baseboard shrinks, twists or expands it with most likely take the track with it. It can be quite distressing to see carefully laid track thrown out of alignment because of the movement of the baseboard, and this can happen all too easily if the conditions under which the model railway is kept, operated or stored are not controlled within reasonably tolerable limits. I have even known track to become distorted after the installation of a central heating system! A previously satisfactory piece of baseboard became affected by the radiator which had to be installed nearby and as a result the baseboard dried out, shrank, and in doing so displaced a length of track. The track, about 2 ft long, was on a curve and was held at each end. It was prevented from moving outwards or inwards, so as the wood shrunk the track tried to lift itself up in the air. No wonder trains started to derail themselves at this point!

Details like this need watching and it is no good building a baseboard, laying the track and forgetting all about it. In particular, you should never lay track in such a position that access becomes difficult at a later date, perhaps because the baseboard is extended, thus making it awkward to reach across to the parts that were first constructed. Inspection, maintenance and cleaning of the track, as well as the recovery of derailed rolling stock, should always be allowed for when designing and building the baseboard. The best remedy for extreme climatic conditions is to be prepared for all eventualities. Use good quality timber, keep the baseboard under constant surveillance all through the year and avoid the obvious trouble spots such as radiators, windows in direct line with the sun, damp patches on walls, water pipes, etc. Wherever possible install your model railway where there will be adequate insulation against heat and cold, ensure that some form of heating is provided which will keep temperatures above freezing in winter, and fix up really adequate ventilation to avoid over-heating in those all-too-rare days of summer heatwave.

Notwithstanding what I have just said the most extreme conditions are to be found outdoors in the garden but, despite the apparent hardships, many model railways in all gauges even down to N have been built outdoors and have survived for many years the ravages of wind and rain as well as extreme temperatures. Railways such as these will not, of course, be the complete scenic models that we build indoors, and all rolling stock will have to be brought indoors after each operating session. Buildings such as stations, bridges and signal boxes will have to be built out of particularly robust materials heavily protected against the elements if they are to be left permanently installed outdoors. Additional hazards with an outdoor model railway can be weeds, falling leaves, shifting stones and soil washed down by the rain as well as cats, dogs, birds, wild animals and insects which can either sit on the railway line or nibble, gnaw or scratch away at the trackwork and the adjoining countryside. But with all these added difficulties there are also some tremendous advantages, particularly the one of space, and the freedom and exhilaration of being able to enjoy your hobby outdoors.

Crichel Down built by Martin Goodall is a fine example of a compact showcase layout, equally at home at exhibitions or, as shown here, on the dining room table.

If really bad weather prevents you from working on the line or enjoying an operating session outdoors there is enough construction work to keep you occupied indoors on the work bench. In fine weather, which can be any day from January to December, the sheer delight of being able to watch a train snaking its way along apparently endless miles of track is something that must surely make up for all the extra hard work. Constructing and operating a garden railway is not a venture to be approached light-heartedly. It is rather more demanding of time than most other forms of railway modelling since there is much more maintenance work to do. This must be done regularly if Mother Nature is not to take over as she surely will do if not resisted, as anyone who has seen abandoned full-size railway branch line will testify. The one big advantage is that maintenance sessions on the railway can also be combined with gardening, something that is rather difficult to concentrate on with an indoor model railway, as some neglected gardens belonging to railway modellers will bear witness!

There are, perhaps, two basic sorts of garden layout. On the one hand there is the type that is built on a wooden framework, trestle or baseboard which is kept well clear of the ground, possibly even running round the garden fence about 3 or 4 feet above groundlevel, or there is the other sort which is built at ground level, either low down on the ground itself or in such a position that the ground is built up to form an embankment either side of the line. The former type is in many respects more like an ordinary model railway built for indoor use, except that the baseboard happens to be outside and everything has to be built to withstand the weather. It is the latter sort, built to run at ground level, which demands the greatest attention, both in the building and in the maintenance, but which at the same time provides the most satisfying result. Here there is a tremendous opportunity to combine your skill as both a gardener and a railway modeller to create a remarkably realistic setting for a layout, using rocks, rock plants, dwarf conifers, bushes, flowers and trees. Despite the out-of scale nature of some of these plants most of these outdoor garden railways provide a very realistic setting for a model train.

To build such a line you can either lay the track on a suitably drained foundation and build a rock garden around it, or else the route for the line can be carved out of the existing terrain. Either way, the work of getting the correct levels and gradients on which to lay the track has to be planned and carried out very carefully, and the track base must be firm and above all very well

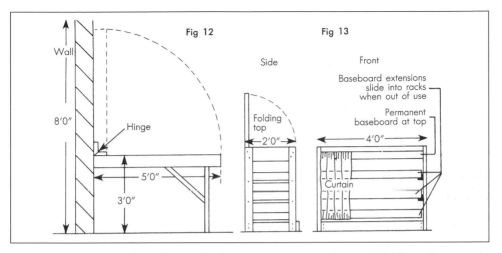

Fig 12 *(left) A baseboard hinged to a wall. When in use, it is swung down and the free end supported by a folding trestle.* **Fig 13** *(right) A rack of baseboard sections, with the permanent section forming the top. Sections to extend the layout stack away behind the curtain when not in use.*

drained. Concrete or stone are probably the best foundation materials, and if wood is to be used it should be well preserved and properly treated. The track will have to be regularly inspected to remove displaced stones and leaves, and the ballast should be picked over from time to time to assist in the drainage and to remove any weeds that take root. Some of the modern weedkillers may be effective, but I would recommend carrying out a sample test application first to ensure that the type you are going to use is not likely to have a harmful effect on the track. One thing is certain; steel rail, even treated steel rail, cannot be used successfully outdoors for any length of time and a non-ferrous metal such as nickel-silver should be employed.

Garden railway modelling is really a subject in itself. Several books have been devoted to this aspect of the hobby and articles appear in the monthly magazines from time to time. In the brief mention here it is enough to know that the garden is an accepted place in which to build a model railway. Some excellent ones have been built which show that, whatever problems exist, it cannot be denied that there are

problems, they can be overcome. I have no personal experience of garden railway modelling and cannot speak with authority on the subject, but I can appreciate the advantages of such a location from examples I have seen, and I feel encouraged to recommend it to anyone who is willing to try.

To come back indoors again, the modeller who cannot find a spare room, or space round the walls of his bedroom or bed-sitter, who hasn't a loft or a basement, who has no room in his garage after he has parked the car, and who does not fancy the garden, still need not despair. Some excellent portable schemes have been tried and tested and have been found to be perfectly acceptable. Some examples are shown in Figs 12-16.

Fig 12 shows a scheme whereby a baseboard is hinged against the wall. When out of use it folds up against the wall and takes up no more space than the depth of the baseboard frame. To allow for any permanent features on the layout, such as buildings and signals, the depth of the frame should be at least 6 in on an 00 gauge layout. To bring the layout into use, the baseboard is simply swung down through 90 degrees and supported at the free end on

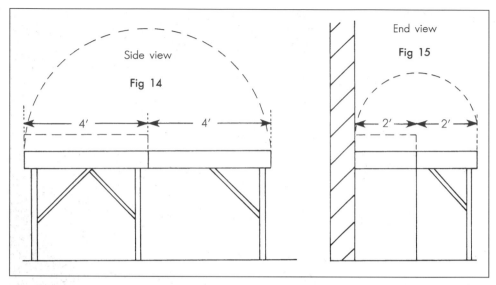

Fig 14 *(left) An extending baseboard built on the principle of a decorator's table.* **Fig 15** *(right) A baseboard fixed to a wall and extendable in width by means of a folding section.*

a trestle. The trestle can be free-standing or it can itself be hinged to the underside of the baseboard. Alternatively, support for the free end of the baseboard can be provided by a chair or some other piece of furniture of the appropriate height. The only restriction on this system is that the height of the ceiling will limit the length of the baseboard, unless two such baseboards are built, each hinged on opposite walls and arranged so that they meet in the middle when they are lowered. Another alternative might be to hinge the long side of the layout along the wall, and in this case the length of the layout can be as long as the wall itself.

Fig 13 shows a simple system whereby a layout is built on a series of baseboards, each of a standard and easily manageable size and which, when out of use, can be stacked away in a specially constructed frame. The frame can be disguised as a piece of furniture, either with curtaining or sliding doors built to obscure the front, and the top can be used to display ornaments in much the same way as a sideboard. When in use the layout would have to be assembled by fitting the separate baseboard section to trestles, which can also be accommodated in the storage frame.

Illustrated in Fig 14 is a simple scheme where a layout consists of two baseboards hinged at one end so that they can be folded together like the covers of a book. When in use, one end of the layout is swung open, thereby doubling the length of the layout. Suitable trestles can be fitted with hinges to the underside of the baseboards, or alternatively the whole unit can be rested on a dining or kitchen table. When folded up, the unit could be slid away out of sight under the bed. A wallpaper pasting table, such as can be obtained from most do-it-yourself shops, is made on the same principle, except that the hinges work the other way so that the tops of the table fold outwards. Also, they usually have a surface of thin plywood or hardboard which is not very suitable for model railways, as explained earlier.

Fig 15 shows a rather similar idea to Fig 12, except that the two baseboard sections are hinged along their side instead of at one end. Here it is suggested that one side could

Below *A bird's eye view of Telford Park, a 4mm scale minimum space tramway layout built by Dick Yeo. The sharp radius curves acceptable with tramways enable this comprehensive system to be accommodated in a glass-topped coffee table.*

be permanently fixed to the wall. The space underneath the baseboard could then be used for storage. The half of the layout which swings down could be supported by trestles when the layout is in use, and out of use it could swing back to form a top to the cabinet, very similar to a sideboard.

A simplification of Fig 15 is given in Fig 16, where the baseboard, a long narrow one, is incorporated into a bench seat which can be made as a permanent feature along the wall or under a window. Removing the cushions uncovers a lid which, when raised, reveals a model railway layout. The snag

Fig 16 *Removing the seat cushions of this bench seat uncovers a lid which can be lifted to expose a baseboard 10 ft x 2 ft, which is suitable for an N gauge layout.*

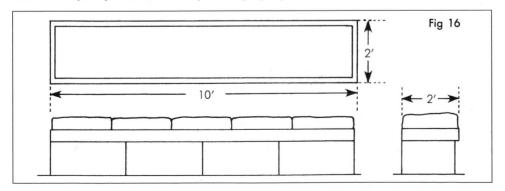

Shute Junction Station on the 00 gauge layout displayed in a simulated attic; one of many exhibits to be seen at Pecorama, Beer, near Seaton, Devon.

(Photo: PECO)

with this idea is that the space is very restricted and too low down.

Many other ideas are possible and may come to mind. A visit to the Peco Modelrama at the Peco head office in Beer, just two miles west of Seaton in Devon, is well recommended as a source of inspiration. Here you will find examples of working model railway layouts in various gauges from N to O built in settings that simulate typical locations to be found around the house or garden. The simulations are very realistic, in many cases cleverly contrived and illustrate, in practical terms, not only how and what space can be utilised to the best advantage but how it can be done and how attractive the end result can be made to be. If you or your domestic authorities have any uncertainties about how a model railway can be incorporated into your home a visit to the Peco Modelrama will dispel the doubts. For the indoor exhibits it is normally open all the year but for the outdoor amenities it opens from the Spring Bank Holiday

to mid-October. Very often the brightest ideas are inspired by the most difficult and unpromising situations. It is probably true to say that a really determined model railway enthusiast will find some room somewhere to create a layout wherever he or she may be. I have even heard of one being built in a submarine! Many articles have appeared in the model railway press showing some of the very small gauge layouts being built in suitcases, on coffee tables, and even in a television cabinet and a violin case! Where there's a will there's a way is a very apt saying, but please remember to keep it a permanent way in the sense that the track is laid down permanently on the baseboard, and, if there is any moving to be done, it is the baseboard that is moved and not the track. One final word on this subject – if you do decide to build a portable or folding type of baseboard, don't forget to remove all your rolling stock from the track and fix all the accessories firmly in place before you put the layout away for the night.

CHAPTER 3
Choosing the type of layout you want

It is perfectly possible to build a model railway without ever first thinking about what type it is going to be, or even what type it is after you have finished. Track can be bought and laid to fill the space available, equipment—including locomotives, carriages and wagons—can be purchased because it catches your eye or it appeals to you, and the whole lot can be made to work and can be operated with tremendous pleasure, just as the fancy takes you. Is there anything wrong with that? It could be argued that if *you* find it satisfactory then this is all that matters, and there is not a lot of point in anyone else worrying about it any further. However, it is a bit like the schoolboy who starts a stamp collection with a bumper pack of pictorials and a tube of glue and proceeds to sick his stamps in the album in no particular order, and with absolutely no thought for the future or even why he is doing it. It may satisfy him at the time, when he knows no better, but the wiser, more mature collector realises that a stamp collection is pointless unless the individual stamps are sorted, properly arranged and displayed in groups or themes.

As with any hobby there are recognised ideal standards, which add purpose to it. Rather than simply accumulating a haphazard collection of unrelated models, it is surely much more satisfactory to decide on a particular period, location and theme for the full-size prototype of your model railway and build up a collection of models and equipment within that framework. Such a model railway with a clearly defined purpose or theme will provide more satisfaction to build and operate and is likely to have a more lasting value and appeal than the first sort. It is largely a personal opinion which I know not everyone shares, but it is worth the consideration at the start before you commit yourself to spending time and money which you may later regret.

When talking about types of railway I have in mind their outward physical characteristics based on known examples of actual railways. Instead of just amassing a whole load of equipment and filling in every square inch of space on the baseboard with sidings and running rails, why not base the layout on a particular aspect of full-size railways that interests you most? If you have an overwhelming fascination for the largest express passenger locomotives you will want a main line setting in which to operate them. Ideally, this should have a length of track which will enable the locomotive to accelerate its train to a realistic express speed. If you like the peace, quiet and slower moving pace of a country town you will find a lot of satisfaction in a branch line layout. You may admire the powerful looks of foreign locomotives or, the opposite end of the scale, the quaint charm of the narrow gauge. All these various types of railways have their different characteristics which can be recreated in model form. Surely, therefore, it is a wise move to get to know something about your chosen prototype before you start to model it.

Surprisingly, not everyone approaches railway modelling this way. To some people the model is the beginning and the end, and as long as one model lines up with another, is reasonably proportioned and looks and works well, it is the limit of their ambitions. I would like to point out that there can be a lot more to the hobby than just that, as very many people have found to their pleasure. The hobby has been growing up over many years and whereas in the early days the measure of a layout was in the amount of equipment, track and rolling stock you managed to cram into a given space, nowadays it is largely judged by the degree of realism and faithfulness to the prototype that it manages to achieve. This is probably due to the higher standard of realism of the individual models themselves. Gone are the days when it was accepted that a manufacturer could produce one model of rather dubious outline and offer it to the public as either 'Flying Scotsman', 'Royal Scot', 'Caerphilly Castle' or 'Lord Nelson' with only the colour of the paintwork and the engine name and number to distinguish one locomotive from another. Now we have come to expect a much higher standard of realism with each individual model offered by commercial manufacturers and home builders. Also, it follows that we should not want to spoil this by displaying and operating such authentic looking models in anything other than an equally authentic-looking setting.

The best way to achieve a sense of realism and authenticity is to acquire some knowledge of the genuine article. The best way of all is, of course, to have direct contact with, or experience of, actual rail-

ways, but not all of us who are interested in making historical models or models of foreign railways are able to achieve this aim. The obvious answer is, of course, to do as much reading about the subject as possible and to study as many photographs and drawings as you can get hold of. Back numbers of the various model railway magazines are probably the best source of information, since the material they contain will be tailored to the requirements of railway modellers, whereas so many other sources of information such as the enthusiast railway books, railway histories and technical books on railways often leave gaps in the sort of detailed information that modellers seek. However, from whatever source, you cannot have too much prototype information and you should aim at building up a library of books, drawings and photographs covering all aspects of your chosen prototype and location. This will stand you in good stead for future construction work, as well as providing you with a background of knowledge which will enable you to create a really authentic model railway.

When establishing a theme and a type of layout which aims at authenticity it is not always necessary to limit your powers of creation to such an extent that you just slavishly copy a particular prototype, past or present. Very often some of the most realistic and attractive looking layouts are really the product of a flight of fancy. Peter Denny's Buckingham Branch layout is a typical example. He has created a most authentic-looking period Great Central Railway layout in a railway location which is completely imaginary. Though the railway system he has modelled never actually existed, at least it might have been possible, and the collection of rolling stock and accessories is authentic for the Edwardian period he has chosen to model. The introduction of a British Railways Britannia Pacific at the head of one of his trains or the parking of a model Leyland National bus in the station yard would, of course, destroy all the atmosphere. Go a stage further and deliberately mix up your periods such as

A GWR 0-4-2T and a BR Class 47 at home together at Talland Junction, an imaginary preserved railway with BR connection built by Dave Peacey, 00 gauge 4mm finescale.

this and introduce a completely unrestricted variety of models and the layout would degenerate into a meaningless collection.

Sometimes, however, it is possible to get away with a freelance layout, by which is meant a model railway that is not representative of any particular company, period or location. But, strangely enough, it is not as easy as it may look. In fact, if it is to be done satisfactory, it calls for as much, if not more, artistry and skill than the layout that religiously follows a particular prototype. With a freelance layout you become your own mechanical and civil engineer which is, after all, assuming a rather large mandate. The classic example of a freelance system is the late John Ahern's Madder Valley Railway. On this layout—which, by the way, is now being looked after by the Pendon Museum at Long Wittenham, Abingdon, Berkshire – locomotives and rolling stock based on prototypes drawn from all over the world were successfully operated together without raising anyone's eyebrows. He even mixed locomotives and rolling stock of different

gauges which necessitated them being built to different scales, but somehow or other they looked perfectly natural in the setting he created. In fact, John Ahern's work was universally admired and has probably inspired more layouts than any other single source. Despite the outrageously varied collection of locomotives and rolling stock he succeeded in knitting them all together and creating an atmosphere, a sense of 'oneness', which immediately stamped the model 'Madder Valley', almost as if it was an actual location instead of the product of one man's fertile imagination. This was due in no small measure to his skill as a landscape, scenic and building modeller as his classic works on the subject, 'Miniature Landscape Modelling' and 'Miniature Building Construction', bear witness.

We can, of course, always invent excuses for satisfying our particular fancies when it comes to rolling stock. The favourite situation these days is to run a preservation line where it is possible to argue a case for mixing a very wide variety of rolling

Two views of the Glen Aros Light Railway, and imaginary 2ft 4½ in narrow gauge railway on the Scottish island of Mull. The model, built to 7mm scale, 16.5mm gauge, connects the Dervaig Granite Company's quarry with the harbour at Port-Na-Ba.

stock. The Bluebell Line in Sussex operates full-size locomotives which probably never met in their lives before they became preserved, and it is very easy to visualise other situations and other preservation schemes which might just as easily have come about. But preservation schemes are not the only source of imaginative projects. If, for example the Channel tunnel had been built 50 years ago when it was first thought of, it might now have been possible to see Continental locomotives as well as rolling stock running on British Rail and vice versa. This could be an excuse for adding a few of the wonderfully detailed Continental models to a British model railway system.

It is sometimes fascinating to imagine situations that might have been, especially if there is some foundation for the theory. History is full of examples of 'might-have beens' if certain events had happened in a different way. What, for example, 'might the Great Western Railway look like today if it had never been nationalised in 1948? What might the Lynton and Barnstaple Railway look like if a preservation society had been formed to save it instead of letting it be scrapped by the Southern Railway in 1935? What might a railway system have looked like in the Outer Hebrides if some important industry had developed in one of the islands which necessitated the construction of a line? As well as the purely imaginary situations such as these there are any number of actual schemes for building railways that never came to fruition. Some got as far as the building of earth works and civil engineering structures which never carried any revenue-earning rails, whereas others, maybe, go no further than the publication of a company prospectus. Many such schemes are revealed in the numerous railway history books that are available from bookshops and libraries, and they afford excellent subjects for imagining what things might have been like if they had been built. Creating a fictional history for such a line can become an absorbing sideline which gives scope for imagination as well as the need for research. Perhaps your own home

town had an idea for building a railway at one time which came to nothing?

I remember reading once of an ambitious post-World War 2 scheme for building a new station at Bath, in Somerset, which would have combined the Midland and Somerset and Dorset Railway station at Bath Green Park with the GWR at Bath Spa. What a place that would have been with S & D 2-8-0s, Midland Class 2 4-4-0s and Black 5s rubbing shoulders with GWR Castles, Kings and Halls and all the rest of the copper-capped brigade! This particular scheme might be too large a project to build in model form, as it was found to be with the full-size original, but there must be many other local schemes of lesser calibre which you may know about or could find out about in your own home area and which might form the basis of a model railway.

When deciding on the type of model railway you wish to build, there are a number of decisive factors which will govern your choice and which you will have to consider at the outset if you are not to experience disappointment later. For example, obviously there is no point setting your sights on a main line system if the space you have available is very limited. Main line express passenger trains require a lot more space in which to operate if they are not going to look ridiculous. In particular, they need wider-radius curves and a lengthy stretch of track on which to run if the train lengths are not going to look unreasonably short. Space therefore is a principal factor in determining the type of layout you can build successfully.

The availability of proprietary equipment may also be a point you will need to consider. If your ability to do a lot of the construction work is limited, you may need to fall back on ready-to-run proprietary items. Luckily, today the trade has introduced a wide range of items to satisfy most popular needs, especially in 00 and HO scales. However, despite the wide choice of accessories and construction aids available, it is simply not physically possible to cater for every single need. Boiler fittings are a case in point. Unless you are prepared to

Many pleasant hours could be spent watching the trains go by at this typical Southern Railway country station. Saunton Sands Junction for Woolacombe built in 3mm scale by John Bateman.
(Photo: Geoff Helliwell)

turn chimneys, domes and safety valve covers yourself, or have them turned for you at a price, you are possibly going to find it difficult to complete models of some of the older pre-grouping railway company locomotives. The amount of spare time you can afford is another important factor to take into consideration. As well as the time needed for construction there is also the question of maintenance to consider. This is something that beginners seldom give thought to until they come face to face with the problem. They find that they are devoting more and more time to cleaning and maintaining track, points and electrical connections and not enough to carrying out operating sessions and further new construction work. The larger and more complex the layout, the more cleaning there is to do and the greater the chance of point blades coming un-soldered, or the electrical wiring coming adrift or of the switches requiring attention.

Another point to consider, assuming you are keen to choose a particular prototype subject as a modelling project, is whether you are going to be satisfied with the limitation you may have set yourself in choosing that particular prototype, bearing in mind that the varieties of different locomotives may have been severely limited. I have in mind, for example, the Southern Railway Lyme Regis branch which would make a very attractive model scenically, but so far as I know there was only one type of locomotive that ran on this branch in latter years. Therefore, I am sure a modeller would begin to feel the limitations of such a modelling project after all the building and construction work had been completed. I think most of us like to see a bit of variety in our motive power and rolling stock, and undoubtedly it adds interest to the hobby. To deny yourself this pleasure would eventually be regretted, I feel sure.

The modern image enthusiast will most likely be tempted to build a main line type of layout since with the demise of the rural byways and branch lines much of British Rail's latter day activity and that of the newly privatised Train Operating Companies (TOCs) has been centered on the development of Inter-City train services and diesel or electric multiple units operating over high density regional or suburban passenger routes. There is perhaps less operating interest in running set-format trains such as HST's and diesel/or electrical multiple units but there were until recently sufficient locomotive hauled trains with Mk 1, Mk 2 or Mk 5 coaching stock to maintain interest and variety. The availability of ready to run equipment in the two popular gauges, N and 00, is certainly very good. One very welcome source of inspiration is the variation in liveries now to be found on Britain's railways. Railway buffs who follow every detail modification to the various TOC fleets of diesel and electric locomotives can enjoy modifying their own models to keep their stock up to date with the latest developments.

Should the lack of space inhibit the development of a fully fledged main line layout you could content yourself with moving diesel locos up and down or in and out of a model motive power depot if this is to your liking. Alternatively there are still a few BR freight yards, oil terminals and such like around which could be used as the basis for modelling. Ideas appear in the railway and model railway press and with modern image modelling a train journey to wherever you fancy is likely to generate ideas of your own.

In talking about modern railways I am thinking primarily of those in the UK, where following the demise of BR's Speedlink it became the policy of BR to concentrate on bulk loads on main trunk routes, most of the smaller station goods yards then being closed.

The situation is not quite the same in America and on the Continent, where the quieter backwaters of the railway system, though declining, are still to be found. Here it is possible to indulge in modern practice using up-to-date diesel locomotives hauling modern wagons in short-length freight trains of less than half a dozen wagons, each containing individual loads. Something akin to this may return to the UK as a result of rail freight coming into the hands of the English, Welsh & Scottish Railway (EWS) in 1996. EWS's parent company, Wisconsin Central, are renowned for reversing the decline in rail freight in their sphere of operations in the USA where wagonload freight accounts for a high proportion of their business. Modern image enthusiasts who pride themselves on keeping up to date look like being kept busy.

Nostalgia can be one of the most persuasive forces in choosing a subject for railway modelling. It is undoubtedly one of the reasons why the hobby is booming so much today. Britain's railways, and in fact railways all over the world, have gone, or are going through, a period of tremendous change which is radically altering their appeal. People still watch them from the lineside, but no doubt for different reasons than they did 20 or 30 years ago. Not many of the people who watched the trains go by then can find the same interest today. To those people 'things ain't what they used to be', and modelling has become a means of creating a three dimensional moving picture in miniature of something that was known and loved in the past, and is no longer there to be seen as a matter of course today. There is nothing wrong in that. If railway modelling is a hobby and a pastime why shouldn't the person – if he wants to – let it pander to his old-fashioned, outdated ideas and let him enjoy his backward-looking sentiment? Your own private model world is the perfect safety valve for expressing feelings such as these. There are enough occasions in our everyday life when we may have to conform to current trends and ideas and in very many instances we see the need and would not have it otherwise. But the sort of person who gained pleasure in whiling away the hours on a country station platform watching a tank engine shunt wagons in the goods yard, witness the local stopping passenger trains arriving and departing, the expresses roaring through and noting the variety of rolling stock and traffic movements, cannot be expected to experience the same pleasure today, when in all probability the station is closed to traffic, the goods yard rails lifted and the buildings and platform razed to the ground.

However, the old order of doing things is perfectly possible in model form and harms no one. There is no denying, with all the material aids there are today, that it is possible to produce some very realistic and convincing effects guaranteed to evoke thoughts of nostalgia from even the most hard-bitten cynic. The period you may wish to recapture will be governed by all sorts of personal motives, but setting a target date in your mind for the period of the model you intend to create will, if you do the job properly, involve the application of a certain degree of discipline in choosing prototypes to model, their colour schemes and insignia, and even such things as posters and hoardings, if you are going to succeed in creating a completely authentic model which, to you, represents a period in your past.

An authentic-looking model layout can be achieved by paying 100 per cent attention to detail – if you have the time to spare. But it is not by any means essential to work to such infinite limits, and indeed in many cases, particularly when it comes to scale distances, it is quite impossible to do so. As long as the atmosphere is established, the exact number of sleepers, paving stones, telegraph poles and other insignificant trivia does not matter at all. In choosing to build a particular model station, for example, many details such as the correct number and length of sidings, size of platforms and radius of points and curves may not be possible to reproduce within the space available. This is where the eye of an artist comes in. An artist can paint a picture which somehow or other looks more convincing and evokes a greater sense of awareness of the subject than the most technically perfect

photograph; yet should this be a portrait, it does not need to show every whisker, every wrinkle or blemish on the skin. The most successful portraits not only succeed in portraying the visual appearance of the sitter, they also tell you something about the subject as a person. The true artist does this with an eye and a feeling for the subject that defies description, but in essence he concentrates the subject matter on to his canvas, emphasising what matters at the expense of the more insignificant detail. In a sense the artist is someone who knows what to leave out rather than to put in, and I am sure this is true about the successful 'authentic' railway modeller. To evoke the sensation of the original prototype requires some degree of faithful observation and copying, but there are many details that can be legitimately shrunk to fit the space available, and some others that can probably be left out altogether.

When it comes to deciding what type of layout you want to build, the sky is the limit these days. Never before has there been so much variety to choose from and never before has it been so difficult to decide, and hence to make a start! This question of choice is sometimes a double-edged weapon. Too much of it and the need to make a decision itself becomes a problem. Provided you can overcome the problems of space, availability of proprietary parts and models, and any possible limitations on your budget or your free time, the question of choice does of course become a very personal one. You are obviously going to build the type of layout that interests you most and the reasons for your choice can be manifold. Let us take a look at the different types of layout you can choose from today, and the possible advantages or disadvantages of each one. I will ignore as far as possible the question of scale or gauge at this stage as we will discuss this more fully in the next chapter.

In no particular order of priority, merit or importance, I would suggest the following broad categories for differentiating between the various types of layouts:

Mainlines ancient and modern: the PW gang stand by to make way for a GNR Mogul and train of teak coaches as it sweeps round the curve towards Mereworth Junction. Gentle curves, by model railway standards, enable full length intercity trains to operate on the MRC 4mm scale club layout New Annington.

Main line

By this I mean a large layout on which you can run main line express passenger trains of at least five or six coach length at scale express passenger train speeds. Even in the smallest gauges and scales such a layout demands a fair degree of space to accommodate the large-radius curves and length of running rails that are necessary if any degree of realism is to be achieved. The sight of an express train chasing its tail round a tight circle of track looks quite ridiculous and unworthy of the attentions of a serious modeller. Five or six coaches are the very minimum you should aim at, as most main

line express passenger trains are usually double this length. Needless to say, any improvement on five or six coaches will add realism to the layout. Station platforms, assuming a station as a necessity, must of course be long enough to accommodate the coaches and, if it is to be a terminus, the locomotive as well. Size and the space available are really the limiting factors when deciding whether you can build a main line layout. One of the desirable features of such a layout is that it gives unlimited scope for operating models of your choice, since there need not be any restriction on the type of locomotives or rolling stock you can legitimately run. You can have the largest express

All the desirable attributes of a branch line terminus are featured in this 3mm scale model of Woolacombe by John Bateman. Note the clever photo montage forming the scenic backcloth.

(Photo: Geoff Helliwell)

passenger engines, goods engines, small tank engines and as much rolling stock, carriages and wagons as you can find room for.

Branch line

Perhaps the opposite end of the scale to a main line layout, the branch line has become tremendously popular because of its space-saving possibilities. Even so, most prototype branch lines occupied (the past tense is more often than not necessary, as most of them are now closed) more space than the average modeller could hope to spare, but a large degree of licence can be used to compress station track plans, sidings and lineside features into the minimum space available without detracting too seriously from the overall effect. Above all, most branch line layouts can be operated realistically with short length trains two or three coaches

being quite sufficient in some cases, with engines that are themselves short in length. The generic description 'branch line' has also come to include the small cross-country through route which was also operated by short length trains and small engines, and had an atmosphere similar to the branch line. However, the important difference with the branch line is that it had a terminus at the extreme end of the line. It is the building and operating of such a terminal station that provides so much of the attraction of the branch line layout. The one possible snag is that generally speaking, you have to exclude the larger, more exciting engines from your stud of locomotives, although you could justifiably circumvent this rule by choosing to model a branch line based on one of the privately preserved railways. Most of these retain the basic characteristics of a branch line, i.e. single track and compact terminal station facilities, yet they operate a wide variety of locomotives covering all periods, pre and post-nationalisation, steam and diesel. Though predominantly passenger orientated even to the extent of running a buffet car and full restaurant car services, the occasional goods train is not unknown. Those with end-on connection to the national network also see occasional through trains thus giving scope for even more variety. For anyone whose main interest is in locomotives and rolling stock a layout based on a preserved railway, either real or imaginary, is one way of combining the best of all worlds. You can even justify installing a short narrow gauge or miniature railway alongside the standard gauge line since a number of preserved railways indulge in this sort of activity.

Modern

By modern we generally mean the contemporary post-steam era of today. Perhaps the odd steam locomotive can be allowed to creep in, but broadly speaking – in Britain at any rate – the motive power will be diesel or electric. Such a layout will, if it is to achieve any reasonable degree of realism, demand a fair amount of space as the tendency for modern railway systems is to concentrate on long haul block trains travelling great distances at speed. The same problems that apply to main line layouts will therefore apply to the modern-style system, in that large radius curves and a reasonably long length of run will be required. The main advantage of modern contemporary layouts is that you can draw inspiration from real-life locomotives and trains which can be seen working any day of the week. Problems regarding the prototype, such as livery, details of construction, up-to-date modifications, operating methods, etc., can be resolved quite simply by going out to see for yourself. The disadvantages, in addition to the big one of space requirements, appear to me to be that, since most modern trains run as block trains or multiple units, which shuttle back and forth, there does not appear to be so much opportunity for variety of rolling stock, train formations and operating methods as there does with the older type of railway system that had a greater emphasis on individual wagon loads.

Modern motive power on the Epsom and Ewell Model Railway Club's 00 gauge Westhill Parkway.
(Photo: Philip Reid)

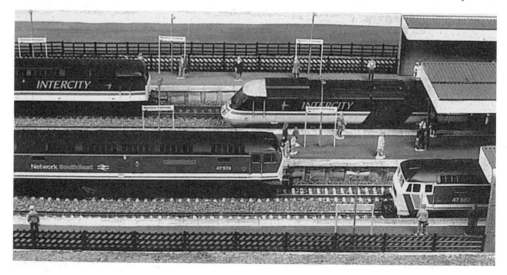

Historical

Using historical in the very broadest sense I mean anything that is not contemporary with today. In Britain this type of layout could be broken down into very clearly defined periods based on events that affected the structure or organisation of our railways. Until recently the most obvious periods and events were: post- or pre-nationalisation, pre-grouping, Edwardian, or early Victorian primitive. Following the privatisation of British Rail we now need to add a new period which I suppose will become known as post-privatisation and hope this will not be confused with the privatised preserved railways or the railways which were all privately owned before they were nationalised. The continental model railway manufacturers operate a well-established and easy to follow system of epoch or era numbers which clearly define the various periods as seen through the eyes of continental railway modellers. The system is particularly helpful when establishing the period appropriate to different livery, lettering and number combinations. Coming back to Britain the post-nationalisation period of the middle to late 1950s perhaps offers the widest choice of prototype material, since during this time most of the locomotives and rolling stock from the four main pre-nationalisation railway companies were still operating together with the standard British Railways designs and there is scope for mixing steam, diesel and electric propulsion together. This period enjoys widespread support from the trade and there is every indication that with the passage of time the flames of nostalgia are being fanned to the extent that the 1950s period is gaining in popularity.

Hitherto the most popular historical period for modelling has been the immediate pre-nationalisation era of the late 1930s and 1940s (but ignoring the war years), and

LNWR 'Cornwall' hauling a NER horsebox and LNWR passenger brake van passing a train of GWR 4-wheel coaches create an old-time atmosphere on the 00 gauge Ashley Bridge layout of Robert Tivendale.

the big attraction of this period is undoubtedly the smart liveries used by the four main railway companies – LMS, LNER, GWR and SR. There is a very wide choice of equipment, kits, finished model and accessories covering this period and no practical difficulty in the way of making a successful model. The GWR is acknowledged as being the most popular of the four main groups and there is no shortage of kits, models and prototype information to enable anyone to make an authentic model based on GWR practice, provided you are prepared not to introduce pre-nationalisation prototypes or mix post-World War 2 locomotives and liveries on a layout based on practice in the 1930s. This sort of discipline takes some watching. It comes easy enough if you have accurate memories of the periods concerned, but you are at the mercy of other people if you were born after this period. Checking up on past practices can be regarded as part of the fun of an historical layout and it is well worthwhile to make a thorough job of it for the satisfaction it undoubtedly gives. You may, however, have to prepare yourself for the time when someone tells you that things were never done that way and you have been wasting your time because you have done it all wrong! It's bound to happen so prepare yourself for it so that it doesn't worry you so much when it comes. If you have got all your facts together and you can prove you are right and the other fellow is wrong, so much the better!

Going back into history still further, the next generally accepted demarcation point in British railway history is the grouping of 1923, when the then comparatively large number of independent railway companies, some of them quite small in size, were amalgamated to make the big four. The immediate pre-grouping period was marred by World War 1, but prior to that we of course had the Edwardian period and this is generally accepted as being the heyday of Britain's railways. Railways spread their tentacles all over the country and carried all the freight and passenger traffic that was worth carrying. Competition was beginning

to be felt though, mainly from the electric street trams, but this only encouraged the railway companies to devise means of combating the opposition which added yet more variety to an already abundant collection of locomotives and rolling stock. Because of this tremendous variety of equipment and the wide diversity of designs, liveries and colour schemes, the model railway manufacturers can only scratch at the surface, and it may not be possible to build up a comprehensive and at the same time representative collection of rolling stock items for every pre-grouping railway company, using commercially produced models and parts. It must therefore be accepted that, for some Edwardian layouts, rather more items must be home-made or scratch-built than for models based on a later period in time. This will depend on whatever pre-grouping railway you have chosen to model since some are supported by the trade more than others. Both the GWR and the Midland Railway for example are very well served with a comprehensive range of locomotive, carriage, wagon and accessory kits. Wagons possibly present the least problem since they were interchangeable from one railway company to another. With the exception of some specialist vehicles and goods brake vans of which you will require comparatively few, the range of wagon kits available will cope with most needs. There is a good selection of locomotive kits available suitable for the Edwardian era and practically all the pre-grouping railway companies are represented as will be seen from Appendix 5, even to the extent of a few ready to run models. Coaching stock is one area where you may have to resort to scratch-building depending on the company you have chosen to model although there are some plastic kits of LNWR and MR prototypes and there are many more etched brass kits available covering most of the major pre-grouping railway companies.

When it comes to scratch-building or assembling kits, perhaps the biggest single problem will be the painting, lining and lettering. Not all pre-grouping colours are available ready-mixed, so careful preparation will be required in a number of cases. Then, when it comes to adding the lining and lettering, the elaborate styles used by most pre-grouping companies will require a fair degree of skill to apply, and there is not the wide range of transfers to help that there is with the post-grouping period. Unless you are particularly skilful as a painter it is very probable that some simplification of the livery details will be required.

Going back to the first days of railways, the early Victorian primitives such as the Liverpool to Manchester Railway present another and different challenge to modellers since, as well as having to construct practically all the equipment yourself, you will also have to do a lot of the research. Just about everything was different in those days—locomotives, coaches and wagons, signalling and even the trackwork which, judging from the early prints we see, appears to have been ballasted with cinders which hid all traces of the sleepers. The GWR 7 ft ¼ in Broad Gauge which comes within this period has attracted a considerable following encouraged no doubt by the activities of the Broad Gauge Society, the availability of a number of locomotive and rolling stock kits and the innate novelty of the prototype. There is unlimited scope for finding inspiration in the early Victorian railways, although a fair amount of digging will be required to establish facts on many items which we take for granted today. Modelling in this period does call for a lot of hard work, but at least you have the satisfaction of doing something different and of arousing the interests of others should you decide to put the results of your work on exhibition. It might also be considered that you are undertaking a worthwhile piece of historical research.

It almost goes without saying that anyone who is interested in modelling based on historical times, whatever period is chosen, is well advised to join the Historical Model Railway Society, which caters for the needs of such modellers. The historical facts that modellers seek are not necessarily those recorded by historians, and more specialised information is required than can usually be found in most history books on railways. Piecing together such information can be a long business if you work on your own. However, it is often possible to find someone in a society such as this who has already covered the same ground and who will be willing to share his information with you. It really is amazing how absorbing the quest for information can become once the interest has been roused, and the need for such research can offer a new dimension to the hobby.

Overseas railways

National characteristics can result in different types of railways as practically everyone knows, and an increasing number of railway modellers in Britain are turning to the continent of Europe or to North America as a source of inspiration for their railway modelling. In many cases this is due to the ever increasing range of high quality, beautifully detailed, locomotives and rolling stock produced by foreign manufacturers. The temptation is difficult to resist when glancing through some of their catalogues and most items are readily available from specialist dealers in the UK. In many cases prices are higher than one is accustomed to pay for British outline models, but some people regard the extra expense as justified in exchange for the high degree of workmanship that most of these models exhibit. An added attraction is the correct scale/track gauge ratio. Many modellers have felt the urge to build a layout based on experiences gained from taking holidays abroad. The ease and frequency with which such holidays can be embarked upon is no doubt another reason why overseas railways, particularly those on the continent of Europe, are increasing in popularity.

So far as the Continent is concerned there is so much equipment available that you can build up a representative collection of rolling stock and accessories for most European countries, especially France, Germany, Italy, Austria and Switzerland. The characteristics of each of these countries' railways differ widely, but perhaps the most popular are the Alpine regions of Bavaria, Austria and Switzerland. The scenic settings possible in model form can be nearly as breathtaking as the originals and they lend themselves well to modelling, since the many tightly curved spirals, tunnels and lines climbing over one another enable a comprehensive layout with immense operating possibilities to be constructed in a very small space. As well as locomotives, rolling stock, overhead electric gear and all the other paraphernalia required to build up a representative Continental railway system in miniature, there is also an unsurpassed range of colourful plastic building and accessory kits designed to a constant scale which enable anyone to build up the authentic scenic setting. Perhaps because there is so much ready-made proprietary equipment obtainable from abroad, very few Continental railway modellers go in for making their own locomotives and rolling stock. The idea has, however, caught on thanks due in no small way to the enterprise of some British manufacturers such as DJH and K's. These two firms have produced some very good kits for locomotives and

railcars, mostly French prototypes but other besides. New kits are comprehensively reviewed in the Continental foreign language model railway press whenever they appear and it is gratifying to see them generally well received.

Modellers of American-type railways, on the other hand, go in for a lot of kit building as well as ready-made items. American models are also very well supported by manufacturers outside America, who find the American market an attractive prospect for building up a lucrative export trade. As a consequence, there is a vast range of equipment available from manufacturers all over the world, but most of it compatible. Quite a lot of this equipment is available in Britain and there are firms who specialise in American prototype models and their importation. American outline locomotive and rolling stock models are reasonably priced and generally represent good value for money which together with the quality and uniformly high standard of most of the products attract a lot of people to this branch of modelling. Another attraction is the scenic possibilities in American-style layouts. They can and usually do reach high levels of

A scene on Bill Lane's HO gauge Detroit & Midwestern RR portraying an imaginary American railroad south of Detroit in the 1920s. The Erie RR Mallet 'Camelback' is a most unusual model.

Power extraordinary as double-headed trains pass each other on the Detroit & Midwestern RR

ingenuity, with wooden trestle bridges crossing rugged mountains gorges in terrain and between towns which look very reminiscent of the Wild West of the cowboys.

I have little personal experience of American railway modelling, or railroad modelling as we should perhaps refer to it, but the advantages appear to be perfectly obvious in that there is no lack of equipment and no shortage of inspiration so far as subject matter is concerned. The only possible difficulty I foresee is to be able to resist buying one of those Union Pacific 'Big Boy' 4-8-8-4s and, having bought one, finding

room in which to operate it. Admittedly most of the commercially made locomotive models of American prototypes are ingeniously designed to enable them to traverse minimum-radius curves, but who wants to spoil the sight of those magnificent beasts by having it practically chasing its own tail? The sheer length of most items of North American rolling stock, locomotives, carriages and freight cars is a bit daunting and for best effect a fair measure of space seems necessary to run representative trains on a continuous run layout. However, there is ample scope for building a compact end

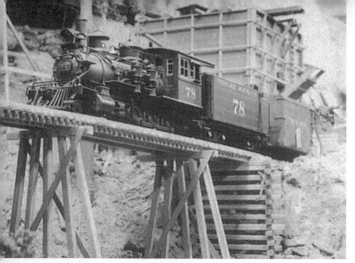

Left Lightweight 2–8–0 No 78 crosses a typical American timber trestle bridge on Leigh Clark's Tuscah Rock Company HO guage railroad.

Hobendorf faithfully portrays a Deutsch Reichsbahn (pre-war German State Railways) branch line set in Bavaria in the period 1923-38. **Above left** Roco HO model of DR Class 58 2-10-0 fitted with coal-dust tender by Gunther. The appropriate vintage lorry confirms the period setting; **Left** DR Class 89 0-6-0T by Fleischmann leaves with a short freight train.

Right *French ambiance lovingly created by Andy Hart and Roger Beacham of the SCNF Society in their imaginative Achaux (HO!) layout set in the mid-1960s. Vintage Renault machinery is represented by the railcar assembled from a K's kit and the lorry by the French firm Top-Models. The express awaiting departure is composed of France-Trains coaches. Under the wires the freight train hauled by a Roco BB300 electric locomotive includes an Inter-frigo van assembled from the erstwhile Airfix kit.*

(Photo: Andy Hart)

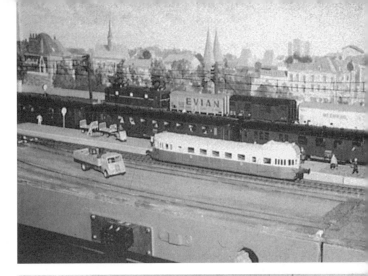

Right *The Achaux baseboard is only 18in wide, but the appearance of extra depth is given by the excellent hand-painted backscene here showing a representation of Chartres cathedral. The Jouef 231-K sits in the platform road awaiting release. An obligatory 2CV is parked in the station forecourt.*

Photo: Andy Hart

Right *John Rowcroft's La Roche is an HO layout based on the Nord Railway in the 1930s. The selection of appropriate vintage rolling stock shown in this view includes a train of wine wagons.*

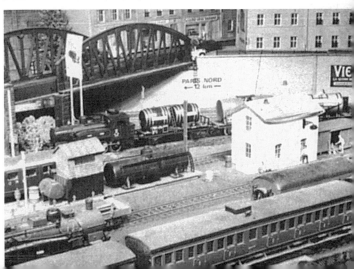

to end terminal to fiddle yard layout based on American short line practice if you are content with this mode of operation.

In talking broadly of Continental and American-type railways I realise that these, too, can be broken down into categories much as I have done previously with Britain's railways. You can go back in history and pick whatever period interests you the most. There is, for example, a wide interest in old-time American locomotives and rolling stock, and consequently there is a fair amount of equipment available in model form covering this period. Continental models tend to favour the more modern post-war era, but older models are not by any means unknown. In contrast to railways at home, those on the Continent have been expanding their traffic at a high rate in post-war years and this is abundantly clear when travelling abroad, especially in France, Germany and Switzerland. Railway wagons appear everywhere, from individual ones in small factory sidings, many of them having to cross public roads to reach their destination, to vast well-stocked marshalling yards and freight depots. To many people's eyes the typical Continental model railway looks over-crowded compared with what we are used to in Britain, and there is an apparent tendency to cram in as much equipment on the baseboard as the space available will stand. To some extent this criticism is valid, but at the same time there are many congested railway centres on the Continent that create this impression in real life, and the Continental modeller can find justification for portraying something similar in his own miniature system. The monthly magazine, *Continental Modeller*, is recommended reading for the average enthusiast modelling overseas railways. For details, see Appendix 2.

Track gauge

As well as the geographical and historical distinctions one can choose from, there is yet another area of choice, namely the one of track gauge. By this I mean the gauge of the prototype, not the model, as model gauges are discussed in the next chapter. When referring to prototype railways we generally talk about standard gauge or narrow gauge. Standard gauge is 4 ft 8½ in, which owes its origin to Britain and its adoption throughout the rest of the world to the fact that British engineers took the gauge with them when they built many of the overseas railways. Narrow gauge is anything less than 4 ft 8½ in, and can cover a very wide range. The most popular narrow gauges are probably 2 ft, 3 ft, 1 metre and 3 ft 6 in, but there are any number of others particularly in the 2 ft to 3 ft range. They can, of course, go down to as little as 15 in as we know with the Romney Hythe and Dymchurch Railway and the Ravenglass & Eskdale Railway. It follows that any of these narrow gauge prototypes can be modelled and you have the choice of deciding either to adjust the scale of your models to suit a particular recognised model track gauge or you can adjust the model track gauge to suit a particular model scale. We will go into this in more detail in the next chapter. The smaller narrow gauge models have a particular charm of their own as invariably the prototypes were built to fulfil a need for transport in a remote area, or where traffic potential was too small or the terrain too difficult to justify the expense of a standard gauge line. The need for economy usually manifests itself in steeper gradients and sharper curves, both of which lend themselves to modelling where space is restricted. The scenery can also be spectacular too. The need for economical operation often results in those delightful mixed trains consisting of both passenger coaches and goods wagons of ancient and long-lasting vintage, all of which make such delightful subjects for modelling.

There is no lack of suitable prototypes on which to base a narrow gauge model layout but there is a tendency amongst modellers working on narrow gauge prototypes to mix their prototypes rather more freely than the standard gauge modellers who invariably prefer to follow one particular company. This freelance aspect of narrow gauge railway modelling is generally tolerated and accepted, but why this should be so, more than it is with the standard gauge, is difficult

Right *Coming round the mountain! Spectacular scenery on Dave Anning's Hengaeau, an 009 narrow gauge layout inspired by the 'Great Little Trains of Wales'.*

Below *'Prince' brings its train of 4-wheel coaches down from the hills at Hengaeau en route to Porthmeir Harbour.*

to understand or explain. Possibly it is because many actual narrow gauge systems, even the best regulated ones, have an independent atmosphere of their own. Certainly many of them have a very wide variety of rolling stock and equipment which is often lacking on the larger standard gauge prototypes, and it is quite possible to find a narrow gauge railway on which no two engines or carriages look alike. To add another of your own invention to your layout is hardly likely to raise many eyebrows.

It is not at all difficult to dream up reasons for building an imaginary narrow gauge system, possibly as a preservation scheme or as a gesture in serving some remote area of country without rail transport. Whatever the reason, you can delight in designing and building your own locomotives, carriages and wagons evolving your own livery, company crest and 'corporate image' if you want one,

and creating a world of your own in miniature which can be good fun. Alternatively, you can pick a particular prototype and create a faithful image of it. Should you wish to choose a British prototype this will necessitate kit or scratch building since, at the time of writing, there are no ready to run models available. However, it is an entirely different picture when it comes to continental narrow gauge prototypes, in particular the Swiss metre gauge Rhätische Bahn (RhB) system and its associated companies. The catalogue of the German firm Bemo contains an absolute plethora of ready to run locomotives, railcars, carriages and wagons from which an authentic model of almost any region of this extensive metre gauge system can be modelled. The RhB and other similar narrow gauge railways on the continent operate as fully fledged transport systems all the year round unlike the narrow gauge railways

A view showing the unique appearance of GWR broad gauge track with its longitudinal sleepers and tie rods. The locomotive is a 'Rover' class 4-2-2.

to be found in Britain today where they operate principally as seasonal tourist attractions.

No talk of track gauges would be complete without mentioning the broad gauges, that is gauges larger than the standard gauge of 4 ft 8½ in. These exist throughout the world, notably the 5 ft gauge in Russia, the 5 ft 3 in gauge in Ireland and part of Australia, and the 5 ft 6 in gauge in Spain, Portugal and parts of India and South America. There was also, of course, Brunel's famous 7 ft 0¼ in on the GWR, but this was dropped as long ago as 1892. Strangely enough, most of these broad gauges, with the exception of Brunel's, appear hardly distinguishable from the standard gauge when seen in the flesh and you have to make a conscious attempt to notice any difference when looking at them. This is some justification at least for ignoring the

difference when making a model of one or other of them.

If you do wish to model one of these broad gauge systems (the Irish railways are very popular amongst modellers and there are some delightful prototypes to be found amongst them to model) the difficulties of working to an exact scale/gauge ratio may make it necessary to compromise. The 7 ft gauge is, of course, quite a different thing. It always was a curiosity and the effect in model form is quite stunning. To choose the old GWR broad gauge is less daunting a task that it was when the first edition of this book was published. The number of models I have seen produced to this prototype gauge convince me that here there is a lot of scope for the really inventive modeller who wants to do something rather different from the rest.

CHAPTER 4
How to decide on scale and gauge

The choice of scales and gauges has never been wider. Each has its merits and its place in the order of things, and each is worthy of full consideration before finally making up your mind which one to follow. A necessary feature of railway modelling is that everything on a layout is, or at least should be, built to a constant scale. There is not the freedom that there is in some other modelling hobbies to change scale from one model to another. The only way you can change is either to scrap or perhaps part-exchange your earlier efforts and start all over again, or else build and operate more than one complete layout. The last suggestion is not so outrageous, as more and more people are beginning to find out. The commercially produced items of equipment for the new smaller gauges are becoming so fascinating that some modellers who have long-established layouts in one of the older, larger scales are now building a second small portable layout on which they can indulge their liking for the new small scale products. The two-car family is now being joined by the two-layout railway modeller!

Scales and gauges are sometimes bewildering for the beginner, but they are the first basic rule or standard by which all railway modelling is categorised and judged. It is thus important to have a ready understanding of the descriptions, codes names and relative position of each scale so that you have some idea of what your fellow railway modellers are talking about. It is also necessary to grasp the distinction between scale and gauge, since these terms are often used together and regrettably sometimes become misplaced.

As far as the railway modeller is concerned, scale means the ratio between a unit of measurement on a model compared with a unit of measurement on the comparable full-size prototype. For example, a model measuring 10 in, based on a full-size prototype which measures 10 ft, would be built to a scale of 1 in to the ft. (A map which shows every mile as 1 in is drawn to a scale of 1 in to the mile; a 1-in Ordnance Survey map is drawn to the ratio or scale of 1:63,360.) Another way of regarding scale is to express it as a ratio. The ratio of reduction of a model built to the scale of 1 in to the ft would be 1 to 12, 1:12 or 1/12.

In railway modelling we have, in the past 40 or so years at least, grown up with the idea of expressing scale as so many millimetres to the foot, eg, 2 mm to the ft, 3.5 mm to the ft, 4 mm to the ft and 7 mm to the ft, etc. The common use of millimetres in railway modelling has until recently been a frequent means of first becoming acquainted with the metric scale. There is probably a well-meaning historical basis for this business of mixing millimetres with feet, but I must confess that I do not know the reason. I only know I have grown up with it and have found it easy to use and to think with.

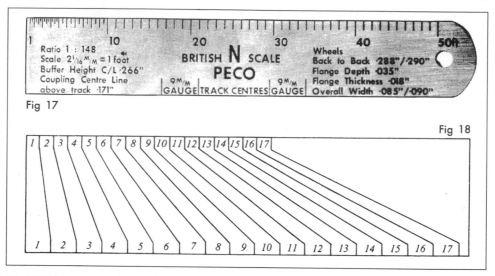

Fig 17 _This handy N scale rule (reduced in size here) is produced by Peco and is available from stockists._
Fig 18 _A simple home-made ruler converting measurements from one scale to another–in this case from 4mm scale (00 gauge) to 7mm scale (O gauge) and vice versa. Each division represents 1 ft._

This is particularly true with 4 mm scale (4mm to the ft), since 4 mm is easily divided by 4 to give the equivalent scale dimension for 3, 6 or 9 in. A 4 mm scale model of a locomotive driving wheel 5 ft 9 in in diameter is 23 mm, and it easily becomes second nature to do the calculation $5 \times 4 = 20 + 3 = 23$ as simple mental arithmetic when the occasion arises. The recent introduction of the new British N gauge scale of 2⅟₁₆ mm to the foot has, however, complicated the thought processes. For a scale such as this, which does not have such a simple unit of measurement, I think it is essential to use a special conversion rule, such as the 'British N Scale' produced by Peco, showing feet reduced to the correct scale dimension. You simply find out the full-size prototype dimension in feet and measure off the scale measurement from the ruler. Likewise, to find the scale dimension in feet from a model, you measure the model with the ruler and read off the dimension in feet. (See Fig 17).

Another useful aid when making a drawing in one scale copied from another drawn to a larger or smaller scale is to construct a ruler showing both the scales you are using, each one drawn along opposite edges of the ruler, with lines connecting relative units of measurement. (See Fig 18.) This way it is simple to translate the dimension from one scale to the other without having to go through any complicated mathematical processes. First, from the drawing you are copying, you simply read off the measurement along the side of the ruler having the scale that corresponds to that drawing, then you read off the corresponding unit of measurement on the other side of the ruler and transfer this to the new drawing you are making.

Gauge or track gauge is, as we have discussed in the previous chapter, the distance between the two running rails. There is also another form of gauge, known as the loading gauge, which refers to the maximum permissible width and height for railway rolling stock to enable it to clear bridges, tunnels, station platforms and other obstructions which come close to the railway line. The _track_ gauge on British, Continental and American standard gauge

(4 ft 8½ in) is virtually the same but, because the loading gauge is bigger on the Continent and in America, it is possible to run much wider and taller locomotives, carriages and wagons on these railways than is permissible in Britain. (See Fig 19.)

In Britain the maximum permitted height and width is normally only 13 ft 6 in and 9 ft 0 in, respectively, less on some lines with particular loading gauge restrictions, and more in a few other cases where the gauge has been built more generously. However, in Europe, rolling stock which is over 10 ft wide can be operated, and in America they can run rolling stock 15 ft high and 10 ft 6 in wide. In South Africa, although the track gauge is only 3 ft 6 in (1 ft 2½ in less than in Britain), the rolling stock can be as wide as 10 ft, which is 1 ft wider than in Britain. It is important to realise the distinction between track gauge and loading gauge and to remember why Continental and American railway rolling stock is so much bigger, wider and taller than in Britain, although the rails are nominally gauged the same distance apart.

You could be forgiven for assuming that if we decide to make an accurate model railway engine to a scale of 4 mm to the ft we would also make the track gauge to the same scale. Assuming a standard gauge

locomotive we would expect the track gauge for a 4 mm scale model to be 18.83 mm (ie 4 ft 8½ in at 4 mm to the foot = 4 × 4 = 16, plus 2 = 18, plus 2½/3 or 5/6 = 18.83). If you are prepared to go to the trouble of making the locomotive yourself to a high-precision standard there is absolutely no reason why you should not use a gauge of 18.83 mm. In fact this can be and is being done on an increasing scale and there are a number of commercially available parts and accessories to assist in the process but, as yet, no ready-to-run models. A model railway built to an accurate scale track gauge requires a higher level of painstaking construction work on track and rolling stock and those who are not prepared to devote so much time to this task, as desirable as it may be, or feel they do not possess the necessary skill, have to rely on the trade for a large part of their equipment.

To produce model railway equipment in large numbers that will sell at reasonably competitive prices commercial manufacturers cannot afford to make all their products to the same high standard of precision as a meticulous worker with time to spare. In addition, to enjoy maximum sales which is essential if prices are to be kept at saleable levels, these firms have to

Fig 19 *Average British, Continental and American loading gauges.*

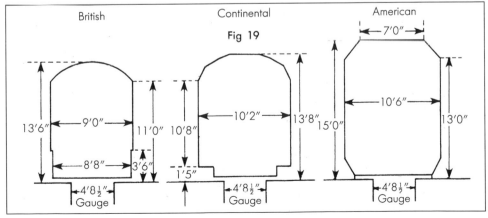

cater for a wide ranging market including inexperienced youngsters as well as the dedicated enthusiasts. As a result, they have to incorporate into their models a certain amount of robustness to withstand relatively rough treatment and the occasional knock and bang. In addition, the rolling stock has to be designed to traverse curves sharper in radius than any that would be found in prototype practice. Therefore moving parts have to be thicker in proportion to their full-size counterparts. Also greater clearance has to be provided between moving parts to give perfectly free movement and to enable bogies to pivot sufficiently to negotiate the sharp-radius curves. The running rail itself has to be slightly wider to give it enough strength and the wheels have to be thicker, with wider and deeper flanges to ensure that they retain their place on the rails. I know these ideas are being successfully challenged by the true scale modellers and I also know that the degree with which manufacturers add thickness and tolerances to their models is being whittled down compared to 35, 20, or even just a few years ago. However, it is probably true to say that, for commercially produced models built down to a price level and capable of going round curves of short radius, it will never be possible for manufacturers to offer exact scale models of British prototypes with the severe limitations of the British loading gauge.

Some working parts, particularly the outside valve gear on locomotives, have to be built differently on the model compared to the full-size engine, and in many cases it becomes difficult in the restricted space available to build a model with the same working actions as the prototype. Bogie sides are another case in point. It is common practice for commercial manufacturers to produce bogies for coaches, vans and bogie wagons out of metal castings or plastic mouldings. To make these with any degree of strength or rigidity they must be proportionally thicker than the full-size bogie if tolerances between wheel and

bogie side are not to be brought to, commercially speaking, unworkably fine levels. So, for commercial reasons, the track gauge for most British outline model railway equipment is something less than the scale dimension of the full-size track. The reason for this is almost entirely due to the restricted width of the full size British loading gauge.

The foregoing explains the subject of scales and gauges and the problems that can arise with them. Now let us take a detailed look at the different scales and gauges that are recognised and commonly used in the model railway hobby today, and consider some of the advantages and disadvantages of each. Beginning with Standard Gauge (4 ft 8½ in) systems and starting with the newest and smallest.

Z gauge

1:220 or approximately 1½ mm to the foot scale; 6.5 mm gauge.

The German firm Marklin astonished the model railway world at the 1972 Nuremberg Toy Fair by introducing this entirely new ultra-small gauge marketed under the banner of the Marklin Mini-Club system. It is a complete system comprising working model outline steam, diesel and electric locomotives, carriages, wagons, track and a growing range of accessories, so that an authentic model railway can be built up by using the products of this one proprietary make. The smallest 0-6-0T locomotive is only 1⅞ in long, a 4-6-2 Pacific locomotive with three working headlights 4⅜ in long, and a Continental coach 4⅜ in long. Models of American as well as German and Swiss prototypes are available. If space is very restricted and you are determined to have a layout, Z gauge could .be your answer. Understandably prices reflect the high degree of precision needed to make such small models. Peco Streamline flexible track is available in Z gauge as are foam ballast inlays to fit the Peco track and Marklin turnouts and crossings.

The excellent appearance of Denys Brownlee's scratch-built trackwork enhances this view of his 2mm scale Leefield layout.

such it is only likely to remain a scale for the dedicated enthusiast. The 2 mm Scale Association serves the needs of the band of enthusiasts who have accepted the challenge of modelling in this scale. The brilliantly successful work that has been achieved in this very small scale leads one to believe that any and all things are possible in railway modelling.

N gauge

1:148 or 2. 06 mm/1 ft scale for British prototypes; 1:160 or 1.91 mm/1 ft scale for Continental prototypes, 9 mm gauge.

N gauge has a track gauge of 9 mm but has two scales—1:148 for British prototypes and 1:160 for Continental prototypes. This is due in the main to the restrictions of the British full-size loading gauge, as explained earlier. N (for 9 mm) gauge was pioneered on the Continent and in a very short space of time has attracted a flood of new equipment from a number of commercial firms, principally in Germany and Italy. To enable British modellers to enjoy the fruits of some of these developments from overseas, the slightly larger British scale was devised to enable mechanisms and certain equipment built by Continental manufacturers for models designed to the large Continental loading gauge to be incorporated in the restricted loading gauge of British prototype models. Trackwork with a

000

1:152 or 2 mm to the foot scale; 9.42 mm gauge.

This was the forerunner of the ultra-small scales but has been superseded in the commercial world by N gauge. with which it should not be confused. Because 000 has not been adopted commercially it is now only used by the modeller who was either formerly established in the gauge before the trade entered into the ultra-small scale field or else because he is prepared to undertake a lot of highly detailed work himself. As

The space-saving properties of N gauge give scope for fully develped scenery and long length trains. Shown here are two views of Brigenshaw by Bernard Taylor; **Above** *Two Class 20 diesels double-head a long mineral train.* **Left** *The high level station forecourt (the tracks are below) shows excellent attention to detail and clever merging of the 3D buildings into the flat scenic background.*

common gauge of 9 mm is, of course, used by both Continental and British scales.

N gauge is developing rapidly, and a wide variety of models is now available. As I feel so assured that the gauge is firmly established I am confident that the choice of products is bound to increase.

There are a number of positive advantages in this gauge. The principal one is the reduced space required compared to the other larger gauges. It is practically half the size of 00 and HO, which for so long were previously accepted as the smallest practical table-top scales. So far N gauge models have

been to a uniformly high standard, and most modellers find the gauge very satisfying to work with. The workmanship, detail and performance are mostly the equal of larger-scale commercially produced models, and in some cases, particularly with regard to performance, appear to be superior to those of larger scales. Perhaps this is due to the degree of precision with which N gauge models have to be made, for they have to be very good to work at all.

One important advantage, which so far N gauge has been able to hold on to, is the universal coupling that has become standard and which means that proprietary equipment of all the different makes can be mixed and operated together. In this respect N gauge has the advantage of being a late-comer, since all the big problems which beset the earlier larger scales and gauges were ironed out by the time N gauge appeared.

I would recommend N gauge to any would-be newcomer to the hobby. It is a practical gauge and so far the wide choice of products are reasonably priced, considering the precision with which they have had to be designed and manufactured. Although the gauge has possibilities for a minimum space layout, the best way to approach N gauge is to continue to think in terms of the space we are accustomed to with 00 and other larger gauges and to expand the layout to fill the space! You can then do all the things that are so desirable, but so difficult in the larger scales, such as use large-radius curves, long station platforms and train lengths (N gauge locomotives are fantastic haulers) and generally introduce a degree of spaciousness and realism which is so often sadly lacking from layouts built to larger scales. The one disadvantage is the difficulty most people are likely to have in scratch-building. It is not impossible, as many examples already produced will prove, but for the average modeller it is certainly not going to be as easy as with 00 gauge and the larger gauges.

TT

1:120 or 2.5 mm/1 ft scale for Continental prototypes; or 1:101.6 or 3 mm/1 ft scale for British prototypes, where it is known as TT3, 12 mm gauge.

TT standing for 'Table Top' was introduced commercially in America by H.P. Products and on the Continent by Rokal of Germany. The UK version of TT, referred to as TT3, was introduced commercially in Britain by Tri-ang in 1957. Scaled at 3 mm to the foot, three-quarters the size of 00, it appealed to space conscious modellers seeking means whereby a model railway could be built taking up less room than 00. A full range of equipment was offered by Tri-ang; locomotives, rolling stock, track and accessories, and other specialist manufacturers supported the new scale with kits and construction parts. Tri-ang continued to develop TT3 for a number of years but the

future of TT3 became less certain as a commercial proposition when N gauge began to establish itself in the early nineteen-sixties. Eventually Tri-ang were forced to cease production of their TT3 range. So far as the commercial side of TT is concerned there are a number of firms producing 1:120 scale TT equipment on the Continent foremost being Tillig which took over the former East German company Berliner-TT-Bahnen. These products are available in the UK from TT International who specialise in Continental TT model railway systems.

Notwithstanding the demise of Tri-ang TT3, the scale of 3 mm to the foot became firmly established and still enjoys an enthusiastic and faithful following in the UK. Much credit I feel must be due to the Three Millimetre Society which organisation offers a wide range of essential aids such as track parts, rolling stock kits and accessories. Anyone interested in 3 mm scale is strongly recommended to apply for membership. Limited commercial support is also maintained by some specialist manufacturers in the trade and Tri-ang TT3 parts continue to change hands on the second-hand market. There appears to be very little to prevent anyone taking up 3 mm scale modelling should they feel inclined. The main advantage is the undoubted saving in space compared with 4 mm scale. Whilst the space saving advantage is nowhere near so dramatic as in N gauge the scale is large enough for modellers with average skill to undertake building detailed and authentic models that would be difficult to contemplate in N gauge. Some excellent models have been produced in 3 mm scale, and 3 mm scale layouts frequently appear at model railway exhibitions throughout the country.

HO

1.87 or 3.5 mm/1 ft scale; 16.5 mm gauge.

When the scale of 3.5 mm to the ft and gauge of 16.5 mm were first introduced in Great Britain in the 1920s they were

A variety of German proprietary model locomotives and rolling stock can be identified in this view of Mike New's HO gauge layout Neuenburg, representing DB practice in Southern Germany, 1950–70.

designated 00. It was only in the '30s, when some British modellers began to adopt the alternative scale of 4 mm to the ft, that a need arose to avoid confusion between the two scales. The term HO, a contraction of 'Half-O', was generally adopted as a designation for 3.5 mm scale, and 4 mm scale models were referred to as 00. The advantage of HO is that it has a true scale gauge ratio as it uses a gauge of 16.5 mm which, with a scale of 3.5 mm to the ft is almost exactly the scale equivalent of 4 ft 8½ in. Because of this HO at one time had strong support from modellers. Unfortunately the trade reacted otherwise and most British manufacturers, including Hornby when they introduced their Dublo range in 1938, adopted 00. With the lack of commercial support, HO lost ground and became little used by modellers of British outline prototypes. However, the reverse happened on the Continent where, because of the advantage of their larger loading gauge there was no incentive to depart from the near correct scale/gauge ratio that HO offered. As a result HO only attracts commercial support from the major manufacturers outside Great Britain where it has probably established itself as the world's most popular scale and gauge. However, British outline HO has been staging a comeback following the formation of the British 1:87 Scale Society in 1994 and a number of kits and accessories have become available from specialist manufacturers. Track of course is no problem since the whole point about the HO/00 controversy is that HO uses the same track gauge as that manufactured for 00.

Robert Twendale uses finescale SMP track and homemade points on his extensive 00 gauge layout Ashley Bridge. The unusual GWR 0-4-4-T No 34 was built from a Ray Rippon hand-cut kit. The prototype was converted from an 0-4-2T in 1895 and sold in 1908.

00

1:76 or 4 mm/1 ft scale; 16.5 mm gauge

This is the most popular scale and gauge in Britain, but is virtually unheard of elsewhere. The reason for this can again be found in the difference between the British and Continental loading gauge. When 00 was first introduced in this country it was with a scale of 3.5 mm to the ft but some modellers and commercial manufacturers considered there was an advantage in using a larger scale allowing a greater clearance outside the wheels for models built within the confines of the British loading gauge. As always with this problem (we have already met it in N and TT gauges) it is the loading gauge width that is the biggest factor. The width of Continental rolling stock is approximately 10 ft which, with a scale 3.5 mm to the ft, means a model width of 35 mm. The maximum width of British rolling stock is 9 ft which, to the same scale of 3.5 mm to the ft, means a model width of only 31.5 mm. Subtract the width of the track gauge, 16.5 mm, from both these measurements and you will see that, whereas Continental models can have a space either side of the rails of 9.25 mm in which to fit wheels, axleguards, coach bogies, locomotive valve gear, etc., British models can only have a space of 7.5 mm, a reduction of nearly 2 mm either side. In an attempt to alleviate the difficulties of the reduced loading gauge and the limited space allowed it was decided to invent a scale of 4 mm to the ft which would give British models the same advantage as the Continentals. The 9 ft width of British rolling stock becomes 36 mm in 4 mm scale, which is much nearer the dimension of Continental models.

Some people regard this levelling of the sizes of HO Continental models and 00 British models as an advantage, since they claim that the similarity in size makes it possible to run the two together. Personally, I find this a very big disadvantage as it seems irrational to me to want to run two models of anything together when they are built to different scales. Everyone knows that locomotives and carriages on the Continent look so much bigger than they do in Britain. This is one of the fascinations of foreign railways, and one of the ways in which the senses become alerted when travelling abroad. Yet when a magnificent model such as the French Jouef 141R 2-8-2 is placed alongside a Hornby 'Evening Star' 2-10-0, the 141R 2-8-2 appears overshadowed by the British locomotive and is only marginally longer, quite contrary to what would really happen if the two full-size locomotives were to be lined-up together. The situation is really brought home, so to speak, when a Continental manufacturer produces models of British prototypes. Lima did this when they first entered the British market. They had a fairly extensive range of British outline locomotives and rolling stock, all to HO scale, but they looked faintly ridiculous if they were mixed with any home produced products. No one manufacturer can hope to retain sole allegiance to his products. At some time or another modellers are going to want to combine the products of one manufacturer with another. Presumably in recognition of this, Lima withdrew their range, retooled (which must have been expensive), and re-introduced the models in 00 4 mm scale. Thankfully Lima and Playcraft British HO models sometimes reappear on the second-hand market which pleases members of the British 1:87 Scale Society so all was not entirely lost.

With hindsight it seems a pity 00 was ever invented. There is no knowing what export opportunities may have been denied to British manufacturers through adopting a scale incompatible with the rest of the world. Such insularity might be considered to be less of a problem all the time the UK railway system was contained within this island but the scene changed dramatically when the Channel rail tunnel was completed in 1993. The solution adopted by the manufactureres with regard to the Eurostar passenger trains has been to produce two models; one for the British market in 00 and one for the Continental market in HO. The two ready to run models of the Class 92 Co-Co electric locomotives used for hauling international freight trains through the Channel Tunnel are both 00 4 mm scale. The Class 92s have not yet begun to range wide the other side of the Channel so there may not be enough incentive at present for Continental manufacturers to introduce HO models of these locomotives.

As much as the distinction between HO and 00 may be regretted there is nothing any of us can do about it now, as 00 has become so entrenched in Britain that there is absolutely no possibility of it ever being dropped in favour of HO. There are, however, a number of advantages with 00. The slightly larger scale does give a shade more space in which to scratch-build and in which to fit locomotive mechanisms. Furthermore, the ease with which you can multiply or divide 4 makes it very easy to convert feet and inches into millimetres. For the scale enthusiast who cannot tolerate the sight of standard gauge rolling stock running on narrow gauge track (16.5 mm is really only 4 ft 1½ in in 4 mm scale) there is always the alternative solution of using a wider gauge to make the track gauge fit the scale rather than reduce the scale to fit the track gauge, as we shall see later.

00 is so wonderfully served by the British manufacturers, particularly for scratch-builders and kit builders. There is every imaginable item of equipment—wheels, castings, transfers, etc—available from the trade so that 00 presents the least difficulty and the best variety of equipment of any of the scales and gauges.

You will find some manufacturers refer to 00/HO or HO/00. In some cases the use of this joint reference to the two gauges is correct, since by using the same track gauge, 16.5 mm, most track components are suitable for either HO or 00 models. This is not strictly true though when one considers the sleepers for HO and 00 gauge track. Sleepers (or ties as the Americans prefer to call them) on British 00 gauge track should really be spaced further apart than on Continental or American HO gauge track, but not everyone is sensitive enough to worry unduly about this and they are content to use either HO or 00 gauge track components, hence the expression HO/00 It is not correct to use the phrase HO/00 to denote the scale or size of a model, since HO uses one scale and 00 another. Airfix were fond of this but, to be fair, they used it largely in an area where it could possibly get by and be excused. It certainly did not apply to their Railway System which stuck scrupulously to 4 mm scale but I refer to their use of HO/00 for some building kits and for their many sets of plastic figures. After all, we do have people in all sorts of sizes, tall or short, fat or thin, and it might be arguable that a figure is either a short or thin 00 one or a tall fat HO one! It is also sometimes possible to mix HO and 00 build-ings and scenic effects together, since who is to argue that a building or tree in HO scale is not really a small 00 building or tree, and vice versa? Slightly smaller HO acces-sories can also be used to good effect to add a sense of perspective to the background parts of a model railway. Even some TT accessories may be used this way. But in the main I do not recommend mixing HO and 00 items together that have a fixed linear dimension, such as a locomotive or an item of rolling stock, since the difference in the two scales immediately becomes apparent when the two are run close together.

At least one manufacturer, in trying to steer a middle course between HO and 00, has tried to introduce an 'International scale' of approximately 3.8 mm to the ft, using of course the same 16.5 gauge as 00 and HO. This has not met with universal approval as the reduction in scale from 00, despite the fact that it is only 0.2 mm per ft, is quite noticeable over, say, the length, width and height of a railway carriage, compared with other similar models built to 4 mm scale.

There is also a small following for American 00, which uses a 19 mm track gauge, but for which there is no commercial support.

EM and Protofour/Scalefour

EM 1:76 or 4 mm/1 ft scale; 18.2 mm gauge. Protofour/Scalefour 1:76 or 4 mm/1 ft scale; 18.83 mm gauge.

I hope followers of these standards will excuse me linking them together, but it is my view, rightly or wrongly, that one evolved from the other and they all share the same ancestry. EM Gauge, for 'Eighteen Millimetre', came about as a result of the growing dissatisfaction with the undersized track gauge used in 00. 18 mm itself was not entirely to scale but in the days in which it was adopted as a standard it was considered near enough and it certainly was a decided step in the right direction. More recently the EM Gauge Society, which has represented this gauge since 1955 introduced revised track and wheel standards which included a revised track gauge of 18.2 mm minimum (0.2 mm wider on 24 in curves) and this has now become the Society's recommended track gauge. Despite the popularity of EM gauge amongst the more enthusiastic and discerning modellers the gauge is not catered for by any of the major producers of model railway equipment and there are no ready-to-run items of rolling stock available. This is probably all that can be said against EM and you need not be influenced by it since converting 00 gauge ready-to-run models to EM gauge is not all that difficult. In the case of some wagons and coaches it may only be a matter of changing the wheel sets. Sprung or compensated wheels, though desirable, are not always essential. Ready-to run-locomotives may not be quite so simple depending on the complexity of the model but there are many component parts avail-able to make the conversion work easier and explanatory articles appear frequently in the model railway press. If you choose to build your locos and rolling stock from scratch or from kits EM gauge is hardly likely to be any more difficult than 00. So far as track-work is concerned, this is the least of the problems since this can be obtained ready made (e.g. SMP flexible track and Marcway points) or easily constructed

Exact scale track and wheel standards can be appreciated in this view of Scalesford, all the more note-worthy since the builder, Sarah Scales, was eight years old at the time.

from component parts or kits (e.g. Peco, Ratio and SMP). Never mind how limited you feel your experience and skill may be, if you are about to embark on 4 mm scale railway modelling think seriously about applying for membership of the EM Gauge Society and starting with EM. The nearer to scale track gauge is so much more satisfying than 00 and for the discerning enthusiast the extra time and trouble is well worth-while. If you are undecided it is best to see a few EM gauge layouts and make a comparison with 00 gauge yourself, since the advantages are better experienced than described.

The inevitable quest for even better and finer standards occupied the attention of a group of railway modellers who produced a set of standards known as Protofour, some-times referred to as P4. There is next to no

Illustrating the perfection of P4 trackwork is this scene from Ray Hammond's Buntingham exhibition layout.

Trackwork built to EM standards is portrayed here is this view of Eastwell. The tufts of grass and weeds on the embankment side contribute to the realism of this scene.

compromise with this system, which is not only a gauge but a set of standards governing track and wheels, and an attention to detail and fine scale standards in areas which have been neglected because of the commercial dictates of the trade. As one would expect, a correct scale gauge ratio has been evolved and the track gauge, which is exactly right for 4 mm scale, is 18.83 mm. Do not be frightened by the two places of decimals. After all, 18.83 mm is only a description of a unit of measurement and once set by an accurate measuring instrument it remains constant. With a selection of tools and gauges set to 18.83 mm it should be no more difficult to build track to this gauge than say to 16.5 mm, 18.2 mm, or whatever else you choose. In addition to the correct gauge, there are standards for the rail section, wheel back-to-back measurements, tyre width, wheel and rail contours and the crossing flangeway and check rail clearances.

Such precise standards rule out the use of rigid chassis for locomotives and rolling stock and a form of springing or compensation is essential for satisfactory running. Whereas for many years there were two societies furthering the cause of Protofour (P4) standards, namely the Protofour society and the Scalefour Society, the two were united in 1987 and now operate as one, known as the Scalefour Society. Protofour is not for the faint-hearted and it requires a degree of precision, accuracy and patient handiwork beyond that required in other gauges such as 00. However, there is growing support for the commendably high standards originally set by Protofour and a number of tools, gauges, wheels and track parts are commercially available which open up the possibility to a wider audience.

Also involved in the furtherance of 18.83 mm gauge is the EM Gauge Society whose rules were changed to embrace all gauges between 18 mm and 18.83 mm in 1969.

Jas Millham opted for S gauge when building his layout Yaxbury. The Dinky Toys lorry appears to be the right size for this scale.

Ratio's easy to assemble track with plastic sleeper bases is available in 18.83 mm (as well as in 18.2 mm) and is approved by the Scalefour Society down to 3 ft 6 in as a minimum radius.

S

1:64³⁄₁₆ in/1 ft or 4.76 mm/1 ft scale; ⅞in or 22.2 mm gauge.

Since 'S' figures prominently in the dimensions, Seven-eighths for the track gauge, one-Sixty-fourth for the scale ratio etc., S-Gauge was adopted as the name for this gauge. It has been around for many years and has an active enthusiast following but has attracted little commercial support outside of America. However at least one firm in Britain has produced wheels and a limited number of locomotive and wagon kits. Other essential parts are available from the S-Gauge Model Railway Society. One advantage claimed for this gauge is that the scale, being larger than 00 or HO, provides greater scope for detailing but at the same time the increase in size is not

as demanding of space as O gauge, it also enjoys a near perfect scale/gauge ratio. Indicative of the following for S gauge and the high standards that can be achieved are the very fine S gauge models and layouts that have appeared at exhibitions and have been featured in the model railway press from time to time. It must, however, be considered primarily a gauge for the modeller who is prepared to construct much of the equipment which in other gauges could be expected to be obtained ready made.

O

1:43.5 or 7 mm/1 ft scale (UK), 1:48 or ¼ in/1 ft (USA); 32 mm gauge.

At one time O gauge was the most popular gauge and it was actively supported by the trade, especially by the mass-production manufacturers who catered mainly for the toy market. The trend away from large homes into smaller labour-saving flats and semi-detached houses, and the development of the table-top layout capabilities of

A fine model of GWR 6930 'Aldersey Hall' leaving Wossford on the O gauge layout of the Ilford and West Essex MRC.

00 and HO between the two World Wars, were largely responsible for its demise. However, although O gauge has for so long been deserted by the popular manufacturers, its appeal to modellers is gaining strength all the time. Much credit for this must be due to the Gauge 'O' Guild. Strong support is coming from that part of the trade which produces parts, accessories, kits and hand-built locomotives, but the latter in particular tend to be rather expensive. O gauge equipment is generally more expensive than the smaller scales and gauges, but it is probably true to say that, because of its larger size, less equipment is required to fill a given space, so overall it may not necessarily consume that much more money.

One big advantage I feel with O gauge, going up the scale and comparing it with other smaller gauges, is that it is the first gauge that results in models having some worthwhile weight and stability built into them. O gauge locomotives have to be solidly and robustly constructed and, in using the traditional materials of brass,

steel, tinplate and wood, finished models sometimes weigh-in at pounds rather than ounces. For modellers who feel more at home with plastic this is a perfectly acceptable material for O gauge and there are some excellent wagon kits in this medium. The Leeds Model Co Ltd produced carriages in moulded plastic before World War 2, long before such methods became commonplace in the smaller gauges. In more recent years there have been a number of relatively inexpensive plastic ready-to-run models useful for starting in O gauge, either as they come from the box or as a basis for conversions. The supply situation fluctuates but names to look for are Lima, Novo Toys Ltd (the former Tri-ang Big Big Trains), RaiMo (the former Pola-Maxi range in kit form) and Rivarossi.

Within O gauge we have Coarse Standard, Unified Standard and Fine Standard. They all use the same track gauge of 32 mm but differ in the dimensions used for wheels, in particular the all-important back to back dimension,

A live-steamer speeds towards the camera on the Gauge 1 Society layout here seen at IMREX 1986.

check rail clearances, etc, Similar moves are taking place as has already happened in 00 in that attempts are being made to bring the track gauge and standard dimensions nearer to scale. One of the most promising is Scale 7 which has adopted a track gauge of 33 mm which is just 0.04 mm more than the true 7 mm scale track dimension of 32.96 mm. As with 4 mm scale though, the track gauge is but one dimension and to adopt Scale 7 standards one needs to be particular about a lot more than just the track gauge. Also like 18.83 mm gauge in 4 mm scale, Scale 7 looks really good and is worth considering if you are making a start and are not committed to anything else.

So many things can be done easily in O gauge that are either impossible or very difficult in other smaller gauges. Real live steam models are, for instance, perfectly feasible and practical in O gauge and track-work can be built just like the real thing, with cast chairs pinned to wooden sleepers. Traditionally track-work is invariably built by the modeller, although Peco have the nucleus of a fine range of O gauge flexible track and point parts suitable for course, unified or fine standard which can provide an excellent foundation for an O gauge layout. If you have the space, a little more cash to spare for your initial outlay and the time to do more scratch-building, I would recommend O gauge and 7 mm scale as a very satisfying scale in which to work.

1

1:30.5 or 10 mm/1 ft scale; 45 mm gauge

The requirements for more space, cash and time to do your own construction work apply even more to 1 gauge, but the advantages are worth it. As anyone who has seen the Gauge 1 Society's stand at an exhibition will confirm, gauge 1 models really steal the show. The sheer size of the models is a real delight. Locomotives look big and heavy and wagons and coaches roll noisily but swiftly and smoothly over the track and pointwork which really looks like the real thing.

Perhaps the ideal setting for a gauge 1 layout is the garden – a garden shed to house the line's HQ, terminal station and

The scenic potential of 009 narrow gauge modelling is well developed in these views of the Dovey Valley Railway by Dick Wyatt; **Left** *Ex-Darjeeling and Himalaya 0-4-0ST (a very popular prototype for modelling) wends its way through a narrow cutting;* **Right** *The approach to Llanymawddwy station showing fine attention to detail and animation of the figures. Note the slate fencing so typical of the Welsh setting.*

rolling stock (provided the shed can be securely locked as there is a ready market for these models!) and the great outdoors to provide a setting for wide sweeping curves and long galloping straights. Power can be by steam, internally or externally fired (that means by a heat source which can either be inside the firebox or outside under the boiler), electricity or clockwork, or any other means of propulsion you like to devise. For the more conventional electrically operated model railway the German firm Marklin produces a very comprehensive range of 1 gauge equipment based on German and Swiss prototypes. The extent of the range as revealed in their catalogue would do credit to any company whatever their chosen scale or gauge. There are several types of ready-to-run steam, diesel or electric outline locomotives, goods and passenger vehicles, track and accessories. The minimum radius, for most of the Marklin locomotives is 3 ft 4 in, the same as their large radius points and curved rails, which means that a basic continuous run layout could be built in an average sized room or garage. Prices are of course higher than one would expect to pay

for compar-able 00 or HO equipment but the quality and detail are superb. Peco Streamline flexible track with flat bottom rail is available in 1 gauge together with a number of component parts for turnout construction. These items can be used with Marklin. Tenmille Products produce bull-head rail Flexi Track and quick assembly point kits together with a growing range of reasonably priced British outline wagon and coach kits. It is true to say that there are British outline ready-to-run locomotives available, both steam and electric propulsion, but for the most part these are tremendously expensive. Scratch-building would seem to be the order of the day so far as locomotives are concerned unless you are not troubled by a limited budget. Make no mistake, 1 gauge can be expensive.

Narrow gauge

The references to gauges have so far been concerned solely with standard 4 ft 8½ in gauge prototypes. However, it follows that, within a chosen scale, you can build a narrow gauge prototype, and the track

A happy gent walks away from the exotic motive power of the Tidmeric Light Railway at Rivendell Station, the 0–16.5 (7mm scale, 16.5 gauge) layout of the Twickenham & District MRC. The track is scratch-built using code 70 rail and PCB sleepers.

gauge would of course be in the same ratio of scale as the model. When building a model of a non-standard gauge prototype you have the choice of either using a gauge which attracts commercial support, thereby making the scale suit the gauge, or of choosing the scale first and fixing the gauge to suit the scale. The former course is preferred whenever possible, since wheels are usually the most difficult items for modellers to fabricate themselves, and by choosing a gauge which is supported by the trade, you are sure to have a ready supply of wheels, mechanisms and working parts. In Britain, real-life narrow gauge systems are flourishing under the post-war fever for preservation schemes, and the popularity of such lines as the Talyllyn, Ffestiniog, Isle of Man Railway, Welshpool and Llanfair, and the Vale of Rheidol no doubt account for the wave of interest in narrow gauge modelling.

Recapping on the previously mentioned standard gauge model systems, you will remember that we have the following established gauges actively supported by the trade, particularly in respect of wheels, mechanisms and track–9 mm (N), 12 mm (TT3), 16.5 mm (HO/00) and 32 mm (O). With a scale of 4 mm/1 ft, the 9 mm gauge of N gauge is equivalent to 2 ft 3 in, which is the exact gauge of the Talyllyn Railway; the 12 mm of TT3 is equivalent to 3 ft 0 in, which is the exact gauge of the Isle of Man Railway and many fascinating, but now closed, narrow gauge lines that used to operate in Ireland. And as we have also shown, 16.5 mm in 4 mm scale is 4 ft 1½ in, which by any standard ought to be a narrow gauge, but the only company I have heard of that operated a line built to this gauge was the Wigan Coal & Iron Company, and I know nothing of its extent or duration.

Apart from this company it will be seen that quite a number of important narrow gauge prototypes can be successfully modelled in 4 mm scale, utilising track and wheel components of other gauges. It is also probably true to say that a fair degree of licence can be allowed with these minor gauges and it can be regarded as permissible to extend the use of 9 mm gauge track to cover prototypes on gauges from 2 ft to 2 ft 6 in, thus allowing many more prototype systems to be modelled in 4 mm scale. The reason for this is mainly the loading gauge used in narrow gauge prototypes. The locomotives and rolling stock are so wide relative to the track gauge that a widening or narrowing of the track gauge of the model can usually be accommodated without difficulty. Also in many cases, particularly with the smaller gauge lines, the bodies are so low down on the wheels and bogies that any alteration made to the underframes of the model to suit practical considerations are largely obscured and can be more easily tolerated and overlooked.

There is a real advantage in trying to stick to a recognised scale as well as gauge when building a model narrow gauge layout, since there are a number of standard gauge items and accessories that can be equally at home on a narrow gauge system. Buildings, road vehicles, miniature people, and what are generally referred to as lineside accessories, are the obvious examples. In this respect, there is a great advantage in choosing a narrow gauge model railway as it is possible to equip such a line built to 4 mm scale with a vast range of items, some designed specifically for 4 mm scale narrow gauge, others that were originally designed and intended for the large standard gauge models, and yet more drawn from the range of track, wheels, mechanisms, wagon chassis and other items intended for N gauge— the best of both worlds in fact! Narrow gauge layouts are also ideal for the person who is obliged to construct a minimum space layout, since the trains can traverse sharper radii and climb steeper gradients than their larger standard gauge cousins. Individual items of rolling stock are shorter and train lengths can be kept within quite minimal dimensions, which restricts the size of station platforms, engine sheds, sidings and other associated items. Narrow gauge models can be made to look very attractive scenically, as anyone who has visited the Welsh narrow gauge railways will acknowledge, and from the operating point of view the wide choice of prototype materials leaves a lot of scope for modelling. Many people operate a narrow gauge system as a feeder to a standard gauge line, thereby combining the two gauges on one baseboard. This opens up tremendous possibilities for mixed gauge track, joint stations

A closer view of Tidmeric track-work with a not so happy gent.

An extensive ground level garden layout composed of LGB track, locos and rolling stock illustrating some of the equipment available from this enterprising German manufacturer.

(Photo: LGB)

where the two gauges meet and for scenic work involving bridges and viaducts over which the narrow gauge can be made to climb and cross over the standard gauge rails. Alternatively, a narrow gauge layout can be developed on a baseboard of its own, either as a subordinate project to a larger standard gauge system or as the sole railway modelling project.

Narrow gauge railway modelling is widely supported by the trade, even down to British N scale. Peco produce wagon kits and narrow gauge locomotive body kits designed for use with the Marklin Miniclub 0-6-0 chassis running on 6.5 mm Z gauge. This combination is referred to as N-6.5. Most developments, however, are in the 4 mm or 5.5 mm scale field, where it is referred to as either 00-9 or HO-9, 00 or HO denoting the scale and 9 the gauge of the track in millimetres. Another method of describing narrow gauge scales and gauges is to denote

the scale by referring to the normal standard gauge, eg 00, followed by N to denote narrow gauge, and then, followed by a figure denoting the prototype track gauge in feet, Thus 00N3 would describe a 4 mm scale 3 ft narrow gauge line. Special narrow gauge track is commercially available, particularly the Peco 'Crazy Track' which is flexible and features authentic looking rough wood grained sleepers arranged in the haphazard fashion so often found on narrow gauge lines. Peco have also introduced a range of 12 mm narrow gauge track intended for 3.5 mm scale metre gauge models. This is generally referred to as HOm. There is no shortage of rolling stock, wagons, coaches and locomotives, and kits of parts are available for converting N gauge locomotives into 00-9 or HO-9 narrow gauge models. There is also a 009 Society. HO3, which uses a 10.5 mm track gauge, is popular in the USA.

The next size up in narrow gauge modelling is the 5½ mm/1 ft scale 12 mm gauge pioneered commercially by GEM using readily available TT gauge track and wheels. A quite comprehensive selection of Talyllyn and Ffestiniog Railway prototype models were on the market at one time but this range of equipment has now been withdrawn by the manufacturer. GEM also produced a series of 4 mm scale equipment on 12 mm TT gauge track for models of the 3 ft gauge Isle of Man Railway. There is a lot of scope for modelling in 00-12 as, apart from the Isle of Man Railway, there were at one time a large number of 3 ft gauge railways in Ireland which now attract a lot of attention from railway enthusiasts and which make excellent subjects for railway modelling.

In 7 mm scale, 9 mm, 12 mm and 16.5 mm gauges would represent scale gauges of 1 ft 3in, 1 ft 7 in and 2 ft 4 in 1 ft 3in is, of course, the gauge of the Ravenglass and Eskdale Railway and the Romney Hythe and Dymchurch Railway, and 2 ft 4 in is as near as makes no difference to the Talyllyn 2 ft 3 in gauge and the erstwhile Glyn Valley Tramway 2 ft 4½ in gauge. Peco produce locomotive and rolling stock kits based on Talyllyn and GVT prototypes in their 'Great Little Trains' series. They also produce special narrow gauge flexible track and have devised a method of converting their 00 points to 0-16.5 standards. Roy C Link and Wrightlines Models also produce a range of locomotive and wagon kits in 0-16.5.

Moving up again to the 10 mm scale, 9 mm, 12 mm, 16.5 mm and 32 mm become the equivalent of approximately 11 in, 1 ft 2½ in, 1 ft 8 in and 3 ft 3 in, which have

very little practical application for narrow gauge modelling except that the latter gauge is not too far removed from either 3 ft gauge or metre gauge. One other narrow gauge standard that has become popular is 16 mm scale using 32 mm O gauge track. This is referred to as SM-32, SM standing for sixteen millimetre. This, of course, represents a prototype track gauge of 2 ft and is an example of narrow gauge modelling built to an existing gauge rather than to a recognised scale. Live steam is very much associated with this scale and gauge, there being many ready to pull live steam locomotives to choose from ranging from the relatively inexpensive Mamod 0-4-0T to the most sophisticated high pressure radio controlled models. For anyone interested there is the Association of 16 mm N G Modellers. One German manufacturer, Lehmann, known as LGB, has introduced a range of giant narrow gauge models to 1:22.5 scale on 45 mm (1 gauge) track, which is near enough the exact scale equivalent of metre gauge. 1:22.5 scale is something like 14 mm to the foot, which makes you realise the giant stature of these models. They must surely be the ultimate in narrow gauge models, if not in commercial model making of whatever scale or gauge.

Metre gauge is a common prototype gauge for narrow gauge railways on the continent of Europe and in other parts of the world, so the potential scope for these models is pretty good. The LGB range is intended for indoor as well as outdoor use, but their tremendous size must surely be best appreciated in a garden setting where they would look delightfully at home wending their way through flower beds and rockeries, and possibly even Scale-Size garden gnomes!

CHAPTER 5
Planning the layout

Having discussed the types of layout that are possible, where they can be accommodated and what scale and gauge we can use, the next important step is to design the plan of the layout and the formation of the tracks.

The complex layout of points, crossings, sidings and running rails at stations, either in real life or in other people's model railways shown at exhibitions, may at first glance appear bewildering to the beginner. But each item of trackwork should have a purpose and a reason for its existence, and there are a number of guiding rules and principles which determine their use and their position in the scheme of things. The factors which govern the use and positioning of tracks, points and crossings in real life should equally apply to a model. However, with the model there are additional practical considerations which must be allowed for, considerations which are peculiar to the world of railway modelling and the practical compromises we have to set ourselves. There are such things as accessibility for maintenance, cleaning or rerailing derailed rolling stock, the necessity for track to double back on itself, thus requiring excessively sharp radius curves, the sometimes awkward shape and position of our baseboards and the clearance available above, below and at either side of the track. These are some of the factors which trouble modellers greatly but which are of little comparative concern in the case of the full-size railway, where in the

majority of instances there is adequate space to provide for all these contingencies.

In other words, we have problems, but of all the difficulties that face railway modellers the designing and planning of a layout gives the greatest delight in solving. Hardly a model railway magazine is complete without a track plan of some sort, and new layout plans often form the subject of regular monthly features. The easy way to design your own layout might be to simply not bother at all, but just to scan through a few magazine back numbers, or some of the excellent plan books that are available, choose a ready-made plan which roughly fits your baseboard area, and build your layout accordingly. Quite seriously though, I do offer this as a practical suggestion as the vast majority of the published plans in books and magazines are the result of years of valuable experience, which you might pay for dearly if you choose to ignore and do without. However, there are some practical points on layout planning which you might like to consider first before you make up your mind whether to choose a ready-made plan or to make up one of your own.

Any successful track layout plan must, if it is to be satisfying to the modeller, fulfil as many of the following conditions as possible:

1 It must fit the space available.

2 It must not be too ambitious and must be within the bounds of practicability to

construct, complete, maintain, clean and operate.

3 It must provide ready accessibility to both track and rolling stock.

4 It must have gradients within easily workable limits.

5 It must have sufficiently large radius curves to suit the rolling stock you intend to operate.

6 It must provide sustained operating interest.

7 It must conform as far as possible to acceptable railway practice.

8 It must provide sufficient working and siding accommodation for the rolling stock it is proposed to operate.

Point number 1 of course goes without saying, and needs no further amplification. The only comment I can perhaps add is that, in some cases, it is just possible to make the space fit the plan. For instance, layouts can sometimes be extended temporarily in various directions, one obvious example being the extension from a baseboard to a window sill or even through an open window and out into the garden. I once had this problem in a garden shed in which I attempted to construct a model railway. The shed was only 7 ft 6 in × 4 ft 6 in, which really was not big enough for the plan I wanted, so I cut a pair of tunnel holes in the end wall of the shed and ran a semi-circle of track outside, thus effectively extending the space available by a good 2 ft 6 in or more. The outdoor section was removable and the tunnel mouths could be sealed up when not in use to prevent animals and insects from getting into the shed. It was not damaged or disfigured at all, as it was a wooden shed made from weather boarding. Where the line left and re-entered I removed the original weather boarding and substituted a replacement length from which tunnel mouths were cut. When eventually the shed was sold to make way for a larger concrete garage, the original weather boarding was replaced and no one was any the wiser.

I am sure I have emphasised point 2 enough already, but it is something that must be considered. We very often come across those magnificent exhibition layouts at seaside towns and big departmental stores, where a vast network of lines can be seen with seemingly dozens of trains moving in all directions. Such layouts are frequently the source of inspiration for a model railway of your own, but you must remember before you attempt to copy anything like it that these layouts are run professionally. They are attended to throughout the whole working day, which is more often than not far more time than can be spared by the average modeller.

Point number 3, accessibility of track *and* rolling stock, is one which needs to be borne in mind at all stages of designing and building the layout. In the planning stage it may be reasonable to expect ready access to a certain point on the baseboard when it is empty and devoid of any obstructions, but it may be another thing trying to reach that same spot to renew an unsoldered joint or to prize out some displaced chips of ballast from between the check rail or switch blade of a point when an item of scenery or a lineside accessory has been installed nearby. The switch blades of points are probably the biggest single item of trackwork liable to give trouble in use and they should, wherever possible, be placed in an open and accessible position. Points and crossings are also the items of trackwork which are most likely to cause trouble to rolling stock, so it is advisable to resist the temptation as far as possible of laying points in tunnels, where they would be difficult to reach when releasing stalled locomotives or rerailing derailed rolling stock.

Access to rolling stock is particularly important and, although it may be possible to build and operate the perfect layout which, with automatic couplings and all the latest electronic devices can be operated 'untouched by human hand', it is often necessary to assist the odd stubborn locomotive that refuses to budge when the current is switched on. Coupling and uncoupling operations can be done automatically, but with some forms of coupling, eg, the popular three-link type, this is not possible and it may be necessary to provide access to uncouple a locomotive or coach from a train. This may rule out the use of an overall roof for a station or affect the siting of an overbridge at the end of a platform. The more coupling and uncoupling required the greater need for accessibility, hence the necessity to position stations and goods yards within easy reach and sight of the operator. On the other hand, locomotive sheds can be relegated to the back of the layout, out of the way, since the locomotives moving into and out of them travel as single self-contained units without the necessity for coupling operations.

It is easy enough to understand the necessity to limit the angle of gradients, point number 4, since a gradient that is too steep will simply not allow a locomotive to climb it. Furthermore, it can cause problems to a descending train, since it is likely to rush down out of control if the gradient is too steep. Some modern electronic controllers do, however, take care of this possibility. Most modern commercially produced model locomotives can, on their own, climb gradients steeper than would be found in real life, but it becomes a different story as soon as a trailing load is added. Some of the older commercially produced model coaches and wagons have a high rolling resistance and literally have to be dragged along by the locomotives. Thankfully, most manufac-

turers have realised this and have done something about improving the wheel bearings to make things easier for the engines. N gauge rolling stock is generally very good in this respect, aided also by the relatively low weight, and quite long trains of N gauge coaches and wagons can be hauled successfully up steep gradients by N gauge locomotives.

With real railways, gradients are deemed necessary by geographical features and the lay of the land. The steepness or otherwise of the gradient depends on the height and size of the hill to be climbed or the valley to be descended. On a model railway there are not usually any hills since baseboards are not only invariably built flat and level but they are purposely built that way. Gradients can be built into a layout just for the fun of it, but this is rather unusual and, more often than not, a gradient is installed to enable one line to climb up over another. In these cases we need to gain sufficient height to clear the tops of locomotives and rolling stock passing underneath, plus the height of the track and the baseboard supporting it. In 00 gauge this usually works out at something like 2½ to 3 In, depending on the thickness of the baseboard supporting the overhead track. If this supporting surface is simply the deck of a bridge it can be quite thin, say about ¼ in or even less—the thickness of a piece of plywood. If, however,

Fig 20 *Dimensions for high-level baseboards using different materials. Figures are for clearances in 00 gauge. Flexible track on foam ballast strip is itself ⁵⁄₁₆ in high in 00 gauge and should be allowed for when planning high-level areas.*

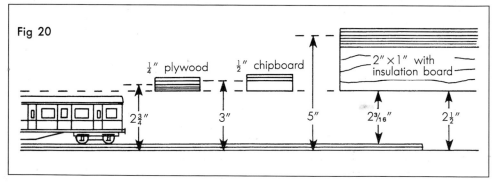

you are building a complete high level baseboard then you will need to allow for whatever thickness you are using, which is likely to be at least ½ in for a piece of chipboard or as much as 2½ in for another open frame baseboard with insulation board covering, as shown in Fig 20.

On real railways, gradients are, in Britain at least, expressed as a ratio of the height the track rises, measured over a given distance. Examples are 1 in 150, 1 in 748 or 1 in 1508. In America, gradients are expressed as a percentage. For example, a gradient of 1 in 25 is 4 per cent, 1 in 50 2 per cent, and 1 in 100 1 per cent, etc. I am always very impressed by the precise definition of some of these measurements and the degree of accuracy that they must represent. Anyone who has ever read any steam locomotive performance articles will know how easily a change in grade can affect things. Gradients that were hardly detectable visually, looking outwards from the carriage window, were all too discernible from the sound of the locomotive exhaust. Yet the majority of these gradients are, by model railway standards at least, modest in the extreme. The Settle Carlisle line has a minimum gradient or 1 in 100, the climb out of Kings Cross to Copenhagen Tunnel is 1 in 107, and most of Shap is at 1 in 125. We have got to get to the extreme cases such as the Lickey Incline (1 in 37¾), Dainton (1 in 36 minimum) and the Folkestone Harbour

Branch (1 in 30) before we reach anything like acceptable model railway practice. When full-size trains were operated with steam locomotives on these three inclines, additional motive power in the form of a banking or a pilot engine, or sometimes one or more of each, was required to assist the train engine up the gradient, Yet railway modellers frequently expect their locomotives to haul trains up similarly steep gradients unaided! For a model railway gradient it is hard to generalise since there is a vast difference in the 'rollability' of most commercially produced rolling stock, but I would suggest that nothing steeper than 1 in 30 is desirable and 1 in 40 is better still. Now, if we are going to clear a 3 in high obstacle with a gradient of 1 in 40 we are going to need a run of at least 10 ft. 1 in 30 reduces the length of run to 7 ft 6 in, but you can see already that the space problem rears its head as soon as the subject of gradients arises. One method which can sometimes be applied to the situation is to lower one track whilst at the same time raising the other, thereby halving the length of run required, as shown in Fig 21.

It almost goes without saying that gradients should be approached gradually and not like a wedge of cheese. The bottom and top of the gradient, where the changes in grade occur, should be curved and smoothed out gently when viewed from the side so that there is no sudden transition. If

Fig 21 *Lowering one track whilst at the same time raising the other can halve the length of track required to clear a given rise.* **Fig 22** *The bottom and top of a gradient should be curved and smoothed out gently to avoid sudden transitions in steepness.*

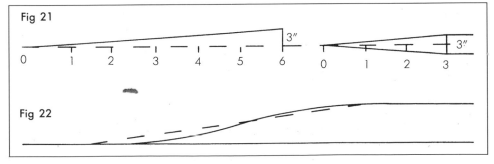

necessary, this gradual easing into and out of the gradient can be done within the overall length allowed, thereby effectively steepening the middle part of the grade, since at least it will allow the train to rush the gradient and, by that time the engine has overcome the worse part, the track will start to level out slightly which will enable the train to keep moving. (See Fig 22.)

It may not always be possible to restrict gradients to straight track but it is preferable to do this whenever you can, or at least to confine the steepest part of the gradient to the straight stretch, since you impose two sets of forces against the movement of the train if you subject it to climbing a gradient round a curve. Another point to watch is to avoid as far as possible having any curves, pointwork or breaks in the baseboard immediately at the bottom or at the top of a change in grade, and certainly do not have such features as points or crossings on the gradient itself. Leave at least one carriage length clear between the start or finish of a gradient before you introduce any of these features. Gradients can cause operating troubles such as stalling and they can be a potential source of derailments, but they *need not* be troublesome if only you respect them and treat them and your rolling stock with respect.

Now, regarding point number 5, it is probably true to say that no one can afford to lay out curves on a model railway in anything like the same way as those on the full-size railway. Even in a garden it is rather rare to come across exactly the kind of curvature you see on the real railway, if only because it is a little unusual for a real train to want to reverse its direction of movement and double back on itself. Ninety degree curves happen on occasions, I will grant you, but 180 degree curves in normal open country must be somewhat of a novelty and 360 degree curves unheard of! Yet on a continuous layout we subject our rolling stock to movements at speeds round curves which would scare the pants off the crew of a real train. I believe the accepted minimum radius curve on British railways which can be

traversed without a continuous check rail is something like 10 chains, which is 660 ft, and in 00 gauge works out at approximately 8 ft 8 in. But this is the *minimum* and most curves are much less sharp than this. High-speed main line curves are not normally made sharper than about half-a-mile radius, approximately 34 ft in 00, yet many of the proprietary 00 gauge systems utilise curves as sharp as 15 in!

In some circumstances, where space is limited and where for instance we have a baseboard only 4 ft wide, we do not have much choice in the matter if we wish to construct a continuous layout, since in a width of only 4 ft it is impossible to plan a continuous run with a curvature of more than 2 ft radius. To allow a nominal couple of inches margin round the outside of the track the curve ought to be about 1 ft 10 in radius in fact. But it should be realised that such sharp radius curves rule out any possibility of utilising a baseboard 4 ft wide for fast main line express passenger trains in 00 gauge, if any degree of realism is to be aimed at and achieved. It is possible to disguise such sharp radius curves or even hide them in a tunnel, but it is better to find a little more space and to increase the radius of the curves as much as possible or, if this cannot be done, change over to a smaller scale. Three feet radius is a generally accepted desirable standard for 00 gauge and should be increased in relation to the scale of larger gauges. For N gauge you might be tempted to think that by application of the rule, 3 ft for 00 gauge, something like 18 in radius would be suitable. But rather than diminish the standards for N gauge I do recommend raising the standard and retaining 3 ft as a minimum radius. This will achieve maximum realism.

Peco have recognised the desirability of large radius curves with their range of 00 and N gauge trackwork, for they have very thoughtfully provided a 5 ft radius point in 00 gauge and a 3 ft radius point in N gauge. This is a brilliant piece of commercial planning and one that deserves a lot of support. It is often in points and crossovers that the

Converging gradients on Dick Yeo's 00 gauge layout Epton. The LT Central Line Underground tube stock ascends above ground towards Epton West whilst the BR 4-wheel railcar descends the branch line from Epton Park. Note the working colour light signals.

effects of sharp radius curves are most felt and noticed. The most undesirable effects are the overhang at the front and rear of a vehicle. The longer the vehicle the worse the effect, and the extreme cases occur with the larger Pacific-type locomotives which can be seen on some proprietary layouts with the front buffer beam pointing in one direction and the curvature of the track in another. When a locomotive such as this pushes wagons or coaches round a curve the buffer heads of the locomotive and the wagon or coach are nowhere near aligning. As soon as normal straight track is reached the buffers side-swipe each other, locking themselves behind the buffer heads (buffer locking, we call this) and the lighter of the two vehicles becomes derailed. The troubles with sharp radius curves are in fact doubled when propelling vehicles over a crossover or reverse curve, since the effect of one

curvature is added to the other, as seen in Fig 23, with the result that even some reasonably short length vehicles can become buffer locked.

In realising that everyone just does not have room to install scale curves on their layout, the time honoured method adopted by most manufacturers is to design their couplings such that the buffers never come close enough together to buffer lock round curves. As referred to in Chapter 10, in recent years a number of continental manufacturers have developed an ingenious close coupling mechanism which successfully overcomes this problem. The manufacturers of British ouline ready to run coaches have not yet caught on to this important development but a close coupling unit which with minor surgery can be fitted to these models and other kit-built coaches has been produced by Keen Systems. For the British

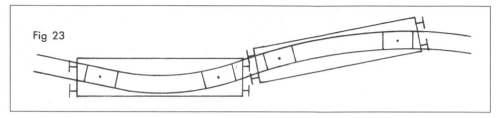

Fig 23 *Buffer locking can become a problem if curves are given too sharp a radius particularly, as here, on the reverse curve.*

railway modeller who in order to see his buffers touching and who likes to use loose three-link couplings, the only alternative is to use as large a radius as possible, 3 ft at the very minimum and preferably something larger, or else limit the rolling stock to short wheelbase four-wheeled vehicles or four or six-coupled locomotives. I must emphasise that the question of radius of curves is entirely related to the type of layout and rolling stock you wish to operate, as it is of course in real life. On a model dockyard layout, coal mine or gas works siding which only sees short wheelbase four-coupled locomotives and wagons, you could probably get away with 12 in radius curves in 00 and a 4 mm scale tramway layout can be built with even sharper curves, but please do not expect the same standards to apply to a main line Pacific locomotive hauling an express passenger train, or to a multi-wheeled locomotive pushing long wheelbase loose coupled bogie vehicles over reverse curves. Plan your curves to suit your rolling stock.

HST Inter-City 125 leaning to the curve on the MRC's 00 gauge layout New Annington. The super-elevated curve contributes to the effect of movement.

Operating interest on an end-to-end layout can be enhanced by the judicious use of curves and in this case by modelling two distinct systems; BR Epton Park in the foreground leading to the junction with LT at Epton West in the middle distance.

One thing I have not mentioned, but perhaps ought to at this stage, is the subject of transition curves. In theory at least, curves should be approached gradually, otherwise an abrupt change from straight track to curved track can have a shock effect on the locomotive and train as it enters the curve. In practice, however, I have found that most model railway rolling stock is fully capable of making the transition without difficulty, even at quite high speeds, but you may – from the appearance point of view if nothing else – make provision for the initial radius of the curve to be a little larger than the main part of the curve, thus avoiding an abrupt change in the track geometry, Similarly, although this has no place in the subject of layout planning, it might be as well to discuss super-elevation of curves. This is the practice of canting the track so that the outside rail on a curve is higher than the inside rail. This can be observed on full-size railways on practically every curve and can be detected readily when travelling in a train. It is done to help counteract the effect of the curve itself, in much the same way that roads are cambered, but in model railways it is not required for any practical reason. It does help to add realism, however, and provided there are no points or crossings on the curve to complicate the matter I recommend adding a little super-elevation wherever you can. On full size British railways the rails are generally canted to a maximum of 6 in, which of course is 2 mm in 00. Either cardboard or balsa wood could be used for packing up the outer rail, but be careful to make the transition as progressive and gentle as possible.

Point number 6, to provide sustained operating interest, is very important, but unfortunately cannot always be visualised in advance. You can try and imagine the operating scope of a layout from a plan on a piece of paper, but the proof of the pudding is invariably in the eating. One important point which affects both the operating possibilities of a layout and its basic shape is whether it is to provide a continuous run by means of an unbroken oval or circuit of track or whether it is to be 'end to end'. The continuous run layout lacks the realism of a full-size railway, since, with one or two rare exceptions no train in real life is made to run over the same length of track, passing the same scenery and lineside settings continuously with only seconds separating each circuit–sometimes derisively referred to as tail-chasing. However, there is a credit side to the continuous layout since it cannot be denied that the sight of a train in motion at a reasonably fast speed, say the equivalent of 60 to 65 mph, is very satisfying and is one of the reasons why some of us take up railway modelling. When observing a model train travelling at such a relatively high speed round a circuit of track you tend to watch the train, not the track or scenery, and it is possible to close your eyes and thoughts to the fact that it is the same length of track each time. By limiting your field of view you only need to watch the engine, the movement of the coupled wheels, valve gear and motion, and the swish of the carriages as they pass by to obtain satisfaction from the sight. A continuous run layout can be disguised to a large extent to cover up the undesirable effects of tail-chasing.

The secret is to achieve a limited field of view and to break up the continuous aspect with tunnels, cuttings and scenery. These will obscure the curves at each end of the layout which are necessary to bring the train round and back again. Another positive step is to try and model the observed section of the continuous run track through a nondescript scenic setting devoid of particular landmarks, which will minimise the effect of passing the same spot on each occasion. It might be particularly desirable, for instance, to avoid bringing the train through the same station on every circuit. A reversing loop which changes the direction of the train can also help. Of course, the best single factor is to make the continuous run as long as possible since the longer the train takes to complete each circuit obviously the less continuous it will appear, but not all of us can take this step. One big advantage with a continuous run layout is that locomotives have a chance to be run-in and this can be quite important with some that have noisy gears and stiff working parts which only become eased after they have been given an airing. Bench runs can help on occasions, but it is my view that there is nothing to beat a run under load round a continuous layout for say half a dozen circuits. The rare exceptions referred to earlier of full-size trains in real life running round a continuous circuit existed for just such a reeason. The one-time Longmoor Military Railway had a continuous run circuit which, amongst other things, was used for running-in locomotive footplate crews as much as the engines themselves. On the Continent there are at least two full-size railway test circuits in current use where new designs of locomotives and rolling stock can be run at different speeds and loadings to show up any faults which may arise before they enter service. In plan vew these test circuits look for all the world like a train set oval. In the 'prototype for everything' category, you could build a model of one of these, the one snag being their size as they are several miles long.

The end-to-end type of layout can take a number of forms, from the simple straight line to a complex system of curves, loops, reverse loops, flyovers and what have you. The shorter the layout the slower the speeds that can be obtained, so if you want to see a locomotive get into its stride and watch it moving for any length of time before it has to come to a halt you will need at least a 20 ft run in 4 mm scale. It always seems to me that the end-to-end layout is best operated by two people each at their respective ends of the layout. One extreme of this idea is to have each end in separate rooms, with a tunnel through the dividing wall. Trains would then be dispatched by timetable and signalled properly with a system of bell codes as the only means of communication between each operator. Such degrees of enthusiasm are not, of course, essential and it is perfectly possible to operate a two-man layout within sight and sound of each other and possibly be a good deal friendlier too! One advantage of two operators is that the

one despatching a train can, after it has got into its stride, leave the control and subsequent stopping to the second operator who can take over the train at a given point on the track. The first despatch operator can then have the pleasure of watching the train pass out of sight without having to be concerned with its control. When a train reappears in the reverse direction after a decent time interval, the first operator can gain considerable pleasure from receiving a train, the formation of which is quite unknown to him, since it will have been made up by the second operator from rolling stock he is holding at his end of the line.

The common formation for a line such as this is to have a terminal station at one end and what is known as a 'fiddle yard' at the other. A fiddle yard is just that! It is somewhere where an operator can manipulate or fiddle with the formation of trains from whatever stock he has available.

At public exhibitions the fiddle yard is often hidden from view. There are any number of different forms a fiddle yard can take, from the simple bank of storage sidings (Fig 24) to the most elaborately engineered turntable affair, such as shown in Fig 25, where different trains on different tracks can be lined up with the entrance and exit roads and at the end of an operating session the trains can be reversed and returned to their starting point. The simple kind of storage bank illustrated in Fig 24 will have to rely on 'hand shunting' to change the formation of the trains, for instance to uncouple the locomotive, reverse its direction and couple it up at the opposite end. Handling such as this is permissible in a fiddle yard, whereas of course it would be frowned on out in the open in the public gaze.

Another alternative is to have a turntable at the far end of the bank of sidings so that the locomotive can at least be turned and transferred from one road to another without having to lift it by hand. (See Fig 26.) Yet another permutation is to have the bank of sidings on a traverser which will allow any particular track to be lined up with the exit road to enable a particular train to enter or

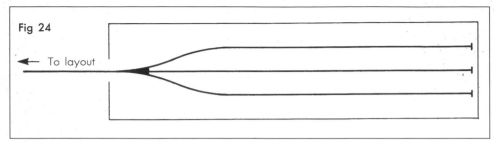

Fig 24 *A simple bank of fiddle yard storage sidings.*

leave the yard. The traverser can he a simple affair, such as shown in Fig 27, which relies on Formica or some other form of shiny proprietary laminate to provide the bearing surface for the movable board or table which simply slides back and forth to line up the required track with the entrance or exit road. The length of the traverser will be governed by the length of train you wish it to accommodate. A small country branch line in 4 mm scale can be operated by a train of three or four coaches which, with the engine, would be something like 4 ft long. This same length would accommodate a 10 or 11-wagon freight train, which is quite a realistic and respectable load for a country branch line. Yet another type of fiddle yard can take the form of a series of reversing loops. This will have the advantage of reversing the direction of the train without the need for a turntable or hand movement, but it will take up a lot more

Fig 25 *A more elaborate turntable storage yard, with tracks long enough to hold both engine and coaches.*

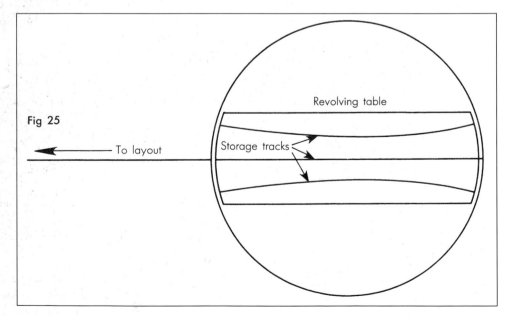

Above *Loft Hill Sandstone 0-4-0ST No. 1 and train exercise the company's running powers over the Winbury branch, REC's O gauge layout.* (Photo: Peter Parfitt) **Below** *Goods ready for delivery or collection in the yard at Winbury.* (Photo: Peter Parfitt)

Passenger and goods facilities form the focal point for most model railways. Shown here are Ashley Bridge station forecourt and goods yard.

Town and country scenic modelling. Stan Ginn's Tramscene and Robert Tivendale's Wenbury Mill, the latter forming part of the countryside of Ashley Bridge.

Above *Prototype Deltic hauling BR red and cream coaches passes single unit power car W55020 whilst A1X Terrier 32678 shunts the yard. REC's EM gauge exhibition layout. (Photo: Peter Parfitt)*
Below *BR(WR) Castle 4088 'Dartmouth Castle' has the 'right away' as Pannier 8745 arrives with a 'B' set and 6769 waits for the road with a freight. REC's finescale 00 gauge layout. (Peter Parfitt)*

Above *BR(SR) diesel-electric 10202 passes Alton's extensive goods yard. H15 30473 and a 700 Class work the yard whilst Z Class 954 is turned on the turntable. Note the third rail on the running lines used by the Alton–Waterloo electric services. REC's 00 finescale Alton layout. (Photo: Peter Parfitt)*
Below *SNCF (French Railways) 'Picasso' railcar under the station roof at Achaux. This classic view composed of Jouef HO station and stock and Peco track shows what can be achieved with commercial products straight from the box (Photo: Andy Hart).*

South for sunshine! The Southern Railway holiday atmosphere is confirmed in every detail in this view of John Bateman's 3 mm scale Saunton Sands Junction for Woolacombe (Photo: Geoff Helliwell)

Above *Winbury Box signalman ready to hand the token to the driver of GWR small Prairie 4549 leaving Winbury on a goods train.* (Photo: Peter Parfitt) **Below** *The highly polished brass, copper and steel of Dean Goods 2336 is admired by the p.w. gang as it heads towards Winbury.* (Photo: Peter Parfitt)

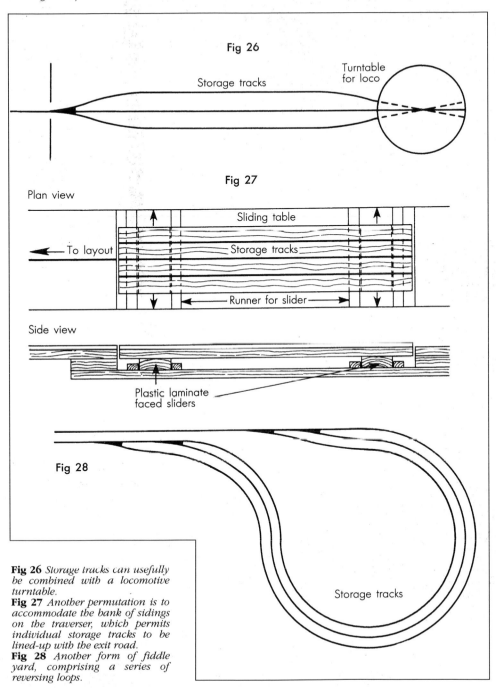

Fig 26

Storage tracks

Turntable
for loco

Fig 27

Plan view

← To layout

Sliding table

Storage tracks

Runner for slider

Side view

Plastic laminate
faced sliders

Fig 28

Storage tracks

Fig 26 *Storage tracks can usefully be combined with a locomotive turntable.*
Fig 27 *Another permutation is to accommodate the bank of sidings on the traverser, which permits individual storage tracks to be lined-up with the exit road.*
Fig 28 *Another form of fiddle yard, comprising a series of reversing loops.*

space since the overall size of the loops will be at least double the minimum radius of the curves you are using. (See Fig 28.)

Possibly one of the most satisfying forms of layout plan is one that combines the advantages of both a continuous, and non-continuous run, an out and back scheme with a continuous run in between. Variations on this basic theme are shown in Figs 29-34 inclusive.

In Fig 29 the train leaves the terminal station at point A, traverses the circuit as many times as required and returns back to A. In Fig 30 the train can leave the terminal station from one platform, traverse the circuit as many times as required and return to the other platform of the same station. Fig 31 is very similar to Fig 30, but the terminal station is on a different level to the normal continuous run which passes underneath the station throat at point B. The track extension at point C is optional since it is not required to provide a continuation of the main circuit, but it could be useful because a triangular junction outside a terminal station can be of great assistance in the manoeuvring or turning of stock. In Fig 32 the train would leave one terminal station at point A, traverse the main circuit and then enter the second terminal station at point B. Fig 33 is in many ways a development of Fig 29 in that it relies on a reversing loop to bring the train back into the terminal station. The difference is that the reversing loop is inside the circuit, which enables the train to traverse the circuit after it has reversed direction and before it is made to return to the terminal station.

Another advantage of Fig 33 over Fig 29 is that a second station, a through station, could be installed on the reverse loop at point B, space permitting, which would provide a number of additional operating opportunities. Fig 34 provides out-and-back facilities using a through station instead of a terminal station. A train can leave from, say, the left of the station and join the circuit at point A, traverse the circuit via the tunnel and the hidden line as many times as required and then return to the station from the right-hand side at point B. In Fig 34 the

part of the circuit behind the station is hidden from view in a tunnel or possibly as an alternative, behind scenic effects forming a backcloth to the station. These suggestions do not by any means exhaust all the possibilities but they do give an idea of some of the basic plans for track layouts which you may be able to make use of in whatever space you have available.

I have deliberately avoided going into detail, not even bothering to mention whether the plans are based on single or double track since in many cases this sort of detail can obscure the basic shape of a layout, and it is this that I am concerned with more at this stage. But in ignoring the details, already some basic facts of life begin to emerge. If any of the track plans in Figs 29-34 are to be developed into a fully detailed layout plan they are going to consume a fair degree of space. Take the most compact one, which is probably Fig 34 If you are working in 00 4 mm scale, the minimum length for the platform forming the station will need to be at least equal to the longest train you intend to operate. You would obviously like to emulate the full-size railway, which sees nothing exceptional in 11, 12, 13, or 14 coach trains, but with coaches in 00 4 mm scale working out at approximately 9½ in long, this would mean a platform length of something like 9 to 11 ft! Reducing our train to, say, six coaches, we can halve the platform length to 5ft, and this is not a bad length to aim at. Now, assuming you start the curves to join points A and B on Fig 34 at a point immediately at the ends of the platform, you will need as much space either end of the platform as the minimum radius curve you are using. (See Fig 35.) Assuming 2 ft radius curves, which really is something less than the ideal minimum we discussed earlier, you will add 2 ft to either end of the station, 4 ft in all, so already in 00 4 mm scale you have consumed 9 ft of space and have made no provision for the insertion of points or turnouts to lead off from the track passing through the station. To make such provision you want to allow yourself at least another

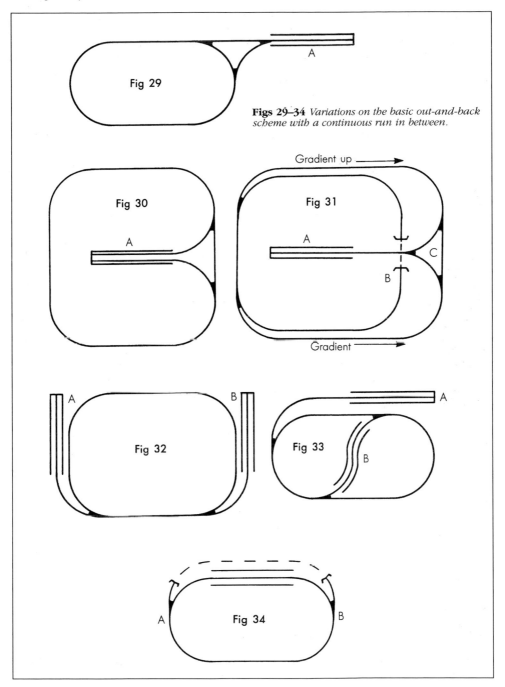

Fig 29

Figs 29–34 *Variations on the basic out-and-back scheme with a continuous run in between.*

Fig 30

A

Gradient up ⟶

Fig 31

A

B

C

Gradient ⟶

A   B

Fig 32

A

Fig 33

B

A   B

Fig 34

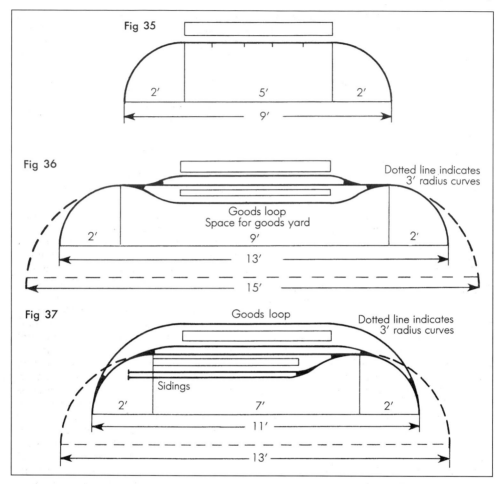

Figs 35–37 *All measurements given in Figs 35–38 are for 00 gauge, and can be halved for N gauge.*

2 ft at one if not both ends of the station. (See Fig 36.) This extra space either end of the platform will enable you to install double track through the station, provide a second platform and put in a goods loop which can lead into the goods yard, south of the station. But it has also added another 4 ft to the length of the station, making a total length of 13 ft, and we still have only a minimum token requirement. Though I spoke of using 2 ft radius curves, in 00 gauge you ought really to be thinking in terms of 3 ft radius

curves which would, in fact, add another 2 ft to the simple plan in Fig 36.

Perhaps this has demonstrated how simple it is to run away with yourself when it comes to planning a layout for a model railway. It is all too easy to think up a scheme which looks all right until you get down to the detailed planning stage and find that you just cannot get that proverbial quart into the pint pot. However, it is possible sometimes to compromise and do some pruning, and the example we have just been discussing is a case in point. Suppose, for instance, that we bring the goods loop around the other side, to the north of the station. It would then be possible to install the turnouts to the loop on the curve leading into the station instead of using up space on the straights. In turn, this would reduce the necessity for having quite so much space for straight track at either end of the platforms. It might also be permitted to stagger the platforms so that, by moving the south side platform of the station to the left, out of centre, it would be possible to install a point at one end from which to bring a siding along the south side of the station. (See Fig 37.) These slight modifications bring the overall length down by 2 ft, which can either be utilised in squeezing the layout into a restricted area or can be used to increase the radius of the curves. Wherever possible the latter is preferable.

The station layout in Fig 37 is really very simple, too simple in fact, and makes no provision for public access to the station, station buildings or any of the amenities we expect to find on a full-size railway. When considering such needs we may well have to revise the plan again and so it goes on! Layout planning is very much a long-term trial and error process, one thing leading to another, and always you have to work within the confines of limited space. To persevere with Fig 37, what have we achieved so far? On the credit side we have a two-road, two-platform station with a goods loop on one side and a siding on the other. On the debit side we have no station buildings, no goods yard, goods shed or public access to the goods yard or station, and no engine depot should we require one at this point on the layout. Luckily we can, if we want to, take the easy way out so far as station buildings and public access are concerned and assume a road crossing the tracks on a bridge, with the main station buildings on the level of the road at right angles to the platform. (See Fig 38.) This is a common working arrangement, especially in towns and congested built-up areas – in fact, just

the same sort of situation we find ourselves faced with in our model. As it happens, there would be a particularly desirable side effect if we used such an arrangement because, you will remember, the station we are developing is to be used in conjunction with the layout shown in Fig 34, where part of the continuous oval passes behind the station in a tunnel hidden from view by a high-level scenic section. The road crossing the station on the bridge could therefore be made to join this high level section, which scenically could be developed to represent a town landscape. This is probably the best solution for this particular dilemma. This practical demonstration shows how layout planning can be approached and how a fully developed plan is often the culmination of a lot of separate decisions which are made step by step as they occur.

The central point of any plan is invariably the station and we have already seen how its length can be governed by the traffic requirements and how the station itself can dictate the ultimate shape and character of a layout. As in real life, the station should reflect the type of traffic you wish to operate. The grander and more express the train, the longer the platform and, unless space is unlimited, the bigger your problems. I think you will begin to see why the smaller type of branch line layout is so popular as, although many actual branch line stations had quite long platforms, in model form we can get away with relatively short platforms provided our trains are kept short. The platform must be long enough to hold the longest train, and in 00 gauge, 4 mm scale, 2 ft 6 in to 3 ft can be ample for a two or three-coach branch line train.

As another exercise in layout planning, let us build up step by step a branch line terminal station. There are, or were, any number of actual stations we could use and the model press is full of examples, but rather than pick on one of these ready-made samples, let us build up one of our own to cover the particular type of traffic

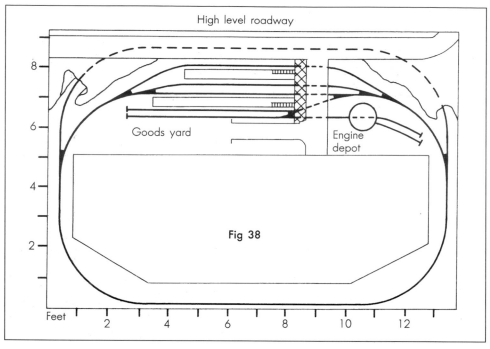

A high level roadway and tramway such as could be modelled as a backscene for the layout plan at Fig 38. Tramscene by Stan Ginn.

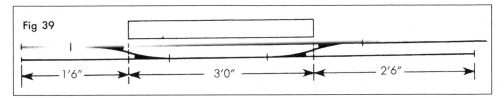

Fig 39 *A track plan for a simple branch line terminal station.*

we wish to operate. Firstly, let us assume the branch line has been built to serve a small country market town some five or six miles from a junction with the main line and about 15 to 20 miles away from a larger commercial centre. The latter will justify the operation of a reasonably comprehensive passenger service since we can assume a residential population and a sprinkling of commuter traffic. For this we need to run a three-coach locomotive hauled train at peak hours and perhaps a diesel railcar or steam-hauled railmotor during the off-peak times. The locomotive-hauled train will require a run-round loop to enable the engine to uncouple and run round the train. We may also need some siding accommodation to stable the early morning commuter train carriages overnight and the railmotor or rail car during the peak periods when it is out of use during the day. So already we need something similar to that given in Fig 39.

Now the overall length of this little lot would work out at something like 7 ft in 00 4 mm scale. The next step is perhaps to consider the goods traffic. We have already established that it is a small country market town, so it is reasonable to assume the following types of traffic:

The attraction of a simple branch line terminal station is conveyed in this view of Crichel Down, the 4mm scale S4 layout of Martin Goodall.

Inward Coal (mainly domestic); general merchandise; parcels; fertilisers; timber; possibly oil and petrol; agricultural machinery.
Outward Agricultural and dairy produce: milk; livestock (eg, cattle, sheep and pigs).

To cater for this traffic we would need the following facilities:
1 Coal bins for coal merchants to unload and store coal.
2 A goods shed to unload inward coming general merchandise and fertilisers and to load outward going agricultural products fruit, vegetables, small livestock, etc.
3 A crane to help offload containers, timber and agricultural machinery.
4 An end loading bay to offload agricultural machinery.
5 A cattle pen for loading and unloading cattle and sheep, and which must be reasonably near road access.
6 A dairy to load milk tank wagons.
7 Possibly an oil and petrol storage depot.

The plan in Fig 41 covers all these points and is probably rather more elaborate than most branch line terminal stations were in practice. But I have attempted to cater for a large volume of traffic and a large number of traffic movements, since we want to provide our model with as much operating scope as possible. For instance, the goods arrival loop is something that may not always be found in a small terminal station, but I have installed it deliberately so that the arrival of a goods train need not interfere with the working of the passenger service. On arrival, the goods train would run into the loop and detach the goods brake van at the end which would be run into the storage siding at A. The engine would then uncouple, run round the train, and proceed to push the wagons into their respective sidings – B for general merchandise and fertilisers, D for coal, C for storage and off-loading when convenient, and E for end unloading of agricultural machinery. It is assumed that the sidings would be cleared as far as possible beforehand of any empty wagons, which would already be made up into a train waiting in the departure road. You will see that,

Ashburton inspired the station building on the 00 gauge Johnshaven branch built by the late Les Parker and his son Richard.

4 m

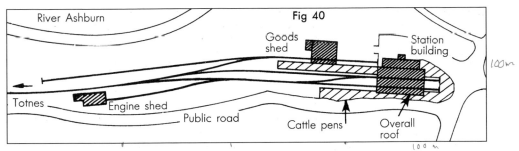

100m

Fig 40 *Ashburton station. This simple branch line terminal station occupies approximately ¼ mile in real life, which is about 15 ft in 00 gauge.*

compared with Fig 39, we have moved the carriage storage road to a bay platform at the side of the passenger station main platform. A bay platform such as this can be very useful for handling parcel traffic or for accepting extra trains during market or fair days. All the loading and unloading facilities listed earlier have been provided and sidings have been incorporated leading to the dairy and oil storage depot. In addition, provision for an engine shed has been made alongside the siding reserved for brake vans. Perhaps a loco coal wagon could be allowed to stand on the brake van siding, which would provide a reserve coal supply for the small locomotive depot.

As I said earlier, probably the track layout of Fig 41 is over elaborate compared to many prototype branch line terminal stations. The very famous Ashburton station in Devon, so beloved by branch line enthusiasts and once the home for locomotives belonging to the Dart Valley Railway, is a case in point. The track layout of Ashburton is shown in Fig 40.

Here a very long run round loop is provided, in fact the locomotive released from the front of the train after it arrived at the station had to travel right beyond the engine shed before it could come forward again to rejoin the train. The whole emphasis is on length rather than breadth and in fact in 00 gauge you would require a space of at least 10 ft in length to accommodate this quite simple design if you wanted to model it accurately, whereas it need only be about 1 ft 6 in wide. A long goods siding is

provided, but access to it is in the middle. If any wagons have to be moved out of the left-hand end of the siding opposite the locomotive shed they have to enter the right-hand end where the goods shed is situated before they can be moved on to the main line. As the engine itself has to make a similar move, only a few wagons can be moved at a time and then only if there are a limited number of wagons on the goods shed road. Frankly, I am not over-enamoured with Ashburton as a track layout for a terminal station as it has such limited operating possibilities, although I join with everybody in regretting the reason for its closure as a branch line terminus. I am sure that it must have been mainly the buildings, particularly the overall station roof, that attracted so many people to it. If you want a much simpler branch line terminal station, but one that still provides some operating scope, Fig 41 could be pruned quite extensively and still leave a number of interesting facilities.

In Fig 42 we have cut out the goods arrival and departure loops. As a result it will be necessary to use the running line for a shunting spur, which is more in keeping with a small branch line terminal. Only one road has been provided for the milk depot and it will be necessary for the bay platform cum carriage siding to be nearly empty before any wagons can be worked into or out of the depot. The oil depot and engine shed can change places if you wish. Dispensing with the goods arrival and departure loops and moving the run round

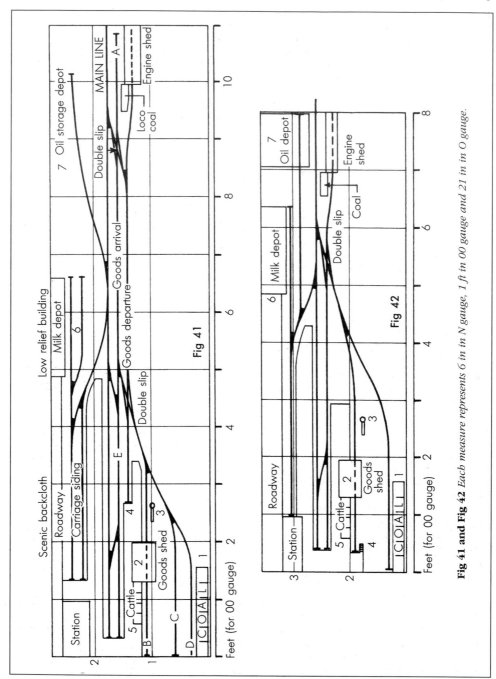

Fig 41 and Fig 42 Each measure represents 6 in in N gauge, 1 ft in 00 gauge and 21 in in O gauge.

Fig 41

Fig 42

loop crossover further down the line away from the buffer stop has had the effect of extending the length of the run round loop, and at the same time has enabled the goods and coal sidings to be extended, which is probably a worthwhile advantage. I think you will agree that Fig 42 is much less cluttered up than Fig 41 and bearing in mind the example set by Ashburton, is probably more authentic in appearance.

In drawing plans for these suggested layouts it is always much easier to use a straight line for most of the running rails but, if possible, it adds considerably to the realism of a station layout if a slight curve can be introduced into the main track roads. Again, Ashburton is a good example as the layout is on a gentle curve, at least it looks gentle on a track plan but it is quite noticeably curved in real life when the eye is nearer to ground level. The inclusion of a gentle curve into the plan of a layout is not always possible if you are using proprietary ready-assembled track since, with few exceptions, the majority of commercially produced points and crossings are designed with a straight stock rail. There are, admittedly, such things as points on curves but the radius of these curves is much sharper than I have in mind for this particular application. If, however, you propose making your own trackwork the introduction of a gentle curve does not present too insurmountable a problem.

If you are intending to purchase ready-made track and points, the points themselves can be an expensive item since a fair number are usually required, even for the most basic layout plan. (Four are needed for the simple run round loop shown in Fig 39). Incidentally, we refer to points as left-hand or right-hand and in Fig 39 we have two right-hand and two left-hand points; the right-hand points are in fact on the left-hand end of the loop and the two left-hand points are shown on the right hand end of the loop, just to be awkward! Two points of the same hand make a crossover from one straight running rail to another, eg, Figs 43 and 44. A crossover on a curve, however,

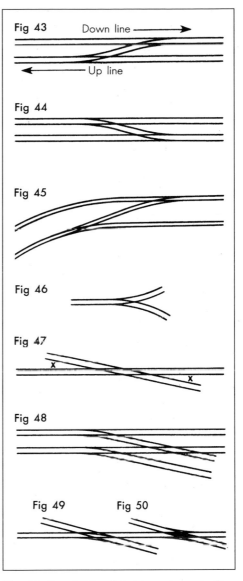

Fig 43 *Two left-hand points make a trailing crossover.* **Fig 44** *Two right-hand points make a facing crossover.* **Fig 45** *One left-hand and one right-hand point make a crossover on a curve.* **Fig 46** *'Y' point.* **Fig 47** *Crossing. 'X' marks the angle – in this case 12 degrees.* **Fig 48** *Double junction, using two right-hand points and one 12 degree crossing.* **Fig 49** *(left) Single slip.* **Fig 50** *(right) Double slip.*

uses points of opposite hands, as shown in Fig 45. Another type much favoured by manufacturers is the 'Y' point, where the two diverging rails curve at an equal radius and angle, eg, Fig 46. The crossing in Fig 47 has a number of uses, depending on the angle of the crossing. A shallow angle such as 12 degrees is used for making what is known as a double junction. eg, Fig 48, where two sets of running lines diverge from each other. Yet another type of point-work is the slip, either a single slip or a double slip (see Figs 49 and 50).

These slip points are very common in prototype practice, particularly in station goods yards. They were always regarded as a bit of a challenge to scratch builders and as ready-made commercial items they were very rare and almost unheard of at one time But such is the development of mass-production technology in the model railway world that several manufacturers now offer double slips in 00/HO and N gauges and Marklin even include one in their Mini-club Z gauge. A double slip virtually combines two points together. The same effect can be obtained by using two points, but at the expense of using more track space (See Fig 51.) Another space-saver combining two points in one is the three-way point (see Fig 52). This is also quite common in proto-type practice and is available from several manufacturers in 00/HO and N gauges.

Fig 51 *Two points placed back to back have the same effect as a double slip, but take up twice as much room.* **Fig 52** *Three-way point – a useful space saver.*

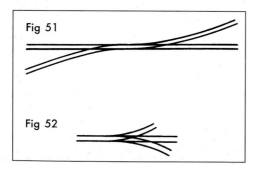

Fig 51

Fig 52

On the full-size railway most pointwork is tailor-made to fit the location and more often than not the points are built on curves and do not assume the straight geometrical form that used to be adopted by model manufac-turers. Points on curves are, however, becoming more common and several firms are beginning to include such items in their range. For really authentic track formations you cannot do better than build your own track, but if you feel you are unable to spare the time or you think it may be beyond your capability, the range of points and crossings available from commercial manufacturers in the two most popular gauges, 00 and N, is such that really comprehensive layouts can be built with very little trouble. But, as I said earlier, points are relatively costly items in comparison, say, to a yard of flexible track. When you find yourself being carried away and sketching in sidings and junctions all over your layout plan, remember that if you are going to purchase your track ready-made, it is probably going to cost more than £6 per point–even a little more after you have purchased the necessary point lever or operating mechanism. We will discuss these later in Chapter 7, Fig 42 is not too bad in that it only uses seven points: four right-hand, two left-hand, one 'Y' point and one double slip. The probable cost of these items in 00 or N could be around £60, which is something that needs to be considered, although it must be emphasised that, once laid, track is a capital investment which need not be repeated and will last as long as the layout. Fig 41 uses 14 points – six right hand, seven left hand and one 'Y' point and two double slips; the probable cost of this little lot could be as much as £120. This is for the point-work alone, to which must be added the cost of the ordinary running rails you will also need.

In case you are worried about these kind of figures I would hasten to add that points and running rails need only be purchased as and when they are laid. It can take several weeks to lay a complete track formation for a station, such as shown in Fig 42, since there is more to it than just connecting points up together, as I will show in succeeding chapters. Three or four points and half a dozen yards of track can be purchased to begin with, and this will enable you to make a start. The rest can follow later as and when funds permit.

Talking about the cost of trackwork, points and running rails reminds me to refer to point number 7 in the list of desirable features for layout planning—conform as far as possible to acceptable railway practice. I think the full size railways are as mindful as anyone of the necessity to keep trackwork down to a minimum compatible with the job in hand. In many cases of railway construction, where single track only was laid, provision was made in the accompanying earthworks and civil engineering structures for laying double track on the assumption that if traffic expanded the second line could be added later. The capital cost of laying a double line and the continual drain on revenue of having to maintain a second line unnecessarily was avoided when it could be, but the relatively slight extra cost of building the earth works and civil engineering structures to double track standard was accepted at the time as being cheaper than having to face the possible total conversion at a later date. Most prototype station track plans, although they sometimes seem to be festooned with points and sidings, are often very simple when you look at them closely and make a detailed study of each particular track and the likely operating movement. These days especially, tracks are not left in

A three-way point and double-slip are both prominent in this view of Buntingham.

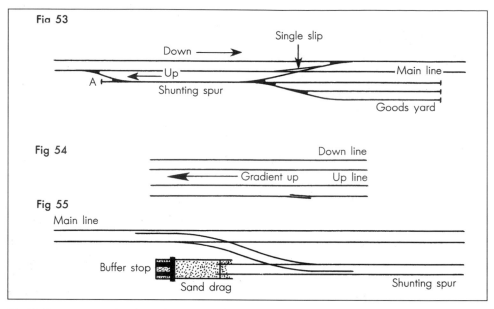

Fig 53 *Shunting spur.* **Fig 54** *Catch point installed at the foot of a gradient on a double track mainline for the purpose of derailing runaway rolling stock running back down the hill, a not uncommon occurrence in the days of loose coupled freight trains. Only the up line is so equipped, in this case with a right-hand point to ensure that rolling stock derails clear of the track and away from the down line.* **Fig 55** *An ordinary turnout employed as a catch point. The shunting spur finishes up buried in a deep layer of sand which, together with the buffer stop, should stop any runaway rolling stock and thus avoid fouling the main line.*

place any longer than they need to be. If you are modelling a modern image layout some provision ought to be made on the plan for a disused siding, or a branch line which perhaps can be made to disappear into a bricked-up tunnel mouth, or even a cutting with a row of hen houses standing where the track used to be.

One of the most basic rules to follow when trying to conform to prototype practice is to avoid the use of facing points on passenger carrying lines. The simplest illustration and practical application of this is the installation of crossover between and up and down main line, The crossover should always be laid in a trailing fashion so that the train has to reverse if it wishes to travel over the points. (See Fig 43.)

This is not to say that facing points never occur, because there are occasions, particularly at junctions where one main line diverges from another, where they are essential. However, in these situations special protective apparatus such as facing point locks and locking bars are needed, which in the old days of manual non-automatic control invariably required the nearby presence of a signal box. On single track lines, where trains travel in opposite directions on the same length of line, facing points cannot be avoided. In these cases added protection is provided by the single line train staff.

Another feature of prototype practice which can be copied so far as through station track plans are concerned is to avoid fouling the main line where possible. A shunting spur can often be laid parallel with the main line to take care of any movements of the locomotive, shunting in the goods yard, without the locomotive itself having to stray on to the main line. (see Fig 53.)

Siding accommodation for full length trains was uppermost in Len Weal's mind when constructing his 00 gauge layout.

Catch points are a necessity in a number of cases to protect the main line against runaway vehicles. Peco have thoughtfully provided such items in their range of N and 00/HO trackwork. A typical installation for a catch point would be where a siding joins a main line, as at A on Fig 53, or on the main line itself at the foot of a gradient (see Fig 54). In the absence of a special catch point, ordinary points can sometimes be used to provide a similar safety facility in the situation such as at A in Fig 53, in which case the short length of track leaving the point would finish up in a sand drag and a buffer stop (see Fig 55). There are any number of government enforced regulations controlling safety arrangements for trackwork which manifest themselves in the layout of stations and goods yards. However, the subject is complex and in practice it need not concern the average modeller beyond the points I have just mentioned.

Lastly we come to point number 8 in the list of features to consider when making layout plans, which is the necessity to provide adequate provision for working and

storing your proposed fleet of rolling stock. It is probably fair to say that however strong-willed you may be you will soon amass a collection of rolling stock which is way beyond your needs, and the problem arises of where to put it all. I think it is impossible, and in fact unnecessary, to provide siding accommodation for *every* item of rolling stock you possess. It is nice instead to ring the changes from time to time and it is a sound practical idea to have a few alternative locomotives or sets of carriages to vary your workings, but which do not necessarily have to be kept in readiness on the layout itself. You only need enough sidings to take care of your immediate working stock and a few spare locomotives. The rest can be shunted into a fiddle yard or put on display some-where away from the layout itself. If you have the room, of course, it is nice to fill up sidings with spare wagons and coaches and the locomotive depot with an impressive stud of locomotives, but I do not think you have to do this just because you are lucky enough to have the stock. And likewise do not feel that it is necessary to stop adding to your stock just because all the sidings are filled up. Imagine your surplus rolling stock has gone off to Thurso or Fishguard or somewhere or, better still, into 'works' and hand shunt them away out of sight for a while. One thing that will be required is adequate length storage roads to receive the trains you are intending to despatch around your layout. You will need sufficiently long goods roads to receive the goods trains and passenger station platforms to receive the passenger trains. Also, loops will have to be long enough for engines to run round the train, turntables and engine sheds long enough to take the largest engine, and bay platforms long enough to take the coaching stock *and* the engine. These are just common sense things which should be in your mind all the time you are preparing your layout plan.

Now we come to the actual job of planning itself. As I said earlier in this chapter, layout planning is a subject that most railway modellers love to get their teeth into. I find it a very relaxing way of passing the time. Instead of a crossword puzzle or a pocket chess set I can find plenty to amuse myself with paper and pencil working out plans for the ideal model railway. At least it's one branch of the hobby that costs nothing! For 00 gauge layouts I always use a scale of 1 in to the ft when planning. Using a ruler with a 12th scale is an advantage since ½ in then equals 1 in. It is necessary to bear a few facts in mind when planning layouts and Fig 57 gives some details of the clearances which should be allowed between parallel tracks and between the tracks and lineside structures such as bridges, station platforms, etc.

When working on layout plans you need to allow a 2 in wide strip for a single track in 00, so it follows therefore that double tracks need to be 2 in apart. I always work on the centre line of the track when drawing plans and only draw a single line rather than go to the extent of marking in both running rails. Tracks should not be brought nearer than 2 in from the outside edge of the baseboard. A fair average length is 9 in for a point in 00 gauge, so you can reckon on a crossover being about 18 in long. As mentioned earlier

in this chapter, bogie passenger coaches in 00 gauge are approximately 9-10 in long so once again your platforms must be long enough to take your longest train. Four wheeled wagons are a shade over 3 in long so you can accommodate approximately four to every foot of siding space. Locomotives can be anything from 3 to 10 in long, according to the type but the average mixed traffic loco is approximately 9 in long. A 60 ft turntable which was quite a common size in prototype steam locomotive days and which is big enough to take all but the largest Pacific type is about 9½ in long. However, if you are equipped with a 70 ft turntable, scale size approximately 11 in, you will take care of any British-type locomotive you are likely to come across.

Station platforms are invariably things that modellers are tempted to skimp on so far as the width is concerned on layout plans, but I do think you want to leave as much space as you possibly can. I think a reasonable *minimum* width might be 1½ in for a single platform and 3 in for a double, that is with a running line either side of the platform, but I emphasise minimum width and something wider can always he made use of. In goods yards one should try and leave room for road vehicles to manoeuvre and to back up to wagons. Where a lorry has to drive between sidings full of wagons I would suggest spacing the sidings at least 6 in apart, centre line to centre line, in 00 gauge.

All this basic information is just for drawing ½ scale layout plans which later become the subject for detailed planning using, where possible, full size templates and plans. Seeing the plan laid out full size on the baseboard may make you change your mind about a number of things and you should be fully prepared to expect this when the time comes. Be careful about sticking rigidly to a plan which you have drawn in ½ scale and do not make too many positive steps which will commit you to it, such as buying all the necessary equipment and so on, until you have started to see what it will look like full size. The figures and dimensions quoted in the last three para-

graphs refer to layout plans for 00 gauge
systems. For N gauge you need to halve the
dimensions, eg, single track needs a 1 in
strip, points are approximately 4½ in long
and so on. 00 gauge plans can, of course, be
used for N gauge layouts and vice versa, but
you must be careful not to fall into the trap
when using 00 gauge plans scaled down for
a N gauge layout of also scaling down the
baseboard so that you only leave yourself
half the space in which to gain access to
some parts of the layout. A gap of approximately 2 ft to provide access to 00 gauge will
still be needed if the layout is N gauge. You
can, similarly, use 00 gauge layout plans for
O gauge, in which case nearly double the
space will be required, whilst TT gauge
layouts will be approximately three quarters
the size of 00 gauge layouts.

Whilst it is perfectly possible to adapt
some 00 gauge layout plans for N gauge,
within the limitations referred to in the last
paragraph, it is as well to bear in mind – and
profit from – the special advantages of N
gauge which sets it apart from the other
larger scales and gauges. Curves of 1 ft
radius are perfectly possible and this means
that a continuous oval layout can be built on
a baseboard not much more than 2 ft wide.
Furthermore, N gauge locomotives and
coaches are only half the length of 00. A
four-track main line only needs a space 5 in
wide, and a station platform long enough
for a six-coach train need only be a yard
long. For the first time for many modellers it
is possible to consider building and operating a main line layout with long fast straights
and scale length trains.

The layout plan shown in Fig 56 has been
designed on this principle. It depicts an
important country station with platforms
served by loops off a double track main line,
the fast roads of which pass through the
station unhindered. Just imagine the sight of
a Peco Jubilee or a Minitrix Britannia romp-
ing through the fast roads heading a 10 or 12-
coach train whilst a Graham Farish 'Black 5'

Fig 56 *An N gauge layout, 10 ft × 2 ft 6 in. Each
square represents one square foot.*

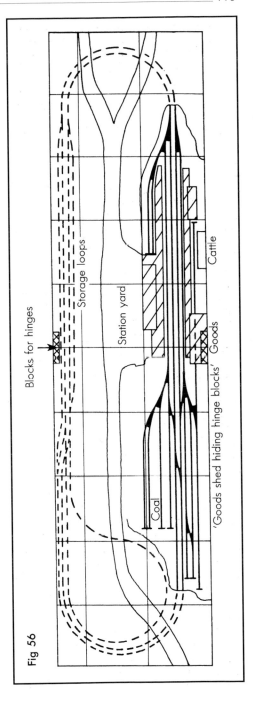

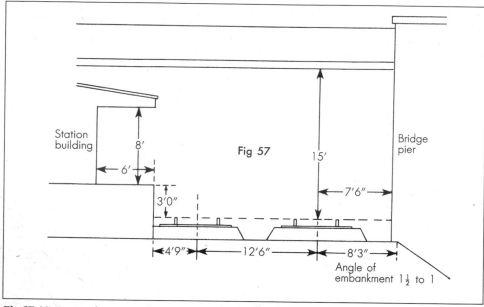

Station
building   8'

Fig 57   15'

← 6' →

3'0"

Bridge
pier

←— 7'6" —→

←4'9"→←——— 12'6" ———→←—— 8'3" ——→

Angle of
embankment 1½ to 1

Fig 57 *Minimum clearances, showing dimensions in feet. It is importnat to remember that additional clearance for platform edges, bridge piers, etc. should be allowed in the case of curved track.*

and train waits on one or other of the platform roads. An extensive goods yard is provided with siding space for approximately 40 wagons, and there is also room for a locomotive depot. All this in an area only 8 ft × 1 ft! The additional space required to incorporate the station plan into a continuous oval layout with hidden storage loops and one or more reversing loops brings the total area to only 10 ft × 2 ft 6 in.

The plan has been devised to enable the baseboard to be constructed in two halves each 5 ft × 2 ft 6 in (less than the size of a door), which could be stored

Right *Only part can be shown here of the long, narrow, continuous run N gauge LNER layout Glenby built by Brian Yallop. D11 'Jutland' heads towards the camera.*

Don Sibley built this compact 4 × 2 ft Dutch narrow gauge tramway in HO. Notice the track embedded in the road surface alongside the quay.

under the bed or hinged to the wall as described in Chapter 2. Such things are within the realms of possibility in N gauge but are less likely to be possible in 00 gauge, where no less than eight baseboard sections each 5 ft × 2 ft 6 in would be required for a comparable layout, which would measure 20 ft × 5 ft overall.

Narrow gauge layouts are also in a world of their own and deserve special attention when it comes to layout planning. This is mainly due to their special, space-saving properties and the remarkable performance of the miniature locomotives and rolling stock. In 00-9, gradients of 1 in 20 and curves of 5½ in are not impossible, so it is obvious that either a lot of narrow gauge layout can be built into a given space or else the space can be reduced to the minimum and still be adequate for a reasonable layout. I have given two plans which have been devised using proprietary 9 mm gauge 00-9 equipment. The larger of the two, Fig 58, measures 4 ft × 3 ft and incorporates a harbour as the main feature. The smaller layout, Fig 58, measures only 3 ft × 2 ft and is suggested as an example of what can be accomplished in the very minimum of space. Both plans can be enlarged with advantage, either by increasing the radius of the curve or extending the length of the sidings, etc.

Apart from the attractive scenic possibilities of Fig 58, its one big feature is that the model railway has a purpose, namely the transport of stone from the quarry to the quayside. It is therefore primarily a freight line, although provision has also been made for operating a passenger service. Trains of tip wagons such as were once made by Jouef or the Minitrains ore wagons would, after loading up in the quarry, run round the continuous circuit for as many times as required to simulate a lengthy run, then leave the main circuit, cross the bridge spanning the river feeding the harbour estuary, and thread their way on to the quayside. As the wagons are unloaded they would be drawn clear and stored in the sidings until there were sufficient to make up a train to run back empty to the quarry.

It is suggested that all the track on the quayside would be level with the road surface. One of the points on the quay is intended to be a Peco 3 ft radius N gauge type which would have its standard gauge sleepers disguised by the road surface. The road surface could be made out of card strips or balsa wood packed up to the height of the tops of the rails. There is room, too, for a reasonably scale-sized ship along the quay. A full-size 300 ton coastal cargo boat measures about 145 ft in length and about 25 ft in breadth which works out at something under 2 ft × 4 in in 00 4 mm scale, making it a distinct possibility on this plan. The quayside would need to be at least 2 in above sea level but the space underneath the model quay could be utilised for hiding the electrical control equipment or for storing spare rolling stock.

Fig 58 *A narrow gauge 009 layout 4 ft × 3 ft. Each square represents one square foot.*

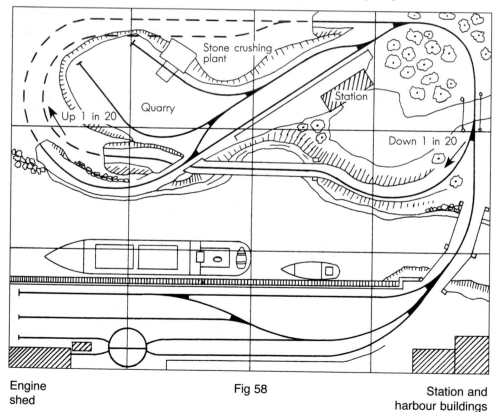

Engine shed

Fig 58

Station and harbour buildings

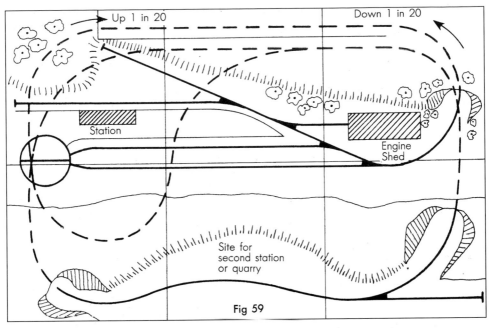

Up 1 in 20

Down 1 in 20

Station

Engine
Shed

Site for
second station
or quarry

Fig 59

Fig 59 *A narrow gauge 009 layout 3 ft × 2 ft. Each square represents one square foot.*

Fig 59 incorporates many features which I consider add interest to a layout, but for which space cannot always be found. Thanks to the forementioned valuable climbing powers of narrow gauge locomotives and the fantastically sharp radius curves some of them will traverse, almost all things are possible in this branch of modelling. The features incorporated are a terminal station with adequate storage space, a hidden continuous run and a reverse loop. It is therefore possible to make up a train in the terminal station, despatch it to run on the continuous circle for as long you like, reverse its direction on the reverse loop and bring it back to the station again. An alternative to the reverse loop might be to install a second station on the lower level with a loop line so that trains could be stopped and reversed and then sent back to the first terminal station.

Chapter 6
Electrical equipment

An accepted requirement of most model railway modellers is that it should be possible to alter the speed and direction of travel of locomotives and trains by remote control. Electric motors powered by electricity conducted through the running rails fulfills this requirement and is the most favoured method of operation for the majority of model railways. There are other methods which I will mention later in this chapter but because rail-conducted electric propulsion is the predominant source of motive power and potentially one of the biggest headaches for newcomers to railway modelling, no book on the hobby would be complete without a detailed reference to the subject.

In the majority of cases, electric model railways today use the two-rail system, where the current is passed to the locomo-

tive through the two running rails which, of necessity, have to be kept insulated from each other. This in turn requires the wheels on one side of the locomotive to be insulated, either at the centre where they are fixed to the axle, Fig 60, or in the wheel itself, usually at the rim or tyre which can be made separate from the wheel centre. (See Fig 61.) The current is conducted to the motor through the chassis on the non-insulated wheel and by current collectors or pick-ups on the insulated wheel. Pick-ups can be a source of trouble if not properly cleaned and adjusted. They can be avoided on tender locomotives by insulating the tender wheels on the opposite side to the locomotive. The non-insulated wheels then become conductors on both locomotive and tender, requiring only a wire or conductive coupling between the

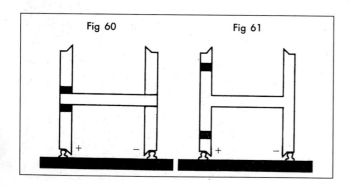

Fig 60 *Two-rail wheel insulated at centre.* **Fig 61** *Two-rail wheel insulated at rim.*

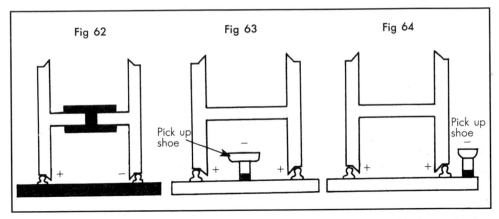

Fig 62 *Two-rail wheel insulated by split axle.* **Fig 63** *Three-rail centre pick-up.* **Fig 64** *Three-rail outside pick-up.*

two to complete the electrical circuit. This system is also applicable to bogie fitted diesel locomotives and DMUs. Another way of avoiding pick-ups is to split the axle across the centre and join the two halves with an insulated collar. (See Fig 62.) The current is conducted through the axle bearings which in turn requires that the two sides of the chassis are insulated. Prior to World War 2 when two-rail electrification was little known, the accepted practice was not to insulate the wheels or track but to install a third insulated rail either inside (Fig 63) or outside the running rails (Fig 64) to complete the necessary electrical circuit.

With the post-war development of plastics, two-rail insulation of wheels and track became more of a practical commercial proposition. Eventually most of the main pre-war manufacturers converted their whole range to the two-rail system and all the major post-war developments have been in two-rail. One manufacturer, namely Marklin of Germany, still sticks to non-insulated running rails and wheels on the three-rail system. Actually, the third rail is no longer a rail but in fact a row of studs

which transmit the current to the locomotive via a skid underneath the engine. The skid is so designed that it is kept clear of the running rails but is allowed to come into contact with at least one stud at any

Mention has been made of 2-rail and 3-rail track. Rarely modelled is the 4-rail track of London Transport shown here on Dick Yeo's Epton.

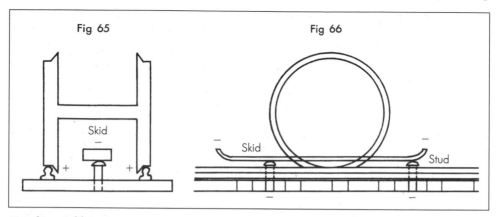

Figs 65 and 66 *Stud contact – cross-section and side view.*

one time. (See Figs 65 and 66.) This is known as the stud contact system and is rather unusual in the smaller gauges. However, it is quite common in O and 1 gauge, where it is a practical alternative for anyone who does not want to go to the trouble of converting all his three-rail rolling stock, or perhaps wishes to operate live steam or clockwork locomotives in conjunction with his electrically powered fleet. Both the studs in the tracks and the skid underneath the locomotive can be made quite unobtrusive and the appearance of the trackwork is very little different from the ordinary two-rail type.

In order to move a locomotive (or railcar, multiple unit, etc., backwards or forwards at a realistic speed we require a variable source of electrical power to be taken to that part of the layout where the locomotive is standing and to where we want it to move. On a very simple layout where there is only 'one engine in steam' this presents few if any problems; just two wires connecting the outlet of the variable source of electrical power, ie the power unit, with the two running rails of the track. However, there are two factors to be considered as the layout is extended. Firstly there is the necessity to retain the purity of the electrical circuit as the track formation is expanded. you will recall it is the running rails that

convey the electricity to the locomotive and the two running rails form part of an electrical circuit. As with any electrical circuit, the two running rails must not be allowed to touch each other anywhere on the layout. There is a danger of this happening with some track formations and these are referred to later in the chapter. The second factor to be considered arises when you have two or more locomotives and you only wish to run one, or you may wish to control more than one locomotive independently at the same time.

With a conventional electrically controlled layout where it is necessary to run one locomotive on a length of track whilst keeping another locomotive stationary it is necessary to electrically isolate that part of the track on which the locomotive is required to remain stationary. The situation arises, for example, when you use a second locomotive to detach coaches from a train which has run into a terminal station. Another example arises in the case of an engine shed or motive power depot where any number of locomotives can be expected to be in close proximity to each other on the same length of track. This is quite simply arranged and is shown in Fig 67. One rail is broken and an on/off switch is wired across the break. The two ends of the broken rail are best joined by an insulating fishplate or rail joiner.

Whist planning a layout, it is important to decide how many track sections will be required and their exact location since the insulated rail joiners must be put in at the same time as the track is laid. It is possible to make alterations afterwards by cutting through the rail with a fine saw and soldering the rail ends to pins driven into the baseboard, but there is less chance of damage to the track if all the insulated rail joiners which are likely to be needed are put in at the start. (You can always bond a wire across those which are not immediately needed.) How many isolating rails and switches you will require will be dependent on the size of layout and the number of locomotives you are fortunate enough to possess but it will be readily appreciated that with some layouts the numbers can rise to an appreci-able amount. It is possible to do away with isolating rails if you think in terms of isolating the locomotive rather than the track on which it stands. In theory it is possible to do this by equipping the locomotive with a hand operated on/off switch though in practice this is rarely if ever done. Overhead electric locomotives fitted with working pantographs do, however, lend themselves to this form of isolation without modifications by the simple expedient of lowering the pantograph. Albeit this has to be done by hand but not an impossible task I would have thought on the average size layout where most parts of the track are likely to be within reasonable reach of the operator.

The ability to remotely control the isolating of locomotives without the necessity for isolating rails is, however, provided for in the very latest electronic multiple train control or command control systems. With these systems the locomotive itself is isolated until commanded or called up by the operator. The calling up process is by means of a coded signal from the controller to an electronic chip or module installed in the locomotive. Each module is programmed to react to a different coded signal and only after the appropriate signal is given will the module, and the locomotive in which it is installed, respond. Modules can also be installed along the lineside to operate points and signals and other such electrically operated accessories. Airfix were one of the first to introduce multiple train control, closely followed by Hornby Railways Zero 1, Hammant and Morgan 5000 and ECM Selectrol. Possibly because they were mostly incompatible one with another or they required total conversion not being interchangeable with conventional power systems they appeared to have a mixed reception on the UK market and for one reason or another are no longer in production. More recently ZTC System have introduced an advanced control system which appears to be very versatile. Their ZTC 511 Digital Master Controller can be set to operate either with an ordinary DC output

Fig 67 *Isolating rail and switch.*

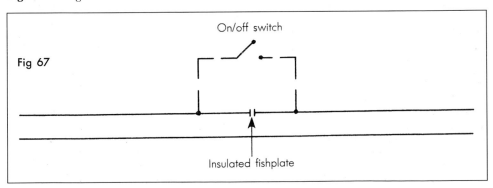

for conventional DC locomotives without decoders or in Digital mode can command up to 100 locomotives with decoders (up to 10 at one time) and up to 1,000 points or signals. In any mode it can simulate the control of a full-size steam engine as it has controls representing brake, reverse gear and regulator, one of the many desirable features of this advanced control system.

Command control systems have attracted a number of manufacturers overseas, noteworthy examples being Marklin Digital HO, Fleischmann FMZ-120 Multi-Train Control, Trix Selectrix and from Japan the Kato Digicon-100. Based on the latest microprocessor computer technology, these systems vary in detail and sophistication but all have the ability to control both locomotives and accessories such as track relays, points, decouplers, etc., and to provide features such as constant train lighting, all with just two wires to the layout. To illustrate the scope of these systems, the Marklin Digital HO, designed for their AC stud contact system, will control up to 80 locomotives and 256 accessories. The Fleischmann FMZ-120, which is fully compatible with existing DC control systems has 119 channels to operate varying combinations of receiver modules in locomotives and accessories, a typical example being 60 locomotives, 200 points, relays or signals, and 72 uncouplers. The Kato Digicon-100 which is also designed for DC systems will operate up to 100 locomotives. A feature of all these systems is an interface to connect with a home computer so that a layout can be programmed to operate fully automatically by computer control.

Clearly the number of locomotives that can be controlled by these systems presupposes a fairly extensive layout which together with the investment needed for the control system might be considered to be beyond the reach of many railway modellers. However, for anyone who is in the fortunate position of being able to consider making such an outlay the various proprietary systems for multiple train control based on micro-processor techniques open

up an exciting prospect. Apart from increasing the operating scope of a model railway it brings the hobby well into the forefront of modern day technology providing a ready challenge to other competing high-tech leisure pursuits. Not all the systems described above are available at the time of writing but details can be obtained from manufacturers' catalogues which in turn can be obtained from dealers in the UK.

The remainder of this chapter is devoted to conventional electrical control systems starting first with the variable source of electrical power or power unit as it is usually referred to. This consists of a transformer to reduce the mains voltage to a level suitable for the motors in the locomotives, a rectifier to convert the alternating current (AC) from the transformer to direct current (DC) and a means of varying the level of the DC voltage output. It is in this means of varying the voltage level that the various types of conventional power unit differ.

The simplest and oldest method is to place a variable resistance in the circuit between the rectifier and the motor. This works on the principle that the greater the resistance in the circuit the less the current that can be delivered to the motor. Thus, by varying the resistance, the motor speed is altered. The second method is also simple and utilises a variable transformer which, as its name implies, supplies a variable AC voltage to the rectifier which converts it to the variable DC output.

The third method is less simple. After DC has been obtained from the rectifier, it is fed to a transistor regulator to obtain the variable voltage. I will not attempt to describe the workings of such a regulator, but power units are available in this category ranging from a simple speed control and reversing switch to very complex ones which can give predetermined rates of acceleration, coasting and braking, in addition to being used as a simple means of controlling the speed of a train in the normal manner.

Besides controlling the speed, we also need to control the direction in which the train travels and two methods of doing this are available on power units. In the first, the control knob or lever has an 'off' position in the centre of its travel, one side of this travel being designated 'forward', the other side 'reverse'. The other method has a separate switch for reversing the direction of the train, thus leaving the whole of the movement of the knob or lever for speed control. The former method is common on variable resistance and variable transformer types, whist most transistor units use a separate switch.

Many conventional controllers of both variable resistance and variable transformer varieties have a facility called 'pulse power' enabling better control to be achieved at low speeds. This works by applying what is known as half wave rectification to the AC voltage rather than the full wave rectification which is normally used, and gives a series of continuous instead of separate pulses of electricity to the locomotive.

All types of power unit in commercial production feature some kind of overload protection. The traditional type is the electro-magnetic cut-out in which a button pops out of the power unit when an overload such as a short circuit occurs. You only have to depress the button in order to reset the unit and continue operation, having of course cured the cause. A second type, called the thermal cut out, is very reliable but unfortunately gives no indication that it has operated. Thus it can cause a little confusion when fault finding, since the

Right *A simple home-made plug-in control box incorporating two panel mounted ECM Comp-speed controllers; Rambler on the left and CB centre-off on the right. The switches are for cab control; top for the high level terminus and bottom for the low level continuous run and fiddle yard. The mimic diagram incorporates studs for electric pencil point control. No isolating switches are included, reliance being placed on the switched track points.*

Below *At the other extreme, Robert Tivendale created this monumental control panel for his Ashley Bridge 00 gauge layout.*

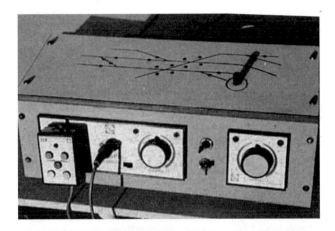

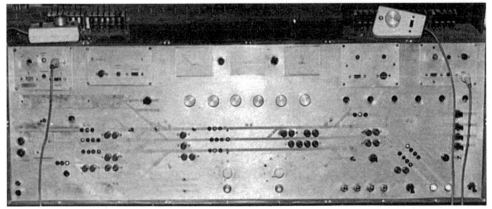

symptom of lack of power and a short circuit are the same. This type is, however, self-resetting after a time delay of a few seconds. Variable resistance and variable transformer units may be fitted with either of these types of cut-out, which do not act with sufficient speed to prevent damage to transistor circuits. Thus transistorised units contain electronic circuitry to limit the maximum current which may be delivered by the unit in case of a short circuit. However, they may have one of the above types of cut-out as well.

When choosing a power unit the modeller must base his choice on a balance of performance and cost. The variable resistance power unit is quite adequate for many purposes and is relatively cheap. The variable transformer power unit will generally give improved control of a locomotive in the low speed area but, as with all good things, you have to pay extra for it. The transistor power unit will give very good control but is, generally speaking, the most costly of all. When buying a power unit, don't forget that if you are going to operate your points and signals electrically you will need the extra uncontrolled outlets available on some units, typically 16 volts AC. An extra 12 volt DC outlet can be useful for a further control unit without its own transformer and rectifier (see below). If your friends own model railways, no doubt you could try out their power units and see how you like them, and if you are going to buy one, your dealer should be able to show you a selection.

As mentioned above, the various components forming a power unit can be obtained separately. Some complete power units have auxiliary 16 volt AC and 12 volt DC supplies, and extra control units of the variable resistance and transistor types can be obtained to 'add-on' and control an extra train. Remember, however, that if the auxiliary supply is AC, a rectifier will be required in the 'add-on' unit in order to give DC for the track.

At this stage, I would like to give a warning. Power units which include a transformer are almost invariably constructed so that it is difficult to get inside them. This is for a good reason since, besides being generally dangerous, mains electricity can be lethal. Under no circumstances should the modeller attempt to open a power unit unless he is a qualified electrician. He should take it to his dealer or send it to the manufacturer for repair.

Having obtained our source of power, we must now consider how to get it to the track by means of wires and connections. Suitable wire may be obtained from your model railway dealer or your local electrical shop. Multi strand flexible wire is better for our purposes than single strand types which may break during the course of installation being unable to withstand the amount of bending required. The designations 7/.0076 and 14/.0076 (metric equivalents 7/0.2 mm and 16/0.2 mm) are used in the trade for wires which are admirable for our needs and which will easily carry all the current we are likely to require.

If the type of track you are using includes in its range a terminal connector, then by all means use it and attach the wire securely to the terminal fixings. If a terminal connector is not available, the alternative is to solder the bared end of the lead to the outside web of the rail. If you are using plastic-based track, apply the soldering iron for the minimum time possible, as it is easy to melt the plastic base if the iron is left in contact with the rail for long periods. You can avoid this by soldering the wire to a rail joiner which is the preferred method.

Normally, tight fitting fishplates or rail joiners should be adequate for conducting electricity across rail joints, but if the layout is likely to be subject to large temperature changes it is advisable to 'bond' the joints by soldering a loop of wire to the outside web of the rail about ½ in each side of the joint. If one is lucky enough to have a large layout, trouble may be experienced with 'voltage drop' which is caused by the resistance of long lengths of rail and joints and manifests itself as diminished power when a train is a long distance from the control point. The cure is to bond the rail joints and, if necessary, to take extra leads from the

Illustrating just how complex some under-baseboard wiring can become.

power unit to the point on the track where the trouble occurs, taking due note of the polarity and using reasonably large-section wire, at least 14/.0076 as mentioned above, and preferably larger.

A subject which often causes confusion is the different types of turnout or point. There are two types, known as 'dead frog' and 'live frog', the difference being that the frog (the 'X' crossing part of the point) is electrically isolated from other pieces of rail in the former type, ie, it is electrically 'dead'. In live frog points, the frog carries electricity although its polarity must change when the direction of the point changes. (See Fig 68a.) Fig 68a also shows that the track which is not selected by the point will be 'dead', since it has the same polarity on both rails.

Fig 68a *Live frog isolating.* **Fig 68b** *Dead frog isolating.* **Fig 68c** *Dead frog non-isolating.*

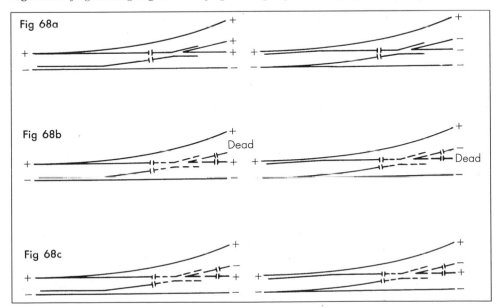

Points with this switching feature are sometimes known as 'isolating' points and are not necessarily live frog types. Fig 68b shows a dead frog point which is an isolating type, and Fig 68c shows a type of dead frog point which is non-isolating, ie, both divergent tracks are electrified, irrespective of the track selected by the point blades.

The question arises as to which is the best type for the modeller to use and, as often occurs, there is no straightforward answer. The best approach is to discuss the relative advantages of each. Perhaps the greatest advantage of the live frog point is that there is an uninterrupted path for the current as a locomotive traverses the point, whereas a dead frog cannot pass current through the wheel which is in contact with the frog. Despite the fact that on a locomotive there should be more than one wheel picking up current on each side, the rocking of a locomotive on any slight unevenness in the track can reduce the number of pick-up wheels on one side of the locomotive to one. This could easily be the one on the dead frog, with the result that the locomotive would 'stall'

Isolating points are preferable to non-isolating ones in conventional electrical control systems since, if you need to leave a locomotive in a siding, it is necessary only to operate the point to the direction against the locomotive when power is automatically cut off. With isolating points it is impossible to run a train over them when they are set against the train – a feature which can prevent many a derailment! When using isolating points it is important that the power supply is connected to the toe, ie, blade end of the point, otherwise it will not be possible for electricity to be passed down the divergent track. If 'kick-back' sidings are included in the layout, such as in Fig 69, then it is necessary to arrange an extra electrical feed to the headshunt in order to take power to the sidings and ensure that it is fed from the 'toe' of point A.

Reference to Fig 70 will show that, when live frogs are used, their polarities on a diamond crossing will need to be switched according to which direction it is desired to run. Since we are not dealing with isolating points but with a crossing with frogs having rails of differing polarities next to them, insulated fishplates will be necessary where shown. All this will be unnecessary, of course with dead frog diamond crossings and with dead frog slips. Live frog slips, however, are very difficult to electrify and this can only be done by using electrical relays which involve techniques beyond the scope of this book.

Fig 69 *'Kick-back' sidings necessitate an extra electrical feed into the headshunt.*

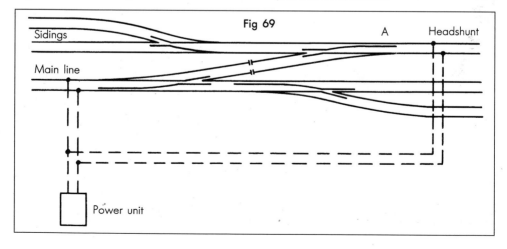

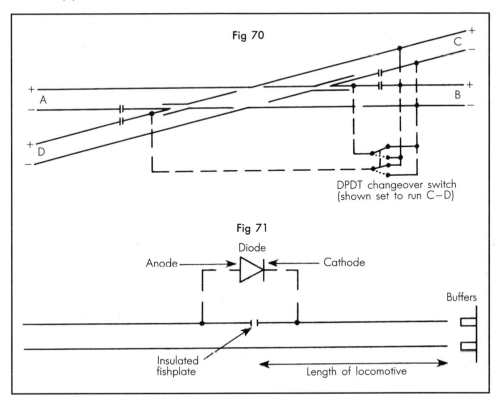

Fig 70

C +
  −

+ B
  −

+ A
−

+ D
−

DPDT changeover switch
(shown set to run C−D)

Fig 71

Diode

Anode ———→ ◁ ←——— Cathode

Buffers

Insulated
fishplate

←———— Length of locomotive ————→

Fig 70 *Live frogs on a diamond
crossing.* **Fig 71** *Using a diode
in the wiring connecting the
isolating section.*

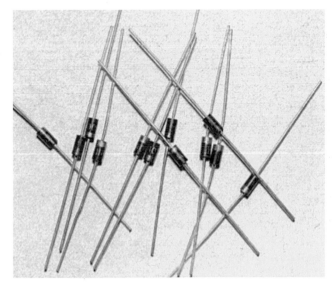

Right Fig 71 *diagrammatically
illustrates a diode; this is what
they look like.*

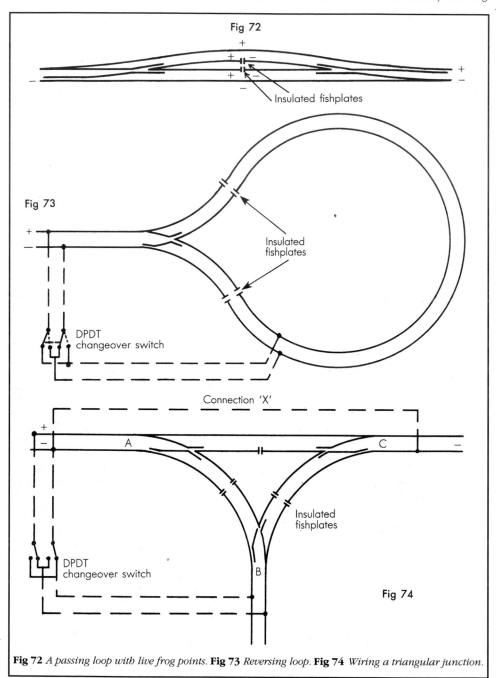

Fig 72 *A passing loop with live frog points.* **Fig 73** *Reversing loop.* **Fig 74** *Wiring a triangular junction.*

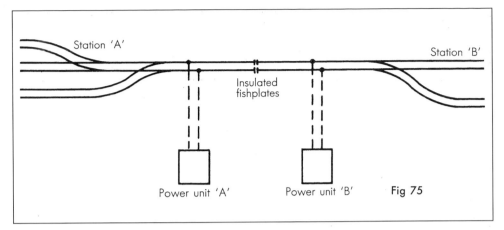

Fig 75 *Two terminal stations in a multiple train operation.*

I previously referred to the necessity for isolating sections in conventionally wired layouts and instanced the case of a train arriving at a terminal station where it is necessary to isolate the train engine. Where it is difficult to see the terminal station buffers from the control position, a useful precaution to prevent a train hitting the buffers is to install a diode in the wiring connecting the isolating section (see Fig 71). Diodes have the property of conducting electricity in one direction from positive to negative (anode to cathode) but not in the other. As shown in Fig 71 the diode will cause the locomotive to stop as soon as it passes the rail break when driven towards the buffers but it will enable the locomotive to be driven away from the buffers when the controller is reversed. The cathode is generally distinguished by a band or lip as an aid to correct installation but should the desired effect not be achieved at the first attempt, simply reverse the connections to the diode. The type of diode used must be capable of passing a continuous forward current of 1–1.5 amps.

Fig 72 shows the arrangement of insulated fishplates necessary to make a passing loop work properly with live frog points. This is necessary since, as is shown in Fig 72, if the two points were set for different tracks a

short circuit would result if the insulated fishplates were not used. Such insulated fishplates are a not required when points with dead frogs are used, since the polarity of the tracks beyond the point is not reversed, as is shown in Figs 68b and 68c.

Reversing loops as shown in Fig 73 require special attention. Tracing the polarity round the outer rail will show that, without the insulated fishplates, a short circuit will occur. The train must be driven into the loop, stopped, and the direction of the point and the DPDT (double pole, double throw) switch changed. The train can then continue its circuit by reversing the controller. The method shown in Fig 73 can be simplified when, as happens in most cases, the point itself can be relied upon to change the polarity of the inner rail. In such circumstances insulated fishplates are not required in the inner rail and the DPDT switch can be replaced by a SPDT (single pole DT) switch.

A few modellers with sufficient space may with to incorporate a triangle in their layouts and this can be done by following Fig 74. The locomotive is driven from A round the curve and is stopped after passing over point B. Points A and B are changed and the DPDT switch is operated. With the controller in the same direction as previously, the locomotive may be driven towards point C and

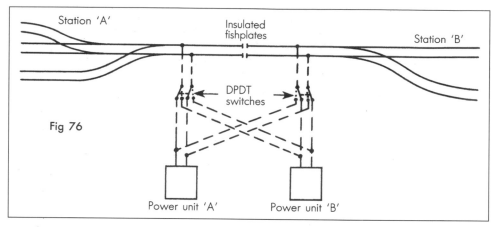

Fig 76 *Cab control; double pole switching.*

any further movement carried out at will. Connection X and the insulated fishplate between A and C are necessary to ensure continuity and avoid short circuits.

Some layouts are sufficiently simple to need only one train running at a time, and indeed on some it would be almost impossible to operate two trains at once for fear of conflicting movements and collisions, etc. Probably the simplest form of multiple train operation is where, as shown in Fig 75, two terminal stations are connected by a single track, but separated electrically by insulated fishplates. In this example, the operators at both stations could shunt and make up trains and, when the time came to exchange trains between stations, say from A to B, operator A would run his train towards the insulated joint whilst, operator B having got his line clear in order to accept the train, would turn his controller knob so as to allow the train to carry on into his section at the same speed, so avoiding jerks. With practice, this can be done to a fair degree of

Fig 77 *Cab control; single pole switching 'common return'.*

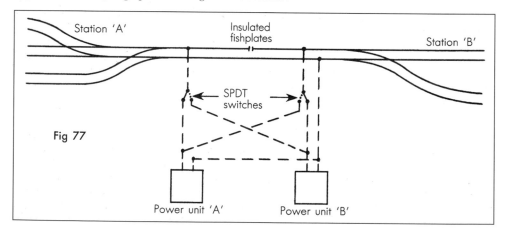

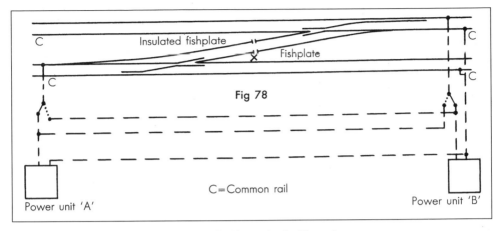

Fig 78 *Switching between separately controlled lines of a double track.*

accuracy, but if it is not, and particularly if operator B has the direction of his controller set wrongly, the train will either have a jerky passage across the joint or will oscillate back and forth, possibly to its mechanical detriment.

This disadvantage may be overcome by allowing operator A to drive the train to its destination in operator B's territory and vice versa. This system, which virtually involves each operator being able to run a train over any part of the layout, is known as 'cab control', the operator position being known as a 'cab'. The switching required to achieve this is shown in Figs 76 and 77, but the exact form required depends upon the types of controllers in use. If you are using controllers which are not completely separate electrically (eg, an 'add-on' unit mentioned previously) then double pole switching is required as in Fig 76. If, however, your controllers are electrically separate (ie, each has its own transformer, rectifier and controller) then 'common return' wiring, as shown in Fig 77, can be employed with the advantage that it uses only single pole switching, ie, the switches themselves are simpler and the number of wires needed is reduced. Neglecting the detail, the principle is the same in either case, which is that the switches connect the track section to whichever controller is required.

The same ideas apply to a double-track line where each track is a separate section, as shown in Fig 78, which includes a crossover. Common return wiring is shown but, for double pole switching, both fishplates between the points should be insulated and the wiring of the two sections to the controllers is similar to Fig 76. Fig 78 shows one insulated fishplate and one described as 'X'. This fishplate may be metal when dead frog points are used since, depending on whether or not it is an isolating point, the piece of rail between the frog of the lower point and 'X' will be either dead or common (see Figs 68b and 68c) with the point set straight and no short circuits will occur. With live frog points, however, 'X' must be an insulating fishplate, since the piece of rail in question would be the same polarity as the frog (ie. live and opposite to common) and a short circuit would result if an insulating fishplate were not included here.

The terminal stations arrangement in Figs 75, 76, and 77 would entail only relatively limited use of the cab control idea, since it would be very likely that the two section switches would be mounted one at each control point. A more flexible use of the cab control would be in, say, a station having both passenger and freight facilities, with separate sections for each and for the main

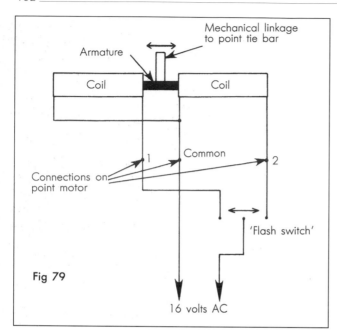

Mechanical linkage
to point tie bar

Armature

Coil   Coil

1   Common   2

Connections on
point motor

'Flash switch'

Fig 79

16 volts AC

Fig 79 *Diagrammatic view of
the operation of a point motor
and its associated wiring.*

Fig 80 Right *Wiring diagram
for an 'electric pencil'.*

Far right *An H & M solenoid
operated point motor and a
Fulgurex point actuator.*

line(s) as well. If there were two controllers, one could work the passenger service, whilst the other shunted the freight yard, but each operator would be able to run his trains on to the main line and towards its destination and the main line, station platforms, freight yard, etc., would each form a section. Switches suitable for model railway use are readily obtainable at very reasonable prices from radio and electronic shops or from specialist model railway electronic suppliers who advertise regularly in the model railway press. One type that is particularly useful for cab control is a double throw switch (otherwise known as a changeover switch) with a 'centre off' position. This will enable one or other of the two cab control sections to be switched off thus reducing the need for some isolating switches on the layout. For larger layouts with more than two cab control positions, it may be preferable to use a multi-way rotary switch. AMR Electronics list four such switches including 1 pole-12 way and 2 pole-6 way.

Fig 79 shows diagrammatically the operation of a solenoid type point motor and its associated wiring. In order to change the direction of the point and electrical pulse is applied to one coil. This attracts the magnetic armature, which is able to slide between the coils. The movement is then transmitted to the point tiebar. The usual means of applying the electrical pulse is with a 'flash' or passing contact switch which ensures that the coil is not permanently connected to the electrical supply, otherwise the coil would heat up and eventually burn out. Similar wiring is required for motor driven point actuators such as the AMR Pointmaster but in this case operation of the unit is via a single pole changeover switch. Limited contacts on the unit ensure that the motor automatically stops before over running its traverse. If a double pole changeover switch is used instead of a single pole switch this can be wired up to change panel light route indicators or live frog connections simultaneously with operation of the point motor.

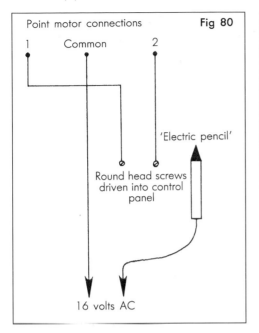

Point motor connections   **Fig 80**

1   Common   2

'Electric pencil'

Round head screws
driven into control
panel

16 volts AC

An alternative method of operating sole-noid point motors is by what is termed the 'electric pencil' and this is shown in Fig 80. The common lead from the coils is taken to the 16 volt AC power supply, as before, but leads 1 and 2 are soldered to the undersides of round-head screws driven into the control panel (see later). The other lead from the power supply is taken to an electric pencil which can be made by threading the leads down the outer tube of an old ball pint pen, soldering it to the metallic point of the pen, and finally pushing the metallic part back into the tube. Upon momentarily touching either of the screws with this 'electric pencil', the point motor will operate in either direction.

If possible it is best to use the 16 volt AC output of a power supply for point operation as this will give better results than 12 volts DC. Most power units are not capable of giving sufficient current to operate more than one point motor at the same time (eg, arranging for both points of a crossover to operate at once) but this can be overcome by using a capacitor discharge power unit.

Such a unit has the effect of storing electrical energy and releasing it when required in a sudden burst. This is exactly what is required to obtain maximum efficiency from a sole-noid operated point motor and there is the added advantage that the capacitor will protect the point motor from burning out in the event of a passing switch jamming. Such units are comparatively inexpensive, simple to install and are readily obtainable from specialist suppliers such as AMR Electronics

AMR also produce a range of plug-in control units for the electronic automation of layouts. Only brief mention can be made here but typical examples are an automatic station stop, a controlled signal stop and a train operated relay. The latter can be used for a number of different purposes such as providing a section and route indicator on a control panel, operating signals, controlling following trains, route setting and controlling the starting and stopping of trains in other parts of the layout. One advantage of elec-tronic automatic train control units is that trains can be gently slowed down to a stop

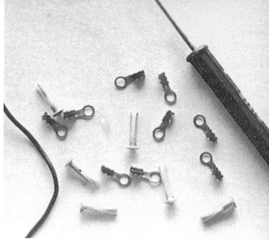

Above left *A homemade electric pencil and mimic diagram with cheese head bolt for studs.*

Above *Peco 'electric pencil' probe, studs and tag washers.*

Left *A battery of capacitor discharge power units for point motors.*

and restarted at realistic speeds. No longer the sudden jerk stop and jump start as is sometimes seen in exhibition and demonstration layouts. There is a lot of scope for the application of electronics to model railways. To find out more about the subject, *Complete Book of Model Railway Electronics*, by Roger Amos (PSL) is well recommended.

Those wishing to illuminate buildings will probably find that the best way is to use 'grain-of-wheat' bulbs which can be obtained from model railway suppliers and which will work directly off the 12 volt DC supply of a power unit. As the name implies, these bulbs are very small and will fit into most buildings so as not to be directly visible through the windows, but will light the building itself in a realistic manner. The 3 volt screw-cap bulbs as fitted to cycle lamps can be used with suitable holders, but remember to connect enough of them in series to use up the whole 12 volt output of the power unit or you will blow the bulbs. Unfortunately, this type is not nearly as unobtrusive as the 'grain-of-wheat' sort. Furthermore, such cycle-type bulbs consume more power than the 'grain-of-wheat' variety and consequently give out more heat. Take care, therefore that your buildings do not overheat when the lighting is left on for a while.

As to lighting the train itself, some manufacturers market locomotives with headlights and coaches with interior lighting, but with conventional electrical control systems these only function when power is applied to the train, ie, when it is moving.

The simplest layouts will have no need of a control panel as such, since a convenient grouping of the switches around the power unit usually suffices. This arrangement is quite all right as far as the owner of the layout and regular visitors are concerned, but when we have to take occasional visitors into account the very least we need is a key to the functions of the switches. This is best done by indicating their purposes on a plan drawn on cardboard (it can also help the owner in case of small lapses of memory!).

An extension of this idea is to make the plan the central feature of the controls and to build the latter around it. Such a control panel can be made from a variety of different materials but ¼ inch plywood is possibly the easiest to work with. This can either be painted or faced with a sheet of Formica or similar plastic laminate. The track plan or mimic diagram can either be painted on the surface of the material or you can use plastic self-adhesive tape. If you are using Formica the track plan can be gouged out of the surface to reveal the dark brown base of the laminate. This can be filled in with paint if you wish. The track plan should indicate where breaks occur for isolating rails or cab control sections.

If you are going to use the electric pencil methods of point control now is the time to drill the holes for the studs. Pilot holes if you are using wood screws (either round head, cheese head or countersunk) or clearance holes if you are using Peco studs or brass bolts which are yet another alternative. The studs should be positioned such that they indicate the route to be followed when the point blades are switched. They should also be positioned sufficiently far apart to ensure clearance for the wiring underneath.

Next to be considered are holes to take any isolating switches or cab control switches.

The switches should be of the panel mounted type and they should be so positioned that the switch lever points in the direction the current is to flow. Once again sufficient clearance should be allowed underneath the control panel for the base of the switch and for connecting the wiring. If the track plan is faithfully followed and the point operating studs and the switches are carefully placed there should be no need for any labelling since operation of the control panel will be self evident.

The control panel should not be rigidly attached to the baseboard, but should at least be hinged to it to allow maintenance and such alterations as may be necessary. The modeller who owns a portable layout must, unless it is all contained on one baseboards, use multi-pole plugs and sockets for inter-connections between the control panel and baseboards and between the baseboards themselves. Unfortunately, such plugs and sockets are usually expensive, but Government Surplus shops may be a source of suitable types. Care should be taken when wiring these plugs and sockets to use only the minimum of solder needed to make a good joint and to ensure that the insulation of the wire is stripped back no more than is necessary, otherwise short circuits may well result from wires touching each other.

Leads between the control panel and the baseboard should be brought together and tied in a neat bundle with insulating tape, or lacing cord, which looks like connecting wire but has cotton instead of wire within the insulation. Connecting wire itself may be used.

Connections between baseboards on a semi-permanent layout which needs to be moved only infrequently can be made by using 'tag strips' – available from radio shops – which may be mounted alongside each other on the framing of adjacent baseboards. The inter-connections are taken to the baseboard side of the tag on each baseboard, the other sides of each tag being bonded together with bare wire.

Having provided power to the appropriate length of track, we must now ensure that it gets to the motor of the locomotive. This is mainly a question of cleanliness, since we rely on passing electricity between two pieces of metal which are in contact with each other and any dirt between them will not conduct electricity.

The track is probably the worst culprit so far as dirt is concerned and the surface of running rails must be kept clean at all times. It comes as a surprise to newcomers to the hobby just how much dirt and grease gets deposited on the rail surface. If you don't believe me, try running your finger on top of a yard of rail after a few hours' running session—the amount of dirt will probably surprise you. The time honoured method has always been to physically clean the rails with an abrasive cleaner (rather like a hard erasing rubber which is sold specially for the purpose) or to wipe the surface with a rag dipped in a solvent such as carbon tetrachloride (sold for removing stains from clothing). *But if you use this, it must be in a well-ventilated atmosphere since the fumes are toxic, and do not smoke until the fumes have cleared, as the smoke you inhale would be highly poisonous.* If you are using proprietary makes of flexible track or point work or track assembled from plastic sleepers and chairs it is advisable to avoid using solvents since these may affect the plastic. This also applies to aerosol switch cleaners.

Physically cleaning the track surface is a time consuming business and there never seems to be enough time to do the job thoroughly. Also there are invariably some parts of the layout where it is difficult to get at the rails properly such as underneath bridges and tunnels, or inside buildings such as goods sheds, engine sheds and stations with large canopies or overall roofs. The installation of a Relco High Frequency Generator between the power unit and the track will overcome the cleaning problem in the most efficient way. This is a very reasonably priced device which not only combats the effect of dirt, oil, carbon deposits and bad connections on the track, it also contributes to self-cleaning all the time it is in use. The generator works by producing a high frequency current which is superimposed on the normal DC supply to the track. When the locomotive wheels are making good contact with the rail surface the HF is automatically switched off but when the contact is poor the HF is instantly switched on, ionising the air gap. This will continue until the DC current is able to flow and re-establish contact with the locomotive. A lamp on the generator gives a visual indication of whether or not the track surface is clean. Relco HF Generators must never be used with multiple train control systems of the type referred to on pages 121 and 122.

Wheels also need to be kept clean and a wheel cleaning brush is available (in appearance rather like a toothbrush) which, when connected to a power unit and pressed against the locomotive wheels, does the job well. Finally, watch for bits of fluff and dirt getting behind locomotive pick-ups; a regu-

Track cleaning using a well worn Peco rail cleaner.

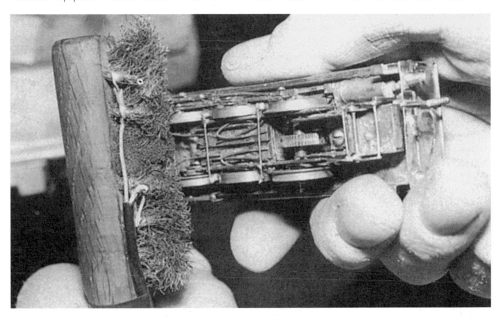

A suede cleaning brush adapted to wheel cleaning. The metal tufts in the centre have been removed and replaced by foam rubber insulation.

lar inspection will ensure that you get no trouble on this score.

In spite of these precautions, it is still possible to get indifferent running and the following advice will help to improve reliability in this respect. Locomotives should have as many current collectors or pick-ups as possible, and in particular this should include all flanged wheels which make contact with the track. If you convert a locomotive to scale wheels, and the radius of the curves on your layout allows it, remember to put all flanged driving wheels on with a current collector for each. Often forgotten is the tender which, if it has metal wheels, can be the source of another couple of current collectors, although leads will need to be run between the tender and the locomotive. The more current collectors a locomotive possesses, the less likelihood there is of the current not being passed from the track to the motor. This provision of extra pick-ups is, if you can do it, a good method of eliminating 'stalling' on dead frog points. Current pick-

ups are best made from thin phosphor-bronze wire or strip bearing lightly on the backs of the wheels.

It will be found that plastic wheels on rolling stock have a far greater tendency to pick up dirt than metal wheels. The best wheels for rolling stock are the metal ones since, besides picking up less dirt, they are usually more accurate in manufacture. Unfortunately they are more expensive, too.

Lastly, although it would not appear to affect electrics, uneven track can be the cause of locomotive wheels failing to pick up electricity. This can be overcome by using sprung or compensated chassis as will be discussed later. If, however, you are forced to run locomotives with a rigid chassis the only recourse is to lay your tracks as flat and as even as possible.

If you still find the technicalities of electrical power a little baffling, a good model railway retailer will always be happy to advise you on the best equipment for your individual needs.

Having covered the requirements for a model railway operated by electricity conducted through the running rails (the two-rail system) for completeness sake mention should be made of some other operating methods available to you. Two forms of motive power which go back to the very earliest days of model railways are of course clockwork and live-steam. Though examples of both have been built for gauges as small as HO and 00 for all practical purposes they are most suited for O gauge and above. They each have their limitations, foremost being the limited running time between winding the mechanism in the case of clockwork and topping up the boiler in the case of steam. At one time they also presented difficulties with regard to remote control though radio control is now very well developed for live-steam locomotives and ready to run models already fitted with radio control are commercially available. Though they may seem expensive they can be regarded as a sound investment if properly cared for and they are certainly great fun to operate.

Clockwork and steam of course have no place in a chapter on electrical equipment but another form of motive power which is allied is battery-electric. With its own on-board self-contained power supply a battery-electric model locomotive can run on any form of track, plastic if you like, so long as it is the correct gauge and you have no problems so far as two-rail insulation and wiring are concerned and nothing to worry about regarding the cleanliness of track, wheels and pick-ups. Running time is of course limited to the life of the battery but this is less of a problem with rechargeable batteries. Because the latest coreless electric motors and spur gearboxes are so much more efficient fewer and smaller batteries need to be fitted. Ni-cad batteries small and powerful enough to fit in 4 mm scale models and giving operating periods of three to four hours in between recharging are feasible. To control this type of battery-electric propulsion there are currently two forms of remote control operation on offer; radio control and infrared. The former is represented by Antenna Models who market a complete radio control system including a ready to run gauge O locomotive. In 4 mm scale Exactoscale Limited have demonstrated their Red Arrow infrared system which operates in a fashion not unlike that used with a remote control TV set. Both systems show great potential for the future.

CHAPTER 7
Laying the track

By now I assume you have decided where the layout is to go, what sort of layout it is to be and what scale and gauge suits you best. You will also have some idea of the track you will require. Now, and really only now, is the time when you can safely make your first purchases and actually start work, assuming that you have already brought the timber and materials for the base board and have got most of this in position.

To a certain extent your initial purchases of model railway equipment will depend upon what scale and gauge you have decided to follow, and whether or not you intend doing most of your own construction work. If you have decided to follow EM gauge or Scalefour, for example, there will not be many items that you will be able to buy ready-to-run and you will have to make some of your own track out of the basic materials and construct, or at least adapt from commercial models or kits, your own rolling stock. However, let us assume you have decided to start with 00 or N gauge, or some other popular scale and gauge which is well supported by the trade, and that, to begin with at least, you are buying all your rolling stock and trackwork ready made and ready-to-run.

First of all, select a retailer who takes the trouble to hold a good stock of model railway equipment. Appendix 4 gives a list of retailers who have at one time or another during recent years advertised in a British model railway magazine and therefore can be assumed to have a keen interest in the hobby. Apart from probably stocking the equipment you want to buy, he is also more likely to have an interest in, and a degree of sympathy for, model railways and therefore be in a better position to advise and assist you. If you tell the retailer you are just making a start and you are not too sure what is required, he will be glad to help you and, with the majority of responsible retailers, you need not fear you are going to be 'conned' into buying something you do not really want. A large number of shops in the model railway trade, certainly in England, have been in the business for many years, some of them since long before World War 2, and they are as keen on the hobby and as anxious to have your custom as you are to make a start. Make a friend of your retailer and I am sure he will look after you.

Now, the first items you will require will be a good power unit, as discussed in the previous chapter; at least one locomotive; at least one bogie vehicle of the maximum length you intend to use; a few yard lengths, say half-a-dozen, of flexible track; a pair of points and some rail joiners. You will need a minimum of two packets of rail joiners (or fishplates as they are sometimes called), one each of the insulated and non-insulated types. The necessity for a locomotive is obvious, since you will want to start things moving as soon as possible, even though you may have only a small nucleus of track parts to lay. In laying your track you will need to check as you go along that you are laying it properly and connecting up the electrical side of things correctly. There is no better method than to use a tried and trusted proprietary model locomotive which can be relied upon to work every time. I recommend buying a bogie vehicle, the longest type you intend using, to enable you to check clearances at vital points. You should have done this already on your track plan, but there is no substitute for a real practical test. You will observe that there can be a considerable amount of overhang with a large bogie vehicle when it passes round curves and over points and crossings. This is not always appreciated, neither is it always possible to make due allowance for it, until you can see and measure it for yourself. Clearances round curves are particularly important where lineside structures, eg, platforms, bridges, tunnel mouths and even the point motors on some proprietary points, are concerned and the sharper the curve and the longer the vehicle the greater the clearance required.

It has been my experience that, however well and detailed I may have drawn up a track plan, I have nearly always felt the need to amend it when it came to actually laying the track. The need for such change usually arises after the rails have been laid temporarily and a couple of items of rolling stock have been put into position, since it is only then that you can really judge your clearances and the overall effect of the plan. It is one thing planning the position of the trackwork, but quite another to judge the effect of the plan with the rolling stock in place. If you have purchased all your track in one go you will be able to lay out each item of trackwork to see how they look in relation to each other on the baseboard. However, if you are only buying a few items at a time and trying to keep within a limited budget, you may not be able to set up enough trackwork to gauge the overall effect. A useful aid at times such as these are the points and crossing plans available from

Peco. A stamped and addressed foolscap envelope, together with a label from a length of Peco Streamline track, will entitle you to one set of plans. These are only available direct from the Peco Technical Advice Bureau, Pritchard Parent Product Co Ltd, Beer, Seaton, Devon, EX12 3NA, England.

In any case, whether or not you use Peco point and crossing plans, you will need to mark on the baseboard the position of each piece of point, crossing and trackwork, and to establish their relationship with each other. My own personal preference is to work out the point controls and electrical feeds at this stage before I actually start laying the track. I have done it the other way round in the past only to regret it later, since it is often easier to drill holes in the baseboard for the electrical wiring or to cut grooves for the point controls before the track is laid than it is after.

The electrical side of the business was explained in chapter 6, but perhaps now is the time to discuss point control. There are a number of alternative methods and the decision as to the best one to use is largely a matter of choice. With some installations, particularly in goods yards and locomotive depots convenient to the operator, it is not necessary for points to be remotely controlled. In these cases a simple point lever is all that is required and is more appropriate to prototype practice. However, where the main line points are concerned, which in prototype form would be controlled from a signal box, or in cases where hand-operated points would be difficult for the operator to reach, remote control is essential. Possibly the easiest and best remote control method is the individual electrically operated point motor. The only disadvantage with these is the cost of the motors and switches, which add at least 50 per cent to the price of the points, manual remote control is, generally speaking, cheaper and the best method is the tried and trusted wire in tube, rather similar in principle to a Bowden cable on a cycle or a motorcycle brake. Either copper or plastic tubing can be used for this purpose, and

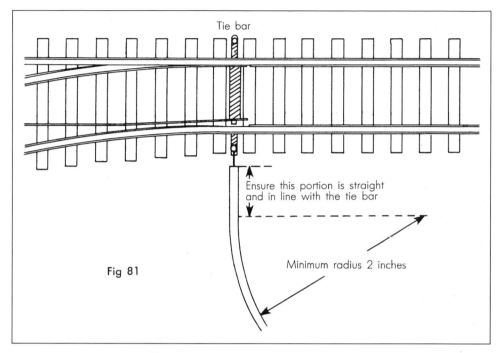

Fig 81 *Wire-in-tube point rodding.*

most model railway retailers maintain a stock of it and the lever frames by which the points can be operated. Ideally, the wire and tube joining the point to the lever frame should be in as direct a line as possible, avoiding sharp bends. Also, at the end of the tube, where the wire joins the point switch blades at one end and the lever frame at the other, the tube should be straight in line with the throw of the switch blade tie bar and the point lever. (See Fig 81.) Where bends in the tubing are essential they should be of not less than 2 in radius, and when bending the tube you should always insert the wire first.

When it comes to installing these point control wires and tubes on the layout I place great emphasis on the necessity of doing as much preparatory work as you can before all the track is laid. Ideally you should lay track from the far edge of the baseboard working forward, connecting up each point

as you go along. Grooves to take the point control tubing can then be cut in the top surface of the baseboard the tubing fixed in place before the next rail is laid down. Fig 82 shows what may be considered as a typical installation. The first point to be laid would be the no 3, together with the two sidings leading from it to the right. With these in place as a fixed datum point the position of the rest of the trackwork can then be planned and the grooves for the point control tubing cut into the top of the baseboard. Points nos 1 and 4 would then be fixed into position, followed by nos 5, 6 and 2. Finally, the running lines which in places overlay the point control tubing can be fixed in place.

Laying the point control tubing in grooves cut in the baseboard surface is far better than laying them on top. The main reason is that, provided the groove is cut with a reasonable degree of accuracy, it will

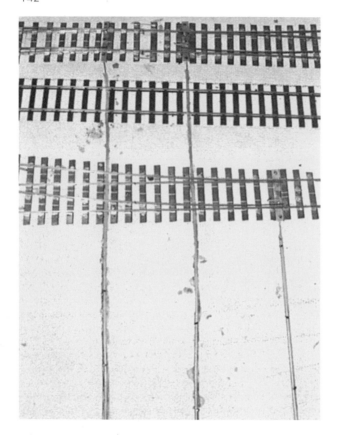

Point control tubing set in the baseboard surface. As recommended the work is proceeding from the furthest point before the track is laid in the foreground.

prevent the tubing from moving, which is essential. An additional advantage is that the tube will be hidden from sight and will not interfere with the running rails that pass over it. Remember, if you are using copper tubing and you lay it under the rails between the sleepers, you must avoid the tubing coming in contact with the two

Fig 82 *Typical layout of point control tubing.*

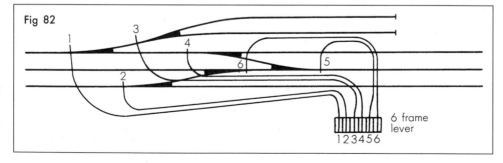

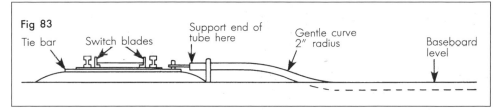

Fig 83

Tie bar   Switch blades   Support end of tube here   Gentle curve 2" radius   Baseboard level

Fig 83 *Bending wire-in-tube, buried in the surface of the baseboard, to match the level of the point tie bar.*

running rails, otherwise it will cause a short circuit. It is imperative that the tubing is held in place and, whereas copper tubing is relatively easy to fix, since you can simply solder it to pins driven into the baseboard, I have found that plastic tubing is rather more difficult. The 'U'-shaped tags supplied specially to hold the tubing in place can, if you are not careful, pinch the tubing and restrict the movement of the wire inside. Burying the tubing in the baseboard surface will of necessity require the tubing to be bent at each extremity to gain height to reach the level of the switch blade tie bar or point lever. However, this can be done very gradually and will not affect the performance (see Fig 83).

It will be appreciated that since the point control tube and wire is sold by the foot or yard, the further the point is from the point lever the more expensive manual control becomes. In some circumstances it is conceivable that electric point operation will be cheaper, but in any case there is a physical limit to the length of control that can be successfully carried out by manual means,

and points more than 6 ft away from the lever should be electrically operated. If the point control wire needs to traverse sharp right-angled corners the best method is to use an angle crank such as that shown in Fig 84. The arrows indicate the line of movement in one direction. It is possible, using these angle cranks, to connect up two sets of point blades to one lever. This is perfectly satisfactory in the case of manual control, but it is not usually possible with electric point motors since in my experience they have insufficient power to move more than one set of blades at a time. One thing to remember with the operation of points is that all things connected with them should be fixed immovably to the baseboard—the point itself, the point lever, point control tubing and the electric point motor. Looseness or slackness in any of these fittings will offer the line of least resistance and, instead of the switch blades of the point moving, it will be the point itself, the control tubing or the lever frame that moves. Peco have devised a particularly neat method of fixing for their own electric point motors which overcomes

Fig 84 *Action of an angle crank. The arrows indicate direction of movement.*

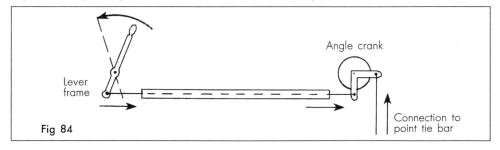

Lever frame   Angle crank   Connection to point tie bar

Fig 84

this problem. They clip to the underside of the base of the point itself, thereby providing immediate positive action without any movement between the point and the point motor. The advice given earlier to make provision for the point controls before the track is laid is even more necessary in the case of Peco points and point motors since to fit the point motor to the underside of the point base a rectangular shaped hole approximately 1½ in x 1 in needs to be cut in the baseboard to accommodate the point motor—an impossible job once the point itself is laid. Should you forget to make provision for this or you are unlucky enough to find you have an obstruction under the baseboard just where the point motor is to go the Peco point motors can be adapted to fit above the baseboard surface. Another type of point motor that is becoming increasingly popular is the motor driven actuator such as the AMR Pointmaster, Fulgurex and Lemaco. These motors provide for a more prototypical slow movement of the point blades unlike the sudden snap action associated with solenoid motors. Apart from being much more realistic in operation they are likely to be kinder to the point blades and tie bar which can be a potential source of weakness in point design.

Before you actually start to lay your track, it is worth paying a visit to your nearest railway line to have a look at the real thing and see the effect you are trying to aim at. Most main line track that has been in use for some time appears a uniform rust red-brown in colour with just the shiny top surface of the rails to break the dullness. New running lines laid today will invariably have concrete sleepers but in the days of wooden sleepers, and currently where crossing sleepers are used for relaying points and crossings, freshly creosoted wooden sleepers appear almost black against the grey stone ballast. However, after a time the creosote fades to a brown colour matching the rust of the rail, and the dirt and mud swept up by passing trains makes the ballast take on a similar colour. A look at the full-size track will emphasise just how important ballast is to

help create a realistic appearance. In practice it forms a well-drained, slightly cushioned base for the sleepers, which also prevents their forward or lateral movement. Visually, the most important point to notice is that the ballast almost reaches the level of the top of the sleepers such that the sides of the sleepers are mostly hidden from view. This effect will be lost if model railway track is laid without ballast. For this if no other reason, track ballasting must be considered an essential aid to realism.

There are at least three proprietary model railway track systems that are ready ballasted; Fleischmann 'Profi-Track', Roco Line and Conrad. These are for 00/HO but the Fleischmann track is also available in N gauge in their 'Piccolo range. Though the products of the three manufacturers differ in many respects they all feature sleepers and ballast integrally moulded in plastic with excellent relief detail such as wood grain in the sleepers. Even flexible track is included in the Roco Line, Fleischmann Piccolo and Profi-Track ranges. The bendable track base can be curved in any direction, down to a radius of approximately 8 inches in the case of Piccolo N gauge.

Most other proprietary model track systems such as Peco Setrack, Peco Streamline or Hornby Railways make use of pre-formed ballast inlays which are sold as separate items. They are accurately moulded to match each item of trackwork making them very easy to fit and very realistic in appearance. On first acquaintance these may be regarded as inessential luxuries which, it the budget is stretched, could be dispensed with but the opposite is true. Ballast inlays possess a number of practical features apart from the obvious one of adding realism to the track. Not least of their qualities is their sound-cushioning effect compared to track pinned or glued to a baseboard. The inlays also help with laying the track, especially lengths of flexible track, since the accurately moulded recesses for the sleepers and sleeper ties help to space the sleepers squarely and evenly. They also help to hold the track into place and the

Examples of 4mm scale ballasted track; granite chippings to the left and sifted ash to the right. Both tracks are Alan Gibson's ready to run Flexi-track (foreground) and assembled from component parts (rear).

process of lining up flexible track into straight lines or round curves is far easier when the track is inserted into a ballast inlay. One of the reasons for this is that the back of the inlay has a rough surface which adheres quite readily to the surface of the baseboard, especially wood fibre insulation board, to prevent most lateral movement. On portable layouts or lifting sections of permanent layouts it is necessary to fix the inlay in place either with a spot of impact adhesive (be careful not to use too much) or by strips of double-sided adhesive tape. On a permanent layout I prefer not to stick the ballast inlay but to pin the track lightly at approximately 9 in to 12 in intervals.

Points need holding down with pins to enable the point-operating mechanism to function, as referred to earlier, and occasionally on the tightest and sharpest radius curves, say 2 ft or less in 00 and 1 ft or under in N, one or two pins in a few chosen sleepers can help the track retain its required curvature. The tighter the curve, the more pins may be required, but this is something you can judge for yourself as you go along. When drilling the holes for the pins (always drill them beforehand, as forcing the pins through may split the plastic sleepers) make sure the pins are a loose fit and see that they

are not pushed home so far that they bend or strain the sleepers and squeeze the plastic foam ballast strip. Another thing to ensure with points is that the straight stock rail is in fact perfectly straight. Sometimes the tension produced by the curved stock rail can bend the point base slightly and curve the nominally straight stock rail out of line. This can be cured easily if a straight edge is held along the straight rail at the time the point is fixed to the baseboard. At least three pins should be used to hold the point in position, one at each end and one in the middle near the frog (the part of the point where the lines cross). Some brands of points have fixing holes ready marked or drilled.

Laying curved track calls for special attention since there are a number of additional points to watch. I have already mentioned the possible need for holding the track in place with pins to avoid any movement. In practice, you will find that track not held in place round curves will spread outwards in the direction of the trains, owing to the persistent force of the train's movement. Obviously this cannot be tolerated, otherwise a break in the running rails will occur at one of the spots where rail joiners are fitted. It is assumed that the position of the curve will be drawn in on the baseboard

A Tracksetta 00 gauge template for 48 in radius curves.

surface. Quite a practical compass can be devised for this purpose using a length of string with a pencil attached at one end. If the baseboard is wide enough the other end of the string can be held or pinned at the correct radius and the curve drawn in with the pencil. If, as is most likely, the centre point of the arc is off the baseboard, the string can be tied to a broom or carpet sweeper handle which, when held upright, can form the centre point for a makeshift compass. One recommended commercial aid to laying accurate radius curves is the Tracksetta Templates. These are available in five different radii for 00 gauge and six for N gauge. The firm also supplies straight sections for 00 and N gauges. They consist of accurately cut stout metal templates which fit in between the two running rails. Slots at intervals in the templates enable you to fit pins into the sleepers whilst the templates hold the track in place. I have found them particularly useful in lining up curves at joins in the baseboard as referred to in Chapter 2, Fig 10.

It will be necessary to square up the ends of the flexible track when laid through a curve, since the inside rail will extend beyond the outer rail. The rail can be cut relatively easily with a pair of wire cutters. The cut will inevitably need cleaning up with a file so make due allowance for this when you make the incision and apply the wire cutters just a shade past the spot where you want the rail to end. It is a good tip to examine the ends of all rails, flexible track

Cutting flexible track in situ *with a mini power drill fitted with an abrasive disc.*

and points, since it will most likely be necessary to smooth the ends of the rails with a file to help them slide into the rail joiners. You will also need to cut the chairs from under the rails at the ends of the track where the rails are to be joined, as most rail joiners are longer than the regulation gap between two sleepers. A very useful little gadget to use when laying double or multiple tracks in 00 and N gauges is the Peco 6 ft Way gauge. This not only ensures that double tracks are lined up exactly parallel to each other on straights and round curves it also makes the job that much easier.

Where moulded foam ballast inlays cannot be used there are a wide range of miniature ballast scatter materials available in different colours and sizes from suppliers of scenic accessories. The miniature ballast will of course have to be fixed with adhesive. One method is to lay the track on a liberal quantity of adhesive and sprinkle the ballast while the adhesive is still wet. When the adhesive is nearly dry the surplus ballast can be brushed gently aside (an old shaving brush is ideal for this) and the remainder lightly pressed into place to ensure it is stuck firmly and evenly in place The snag with this method is that there is little time to adjust the position of the track before the adhesive begins to harden off. With a yard length of flexible track you have to move quickly which is likely to give rise to errors. A better method is to lay the track first, pinning it down where necessary, and then after you have checked it and found it to be exactly as it should be, sprinkle the ballast dry and tamp it into place around the sleepers. Make sure the ballast is spread evenly and when you are satisfied there are no high, low or bald spots, fix the ballast with drops of adhesive. A glass medicine dropper is ideal for this purpose. For adhesive I normally use Evo-Stik Resin 'W' wood adhesive diluted with an equal measure of water to which has been added a few drops of washing up liquid detergent. The latter breaks down the surface tension and ensures the adhesive spreads evenly. Make sure the adhesive reaches all of the ballast

but try not to be too liberal with the application since it can lift the ballast, even granite chippings, and float individual grains away to parts where you don't want them to be such as the sides of the rails or the tops of the sleepers. Any misplaced ballast can be carefully tamped into place whilst the adhesive is still wet, likewise any bald spots can be filled in with a few extra grains of ballast and another drop of adhesive. Make a final inspection before the adhesive dries then leave well alone. If left overnight it will be firmly set the next day. Whatever else you do, make sure you keep the ballast and the adhesive well clear of point tie bars and switch blades. It is vital to preserve the free movement of these parts.

Mention should also be made of the very good 'bonded ballast' system used in the USA. The ballast (granulated cork) is placed loosely in position round the track after the track is laid. This is then sprayed (using an old hair or scent spray) with an adhesive consisting of water with ⅙ part size or artist's polymer varnish. This is transparent, sets the loose ballast solid with the track and the edges of ballast can be shaped and adjusted while setting. Another method is to mix the ballast with glue powder, sprinkle the dry mixture evenly between and to the sides of the sleepers and spray the track with water.

Laying track may at first glance seem an easy, quick thing to do, especially when you are using ready-made proprietary items, but there is a bit more to it than meets the eye. The point control, electrical feeds and ballasting have all to be considered and it is far better in the long run to move slowly and surely than in great haste. After all, the track is likely to be left down for a long while, and it is best to ensure that it is laid properly in the first place. It is understandable that there could be a feeling of impatience to get something running, especially if this is your first model railway. Give yourself the occasional break from the slow, tedious process of laying points, crossings and sidings and get on with the far more satisfying job of laying the main line. You will find this easier and quicker, thereby raising your spirits

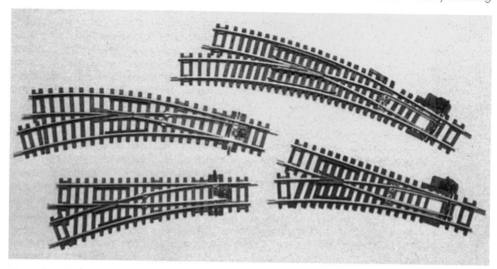

Curved and straight left handed points; Peco Setrack on the left and Hornby Railways on the right.

again. In fact, it could be preferable to obtain some practical experience in track laying at the country end of your layout where the track is most likely to be straightforward and devoid of complicated pointwork.

Certainly, if you have a lifting section across a doorway, it would be best to start here. When laying track across such sections it is essential to line up the tracks correctly from all angles and great care should be taken here. If you have to err at all, err on the side of cutting the rail overlength for the lifting section, assuming that this lifts upwards, since it will not matter if the ends of the rails slightly overlap the fixed base-board section. On the other hand, if the rails on the fixed section were to overlap the lifting section they would either become damaged when the section was raised or they might prevent it from being raised at all.

Most of the foregoing has been written on the assumption that you are going to use proprietary ready-made track. There is no shortage of suitable material and if there is one area of model railways that is blessed by the trade it must surely be trackwork. One particularly noticeable development in recent years has been the improvement

made to the fixed geometry track associated with toy railways and train sets. At one time most of this had to be discarded when a youngster grew up and made the transition from a toy railway to a model railway but, so far as 00 gauge is concerned, this is not the case today. Peco Setrack, which is compatible with other track systems conforming to the British standard geometry, is complementary to the more advanced pointwork and flexible track in the Peco Streamline range. A fixed geometry track such as Peco Setrack holds considerable advantages for the younger or less experienced railway modeller. Because the rails are fixed in length and curvature and each section of track has the rail joiners fixed in place at each end, a layout can be planned and laid in a very minimum of time. Furthermore, if the layout is found not to be interesting enough it can be dismantled and re-laid in a different form, again and again. The standard radius curves will ensure that the layout is workable when finished provided the right number of track sections have been used. It is a very good way of cutting your teeth on a model railway and, as I said before, there is no need to give it all away when you are ready to move on to more advanced schemes. Admittedly, some of the curves down to 14½ in radius would be unrealistic in a scale model railway setting but you might be able to hide some of them in tunnels or incorporate short pieces between two flexible track transition curves in the less noticeable parts of the layout.

Despite the enormous variety of brands of track in most of the popular gauges there are many people who have had occasion to make their own for a number of good reasons. Foremost are the finescale modellers who apart from any consideration of a true scale track gauge, seek a finer scale rail section than is generally offered by the majority of proprietary track manufacturers. The rail used in most proprietary 00/HO gauge track systems is in what is called Code 100 section. In N gauge Code 80 rail is generally used. These figures refer to the depth of the rail expressed in thousands of an inch; i.e. Code 100 is 100 thousands of an inch (0.1") and Code 80 is 80 thousands of an inch (0.08"). Whilst to the human eye these track sections look commendably close to scale (and they certainly are close to scale compared with the very coarse section rails of years gone by) it has to be accepted that Code 100 rail in 00/HO represents the very heaviest track you are only likely to see on modern day lines and this should be of a finer section as recognised by Peco who are

adding Code 75 flat bottom rail to their Streamline range. Another point is that most proprietary track systems use flat bottom rail, universal in Continental Europe and America for decades but seldom found on British railways in pre-nationalisation days. To be really authentic, a steam age model railway based on one of the Big-Four railway companies or early BR days should use bullhead rail (Code 75 in 4 mm scale) laid in the distinctive shaped chairs that are a feature of bullhead track. Such considerations depend on the standard you aspire to and the level of authenticity you wish to achieve. It is hardly likely to be a matter of great concern in N gauge since this amount of detail is barely visible in such a small scale. Nevertheless, mindful of the exaggerated height of Code 80 rail in N gauge, Peco have introduced 'Super-N' in their Streamline flexible track range which retains the robust quality of Code 80 rail but shows a visible profile of only .05". The realism achieved will do much to enhance the quality of N gauge model railways and it is hardly likely it can be bettered by handmade track. At the opposite end of the scale, Peco 0 gauge track which has been available now for many years has always been based on finescale bullhead rail standards and is held in great regard by O gauge modellers. The range includes turnouts and crossings and track parts should you wish to construct

A selection of different rail section codes. From left to right: Alan Gibson O gauge Code 125, Peco Streamline 00 gauge Code 100, Peco flat bottom rail Code 82 (correct section for 4mm scale), Alan Gibson EM Code 75 and Peco Streamline old style N gauge Code 80. Peco Streamline is now available in Code 55 for N gauge and Fine Standard Code 75 for 00 gauge.

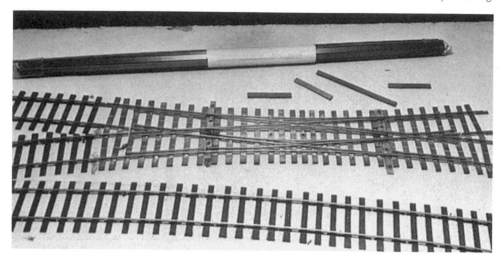

Above *A hand-built double slip using SMP Scaleway copper clad sleeper strip.*

Left *A J & M roller type track gauge on SMP Scaleway track.*

your own. O gauge trackwork is also very well supported by other specialist manufacturers who produce ready made pointwork, kits and component parts.

It is in the realm of 4 mm scale modelling where finescale modellers have long felt the need to make their own track though the requirement for this is diminishing rapidly. Scale flexible track is now available in all 4 mm scale gauges, 00, EM and 18.83, and the

quality is such that it is hardly conceivable it will be necessary to make track other than pointwork in future. Pointwork can be obtained ready made in EM gauge but not so far as I am aware in 18.83. Apart from the desire for greater realism which necessitated the building of track at one time there was generally a worthwhile saving in cost compared with ready made prices. This is hardly likely to be the case with the advent

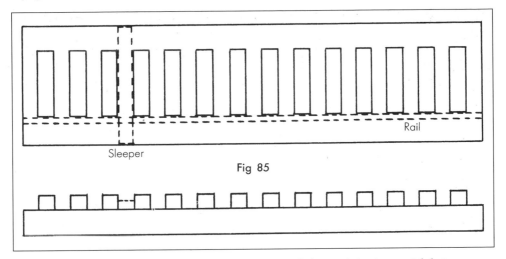

Sleeper

Fig 85

Rail

Fig 85 *A jig for making track, using rail soldered to copper-clad printed circuit material sleepers.*

of finescale flexible track but it may still be true with regard to pointwork due to the high degree of fabrication needed. Hand built points and crossings can also be tailored to suit your own specific requirements which is an added incentive. There is a wide range of component parts; rail, chairs, sleepers, ready-machined point blades, etc., available from specialist suppliers to make track building a relatively painless task which, though demanding of care and attention, does not require any particularly high level of skill. All you need is time and patience.

In the smaller gauges below O gauge, one of the most popular methods of track building which has been developed over recent years is the method of soldering rail to sleepers cut from copper-clad plastic, similar to that used in printed circuits. Strangely enough this goes back to the old pre-war days when practically all so-called scale 00 gauge track was built by soldering the rails to brass sleepers. This, of course, was the three-rail track, since the brass well and truly conducted the current across to the two running rails. With the printed circuit material, however, it is a perfectly simple matter to scratch the top of the sleepers lightly with

a saw blade after the rails have been soldered in place. This will make a gap in the copper cladding which will in turn effectively insulate the two running rails. Sleepers can be purchased ready cut or alternatively, you can cut your own from sheet material—not to be recommended unless you have a strong guillotine or access to other suitable machinery. Another method is to use thin wooden sleepers stuck to a sleeper base and to solder the rails to the heads of pins driven into the sleepers. The uniform size of the pin heads help to ensure that each blob of solder is roughly the same size and shape which assists in creating the illusion of a cast metal chair. A similar method to this is the one recommended by the Protofour people.

Whatever you are working with, an accurate track gauge is essential and there are a number of different types available. The use of jigs is also advised whenever scratch-built track using copper-clad printed circuit material sleepers is built, not only from the point of view of accuracy but also because of the speed with which it enables the work to be done. The simplest form of jig is shown in Fig 85, and it consists of blocks of wood glued or pinned to a wooden base. Sleepers are laid in the gaps left between each block and one rail is laid along the edges of the blocks and soldered to as many sleepers as are slotted into position at any one time. The rail and the sleepers can then be removed from the jig, the rail slid along and soldered to another batch of sleepers inserted in the jig, until sleepers have been soldered throughout the whole length of one rail. Not until the track has been laid in position and ballasted will the second rail be soldered into place and this is when the track gauge will be required. This method will enable the track to be curved into any desired formation and multi-radius or transition curves will present no problem. A similar system can also be used for constructing points.

The importance of joining rails properly cannot be over-emphasised. Apart from the necessity to provide electrical continuity which we discussed in Chapter 6, it is essential that the rails be connected thoroughly to avoid the possibility of misalignment and derailment of the rolling stock. This is particularly true of pointwork and curved track, where there seem to be so many opposing forces intent on removing passing trains

from the rails. When laying flexible track round curves, it is preferable to avoid having a rail joint too near the point where the curve starts and finishes. If by mischance you find it necessary to have such a joint, you will possibly find it necessary to bend the rail between your fingers into the curve required, rather than let it bow into its own curve. Fig 86 is an exaggeration of the bad effects of joining flexible track at the point of transition into a curve, whereas Fig 87 shows the correct method. With joins between two curved rails on the curve itself the effects are not quite so bad, but it is important to watch the joints carefully and perhaps solder the rail joiners in position.

I mentioned earlier the point about curved track and the necessity to cut the inside rail shorter than the outside rail. It is quite amazing how a slight adjustment to the curvature can affect the relative lengths of the two rails and it is important to get measurement as accurate as possible before you let the saw cut into the rail. It is preferable to ask someone to give you a hand, since the rails often slip unnoticed when you are marking them

Fig 86 *An exaggerated drawing of the bad effects of joining flexible track at the point of transition into a curve.* **Fig 87** *The correct method.*

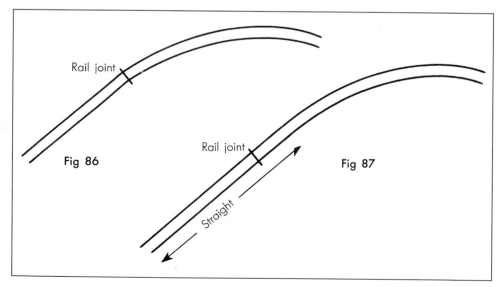

for cutting, especially if you are tackling a yard length of track and you have to take your eyes off one end to deal with the other. Another helpful aid when using proprietary flexible track is to try and arrange it so that two or three sleepers extend beyond the end of the rails at the end of a section of track, thus allowing the rail from the next section to be led into them. This is not essential but sometimes it helps The situation can arise when one rail is shortened when it has been laid round a curve: the subsequent rail joint mid-way along a length of plastic sleepering can be just that little bit less strained than a joint between the ends of two separate lengths of sleepering.

In most gauges different proprietary track units can be joined to flexible track where the rail section is not too dissimilar. For trackwork in tunnels and other locations where it is hidden from view it is sometimes an economic proposition to use second-hand or sale price items of proprietary track instead of using brand-new flexible track, especially since second-hand curved rails are invariably cheap items to buy. Another method of economising with scratch-built track in tunnels is to dispense with all the sleepers, leaving, say, one out of every four or five, just sufficient to hold the track in place but without making any attempt to realism. Sleepers can, in fact, be dispensed with altogether if you care to solder the rail to pins laid directly into the baseboard.

Thankfully wheel standards and track standards (the two go inseparably together) have improved tremendously in recent years and with the current range of products from the commercial manufacturers in the two most popular gauges, N and 00, we do not have the wide disparity between coarse and fine standards or between the standards of one manufacturer and another that once bedevilled the hobby.

CHAPTER 8
Scenic settings

In the early days of model railways, and I am thinking largely of O and 1 gauges in the pre-00/HO era, scenic effects were virtually unheard of. Practically no attempt was made to embellish the model railway beyond the bare bones of rolling stock, essential railway buildings such as stations and signal boxes, signals, and of course the track. Even the track itself was neglected from the appearance point of view and in the majority of cases it looked very crude with thick, heavy rails and widely spaced sleepers. Yet somehow or other these were accepted, and the obvious faults, at least they appear obvious now, were either ignored or glossed over. Very soon we began to see an improvement in track and additional sleepers were incorporated to make it look a little more presentable. Even so, the whole effect was often marred by fixing the track to wooden battens which raised it high into the air and no attempt was made to hide the unsightly effect by sprinkling the whole lot with a good covering of ballast The remedy always seemed so obvious, but in only a few instances did it appear to have been considered or applied. There probably was a good reason, but it has always escaped me.

The coming of 00 gauge seems to have done more to change things than anything else, especially when the two-rail system of electrification overcame the necessity to fit the unsightly and unrealistic third rail. At one time it appeared to be accepted that you had to make concessions and some departures from the real thing if you were going to make a practical success of a working model railway. But when people began to realise that there was less and less necessity to depart from the real thing and fewer concessions needed to be made the quest for realism became greater, until we have reached the state of perfection we know today. This change in attitude was resisted at great length and even now there are many people who feel that scenic effects are to a certain extent overdone. 'Too much scenery and not enough railway,' some people say. As with many judgements about model railways this is largely a matter of opinion, but it is probably fair to say that the majority of people accept the need for a certain amount of scenery to embellish their model railway and that few are considered complete without it.

Another factor which has had a considerable influence on the changed attitude to scenery is, I think, the increasing number of illustrations of model railway layouts that appear in books and magazines. You can often be quite oblivious to the faults in the appearance of your own layout, since it is possible to be so absorbed in its operation that you never notice them. This is probably a slight case of familiarity breeding contempt. Yet the moment it is photographed and a copy of the photograph

Varying types of fencing contribute to the air of authenticity on Keith Gloster's Camelot Halt.

is examined critically or, worse still, published in a magazine, the areas at fault will stand out like sore thumbs just as much to you as to other people. Critical examination of other people's layout photographs has probably made us more aware of the obvious visual pitfalls and has made it much easier for us to diagnose and apply the remedy to our own layouts.

When considering what can be done to add a scenic setting to the bare bones of our model railway, we can best start with the track itself. We have already discussed in the previous chapter the necessity for ballasting, strictly speaking a scenic addition since it is perfectly possible to run a model railway without ballast, but it looks so much better with it. Another aid to realism is to paint the rails a rusty-brown colour as it is most unnatural for the whole depth of the rail to be shining bright. Only the top running surface of the rail is in this condition and this can be achieved by wiping the top of the rail with a rag after it has been painted. It is probably easier to paint points before they are fixed in position, but it is not possible to do this with flexible track, since the chairs and sleepers will more than likely slide along the rail during the laying of the track and this will reveal patches of unpainted rail. Be careful not to get paint on to, or too near, the moving parts of the points, as one coat of

paint is sufficient to stop the switch blades from functioning. Also, when using proprietary points with plastic sleeper bases, it is advisable to experiment first on a small section of track with the paint you intend to use because some types of paint can have a harmful effect on plastic. While we are dealing with colour it might be as well to mention that not all track is brown. There are many places on a railway system, especially in the old steam days, where coal, ash, water, oil and soot were deposited and covered the whole track, sleepers, ballast and rail, with a black gooey mess. Locomotive depots are the obvious places for such treatment, but other spots are the ends of platforms where engines frequently stand at the head of a train, or in coal yards and goods depots. Frequently, little-used sidings can be found that rust very quickly, and it is sometimes effective to model such a siding using brass rail instead of nickel silver. There is an added advantage in that brass rail is usually cheaper.

Moving outwards from the rails themselves, the first item we are likely to meet with, at least on an open country stretch of line, will be the boundary fence. On British railways anyway, it is an essential statutory requirement since by law all lines have to be fenced. There are a number of different types of fencing to be found on the full-size

4mm scale rabbits with wire and post fencing on Dave and Bev Lowery's Bevleys.

railway, as anyone keen enough will observe. In all gauges our requirements are fully met by the trade and a number of different types of fencing are available from several different manufacturers and suppliers. One recent innovation has been the use of etched-copper techniques to produce iron railings, chestnut paling, chicken wire and even barbed wire—in N gauge as well as 00! Parts for typical railway post and wire fences are available and so are field gates, wicket gates and stiles. Of course, you can construct most types of fencing yourself out of basic raw materials and in some specialised applications this may be necessary. But out in the country section of the layout, where several yards of fencing are required on both sides of the line, the installation of ready-made proprietary fencing can save a lot of time. Just a word of warning though—some proprietary fences are made from white plastic material. Now, fences painted white may be found around stations or specially protected areas, but it is most unusual to find ordinary lineside fencing painted white. Some concrete fences and fence posts appear an off-white colour, but usually wooden fences are creosoted, if they are protected at all, and over the years they become almost black in colour. This effect can be achieved by dabbing on washes of black and brown paint in haphazard fashion. A useful paint to have at

hand for a large number of model railway applications is Humbrol Track Colour, which is a dull rust-brown. 1t is worth while buying a ½ pint tin since there are so many potential uses for it.

There are very few railways that run through the countryside as flat as a model baseboard, and some means are called for of adding realism and variety to an otherwise monotonous landscape. Although the track base itself may need to be level, inevitably the country on either side of it will rise and fall. The rising bit is simply done on a model railway, since we can build up from the baseboard level without difficulty, but the falling part is a different matter, and we will deal with that later. The rising parts, ie, the land either side of the track that rises above the level of the track in the form of hills, cutting and tunnels, can be represented by an almost endless variety of methods and materials. To a certain extent what you use is dictated by the size of area and type of hill, cutting or tunnel you wish to represent, but let us assume a normal rolling or undulating countryside. For scenery such as this, the generally accepted method is to build some sort of framework over which can be stretched a suitable covering material. Fig 88 shows a cross section of a typical stretch of lineside scenery modelled in this fashion. When planning the framework for a scenic setting

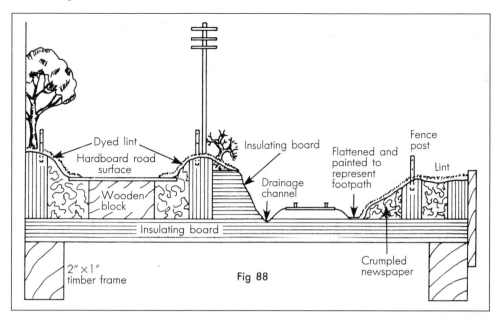

Fig 88 *Cross-section of a typical stretch of lineside scenery. Dyed lint, representing grass, is laid across a foundaton made from pieces of insulating board. Note how the tree, telegraph pole and fence posts fit into the insulating board. Crumpled newspaper helps to support the lint*

such as this, it is a good idea to take the fencing line as a datum point for working out the height and shape of your high ground. Inevitably the fencing will follow the contour of the land either side of the railway line, since it would have been the railway in all probability that was responsible for cutting into the land and changing its shape in the first place. Anything within the cutting will be railway property, so the fence that runs along the cutting edge will mark the end of that property,

Now we need to establish a reasonably reliable foundation on which to build the boundary fence, so the framework we use for hills and cuttings can also provide the foundation for the fence. My own personal preference for making such a framework is to use offcuts of insulation board which are left over from the baseboard itself. These can be cut roughly to the shape of the hill and glued on edge to the baseboard. The open spaces between the framework

should be filled in with something to stop the covering material sagging, and crumpled newspaper is very suitable for this, It can be simply rolled and screwed up in the hand, then glued and pinned into position. The material I have found most effective for covering hills such as these is medical lint, dyed green. An 8 oz roll of lint measures 4 yd long and 9 in wide and a packet of dye costing a few pence is more than enough to colour the lot. Ideas vary as to what constitutes a natural grass green, depending on the time of the year, the dryness of the weather, and other variable climatic conditions, but I try to avoid too bright a colour and prefer olive green. The lint should be glued along the edge alongside the track and over the framework of the hills. Joins in the material can be covered up by carefully brushing with a stiff nylon nail brush, which is also an effective method of bringing up the 'pile' in the material to give a realistic grass effect.

Alternatively, the lint can be coated with a size solution and painted, using matt oil paints or poster colours.

There are any number of alternative covering materials and one variation which has had the accolade of being demonstrated on television is the Jack Kine method which consists of building up a framework of card strips over which are pasted 2 in squares of tarlaton (a type of thin open muslin) or buckram. The paste used is a modelling compound specially formulated by Artex which when mixed with water can be worked into the landscape to form varying textures and finishes. Full details of the method are given in an instruction booklet which is supplied with the Jack Kine modelling powder and having seen this remarkable material and method of scenic modelling demonstrated several times I can vouch for its excellence. Another popular method is to use a proprietary material known as Mod-Roc, which is a form of plaster-impregnated bandage. Alternate layers can be soaked and placed across each other to build a cover over the scenic framework, and when the plaster dries, which it does quite quickly, it forms a thin but reasonably robust 'crust'. The surface can then be painted to represent a basic earth colour and sprinkled while the paint is wet with the various scenic dressings which are available from model shops. I advise that you experiment with scenic dressing and I would hesitate to recommend any specific brand or colour. I do, however, suggest that a mixture of two or more colours gives the best result, say yellow and green, or two shades of green, when it comes to representing grass. There is endless scope for imagination and originality in the application of these materials.

Another very useful material to use when building up a scenic landscape is expanded polystyrene. You can buy this is in the form of ceiling tiles, or you can do as I do and beg, borrow or scrounge odd pieces used for packaging which in normal circumstances would only be thrown away. I keep a cardboard box to store the odd bits in and add to it any time a piece comes my way. 'Never throw anything away' is the model makers' maxim – 'you never know when it might come in useful.' Expanded polystyrene is so light that it is absolutely perfect for portable layouts. It is even possible to carve out the track bed for a layout from a solid block of expanded polystyrene, using a soldering iron or some other heat source to burn your way through the material but this is not recommended. The fumes given off can cause rapid loss of consciousness and adequate ventilation must be provided. Where weight is no problem almost any material can be used as a foundation for the scenery-blocks of wood, chipboard, softboard, cardboard, or anything that comes to hand and is not otherwise wanted. Similarly, there are countless alternatives for covering surfaces. Old worn-out sheets, shirts or blankets can be used and these can be pre-soaked in size to hold them stiff when set. Alternatively, you can consider pasting paper over a chicken wire frame or spreading a coat of plaster over some stiff hessian or rug canvas. Again, I can only recommend that you try the different methods and find which one suits you best. It might be as well, before you place your covering material, to establish where any firm and flat surfaces such as roads or foundations for buildings are to be positioned, since it is preferable to fix these first. They can be made of pieces of hardboard and cardboard supported on wooden blocks.

A rocky landscape is easy to build with the materials available. We have already mentioned the possibility of expanded polystyrene, but one of the best and most widely used materials for simulating rocks is cork bark. This is available in packets from most model shops and is easy to apply and most effective in use. It is, of course, very light in weight which makes it suitable for portable layouts. The cork bark should be pinned and glued to the baseboard, with perhaps a light supporting wooden framework behind, and any gaps between different pieces can be filled in either with

Cork bark used to splendid effect to create the rock landscape on Roger Desouter's HO gauge Wintertal.

offcuts of cork bark or with plaster. The softer limestone rocks, or such features as sand and chalk pits, can be represented by gluing layers of soft insulation board on top of each other so that the rough edges face outwards. The edges can be roughened up still further with a stiff wire or nylon brush to represent a lush growth of foliage, ferns, etc., which often congregate in places such as these, especially if there is any water around. Alternatively, the edges of the insulation board can be smoothed over with plaster which, if left in its natural colour, will look like a chalk pit. Plaster can also be used on its own to represent rock faces, where paint will need to be added to complete the effect. A favourite dodge is to imprint the impression of a piece of coal on the face of the plaster before it finally sets. Even a lump of coal itself can be used to

represent a rock face and so can actual pieces of stone or rock, but this will give you a weight problem which will rule out the use of these materials in a portable layout. Smaller, lighter pieces of rock or stone can, however, be used in places such as river beds, rocky streams and at the foot of a cliff or cutting, where loose boulders can be expected to be lying around. Small pieces of real coal can also be left lying around on the coal yard siding and employed as loads in wagons and locomotive tenders and bunkers.

Water always adds interest to any scenic setting, in real life as well as in miniature, and I suggest finding an excuse for simulating a water effect somewhere on your layout, whether it be a harbour at one extreme or a duck pond at the other. How you can best do this will depend on the particular location. For a large, deep water area like a harbour or river, I find a sheet of ripple glass such as Stippolyte gives a realistic result, especially if it is held about 1 in clear of the river bed. The higher the glass is held above the bed the more obscure the river bed becomes and the more realistic the whole affair looks. There are many simple ways of achieving extra realism, such as streaks of green paint applied to the underside of the glass to represent weeds floating in the water, or actual rocks placed on the bed of the river so that they just show below the surface of the glass. The river bed or harbour bottom can be a piece of hardboard painted according to the type it is to represent. If the scene is set in a heavy industrial area it could easily be painted black! On the other hand, a tidal creek could be painted sea green,

Varnish is the medium used to simulate the babbling brook in this skilful piece of scenic modelling on Wigleton by Tony Hills.

with perhaps the natural hardboard colour at the edges to represent the sand banks just appearing below the surface. The natural hardboard colour will also be perfectly satisfactory for the average muddy brown river.

On a portable layout you will hardly want to use glass for obvious reasons, in which case you can use other lighter and potentially less vulnerable materials such as clear plastic. Another method which is very popular especially for smaller streams, is to apply successive coats of varnish. Allow each coat to dry before applying the next and, over a period of time you will build up a thick semi-clear layer which looks very much like a smooth flowing stream or brook. This method is particularly suitable for waterfalls and streams, where the

varnish can be allowed to tumble and find its own level just as the water would do. One of the most realistic artificial rivers I have ever seen was on the Johnshaven Branch constructed by Les and Richard Parker, which has been exhibited on several occasions. Here the material used is a sheet of silicon rubber known as Midland Silicon, and the effect is quite tremendous.

Foliage, bushes, trees and plants present quite a challenge to modellers, if only because in real life there are so many of them. There are a number of commercially made models available but this is perhaps one branch of the hobby where the quality of the product is relative to the price. At the lower end of the scale the cheaper, mass-produced trees, which either make use of plastic mouldings or resemble cone-shaped bottle brushes, leave much to the imagination. Of the two, perhaps the bottle brushes are more useful for creating a cheap conifer forest. The most realistic models are quite expensive, reflecting the level of skilled handwork that goes into their production. Tree kits are a happy compromise and there are a number available using cast white-metal trunk and branches and either rubberised horsehair sprinkled with scenic dressing or a foam rubber foliage material. For the smaller trees and bushes, green lichen — which can be bought in packets from most model shops — is ideal, either glued direct to the ground to represent bushes and hedgerows, or placed on suitable twigs which can be made to look like tree trunks. Home-made trees can be fash-

ioned out of multi-strand wire, bound with tape at the base and progressively unwound towards the top of the tree to represent the diverging branches and twigs. The branches can be dipped in glue and sprinkled with green-dyed sawdust, scenic dressing or dyed tea leaves for summer foliage, or they can be left to represent the bare winter branches. Various other ways have been demonstrated or described in the model railway press from time to time and, as with most other aspects of scenic modelling, there is considerable scope for ingenuity in adapting different materials and devising new methods.

I mentioned earlier the rise and fall of the countryside and said that the rising part was easy enough but that the falling part is

This 4mm scale oak tree cleverly fabricated from a Britains tree kit and Jack Kine's scenic materials is another attraction from Wigleton.

Robert Skene, renowned for his tree modelling makes all the trees on the Yakima Group's Yakima Valley Railroad, a 7mm scale 16.5mm narrow gauge line set in Colorado.

A realistic grouping of trees, bushes and undergrowth lining the embankment aside Sandalmouth station on New Annington. Twisted wire, stretched pan scourers, teased out carpet underlay, flock powder and Woodland Scenics foliage are some of the materials used.

another matter. The difference lies in the fact that we usually build our model railways on a flat baseboard, below which we cannot normally go. With the open framework type of baseboard we can sometimes cut and lower a section of the framework to build some scenery below the level of the railway line. Figs 89 and 90 illustrate two alternative schemes. The first illustration shows the railway line crossing a shallow valley on an embankment; the small bridge or culvert is optional. The second illustration shows the line carried across a river by a bridge, such as the Dapol (ex-Airfix) Girder Bridge.

In an undulating landscape a railway is just as likely to burrow through hills and cuttings as it is to be carried above the surrounding countryside on embankments,

bridges and viaduct. It follows, therefore, that wherever you can it is desirable to build scenery *down* from the track and baseboard level as well as up. In a scheme such as that in Fig 89, the insulation board forming the baseboard surface and track bed would be cut to approximately 2 in wide (assuming a single track in 00 gauge) for the embankment section, and the embankment sides and valley floor can be built up by using dyed lint or whatever surfacing material you have decided on. The bridge or culvert can be a simple cardboard structure faced with brick or stone paper or can be adapted from ready-made proprietary parts. Fig 90 is perhaps self-explanatory and you can see that I have used a sheet of Stippolyte glass to represent the surface of the river, as described earlier.

The river banks can be formed from strips of insulation board and shaped to represent sloping banks with a level tow path either side of the river. The insulation board can then be covered with dyed medical lint to represent grass and the ragged edges painted with dabs of brown, grey and green paint. The banks themselves can form unlimited scope for artistic enterprise in the application of paint, lint and lichen to represent weeds, rushes and overhanging trees. There is also scope for modelling landing stages, boat houses, boats and marine equipment of all kinds. If the railway is planned in detail before constructing the baseboard, it is an advantage to consider features such as these when the baseboard framework is being constructed. If, however, you already have your base-

board in place, it is a relatively simple matter to adapt It, especially if you are using insulation board since this can be cut so easily, even when *in situ.*

To augment the natural scenery and scenic effects there are any number of man-made items which either form part of the actual railway scene or are frequently to be seen adjoining the line. The obvious ones are, of course, buildings and bridges, but there are others like telegraph poles, overhead electric pylons, roads, level crossings, road vehicles, and street furniture such as lamps, road signs and advertising hoardings, etc. Model railway buildings fall into two categories, depending upon which side of the railway fence they are to be found. On one side are the railway-owned properties such as stations, engine sheds, goods

Fig 89 *Dropping the datum line of the baseboard surface to provide scope for embankments and bridges.*
Fig 90 *A bridge across a river.*

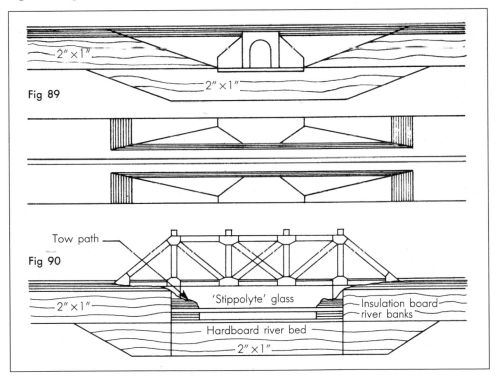

This page *The opportunity to build below track datum level gives scope for modelling attractive features such as this culvert on Camelot Halt and the bridge over the stream on Yaxbury.*

Right *The narrow gauge feeder on Jack Browne's HO Spindelbahn Region climbs to a high level terminus giving scope for dramatic Swiss mountain scenery and the high viaduct shown here. Note the realistic waterfalls.*

Right *An aqueduct is an attractive and unusual feature on the Twickenham & District MRC's layout Rickenham.*

Below right *Stone viaduct and girder bridges on Mereworth Junction. Dental plaster was used for casting the viaduct. Note the safety escape gaps in the parapet and the bracketed telegraph pole.*

The road overbridge and goods shed shown here on Barrie Bean's EM gauge Taunton North were constructed from Linka System moulds.

sheds, signal boxes, etc., and on the other side the privately owned properties such as houses, shops, industrial premises, farms, etc. Ready-assembled or simplified easy-to-assemble models of railway-owned properties are generally featured in the range of items produced by the main model railway manufacturers. Most of these are acceptable as starters–a quick and easy way of adding the basic necessities to your layout.

However more individual styles can be offered by the manufacturers who specialise in building construction kits. The most widely available kits for British style buildings take the form of printed card parts. Some very attractive and, in some cases, authentic models based on actual prototypes can be made from these kits. Although the beautifully printed and well-detailed parts save much of the hard work,

Robert Tivendale used plasticard to construct the buildings on his 00 gauge Ashley Bridge. Plumber's hemp was used to make the thatched roofs on Wenbury Farm shown here.

each model takes time to make especially if closer attention is paid to improving the relief details. Some of the smaller buildings are available in cast white metal kits and another method of establishing relief detail in model buildings is to use moulded plaster. Ossett Mouldings and Linka were foremost in this field and currently S. D. Mouldings provide a range of ready assembled castings for N gauge in stone bearing plaster. There are a few British-style moulded plastic building kits such as Dapol, Cooper Craft, Hornby Railways, Peco, Ratio and Wills Finecast, but the most prolific sources of plastic building kits emanate from the Continent where, of course, they are built to Continental styles of architecture and to the Continental scales, 1:87 for HO, 1:100 for TT-3 and 1:160 for N. A notable exception is the Danish firm Heljan whose extensive range of 00, HO & N building kits includes a number of authentic British style railway buildings in 4mm scale. Admittedly some of the Continental kits are unsuited to British layouts. I have in mind the typically Bavarian and Alpine buildings

with low pitched overhanging roofs. But many more can easily be adapted, in some cases simply by leaving off the Continental embellishments such as window shutters, a feature not often found in Britain. The question of scale need not be all that important especially if the buildings are placed nearer the back of the layout where in all probability most scenic buildings will be placed. The quality and attention to detail in these Continental kits has to be seen to be believed and they have the added attraction of being moulded in different realistically coloured plastics, sometimes multi-coloured, which give a natural realistic random effect. Therefore, there is absolutely no painting required and this more than offsets the slightly higher cost of these kits.

As nice as all these building kits are, and let there be no mistake, some of them are superb little gems, there is no substitute for the scratch-built tailor-made model. There are many different styles of architecture and even in these days of 'shoe box' office blocks there is still a lot of individuality to be found in buildings, particularly railway

Fox Hatch by Derek Bunting showing the effective use of printed card building sheets and papers.

stations. Many railway companies had an individual 'house style' (no pun intended) and numerous small characteristics such as chimney pots, barge boards and awnings, bore the stamp of the owning company. The types of material used in the construction of the building, whether wood, brick or stone, varied according to the company or location of the line and there were even variations in the type of brick and stone used. There is little doubt that a model built to represent an authentic railway in an authentic location ought to have authentic-looking buildings in the style of the owning company and with representative local materials. Appendix 2 gives details of a number of books devoted to railway architecture and the model railway magazines frequently include articles on buildings illustrated with photographs and plans. All of these provide a valuable source of inspiration and information. There is, however, no real substitute for field observation and a visit to a railway station taking with you a camera, notebook, pencil and tape measure, will pay dividends. There is little doubt that a model of an authentic railway station will be admired much more and will add more atmosphere to your layout than a

kitbuilt structure which has possibly already been seen on countless other model railway layouts. I would suggest using building kits as an expediency, to get something assembled quickly, and then after the rest of the layout is finished you can again turn your attention to the buildings and replace them one by one with scratch-built models. But remember if you do intend doing some field observation in a particular area there is no time like the present. To delay the job for a week or two may be too late, since many of the most interesting railway structures are being pulled down or rebuilt beyond all recognitions and if your interest is primarily in the past it is important to get out and about now,

The materials which can be used for making scratch-built buildings are generally simple to work with, easy to come by and inexpensive, which is not something we can always say. They need not be difficult to construct or call for a great deal of manipulative skill or architectural knowledge. What model building construction does need, however, is an artistic eye, an appreciation of colour, a keen sense of observation and in some cases the ability to concentrate the subject matter in such a way that the overall

Right *Strip wood in appropriate sizes suitable for modelling timber buildings is available from specialist suppliers. The effect can be seen in this HO freight depot in Leigh Clark's Tuscab Rock.*

Below *Meticulous attention to detail is apparent in this superb model of the 'Rovers Return Inn' by Stan Ginn.*

effect is retained without overburdening the model with a lot of unnecessary detail and without spreading it over too large an area. Some railway buildings would take up more space on the baseboard than we have

room for and it is sometimes permitted to reduce the ground area by perhaps restricting the length or width of a building, so long as it does not unduly affect the overall appearance.

Left *Buntingham signal box and part of the water tower on Ray Hammond's 4mm scale LNER layout closely resemble the full size structures on the now closed GER branch line terminus at Buntingford. Notice the point rodding and the signal lever seen through the open window.*

Right *Signal boxes can take many shapes and forms. The two shown here on John Woodman's extensive 00 gauge layout were cleverly adapted from proprietary kits, bits and pieces. The one spanning the tracks was inspired by the ex-SER box still standing at Canterbury West.* (Photo: NCS)

Balsa wood is a good basic material to use for the main structure of buildings, It cuts easily, is light in weight, does not twist or warp and can be stuck easily with balsa cement. It can be obtained in a wide range of thicknesses, thereby allowing the correct depth to be given to window and door openings. As an alternative to balsa wood, card (either the normal paper fibre type or the modern plastic or styrene sheet variety) is often acceptable, but it can bow or warp if subjected to heat or damp, especially when building papers are glued to the outside. If you prefer to use card rather than sheet balsa I would suggest gluing a framework of bracing struts made out of balsa or hardwood strip behind the walls. The printed paper building sheets representing brick or stone can be obtained in a variety of styles and can be thoroughly recommended. An advance on these printed sheets is, however, to be found in the embossed card or moulded plastic sheets which show the individual brick or stone course in relief. These moulded plastic sheets generally require some painting since they are invariably moulded in a basic brick colour, which does not differentiate the pointing. The pointing can, however, be picked out quite easily by applying a wash of matt cream cement coloured paint over

the whole surface of the plastic sheet. Before the paint has a chance to dry, wipe the surface with a tissue or cloth so that the paint is removed from the surface of the bricks leaving sufficient behind to fill up the pointing. You may find this leaves a faint smear on the surface of the bricks but this all helps to produce a realistic weathered appearance to the otherwise shiny plastic. A similar effect can be achieved using dry powders such as talcum or even ordinary domestic scouring powder. Thus, whether you prefer plastic to printed paper sheets may depend upon your skill as a painter. My view is that where brickwork is concerned the relief effect is less important than accurate colouring, and I think it is no easy task to match the accurate random brick shades that some producers of the best brick papers manage to achieve.

With stone work, however, I consider the relief effect of moulded plastic. provided it can be painted reasonably well, is worth the extra expense and effort. Roofs should be given particular attention, since they are invariably the parts of the model which we see the most. For this reason, moulded plastic or embossed card roof tile sheets are to be preferred and are essential in the case of the more highly profiled roofing materials such as pantiles. Printed paper sheets are

passable in the case of the smoother slate roofs, a favourite dodge being to cut out the roofing tile papers into strips and overlap each succeeding strip. This is a long and tedious process, but it is worthwhile if you can do it neatly and evenly and you have the time to spare. If you are in any doubt on any of these points it is probably better to leave well alone. The process can also be used to represent weather boarding on timber buildings, but the same reservation applies, and you may find it easier just to score the planks rather than build them up one by one. However, weather boarding can also be bought ready-made in moulded plastic which is probably a lot more satisfactory. Finally, when it comes to mentioning ways of representing surfaces of buildings, excellent relief detail as well as authentic texture can be created by using plaster, modelling clay or the special types of modelling compound developed for the purpose such as Das self hardening modelling clay or Peco Scene Texture Modelling Compound. These materials can be moulded or carved to represent stonework in any shape or form either as low standing walls or else applied as a thin coating to complete the facing of a building.

Plastic card or styrene sheet is a tremendous asset to miniature building construc-

tion because it simplifies making many smaller detailed architectural features, such as foundation and corner stones, window frames, bay windows, doors and door frames, dormer windows, sills, lintels, barge boards, cornices, facias, buttresses, plinths, canopies, balconies, chimneys, steps and staircases, to name several. The advantage or plastic card is that it can be cut and cemented together so easily. It is not necessary to cut right through the material, you just score it with the tip of a craft knife blade, bend the two halves of the material either side of the score mark and the pieces will snap in two. After the light application of a brush full of liquid cement the two pieces can be joined together again in any position. The liquid cement evaporates very quickly and leaves little or no mark, unlike glue for example, which can leave a blob mark unless it is put on sparingly, when it may not have sufficient strength. To cement two pieces of plastic card together you should use tweezers to avoid undue handling of the material, because there is a danger that the liquid cement will get on to the fingers and dissolve the card, leaving an impression of the finger tip on the plastic. One particular asset of plastic card is that it is possible to cement two pieces together along their edge and, because the liquid cement dries so quickly, they can be held together long enough for them to set firm. If, after you have cemented the two pieces together, you find they are in the wrong position, a quick stroke with another brush full of liquid cement is enough to free the two parts so that they can be repositioned and cemented together again.

Umbrella ribs have been suggested more than once for guttering, which is all right if you have a ready source of such material. However, an alternative which is probably better, at least in the smaller scales, is to use plastic rodding which can be obtained in a number of different sizes, and to flatten or scrape along one side to produce a 'U'-shaped cross-section. The fact that it is a solid 'U' will not be visible In the finished model, especially if the top part is painted black. Plastic rodding can also be used for the down pipes, which can be bent in almost any fashion by warming them between the fingers, in hot water, or over a candle flame. One method of fixing them to the walls is to use handrail split pins which can be made to look like downpipe brackets.

Whereas just about every part of a building can be scratch built from basic raw materials. there are very many excellent ready made accessories available to aid architectural modellers. Such items as guttering, downpipes, chimney stacks, doors and windows, etc., are available from a number of manufacturers either in moulded plastic, cast whitemetal or etched copper. Etched copper frets feature prominently in the extensive range of detailed scenic and architectural accessories produced by Scale Link Ltd. The more ornate of these frets such as those representing cast iron brackets, wrought iron balconies and gates, valence boarding, roof trusses, barge boarding, fancy ridge tiles, etc., contain an amount of delicate tracery that would be extremely difficult and time consuming to produce by hand.

There is much to be said for making the same approach to designing and scratch building models of buildings as do many builders of full size buildings who build brick courses around standard size joinery, doors and windows, etc., rather than make the joinery fit the openings in the brick-work. Study the catalogues of specialist firms making model doors and windows, select whichever best suits your needs and cut out the door and window apertures in the walls of your model to fit. This applies particularly to windows since they can so readily make or mar a model and they are not the easiest of things to make convincingly by hand. The availability of such ready made items is a comparatively recent innovation in modelling circles. Even now it may not be possible to find exactly what you are looking for in which case you will have to make your own window frames and doors. Doors can easily be made from plastic card, scribed to represent planking where necessary or laminated with plastic card to represent panelling. Window frames, in particular the glazing bars, are, however, more of a problem. They can be built up from strips of thin plastic card cemented to the glazing but care is needed to avoid spoiling the glazing material. A cleaner method is to cut glazing bars from self-adhesive labels but the lasting quality of the adhesive is open to doubt. The above pitfalls can be avoided by drawing glazing bars directly on the glazing material using white or coloured inks. Whatever method is adopted be sure the windows are cleanly glazed to capture the reflection of light that normally comes from glazed windows.

If you want to hide the lack of detail inside the building you can always draw curtains across behind the window, which will also add a splash of colour and realism to the finished model. Whilst it is by no means essential to furnish the interiors of buildings, since in miniature they are so dark that nothing can be seen in normal lighting, it might be necessary to fit interior partition walls in some locations. It would spoil the effect if you were able to see right through the building from one side to the other or down from the third floor to the basement. Apart from the extra realism it will also add strength to the building if an

Above *Motive Power Depots are an attractive as well as useful feature on any layout and space can usually be found for them. The mainlines in the foreground curve to the right giving corner space on the baseboard for this comprehensive MPD on Ashley Bridge.*

Left *A fine collection of industrial locomotives can be seen here as the sun clears the smoke haze to start a new day at Eastwell MPD.*

intermediate floor and interior partition are included. The fitting of lights inside miniature buildings can add a large measure of interest to a layout but at the same time it is necessary to provide ready access to the building interiors. This can be achieved in a number of different ways, but the most effective is to fit the roof so that it can be lifted off the sides rather than make the whole building lift off the baseboard surface. We generally look down on to a model railway and any gap that it may be necessary to leave around the edge of the roof and the walls of the building can be largely obscured by the overhanging eaves. If the whole building is removable from the baseboard it may not be possible to hide the gap around the bottom edge of the

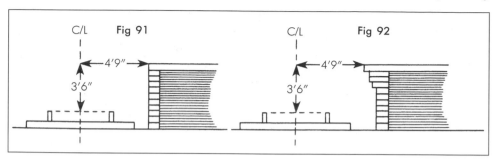

Fig 91 *A simple brick platform wall.* **Fig 92** *A platform wall with a protruding edge.*

building so easily and if there is one give-away feature that detracts from the appearance of a model building more than any other it is the sight of the building standing suspended above the baseboard, albeit by only the barest fraction of a millimetre. The base lines of all buildings should be well and truly wedded to the ground on which they stand, and it is a useful aid to sprinkle some scenic dressing around the foundations to help simulate this effect as much as possible.

Apart from the painted woodwork and curtains, a welcome splash of colour can also be given to painted walls of buildings which need not always be white, cream or grey. A few stucco or plastered wall buildings can liven up and add variety to a row of houses built of brick or stone. The roughcast effect can easily be achieved by using sandpaper or glasspaper of the appropriate grade and suitably coloured. Such material is also useful for gravel or stone paths and terraces or station platforms. Station platforms are almost a subject in themselves. There appears to be an unlimited variety of styles and materials used in their construction, from the simple timber wayside halt built out of old railway sleepers to the modern pre-cast concrete structures of today. In Britain, the most common form is a brick or stone retaining wall surmounted by paving stones forming the platform edge, behind which there is a mound of earth and rubble finished with tarmac, paving stones or some other suitable surface. In many cases there is only a paved surface near the station buildings and gravel or ashes suffice elsewhere. One method of representing ashes or tarmac, another common form of platform surface, is to use cork sheet. Painted matt black and toned down after the paint is dry with a rubbing of domestic scouring powder, it takes on a flecked grey colour, realistic in both texture and appearance. Provided the cork sheet is thick enough, ⅛" thick is ideal, the cork will readily accept pins which can be inserted in the base of such items as milk churns, figures, etc., so that these items can be pinned in place but readily moved when required. The pin holes make little or no impression in the cork surface whenever items are moved from one place to another. The retaining wall can be a simple brick one ending abruptly at the top, or else it can have one or more courses of bricks brought forward at the top to support a protruding edge, eg, as shown in figs 91 and 92.

One aspect of real railways that never ceases to amaze me is the number of huts and small buildings that you can usually see scattered around stations, station yards and goods depots, to say nothing of the main line itself. Alongside the main line they provide shelter and tool storage for the permanent way staff and a number of them fulfil a similar function around the station and goods yards. The huts come in a variety of structures from brick-built to corrugated iron and even the familiar railway van or coach body. The railway coach body minus bogies that you find dumped along the lineside, or possibly resting on wooden or brick-built blocks, is now almost a hackneyed subject amongst scenic railway modellers. There has been at least one commercially produced model of this most scenic feature that I know of, but far less commonly seen in models is a wagon body used in the same way, whereas in real life they appear in large numbers on both sides of the railway fence. They are popular amongst farmers and many can be seen miles away from the actual railway, but still bearing signs of their former lettering and painting details.

Reverting back to railway uses, old wagons are often converted to mess wagons, either on or off their chassis, and the conversion usually takes the form of the insertion of a couple of windows and the inevitable addition of a stovepipe through the roof. For small details, such as huts and old wagon and coach bodies, etc., it is worth giving a little thought to the subject and paying attention to those you see in real life, since often a lot of small items pass unnoticed individually but collectively add up to a sense of realism. I mean such things as the use of an old enamel advertising sign to patch up a rotting body panel; an extra piece of roofing felt nailed to the roof (which can be represented by sticking on a square of tissue paper painted black), a broken window pane; a lean-to fitted at one end or side of the body to provide additional storage, perhaps for a bicycle or wheelbarrow, etc; a water tank on the roof and guttering draining into a water butt; old wooden boxes stacked at one end, and perhaps storage for firewood and boiler fuel. You can spend hours detailing mundane structures such as these and there is no end to the variety of work you can find when adding realism to scenic models.

Scenery is not only decorative, it can also perform a useful function on a model railway as an aid to illusion. We have already discussed in the chapter on layout planning the desirability of breaking up the circle effect of a continuous run layout. Tunnels built at each end of a continuous oval will not only help to conceal this, they will also hide the curves, thus permitting the use of a sharper radius without offending the eye unduly. There is something fascinating about the sight of a train entering or leaving a tunnel. The tunnel mouth itself can provide scope for an interesting architectural feature, since there is so much variety in their style and method of

The landscape modelling either side of this tunnel mouth on Mereworth Junction shows careful attention to detail.

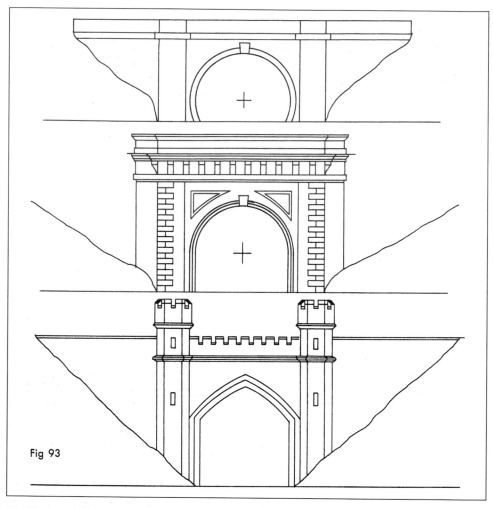

Fig 93 *Three different styles of tunnel mouth.*

construction (See Fig 93). Tunnel mouths can be purchased ready made in N, HO, 00 and O gauges in a variety of styles, or they can be built by hand using balsa wood covered with brick or stone paper. If the tunnel is to be installed on a curve or near the entrance to a curve, do not forget to allow extra clearance for the overhang either side of the longest vehicle in your rolling stock fleet, or for the outward swing of the front buffer beam of your longest locomotive. The general construction features already described for scenery can be applied when building the rising ground between the two tunnel mouths, ie. a framework over which can be stretched a covering of some suitable material. Rarely will it be necessary to build a lining actually inside the tunnel, although you may feel it is a good idea to have one for the first few inches inside the mouth of the tunnel,

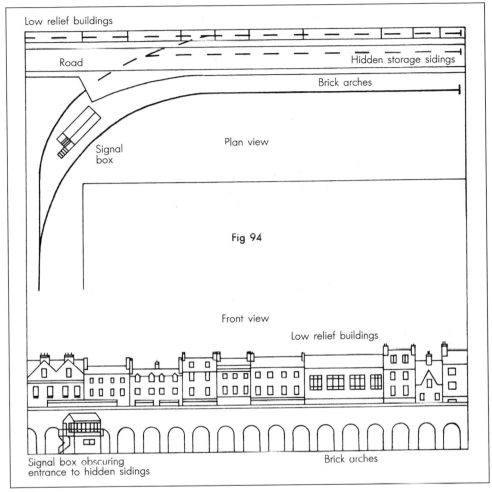

Fig94 *High level road and low relief building obscuring hidden storage sidings. The entrance is obscured by the signal box.*

especially if at that point the tunnel is in line with the viewer and clearly visible. The tunnel mouth itself can be supported with a framework of wood blocks or strips, or alternatively expanded polystyrene is a useful material to use. Blocks of expanded polystyrene can be built up to make an arch entrance to the tunnel and the tunnel mouth can be simply glued in place. Don't forget to paint some telltale black soot marks an the tunnel arch if you

are modelling a steam railway. You can use a lighted candle to do this job, but I do not recommend it if the tunnel is made of inflammable material which it is most likely to be!

Another way in which scenery can be applied for practical purposes is to disguise the entrance to a fiddle yard or a bank of hidden storage sidings. A gap in a scenic backcloth can sometimes be used this way, as shown in Fig 94. The backcloth in this

A road overbridge forming a natural break with the fiddle yard on Buntingham.

instance is a row of buildings facing on to a high level road, the road being supported by a retaining wall made to represent a row of brick arches (easily made using brick paper or embossed plastic sheet). The buildings facing on to the street can, if they are normally viewed from one side be built in low relief, that is they only have a false front to them and have no back or depth, thus reducing by at least half the space taken up. Kits for such low relief models are made and sold specially, but alternatively you can adopt a number of ordinary kits, simply by cutting them in half, or you can make up your own. The scenic backcloth effectively becomes a tunnel and the entrance to the 'tunnel' can either be disguised as an ordinary road bridge, or else there need be no proper entrance at all, and the railway line simply disappears behind a building or a row of trees.

Scenic features can also provide operating scope for a model railway. The obvious example is, of course, the station itself which provides a focal point for the operation of the railway, from where the traffic originates. In discussing the plan for a country terminus in the chapter on layout planning, I mentioned a dairy and a petrol and oil storage depot as a source of traffic for the railway. Lineside industries such as these can make interesting scenic features in their own right. There are any number in this category that not only provide traffic for the railways, but form interesting subjects for modelling or adding scenic interest. Timber yard, iron and steel merchant, scrap merchant, stonemason, brickworks, power station, gasworks, stone crushing plant, quarry, coalmine, cement works, oil refinery, tar distillery, whisky distillery, china clay works, army depot (scope for army vehicles and tanks travelling on bogie flat and well wagons, to say nothing of squads of soldiers lined up on the nearby station platform), canal wharf, harbour (either deep sea, river estuary for coastal shipping or inland waterway), or simply a straightforward factory are just some examples of what I mean. Any one of these industries can provide traffic for the railway, and some will require special wagons possibly privately owned and painted in attractive and colourful liveries. Also, at the same time, the industrial premises themselves can provide unlimited scope for creative modelling and for artistic expression.

There are bound to be a number of places on the model where the railway comes in close proximity to the road and road traffic, for example in station fore-courts, goods yards, level crossings, road over and under bridges, and in the straight-forward case of a road running alongside the railway line. In all these cases there will be an opportunity to display a collection of road vehicles, and here special care is needed to select the right vehicles in order to create an authentic atmosphere. It is regrettable that of all the hundreds, if not thousands, of miniature die-cast model cars and commercial vehicles that are mass produced as toys, but which are made to

such incredible precision as to raise their status to the level of scale models, so few are built to a scale which makes them suit-able for incorporation into the scenic effects of most of the popular model railway gauges. Two notable exceptions are the ranges of 1:76 scale diecast vehicles produced by E.F.E. Exclusive First Editions and Corgi's The Original Omnibus Company. The models so far produced by these two companies are perfect for 00 gauge 4 mm scale layouts set in any period from the 1950s onwards. For HO gauge

A busy street scene forms the high level backcloth to Ashley Bridge.

Continental building kits are a valuable source of material for modelling lineside industrial premises. The timber yard wood treating plant prominent in this view of John Woodman's 00 gauge layout was constructed from one of the extensive range of Heljan kits. Super-quick parts can be identified in the high-rise signal box.

(Photo: NCS)

Industrial premises underneath the arches on John Woodman's layout. Cooper Craft and Merit supplied the kits for the lorries
(Photo: NCS)

Continental modellers there are a number of firms that produce a wide range of road vehicles, both mechanical and horse drawn, and these are available in Britain where in a few cases their use can pass muster on the larger British 4mm scale 00 gauge layouts. But true scale 4mm models suitable for British 00 gauge modellers were few in number before E.F.E. models were introduced in 1989. For instance, Dinky Toys produced a few cars before World War 2 that were suitable for 00 gauge and at one time hardly a layout was complete without one or more of them, together with at least one example of their fine double deck bus. Despite the fact that the bus was modelled on a London Transport STL type, which was practically unheard of outside London, the model looked good repainted in other liveries and served its purpose in providing suitable passenger road transport on many a model layout based on country and provincial practice. Alas, this model is not available today, unless you can track down a second-hand example, and the cars that were also supplied are very difficult to obtain even second-hand

It can be quite entertaining trying to find past or present die-cast models that may be suitable for use in a model railway scenic setting. Some of the Matchbox and Lledo Days Gone models are produced to something near recognisable model railway scales, but these prolific suppliers produce the vast majority of their models in a size which will fit their packaging rather than to a scale which will suit railway modellers. A number of Yesteryear, Dinky Toy and Corgi Classic models are suitable for O gauge. Modellers in this gauge are fortunate in that 1:43 is an internationally recognised scale for collectors' models.

Therefore, so far as 4mm scale road vehicles are concerned, chances are there will be some types of road vehicle that will not be available ready-made. Luckily, commercial vehicles such as buses and lorries are perfectly practical models to make. They can be scratch-built from simple materials like card (the paper type or plastic card and styrene sheet) and wood, and only the wheels need to be obtained commercially. Special wheels for lorries and buses can either be bought ready made or they can sometimes be modified from other kits. Generally speaking, older vehicles,

such as those built during the 1930s, 1940s and early 1950s, are easier to make than the more modern ones, since the later vehicles contain a large amount of body pressings with multiple curves and, even worse, they invariably include multi-curve windscreens and windows. Even these features do not rule out home construction entirely, but they do make the job that little more difficult, since the glazing material has to be specially moulded to help create the shape of the original, whereas bodywork with flat plain glass windows is so much easier to model.

Windows are one of the biggest difficulties with model cars because in 4 mm scale they are rather small and difficult to glaze individually using flat strips of clear styrene sheet. It is possibly best to mould the entire top half of the bodywork out of perspex and simply paint on the roof and window pillars, or even carve the bodywork out of wood and just paint the windows on. On the other hand buses and lorries with predominantly flat sides are relatively simple to make using two sheets of card for each side with the windows cut out and a strip of glazing material sandwiched in between. Each of the three layers of material forming one side should be cut progressively shorter at the corner ends so that they form steps which will fit into each other

The Bristol Lodekka. One of E.F.E.'s superb range of authentic 4mm scale diecast models.

when two side panels are placed together at the corners (see Fig 95). Not only will this give added strength to the corners, it will also provide a sufficient depth of material at the corner to enable it to be rounded in prototype fashion, using at first a craft knife, followed by a file and sandpaper to smooth the surface. On a bus, the rear dome is usually the part of the bodywork with the most curves and a smooth gentle curvature at this point can often be obtained by using a block of balsa wood for the roof which can be made to smooth into the sides and rear panel (See Fig 96).

The importance of road vehicles has now been fully appreciated by the trade and there are a growing number of kits available in N and 00 gauges covering horse drawn vehicles, traction engines and steam lorries as well as cars, lorries and buses. A few of them are in plastic but the majority are cast white metal. Bus models predominate due in part to the hobby of bus modelling which is a recognised branch of model making in its own right but it has a very welcome spin off for railway modellers. There are a number of specialist firms catering for the needs of bus modellers

notably Mabex and Bus Fare who between them produce a commendably wide range of water slide transfers of bus fleet names, destination blinds, bus stop signs and advertisements. If you would like to find out more about bus modelling and the Model Bus Federation which has supported the hobby since 1968 *The Model Bus Handbook* by Ian Morton, published by British Bus Publishing, is recommended.

The bus modelling fraternity appears to go in more for the post-war or modern day prototypes which form the majority of bus model kits. This is, of course, no disadvantage to the railway modeller modelling the contemporary railway scene but one of the most popular periods for railway modelling is the late 1930s when the big-four railway companies were at the height of their existence. There does appear to be a tendency with some model railway layouts based on this period to include vintage and veteran cars and an over-abundance of steam vehicles more reminiscent of pre-World War 1 rather than pre-World War 2. It is important to get the right model when selecting road vehicles and to ensure that you have a type appropriate to the period

Fig 95 *Stepped card corners are strong and easily rounded.* **Fig 96** *A square piece of balsa is ideal material for a bus roof.*

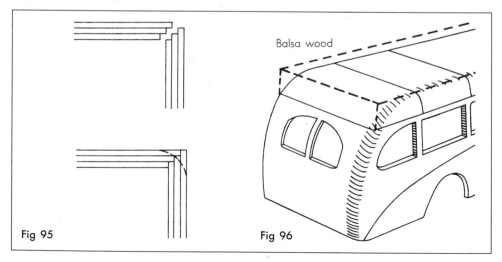

Balsa wood

Fig 95

Fig 96

Above *The horse-drawn dray and showman's tractor are contemporary with the 1930s setting of Paul Skinner's 00 gauge SR branch line Ashmouth.*

Right *A vintage vehicle rally explains the presence of this ancient bus seen passing the 'Signal Inn' on Dave Peachey's preserved railway Tallund Junction.*

you are modelling. To come back to the 1930s and knowing that not everyone can remember them; horse drawn vehicles especially railway owned ones, were abundant at that time and there is no shortage of kits for these.

Despite the predominance of modern day bus kits there are sufficient bus model kits covering the 1930s to suit most people's needs. Several manufacturers are now producing kits for car models and there is one firm, Scale Link, who concentrate on the 1930s period which is of great benefit to modellers of both the pre and post nationalisation scene. It should be remembered that pre-war cars had of necessity a long working life and some of the more common or garden types such as the

Y Model Ford or Austin Ruby could still be seen in day to day use well into the late 1950s. There is little prospect that the toy market will ever produce any popular saloon cars in recognised model railway scales but if you are prepared to make your own there is no shortage of kits, at least in 4mm scale, and scratch building cars now seems hardly necessary.

Some of the manufacturers of die-cast miniature road vehicles produce lorries suitable for model railway use and it may be possible to find a softskin military vehicle kit which can be constructed either as intended or converted for civilian use. Mention must be made of the never to be forgotten Scammell mechanical horse and trailer. Most model railways portraying the 1930s onwards can justify one or more of these. There were two basic types of 3-wheel tractor unit; the original pre-war type dating from around 1933 and the post-war Scarab which is distinguished by its more rounded streamlined shape. As with private cars, the pre-war Scammell mechanical horses lasted well into BR days and could be seen alongside the post-war Scarabs whereas of course the Scarab could not be seen in anything other than BR livery. It is rather necessary to get this sort of detail right!

Luckily, there are kits for both types available in 4mm scale.

Trams also have a great following and they can form an excellent scenic feature on a model railway, with the added advantage of being working models. E.F.E. makes an excellent die-cast model which can be motorised and there are several plastic and cast metal kits available in 4mm scale, together with a number of accessories. To find out more about this subject, *Tramway Modelling in 00 gauge* by David Voice (Lancastrian Transport Publications) is recommended. A number of working roadway systems can also be incorporated in a model railway layout although I have never been particularly impressed with the realism or practicality of any I have seen. There are some working scenic models that can form arresting scenic features. The Continentals are great ones for scenic attractions such as working cable railways, working windmills, waterfalls that are operated by a concealed electric pump, chiming church bells, flashing neon signs and various other ideas which add rather more novelty than realism to a scenic setting. Nevertheless, they are still desirable provided they are not overdone or obviously installed just for effects sake.

The attraction of tramway modelling can be gauged from this impressive line-up outside the depot on Dick Yeo's Telford Park.

A harbour can provide a most attractive and practical scenic feature on a model railway. This is recognised by a number of Continental manufacturers who produce both static and working boat models and dockyard accessories which can be incorporated in HO gauge model railways. Whilst it may be possible to adapt some of these to 4 mm scale there are otherwise very few models or kits available to British 00 gauge modellers. The majority of ship kits seem to be galleons, liners or battleships, which are either of the wrong scale or the wrong vintage for a model railway. What would be most desirable for an 00 gauge layout would be a nice 4 mm scale model of a typical 300-ton coastal cargo vessel, the sort that sails up river estuaries to take on loads at small docks all over the country and also many other parts of the world. Apart from being a scenic addition, such a ship would also be an excellent model to make in its own right and the techniques of plastic kit manufacture would appear to be ideally suited to producing the usual deck trappings, winches, derricks, lifeboats, dinghies and other nautical paraphernalia which usually accompany such vessels.

In the absence of almost any suitable kits, you have to be prepared to scratch build if you want to add a boat or boats to a harbour setting, but thankfully this is not such a difficult task and is one that can give a lot of pleasure. Balsa wood or ordinary hardwood is perhaps the best material to use for the hull, the plastic card can be used to build up the superstructure and deck fittings. The model itself can be a long-term project that can be fitted in as and when time permits and can be regarded as a kind of relaxation when something other than model railways is required. There are many more types of suitable ships and boats other than 300-ton coastal cargo vessels that would look equally at home in a harbour setting alongside a model railway. However, it is a good idea to select a vessel which will provide an excuse for operating traffic to and from the harbour, thereby justifying the construction of the harbour branch and the running of trains to and from the quay. For example, you could operate a passenger ferry service and run trains on to the quay, such as is done at Weymouth for the Channel Islands service or at Ryde Pier Head on the Isle of Wight. However, most of these models demand more space than can usually be spared in the majority of scales, but they might make ideal subjects for N gauge. Coming down to a much smaller size, canals form a very interesting scenic subject for a model railway and almost any space can be utilised for adding at least one canal feature. Locks and lock gates are perhaps the most noteworthy features of such systems, which can be easily fitted into either the corner of a layout or else across the width of a baseboard, where the railway line can perhaps cross the canal on a bridge similar to the one shown in Fig 90. Langley Miniature Models supply kits in N and 00 gauges for modelling canal scenes.

Lastly, on the subject of scenery, we come to the animal kingdom—farmyard animals and, most important of all, human beings. Luckily there is no shortage of material here in almost any scale. The Continental manufacturers look after their own scales of N and HO very well. For British N gauge Peco have their 'Petite People'. Both 4mm and 7mm scale modellers are extremely well catered for by a whole host of manufacturers too numerous to mention individually. New sets of figures covering different historical periods, fashions or occupational groups, feature fairly regularly in the advertisement and review pages of the model railway press. 1 gauge modellers can make use of the wide range of Britains' models, which include a number of farmyard items ideal for a model railway. Some modellers are particularly adept at miniature figure conversion. This is easily enough done with plastic figures, since it is possible to cut them in half and fit the top half of one figure to the lower half of another, thereby changing its shape in as many ways as you like. Similarly, running figures can be

Figures from the Dapol (ex-Airfix) Railway Workmen series can be recognized in this further example of superb scenic modelling by Tony Hills.

converted to standing figures and standing to sitting figures, or any other combination you want. Simple conversions, either by the use of the craft knife or the paint brush, can also be done to alter dress and uniforms to make, for example, soldiers into ticket collectors. To add variety to your layout don't just take your figures at face value, but see what you can do to alter their pose, shape or dress, to represent a variety of figures not covered by the normal range of commercially produced models.

Farmyard animals can often be adapted in the same way, altering the position of the head, limbs or tail, or repainting to represent different breeds appropriate to the district or period of time being modelled. Not so far fetched in the case of cattle where different

breeds had at one time strong regional preferences amongst farmers and the popularity of breeds has changed markedly over the years. On modern day layouts, farmyard animals will have to be relegated to the lineside fields since they are no longer carried by rail but in the days of cattle wagons and cattle docks a rural country station could put on a very animated scene. With human figures, which normally stand on a heavy base, it is desirable to remove as much of the base material, all of it if you can to improve the appearance of the figure. Then you can either glue the figure in position to keep it upright or you can fix a small length of pin in one of the legs (Peco track fixing pins are ideal) leaving the pointed end to project about ⅛in from the sole of the foot. With

Right *The station cat attracts the ticket collector's attention on Winbury station, the REC O gauge layout.*
(Photo: Peter Parfitt)

Below *Farmyard livestock was at one time an important source of railway revenue. Cattle and sheep await loading at Buntingham.*

plastic figures I find it preferable to drill a force fit hole for the pin using one of the miniature 12 volt variable speed electric drills. The pin is useful not only for fixing the figure to the baseboard but also for holding the figure in a pin chuck to facilitate cleaning up and painting. You should be careful to remove all flash and moulding marks from the figure. A scraping with a craft knife will usually achieve the desired result.

The smaller scenic features, such as human figures, milk churns, platform barrows, luggage on platforms, street furniture (eg, lampposts, pillar boxes, telephone kiosks, sand bins, fire buckets, posters, hoardings, notice boards, etc.) are the sort of things that can always be added to a model railway layout at any time, as and when funds and time permit. In actual fact they cost very little individually, but collectively they could amount to a considerable sum, if only because there are so many of these features that you can add to a layout.

This is perhaps one of the attractions of a model railway—it is never really finished. However complete the layout may become there is always somewhere where a little added detail can be attended to. The commercial model railway trade is bringing out new accessories all the time and new ideas are always being discussed in the model railway magazines which give you inspiration to alter or make additions to your layout. One small enterprising firm brought out a range of 4 mm scale model birds in different shapes and sizes, some with wings outstretched and others perched as on fences or roof tops. It is quite amazing the amount of extra realism these models give to a scenic setting, yet how often do you see features such as these modelled? After the main expense of equipping the layout has been completed, small details like this can always be added to make a valuable contribution to the overall effect of the layout.

CHAPTER 9
Locomotives

Of all the many different and separate items that go to make up a complete model railway the one that probably has the greatest universal appeal is the motive power—the locomotives, whether they be steam, diesel or electric, that haul the trains. There are exceptions, of course, and for example there are some people who specialise in railway signalling electronic control, architecture or a scenic landscape setting who may pay scant regard to the locomotives and the rest of the rolling stock. However, the majority of us build our model railways so that we have somewhere on which to run our locomotives and their carriages and wagons.

It is important not to lose sight of the fact that most locomotives were built for a purpose. Some cynics may argue that certain classes of locomotives were built just to satisfy the vain glory of a particular locomotive engineer. There are certainly cases where there seems little justification for the introduction of an entirely new class of locomotive, and an existing and, on the face of it, perfectly adequate design appears not to have been persevered with because of a personality change in the locomotive design office. But this is not by any means true in all cases and there are probably more examples of locomotive engineers perpetuating the designs of their predecessors than there are the other way round. Consider, for example the continued construction of the Great Western Railway 'Castle' Class from

1923 when the first was built until the last one which was constructed as late as 1950. The building period of 28 years not only covered the reign of two Great Western Railway Company locomotive engineers but also the transition into the Western Region of British Railways. On British Railways the classic example of longevity of a locomotive design is the J72 Class of 0-6-0T designed originally by Wilson Worsdell for the North Eastern Railway in 1898. Seventy-five were built by the NER before the grouping, another ten were built by the LNER after grouping and a further 28 were made by British Railways after nationalisation. The final eight locomotives were built in 1951, 53 years after the construction of the first J72 in 1898.

The design of a locomotive is influenced in a great number of different ways. The weight and speed of the train, the length of run, the ruling gradient, the curvature of the track, the condition of the permanent way and the civil engineering structures are probably the most important factors. This is, of course, ignoring the all-important aspect of power source; steam (coal, oil fired or wood burning), diesel (electric, hydraulic or mechanical transmission) or electric (overhead, third rail or battery) to name some of the most important types. A steam locomotive carries its own source of power, namely the boiler and a heavy long-distance train will of course demand a big locomotive with

The former Airfix 00 gauge model of GWR 'Castle' Class 4–6–0 No. 4073 'Caerphilly Castle'. After Airfix ceased production the model passed to Dapol and is now being produced by Hornby Railways – a production history almost approaching that of the full-sized engine.

a large boiler to provide a plentiful supply of steam. A heavy but relatively slow-moving freight train will need maximum power for starting and for plodding up the gradients which, with a steam locomotive can best be met by a larger number of relatively small diameter coupled wheels. On the other hand, the requirements for a high-speed passenger train steam locomotive are best met by large diameter driving wheels.

Since it is necessary to keep the weight of high-speed reciprocating and moving parts down to easily manageable proportions, and because it is necessary for the rigid part of the locomotive chassis to pass round curves with ease, the number of coupled wheels on express passenger locomotives has to be kept within limits – more often six but, rather exceptionally, eight in number. With the most powerful locomotives, poorer quality coal will demand a larger and wider firebox which, because it cannot be contained within the space between the frames and the coupled wheels, will invariably require the added support of a trailing pony truck or bogie. Leading bogies or pony trucks are required at the front end to spread the weight of the locomotive over as many axles as possible, to keep the individual axle weight down and also to guide the locomotive into

curves at speed. This is why the majority of latter day large high-speed passenger steam locomotives tended to have the 4-6-2 wheel arrangement. In contrast, heavy goods engines were invariably of the 2-8-0 or 2-10-0 type and their smaller diameter coupled wheels allowed them to carry boilers with large fireboxes without the necessity for trailing pony or bogie carrying wheels. A short-range medium or lightweight goods engine can be built on an 0-6-0 chassis. If the range of operation is limited to short transfer goods, branch line or shunting duties, sufficient water for the boiler and coal for the firebox need not be carried in a separate tender but can be accommodated on the locomotive chassis in tanks alongside the boiler and a bunker behind the cab. A locomotive intended for very sharp radius curves will, however, need to have the rigid wheelbase as short as possible. This is why many dockyard, colliery or factory shunting locomotives have only four coupled wheels or, if they have six, why they are close coupled.

With most locomotives the reason for their particular shape, style or design becomes obvious once the subject is given some thought. It is certainly no accident or personal whim on the part of the designer that some classes of locomotives had more or less wheels than others, larger or smaller boilers, tenders or side tanks, or the many other distinguishing features which make one type of locomotive different from another. They were designed for a particular purpose and the design that was ultimately evolved was considered to be the most suitable for that purpose, It follows, therefore, that if we want to make our model railway as authentic as possible we have to consider the same factors when we choose a model locomotive for our layout. If we have the space to run heavy main line express passenger trains or long haul mineral or goods trains we can justify having a fleet of large 4-6-0, 4-6-2, 2-8-0 or 2-10-0 tender engines. If, on the other hand, our layout is restricted by the space available and we have to run lighter, smaller trains, we may have to limit our stud of locomotives to smaller 4-6-0, 4-4-0 and 0-6-0 tender engines, or the even more compact tank locomotives of possibly 2-6-4T, 2-6-2T or 0-6-0T designs.

There are, of course, exceptions to these guide lines as there are with most rules. For instance, immediately after World War 2 the Southern Railway started a big engine policy and built a fleet of 4-6-2 locomotives that were designed to operate both heavy main line passenger trains as well as relatively lightly loaded feeder services in the remoter outposts of the Southern Railway system in the West Country. For someone who likes Pacific type locomotives but does not have the space for a large layout this is a golden opportunity to have the best of both worlds since you can build a small country branch line and still operate large locomotives. This is also an illustration of applying knowledge of actual railway operation and drawing from authentic locations and authentic railway practice. If you search hard enough you will most likely find an example of almost anything for which you are looking.

If, as I strongly recommend, you are modelling your railway to represent a particular company or a certain period in time

An example of a short wheelbase 0-4-0ST industrial locomotive shunting the tin works at Wheal Louise.

The LMS 2P 4–4–0 is a nice compact design suitable for a wide range of duties on limited space layouts. The 00 gauge ex-Airfix/Mainline model shown here can be improved by close coupling the engine and tender.

then, if you are to retain an air of authenticity, your choice of locomotives should be further restricted to the types of classes that are representative of that company or could reasonably be expected to be seen in service during the period or in the geographical location you have selected to model. I have already mentioned in Chapter 3 some of the many varieties or types of model railway you can build. The fact that there are so many accounts for the commendably wide range of ready-to-run model railway locomotives that are currently available. Yet, despite this there is still a persistent clamour for more and it is not difficult to understand this when you consider the tremendous number of different

The ubiquitous LMS 'Black 5' as modelled by Len Weal from a DJH 4mm scale kit.

Private owner wagons and new colour schemes added variety to the BR scene. Lima Class 50 'Royal Oak' in Network SouthEast livery. **Below** *HST Inter-City 125 approaching Sandalmouth speeds by a freight working to Dyers End on the MRC 00 gauge layout New Annington.*

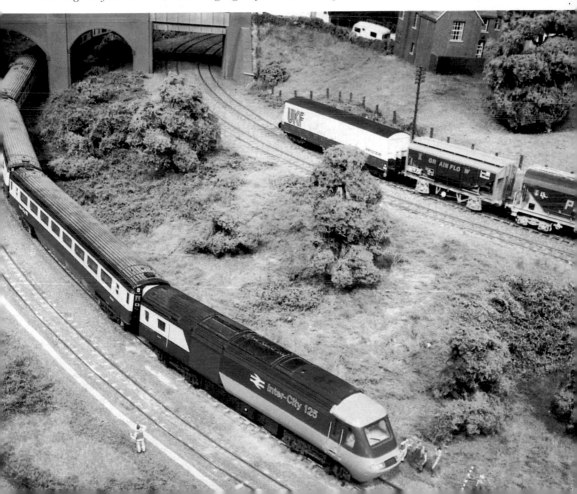

Facing Page *SR Schools Class 900 'Eton' passes a LB&SCR A1X Terrier 2635 on the REC's EM gauge exhibition layout.* (Photo: Peter Parfitt)

This page *BR Britannia 70004 'Iron Duke' with express passenger headlamps roars out of the tunnel on the REC's finescale 00 gauge layout* (Photo: Peter Parfitt)

Above *SBB (Swiss Railways) RBe4/4 railcar and driving trailer overlook the Faller 'Rustic Pavilion' on the HO standard gauge Spindelbahn Region.* **Below** *RhB (Rhatische Bahn) Ge4/4 II No 610 'Viamala' on the HOm Swiss metre gauge layout Bernhardingbahn.*

FO (Furka Oberalp) Ge4/4 III BoBo electric traversing spectacular Swiss mountain scenery on the HOm metre gauge Bernhardingbahn line.

Above *A fleet of Class 33s await their turn of duty on the REC's Recborough & Whittleton N gauge exhibition layout.* (Photo: Peter Parfitt) **Below** *Network SouthEast personified in the Epsom & Ewell Model Railway Club's exhibition layout Westhill Parkway.* (Photo: Philip Reid) **Facing page** *Much research was needed to create this faithful 4mm scale model of Alton station as it was in the 1950s. The white building was demolished to give way to a car park and the goods yard has long since disappeared. M7 30028 awaits departure on a Meon Valley train.* (Photo: Peter Parfitt)

Fitting lights to buildings and rolling stock can pay handsome dividends as can be seen here by these realistic night scenes. The station forecourt at Ashley Bridge and the main station at Wintertal.

locomotive designs and classes there have been in the past and still exist in one way or another today. Many attempts at standardisation and rationalisation have been made by locomotive designers to limit or reduce the number of classes. The trouble with standardisation is that every locomotive designer has his own idea of what should be a standard class. When a change of leadership, ownership or organisation takes place, a new set of standard designs emerges. We thus had the picture in Britain in the 1930s and early '40s of the four main groups, the GWR, LMS, LNER and SR, each attempting to rationalise their stock of locomotives obtained at the grouping and trying to establish a range of standard designs which, when the companies were nationalised to become British Railways, were added to by yet another set of standard designs. Even more variety of motive power came when the diesel locomotives began to emerge in the late 1950s.

It is absolutely impossible for one manufacturer to keep abreast of all developments such as these. Model locomotives are expensive things to produce and the cost of tooling, making moulds and dies, etc., can run into several thousand pounds. All the manufacturers can hope to do is to produce a range of models which, as far as can be judged, will be popular amongst the majority of people and which possibly has been requested by customers. Even so there have been some surprising choices of prototypes and one wonders what thought processes have been responsible for some of them. Some locomotives have more visual appeal than others. Some for reasons unconnected with the hobby attract widescale publicity. The 'Flying Scotsman' is a case in point. Who amongst the general public has not heard of this locomotive? Other locomotives that perhaps are potentially more useful for the railway modeller because they are, or were, to be found all over the railway system and thus can be used on a variety of different duties, are slow to attract the manufacturers' eye. Perhaps the most ubiquitous steam locomotive ever to run on Britain's railways was the LMS 'Black 5' 4-6-0. No less than 842 engines

of this handsome class were built over a period of 16 years from 1934 and they could be seen anywhere on the LMS system, stretching from Wick in Scotland to Bournemouth on the South Coast, on all kinds of duties, passenger as well as freight. As a further incentive for its choice as a model the class had a lifespan covering both pre- and post-nationalisation periods, right up to the very last days of steam on BR in 1967, and no less than 15 locomotives from the class are currently preserved. It was 1973 before a ready-to-run model of one of these locomotives became available in 00 gauge and 1978 before an N gauge version was introduced.

Another oddity, or so it appears to me, is the ex-South Eastern Railway R1 Class, which was selected by Hornby-Dublo as the basis for their model 0–6–0T. Only 13 of these R1 locomotives were ever built and in actual fact there were detailed modifications to the class affecting their appearance which reduced to six the number of actual engines identical with the Hornby-Dublo model. Consequently this class of locomotive was not a very common sight on the Southern Railway, likewise the ex-London Brighton and South Coast Railway E2 0-6-0T, which has been faithfully modelled by Hornby Railways, but was nonetheless a comparatively rare Southern Railway class. Only ten of these locomotives were ever built and there are detailed modifications on this class which reduce the number of engines comparable with the model to five. Furthermore, they were not successful when tried on passenger trains and they spent their time mostly on shunting or short trip freight workings. Not an engine likely to be in great demand by Southern Railways modellers as grateful as they may be for any consideration by manufacturers in this most neglected of railway companies.

I always feel that a railway modeller should have a balanced stud of locomotives which is representative of the company or region which he is modelling. By balanced stud I mean a collection of models of different classes which could commonly be found at the majority of locomotive sheds of the company you have chosen to follow.

Very few GWR layouts can afford to be without one or more 57XX Class Pannier Tanks. The former Mainline Railways 00 gauge version (since produced by Replica Railways and Bachmann) is an extremely faithful model.

Normally speaking a balanced stud is likely to include representatives of the large classes, ie, those which were built in the largest numbers. Some railway companies are easier to cater for in this respect than others. The GWR for example, through its policy of standardisation, had comparatively few basic classes of locomotives but each class was built in large numbers and could be found in most parts of the system. Partly for this reason GWR 00 gauge modellers are well able to build up a balanced stud from the following list of locomotive classes for which ready-to-run models have been produced: King, Castle, County 4–6–0, Hall, Saint, Manor, 28XX 2–8–0, 43XX and 93XX 2–6–0s, County 4–4–0, Collett and Dean Goods 0–6–0S, 61XX and 4575 Prairie Tanks, 56XX 0–6–2T, four types of 0–6–0T Pannier Tanks (2721, 57XX, 8750 and 94XX), 14XX 0–4–2T and, not least, a Diesel Railcar and Parcels Car. Though not a standard GWR locomotive the Dapol Terrier, GWR No 5, could be added to this list.

On the other hand the Southern Railway enthusiast has never been so well served. At the maximum extent, allowing for some items no longer in production, the following is the sum total of 00 gauge ready-to-run models that have appeared over the past 20 or so years; West Country/Battle of Britain 4–6–2, Lord Nelson and King Arthur 4–6–0s, Schools and L1 4–4–0s, M7 0–4–4T, and A1X Terrier, R1 and E2 0–6–0Ts. Thanks be to Hornby Railways for most of these items. Were it not for this manufacturer S.R. 00 gauge modellers would have a very lean time. To a certain extent one can understand the dilemma of manufacturers when faced with the multitudinous classes that made up the Southern Railway. Many of the classes were small in numbers and had a limited regional distribution over the system. There is, however, one class I can think of which ranged wide from Kent to Cornwall and numbered 80 locomotives in the class and that is the N Class Maunsell Mogul. An 00 gauge model is believed to be under consideration.

The LNER is another difficult railway for manufacturers to cater for. In many ways it is similar to the Southern Railway since it

Above *'Springbok' the first of the LNER Class B1 all-purpose 4–6–0s was introduced in 1942. The 4mm scale model shown here in BR livery was made from a Nu-Cast kit. Replica Railways and Bachmann have since introduced 00 gauge ready-to run models of this locomotive.*

Below *As with most SR modellers, kit built locos form the mainstay of the loco stud on Paul Skinner's Ashmouth. The ex LB&SCR 'Gladstone' 0–4–2 in the foreground was made from a GEM kit. The Adams Radial and Brighton Terrier are from K's kits using Airfix 5 pole motors*

also had strong regional tendencies. Large numbers of locomotives from the constituent railway companies continued to be built after the grouping and it was very late in the life of the company before it embarked on a measure of standardisation like the GWR and LMS. In 00 gauge there has been no shortage of express passenger locomotives since no less than three manufacturers chose to produce the A4 Pacific and two the 'Flying Scotsman'. For the middle range of mixed traffic and passenger locomotives there are models of the V2 Green Arrow 2–6–2, B1 and B17/4 4-6-0s and D49/1 Shire 4–4–0. There is then quite a gap in the range of ready-to-run models down to the J39 0-6-0, V1/V3 2–6–2T, N2 0–6–2T and four 0–6–0Ts (J50, J52, J72 and J94). Noticeable absentees are heavy goods locomotives which were very much in evidence on the LNER as they were with most pre-grouping railway companies. Not quite a balanced stud for the LNER but there has been a marked improvement in recent years.

To complete this summary of the big four railway companies in 00 gauge and to turn attentions to the LMS, this company is much better served. Once again we have seen the spectacle of manufacturers choosing to duplicate the models of rival firms so that we have been offered two Duchess 4–6–2s, three unrebuilt Scots (if one model which is under scale is included) and two rebuilt Scots. From there on the list includes a Princess 4–6–2, a Jubilee and a Patriot both rebuilt and original, Black 5, 8F 2–8–0, Crab 2–6–0, Compound and 2P 4–4–0s, 4F 0–6–0, Fowler 2–6–4T, Ivatt 2-6-2T, Jinty 0–6–0 and lastly Caledonian Railway and LYR Pug 0–4–0 Saddle tanks. This is a very well balanced stud from which the majority of LMS enthusiasts can find enough ready to run motive power to operate a representative 00 gauge layout covering most regions of the system and all types of traffic.

Modern traction enthusiasts are fortunate in that there really are no serious gaps in the ranks of 00 gauge ready-to-run diesel and electric locomotives. To list all models which have been produced would include practically all classes currently in service as well as most of those which were introduced by BR and have now been withdrawn from capital stock. The anxiety to produce new models is best illustrated by the Class 58 which entered service on BR after the model was on sale. Manufacturers have at last turned attention to diesel multiple units (DMUs) which have for many years been such a mainstay of BR's services and look to be increasingly so with the newly privatised Train Operating Companies (TOCs). The availability of ready-to-run models is detailed later in this chapter and also in Appendix 5.

The products of at least eight different manufacturers have been included in the foregoing lists of models but clearly it can be seen that the 00 gauge modeller in Britain today can build up a varied stud of locomotives covering most of the popular periods and companies (SR and possibly LNER excepted) in a way that he has never been able to achieve or even dream about before. The added marvel is that all the models are compatible in respect of couplings and wheel and track standards, so that they can all run on one and the same layout together. Furthermore, the universal standards set by manufacturers in their attention to detail, accuracy of outline, paint finish and faithful reproduction of liveries, which have reached such heights of perfection, ensures that no one manufacturer's product looks out of place alongside another. There has been such an improvement in the quality and authenticity of ready-to-run models in recent years that it is to be hoped that, with the important exception of track gauge any vestiges of compromise that were once considered to be necessary in the early days of model railways are gone forever, now it has been shown that these departures from scale which always were of doubtful necessity, can no longer be tolerated by the discerning modeller.

The main European manufacturers catering for the needs of Continental model railway enthusiasts generally show an awareness for a balanced stud of locomotives in

Above *Both Lima and Hornby Railways model the BR Class 37 in 00 gauge. No. D6724 shown here in early BR green livery is based on the Hornby version. It has been converted to EM 18.2 mm gauge and modified to include split headcode boxes and correct bogie side frames from a Kitmaster Deltic.*

Right *A well-balanced stud of German HO locomotive models are seen here in this view of Mike New's Neuenberg.*

Two superbly-finished HO locomotives made from DJH kits by Andy Hart of the SNCF Society:
Above *SNCB (Belgian Railways) Class 1 Pacific on John Rowcroft's Nord Railway La Roche; and*
Below *SNCF (French Railways) Ouest 231-D about to depart from Achaux for Paris.*

(Photo: Andy Hart)

the wide variety of models they produce. To a certain extent the problem has been simplified by the fact that most of the Continental railways were nationalised many years before their British counterparts, thereby achieving a greater degree of standardisation of locomotive classes. Fewer classes of prototype locomotives make it easier for the model manufacturers to cater for majority tastes. Also the fewer the classes the larger they become, thereby giving each

type of locomotive a wider distribution. In Germany, for example, the standard DB class 38 (ex-Prussian P8) 4–6–0 dates back to 1906, whereas in Britain the BR standard 4–6–0s did not appear until 1951. Close to 3,800 locomotives of the DB class 38 4–6–0s were built. Other large German classes include the ex-Prussian G8 0-8-0 which numbered approximately 5,000 and the World War 2 austerity class 52 2-10-0s of which more than 8,000 were built. These massive production totals cannot be matched by any British locomotive class, where quantities of 800 are considered to be high. It follows that the larger the number of locomotives produced in any one class the more common it becomes and the fewer different classes that result makes it much easier for model railway manufacturers to cover the needs of enthusiasts for a balanced stud of locomotives.

By combining the products of Piko, Roco, Fleischmann, Liliput, Marklin, Rivarossi and Trix it is possible in HO gauge to build up a comprehensive stud of German ready-to-run locomotive models. Even in N gauge, German locomotives are well represented, with several different Pacific designs, 2-10-0, 4-6-0, 2-6-2, 2-6-0 and a host of different tank engine classes to choose from, to say nothing of diesel and electric locomotives and railcars. Arnold, Fleischmann, Minitrix and Roco are responsible for most of these. The principle manufacturer of French locomotives in HO scale is Jouef but other suppliers include Fleischmann, Fulgurex, Lima, Metropolitan sa, Roco and Rivarossi. Some British firms notably DJH and K's also produced cast-metal kits of French locomotives. Also in HO, the Italian firms Lima and Rivarossi produce a comprehensive range of Italian locomotives and the Austrian firms Kleinbahn, Liliput and Roco include a representative selection of Austrian locomotives in their international ranges. Swiss locomotive models (some steam outline as well as electric) feature in the catalogues of most European manufacturers including Hag which originates from Switzerland. To complete the Continental picture, several manufacturers include Belgian, Dutch and Swedish locomotives in their ranges and there are just a few Norwegian, Portuguese and Spanish locomotives available. One factor which assists manufacturers catering for Continental modellers is that large numbers of German locomotives were used as reparations after World Wars 1 and 2 and were absorbed into the stock of other railways, such as the French, Belgian and Austrian. In fact, at some time or another,

German locomotives could be seen over practically all the standard gauge lines in Europe.

In America the situation is potentially not so easy as far as steam locomotives are concerned since there were many railway companies which built their own individual designs. Even so, it was the practice of a number of other railroads to buy their locomotives from builders who offered a range of 'standard' designs. This practice has become even more noticeable with the advent of diesel locomotives, and in many cases it is only the livery that distinguishes one railroad company's locomotive from another. Many European and Japanese manufacturers produce ready-to-run models of American prototype locomotives – both steam and diesel – and consequently it is possible, by combining the products of several different manufacturers from within the USA itself, as well as from Japan and Europe, to assemble a comprehensive and representative stud of locomotives for practically any major American railroad. Many railway modellers in the UK have turned to modelling American railroads because the performance of most American outline diesel-electric locomotive models is so good and is often superior to the British outline models to which we are accustomed. This quality comes at a very affordable price, certainly no more than the prices charged for British models and there are several UK dealers from where supplies can be obtained. The best running models take advantage of the Bo-Bo or Co-Co diesel-electric configuration where it makes sense to take advantage of the room available in the model to install a centrally mounted motor with flywheels and a drive system transmitting power to both bogies. Such is not generally available for comparable British models and the Continental European models that are so equipped can be much more expensive. There are of course many other reasons for deciding to model American railroads but the prototypical performance of present day American diesel locomotive models with their sure-

Illustrative of the fine detail incorporated in Japanese built brass models is this GEM (USA) 'Camelback' centre-cab 0–6–0 switcher operating on Bill Lane's Detroit & Mid-Western Railroad.

footed slow speed capabilities together with their excellent value for money can be a persuasive deciding factor.

So far as British prototype railways are concerned, although it is possible to build up a balanced stud of locomotives from ready-to-run products, there are some railway companies not so well blessed or there are some regional locations within the best served companies where it is necessary to resort to constructing your own model to fill in one or more gaps in the stock list. Resort is probably the wrong word to use, however, since we do not make our own model locomotives simply because we need to. The majority of railway modellers also *enjoy* making them.

For many years the traditional method of building model locomotives was to use tinplate, brass or nickel-silver sheet cut, bent and soldered together. For many people this is still the preferred method, but the higher standards of the art demand a fairly fine degree of skill and patience which not all of us possess in sufficient quantities. Fortunately, many of the specialist model railway firms have come to our aid with a

range of locomotive kits which today is truly outstanding. Their numbers are continually being expanded and new firms are entering the field to widen the choice of models even further. Appendix 5 gives a list of representative classes of locomotive from the pre-nationalised railway companies and British Railways, showing what ready-to-run models and/or kits are available in the popular N, TT, 00 and O gauges. It will be seen that, in the most popular 00 gauge at least, the kit manufacturers have filled in most of the gaps in available ready-to-run models left by the larger manufacturers.

Excluding injection moulded plastic for which there are but few kits available, the majority of locomotive kits fall into one of two categories; etched sheet metal (generally brass or nickel-silver) and cast white metal. These categories refer to the predominant material out of which the main 'bodywork' structure of the locomotive, eg the footplate, boiler, smokebox, firebox, cab and tender (or tanks and bunker in the case of a tank locomotive), will be constructed. Most etched brass or nickel-silver kits will include some white-metal castings or maybe turned brass fittings for the chimney dome, safety valve, smokebox door, buffers, etc., and a number of cast white-metal kits may incorporate some etched brass or nickel-silver fittings such as smoke deflectors, valve gear, etc. Chassis components, where supplied, generally take the form of etched brass or nickel-silver frames and stretchers though profile milled brass is one alternative. Cast white-metal chassis are not now so common as they once were. Etched brass or nickel-silver kits usually take the form of one or more frets wherein all the parts have been photo-etched to shape. The photo-etching process also takes care of any relief detail needed as well as score lines on the reverse to assist bending when parts have to be bent to shape. To remove each part from the fret it is necessary to break the small metal tabs which hold them in place. This needs to be done carefully but can be accomplished in a number of different ways, e.g. cutting with a pair of cutting edge pliers or fine hacksaw blade, filing with the edge of a fine needle file, or when sufficient tabs have been removed, bending the part backwards and forwards until the remaining tabs break. A number of these kits are cleverly designed so that parts interlock by means of tabs and slots which is a great advantage when it comes to assembly. It is possible to assemble etched brass or nickel-silver kits

The components of an etched metal kit, in this case the Anchoridge Steam Heritage kit for the LNER K3 2-6-0 with chassis partly assembled.

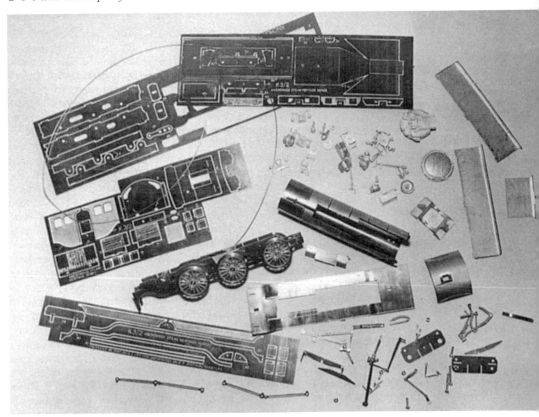

LNER P2 2–8–2 constructed from a Proscale etched brass kit and awaiting a visit to the paint shop.

using cyanoacrylate adhesives such as Loctite Superglue-3 but generally speaking it is more satisfactory to use solder.

It is easy enough to give reassuring advice about soldering and to say that there is really nothing to fear or worry about, but the person who has met with little success in his early pioneering days will take a lot of convincing. Soldering is a knack which can only be mastered after a degree of practice and the best advice I can give is to suggest practising on some scrap pieces of brass, nickel-silver or tinplate before you risk making a mess of a relatively expensive kit. Successful soldering requires that the metal pieces to be joined are both scrupulously clean and they are heated by the soldering iron sufficient to ensure that the solder flows evenly. Should the solder not adhere evenly and perhaps run off in a blob this will in all probability point to the fact that the work pieces need more heat or else they need to be rubbed over with a fine file or emerycloth followed by a further application of flux. Having achieved an even flow of solder into the joint you are making it then becomes essential not to disturb the assembly whilst the solder remains molten after the soldering iron is taken away. Thankfully it takes but a

few seconds for the solder to solidify although the heat will be retained for some considerable period of time after the solder has set. It is perhaps this aspect which is most frustrating to anyone who is more used to assembly by glue or cement since ways and means of holding parts together have to be devised without using the hands and fingers. It is generally possible to improvise a jig using one or more pieces of wood, offcuts left over from making your baseboard for example. It is not possible to describe every situation but each set of circumstances will suggest its own solution. Once an assembly begins to take shape and becomes self supporting the task becomes easier although you do have to take care when soldering further parts to the assembly not to heat it too much so that the solder melts on previously assembled parts. It is, of course, possible to use different types of solder which melt at different temperatures and to make the first prime assembly using the highest melting point solder. However, this usually means using silver solder which is again an art in itself, requiring different techniques from ordinary soft soldering. Possibly the easiest way to solve the problem of having lots of separate parts together in close proximity to each other is to make a series of separate sub-assemblies which can eventually be bolted together. Sub-assemblies such as these can also be an asset when it comes to painting since it is often difficult to get at some parts of a locomotive model after it is completed. The worst part is the underside of the boiler and it is frequently a practical idea to make the boiler, firebox and perhaps smokebox as a separate assembly which can be removed from the running plate and cab. To return to the subject of soft-soldering again, there is no value in leaving large blobs of solder at a join between assembled parts unless you are deliberately trying to fill up space or build up sufficient thickness of material for subsequent shaping, eg the front corners of a belpaire firebox. Large blobs of solder do not necessarily add strength to the join. It is far more desirable to give the parts to be assembled an overall thin coating of solder (referred to as tinning), which will fuse together when the two parts are brought into contact and the

hot iron applied. Only a little additional solder is then needed to complete the joint.

One of the advantages of solder is that it is much quicker than glueing. The solder 'sets' in seconds as soon as it cools, whereas most glues take quite a long while to set thoroughly and there is a danger all the time that the parts may be disturbed and become misplaced. After a soldered joint has set it is a pleasure to clean up with a file and emery cloth and to feel the solid construction of the finished assembly. Finally the model should be washed and scrubbed in mild detergent to remove all traces of the solder flux and metal dust which is liable to lurk in unsuspecting places and will only reappear when a paint brush is brought to bear! There is little doubt that there is a great deal of satisfaction in handling a model constructed from sheet nickel-silver or brass and, if not to begin with, I recommend you to try your hand some time at locomotive building this way.

Despite their superficial similarity there were a number of different classes of GWR pannier tanks. Larger driving wheels (5ft 2in) and auto-gear for working push-pull trailer cars distinguished the 54XX Class. Shown here is No 5412 modelled in O gauge from a Castle Kits cast metal kit. (Photo: Peter Parfitt)

The LMS ex MR 'Flatiron' 0–6–4T is one of a number of Southeastern Finecast cast metal kits designed to fit proprietary ready-to-run chassis, in this case the Wrenn ex-Hornby-Dublo R1 0–6–0T.

When you do decide to build your first sheet nickel-silver locomotive, whether from a kit or from your own home-cut parts, it is a good idea to choose a simple locomotive design preferably one with a straight running plate without drop ends and with a parallel boiler. Taper boilers can be a bit troublesome to a beginner, whereas parallel boilers need be nothing more than a length of brass tubing—and it is sometimes possible to find tubing of exactly the right diameter. Tank locomotives often provide suitable prototypes for beginners since the large flat area of the tank and the bunker sides forms a solidly constructed unit which can be jigged up between blocks of wood during assembly to facilitate soldering. A perfectly flat surface, such as a sheet of plate glass, is a great aid to accurate assembly.

The choice of a simple straightforward locomotive design is also recommended for your first attempt at assembling one of the cast metal locomotive kits. The type that has been designed to fit on a proprietary chassis is perhaps the best since you will not have the added worry of getting the chassis to

work properly. Another modification you may need to make is changing the driving coupled wheels. This may arise because you need to fit wheels of a different size or, if you are making use of an older chassis with course standard wheels, you will have need to replace them with finer scale wheels. Romford wheels are ideal replacements but their axles are smaller in diameter than Hornby Railways. However, special brass bushes are available to enable such a conversion to be carried out, and most model railway retailers stock them. The Hornby Railways wheels can be removed by knocking out the axle from the wheel. I have an old nail with the pointed end cut off which I use together with a light hammer to tap out the axle. This can be done fairly easily, provided you give support to the chassis frame as close as you can either side of the axle. Extra resistance will be felt with the driving axle since this also needs to be knocked out of the worm wheel. It is even more important to ensure that the chassis frame is well supported for this operation, otherwise it is all too easy to bend and ulti-

Above *The Grange Class was a firm favourite of GWR locomen but none of the engines has been preserved. Shown here is a fine 4mm scale model of No. 6868 'Penrhos Grange' made from a Premier (ex-M&L) body kit fitted to a Mainline 'Manor' 4–6–0 chassis.*

(Photo: Peter Parfitt)

Above right & right *Two 2–6–2T locomotives from the Nu-Cast range of 4 mm scale cast metal kits; LNER V1 No 465 and LMS Stanier 3P No 165. No. 165 was actually made from a Cotswold kit before this manufacturer's range was acquired by Nu-Cast. Bachmann have since introduced a ready-to-run 00 gauge model of the LNER V1.*

mately break it. I have found in practice that it is rare to find all axles revolving freely in their bushes immediately they are inserted, and it is often necessary to bore out one or more of the holes very slightly to overcome a tight spot. The boring out can be done quite easily with the tapered handle end of a file, but take care to ensure that the hole is bored out evenly and is not enlarged too much. Finally, a small piece of very fine emery cloth wrapped round a length of rodding, dowel or stout wire, inserted into the bush and twisted a few times will ensure a smooth bearing surface to present the very minimum resistance to the axle. In case you think this is too crude, which I admit it is, the preferred method is to use a ⅛ in diameter parallel reamer and a tap wrench but these two little items will cost around £10. It rather depends on how many locomotive chassis you wish to make but money spent on tools is always a good investment.

As anyone will find out when they strip down a Hornby Railways six-coupled chassis, the coupling rods are fitted rather ingeniously in that the coupling rod is only held in place by means of a 10BA bolt to the centre driving wheel. In the case of the leading and trailing wheels, the crank pins are fixed to the coupling rod and simply fit loosely into the wheel faces. If you wish to retain this system there is normally adequate material in the Romford wheels to drill out the relatively large crank pin holes to take the Hornby Railways types. A No 51 drill is required for the front and rear wheels and a No 54 drill for the centre driving wheel. No 54 is the correct size for tapping out a 10BA thread to replace the Hornby Railways crank pin screws. Some kits take a proprietary chassis without modification, whereas others require the chassis to be adapted in some way, possibly involving the removal of certain areas of the die-cast metal chassis block. In many cases this is easily enough done with a hacksaw blade, but it is sometimes preferable to strip the chassis first to avoid damaging the wheels and motion and to ensure that no metal dust from the hacksaw gets into the commutator of the electric

motor. If you do dismantle a proprietary chassis in this way remember to make some notes as you unscrew each nut and bolt and remove each part so that you know where they go back again when the time comes to reassemble them. It is also a wise precaution to have a small box or container at hand so that the parts can be put in straight away without fear of losing any.

The parts in most cast metal kits require a great deal of cleaning up and preparation before they can be assembled. Very often 'flash' from the casting process needs to be removed and marks where the two halves of the casting mould were brought together need to be cleaned up. In some cases parts have also to be bent flat or straight and this can be done easily since the metal is relatively soft and responds well to careful manipulation. The parts should be held firmly and only a slight deflection made at any one time, gradually applying even pressure so that the parts are eventually brought back to shape. It is very important that parts which should be assembled vertically are, in fact, vertical. Cabs on locomotives are a notoriously bad spot for this since any lean forward or backward at this point, however small is immediately noticeable and stands out like a sore thumb.

Sometimes you will find that certain parts do not fit together very well. This may be due to bad design or it may be that they have shrunk or become distorted after removal from the mould. It will depend on each individual case, but you should be prepared to do some filing or trimming with a knife to get some parts to fit properly. Always be careful when faced with problems such as this, for you may be trying to fit the wrong two parts together! Parts often look very much alike and the illustration in the instruction sheet may not be all that helpful. I cannot emphasise too strongly the necessity to study the instruction sheet carefully and check the fit of *all* parts before you actually start to fix any two of them permanently. It has been known for instruction sheets to make mistakes and this is another reason why I consider it necessary to go through a dummy run with *all* parts. If you come across any snags and it is late in the day it is sometimes a good thing to go to bed at this point. The solution to assembly problems can become crystal clear in the morning!

Assembly of cast metal kits can be accomplished in a number of different ways. The most common method is to use a clear cellulose adhesive. I have some models assembled in this way which have been in use for 20 years or more and they are still perfectly sound today, largely I suspect because a number of parts on such kits are designed to interlock with each other, thereby adding strength to the joins. But in cases where moving parts or those under stress are involved (for example fixing points where the body is connected to the locomotive chassis) I recommend the use of something stronger, such as an epoxy resin adhesive or the special type of low melting point solder which is available for use with cast metal kits. One of the objections to epoxy resin adhesive has been that it takes time to cure or set, particularly because the parts cannot be heated in the oven as the adhesive instructions recommend since the heat would simply melt the cast metal. However,

there are fast set epoxy adhesives available that have the advantage of holding parts together after approximately five minutes before being left to cure finally. There are also the latest cyanoacrylate adhesives such as Loctite Super Glue-3 and Slater's Plastikard Cyanobond 'Kung-Fu Glue' which as previously mentioned can also be used for sheet metal as well as cast white metal kits. I am still a bit wary about these glues, having heard some awful tales about what they can do, but with a little practice you soon get used to them and avoid the all important thing of not getting the stuff on your hands. I prefer to use cyanoacrylate adhesives on fitting smaller parts such as footplate steps but definitely not chimneys, domes and safety valves where I like to take my time and stand back to view the model to make sure they are upright from all angles. For those who prefer soldering, and most people do once they have broken the ice, special low melting point solder and a 12 volt iron which can be controlled by a normal model railway power unit take the worst headaches out of the job. Be careful though, since a cast metal kit can turn into a pool of virtually valueless molten metal quicker than the time

The LMS 'Crab' 2–6–0 was a distinctive but wide-ranging mixed traffic locomotive with great appeal to LMS modellers. No 2743 shown here was made from a DJH kit. Graham Farish have since introduced a ready-to-run N gauge model of this locomotive.

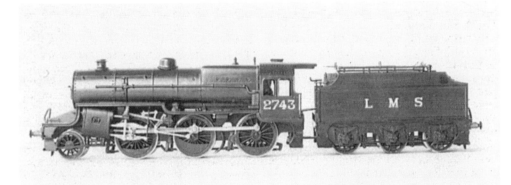

it took you to hand over the cash to pay for it, so if you are in doubt about your soldering ability, stick to glue! On the other hand, once the technique has been mastered, a soldered cast metal kit is quicker to assemble and is unlikely ever to come apart, provided it has been carefully made.

There is a great deal more to building locomotives from cast metal kits than simply sticking them together. The finished assembly also needs a lot of attention to fill in cracks and gaps between parts and the minute blow holes or pit marks that sometimes appear on the surface. I have used a proprietary brand of wood stopping paste known as 'Brummer' stopping for all such jobs, and since the tin I bought many years ago is still going strong I see no point in changing to any other method! The paste is soluble in water and, since only very little is required each time, I find it satisfactory to wet the end of the finger and transfer the paste on the finger tip to the locomotive body where it can be rubbed in. Sometimes a craft knife blade or the end of a screwdriver can be used to get at areas which cannot be reached by your fingers. The paste dries reasonably quickly, after which it can be smoothed down to provide an almost indiscernable cover to a badly fitting join, hole or gap in the cast metal parts. There are also several proprietary putties or body filling pastes such as Isopon which are useful for filling in the larger gaps and even for building up extra detail.

It is advisable to inspect the assembled body again after the first undercoat to ensure that there are no imperfections in the surface or at any of the joins and that the stopping paste or putty filling has been thoroughly smoothed into the surrounding surfaces. Boiler mountings also need special attention when assembling cast metal kits. Apart from the obvious necessity to fix them upright, the flare at the base of the chimney or dome often needs special attention to ensure that it blends in perfectly with the top of the boiler and that the flare itself is kept as thin and as unobtrusive as it is on the prototype. For detail points such as these it is essential to have as many good photographs of the full size locomotive you are modelling as you can lay your hands on and also at least one detailed drawing. Gathering facts around you of the locomotives and rolling stock you think you may one day want to build is one of the fascinations of the model railway hobby. Squabbles do arise from time to time about the accuracy of published drawings, but on the whole the hobby is well served with prototype information and new drawings appear regularly in the model railway press.

It is, of course, perfectly possible to assemble a model railway locomotive kit without the use of prototype drawings and photographs but if you want to make a really authentic job then drawings and photographs are essential. The range of drawings produced by the late John E. Skinley are perhaps the best known. The Ian Allan books of locomotive, carriage and wagon drawings in 4 mm scale are also good value for money and, although at first glance you may think that you will never need all the drawings in these books you will be surprised at the inspiration they will give and the pleasant hours you can spend studying them. For accurate and authentic models you simply cannot have too much prototype information.

One of the big advantages with cast metal kits over any other form of locomotive body building is their weight. This can be demonstrated easily if you care to make one of these locomotive kits that fit to a proprietary chassis and compare the performance of the chassis fitted with the original plastic body with its capabilities when fitted to the new cast metal one. The extra weight provides greater adhesion and hauling capacity and often has a beneficial effect on the noise of the motor and gear train, which in turn creates the illusion of smoother, silent power. It is not an exaggeration to say that cast metal locomotive kits have revolutionised model railways. They have vastly extended the scope and variety of locomotives beyond the ready-to-run models and they have made scratch-building possible to anyone with average manual dexterity.

Some people despise cast metal kits because of the thickness of the parts. With one or two exceptions I fail to see the justification for this since it is an easy matter to taper to a scale thickness the visible ends of such parts as cab roofs, smoke deflectors and tender sides. Note that I say the visible ends, since it is only the edges of these parts that can be seen and it is only at these points that any thinning is really necessary. The parts can be tapered to a scale thickness at the edge without detracting from the appearance or weakening the structure in any way. It surely does not matter that a cab roof is not the scale thickness throughout the whole of its length since it will, after all, only be the edge that is seen. One advantage with cast metal as opposed to plain sheet metal parts is the relief detail that can be incorporated. Etched brass kits are, of course, the exception. This is perhaps a little overdone in some cases, and on certain models rivets look more like saucepan lids. However, where they do offend they can always be removed and the state of the art is improving all the time so we may be spared these oversize details in time. It is a funny thing how points like this always look worse in photographs. In actual fact, over-scale relief detail is much more bearable than photographs would have us believe.

When it comes to building model locomotives, plastic has not had the same revolutionary effect on railway modelling as it has for example in the field of solid scale model aeroplanes, where there is a vast range of constant scale plastic kits available at commendably low prices. The accuracy and attention to detail in these plastic aeroplane kits show a degree of sympathy for the prototype on the part of the designer, tool maker and manufacturer which is not so apparent in all cases in comparable locomotive kits. Plastic is, however, very

Whereas the GWR 56XX Class 0–6–2Ts were more frequently seen operating in South Wales, preserved examples have now spread as far as North Yorkshire. This ex-Mainline Railways 00 gauge model has been given a repaint, new lettering and number plates and some added details.

successfully used for complete ready-to-run model locomotive bodies and I see no basic reason why it should not be more widely used for kits and home construction work. However, the cost of tooling-up being what it is, manufacturers – if they are to be commercial – are only interested in models which will have very wide sales. Unfortunately, many locomotives that would form ideal subjects for models are not million-sellers. Such plastic locomotive kits that do appear on the market sometimes have a limited production run so I recommend you to buy as many as you think you are likely to need when you see them. As straightforward static models they can be made to look attractive on the mantlepiece or railway bookshelf, or they can be displayed in or around the locomotive depot on the model railway itself. In many cases they can also be motorised using special adaptor kits for the locomotive chassis, by modifying an existing proprietary model locomotive chassis or, in the case of a tender locomotive, by fitting a motorised chassis into the tender. This form of tender drive is frequently adopted by manufacturers of ready-to-run models, the advantage being that one basic design of motor unit can be used to power a variety of different locomotives. Most locomotive tenders are capacious enough to take a fair amount of ballast weight as well as the motorised chassis itself. Ballast weight for adhesion is a factor which has to be given serious consideration with plastic-bodied locomotives, and as much weight as possible should be inserted in the body above the traction wheels.

As well as making attractive models in their own right, many plastic locomotive kits are capable of modification or conversion into other prototypes. In any case, practically all plastic model locomotive kits are capable of improvement by the constructor and it is seldom good enough to make the model straight as it comes in the kit. Some of the details I mentioned with regard to cast metal kits also apply to plastic kits, eg attending to the flash which sometimes adheres as a result of the moulding process,

and the marks where the two halves of the mould have come together. These blemishes, and any others, should be thoroughly cleaned up before you commence assembly. Also the thick visible edges of cab roofs and sides, smoke deflectors and the tender body (as I mentioned with cast metal kits) can all be reduced in thickness to near scale proportions without weakening the structure in any way. Most of the former Airfix kits made a point of moulding the lining detail on the body parts. I always think it is rather like moulding RAF roundels on the wings of an aircraft model and I am sure aeromodellers would soon be up in arms about that. The lining detail is fairly easily removed, although in one or two cases care has to be taken not to erase other detail which *is* wanted. I have found a ¼ in wood chisel to be my best tool for removing moulded plastic lining. Such a tool would be ideal for removing the colour separation bands on the earlier Hornby Railways' models of the Class 47.

A desirable modification which can be made to some plastic ready-to-run and kit model locomotives is to fit wire handrails instead of the solid plastic one moulded on to the model. With ready-to-run models the problem is not so persistent as it used to be since the manufacturers that erred in this respect have come to appreciate the improvement that separate wire handrails make. Most new models are being introduced with this feature and there has been at least one case where a model was originally produced with solid handrails and has now been modified. However, where you do wish to replace old solid plastic handrails it is necessary first to remove them (once again the ¼ in chisel is useful for this), and drill holes in which can be fitted either the specially made metal or plastic handrail knobs produced by some manufacturers or else the handrail split pins which are also available from most model railway suppliers. Split pins are not everyone's favourite but they do have the advantage of being adjustable so that the space behind the handrail can be varied to suit any location.

The M & L Premier conversion kit was used by Robert Tivendale to convert the Mainline Railways GWR Mogul to one of the later 93XX series with side window cab. Bachmann have since introduced a ready-to-run 00 gauge model of this locomotive.

Furthermore, they are easy to fix simply by spreading the split ends inside the body and holding in place with a spot of epoxy adhesive. I have found they can corrode if a water based fixer such as Polyfilla is used. Handrail wire is available from model railway retailers and can be bent easily with fingers and pliers. On a locomotive boiler handrail, remember to thread on whatever handrail knobs or pins you require for the front of the smokebox before you fit the handrail wire into the knobs or pins alongside the boiler. I suggest that you cut the wire overlength and drill a couple of holes, one each side of the cab spectacle plate, to take the loose ends of the wire. The wire can then be bent inside the cab to hold it securely in place. Not all handrails are secured by knobs and many are simply 'U'-shaped pieces of wire. When fitting handrails such as these it is advisable to bend over the ends of the wire behind the assembly, thereby fixing the wire firmly in place. If the spread-over ends of the wire are also sealed by a piece of plastic card or dabbed with a spot of epoxy adhesive they should withstand handling.

One of the finest finishing touches for a locomotive is the fitting, where appropriate, of the correct type of engraved metal name and/or number plate. These sometimes appear expensive items but the improvement they make cannot be measured in monetary terms. There is such a wide range available from a variety of different manufacturers that few retailers can be expected to stock them all but most good shops keep a fair selection. Some proprietary brands are available already trimmed to the correct size and shape but there are others where this has to be done with scissors and a file. This is no great problem as the metal is thin and cuts easily but care needs to be taken, especially with curved nameplates, since they can distort easily. When filing, it helps to handle the plates with a good quality pair of tweezers placed close to the edge being filed. It is preferable to fix the plates with an epoxy adhesive which will enable you to manipulate the plate into exactly the right position before the adhesive sets. In the case of metal models, soldering is not recommended nor necessary Where a nameplate has to be fixed on edge to the top of a splasher it is advisable to stick the plate to a concealed backing plate in the form of a piece of plastic which can in turn be cemented to the splasher top.

In talking about plastic locomotives we have so far only mentioned ready-to-run models and plastic kits. Another medium which can also be used with great success in locomotive body building is plastic card, or styrene sheet as it is sometimes referred to. This is an excellent raw material for making cab side sheets, tender bodies, belpaire fire-boxes, coupled wheel splashers, tanks and bunkers for tank locomotives or any number of different features. Admittedly working parts in plastic are not suitable for serious or prolonged use in model locomotives but, as we have shown earlier, it is perfectly possible to combine a plastic locomotive body with a metal chassis. It is also possible to combine plastic and metal together in the case of body parts. Such fittings as chimneys, domes, safety valves, buffers, name and number plates, handrails, smokebox doors, handbrake columns, etc., which are produced in metal by various model railway accessory firms and which are usually readily available from most retailers, are quite capable of being fitted to an otherwise all plastic model. Even a piece of brass or copper tubing can be used to represent the boiler. In fact, it is probably worthwhile having an item such as the boiler made out of metal to give added strength and rigidity to the finished model, though plastic card is well capable of standing up on its own right. It is possible, using laminations of two or more sheets of plastic card, to make a very robust structure and you are nearly always able to hide bracing struts and reinforcements behind the assembly and out of view. Before the days of plastic card I once made a GWR 57XX Pannier Tank from ordinary card of the sort used for filing cards and postcards and reinforced the model with 1 mm plywood and ⅛ in obeche. A liberal coat of shellac afterwards ensured a pretty strong model which, because of the solid square-shaped construction of the Pannier Tanks, lasted for quite a long while. The body

outlasted the mechanism, in fact! Although the 4 mm scale model was only wood and card I was able to ballast it with lead shot and it turned the scales at 12½ oz. I would suggest not being the least bit shy about using unorthodox materials for locomotive building. Use those materials you find best, since it is more likely you will meet with success that way. A good plastic or plastic card model can often fool the expert—if not at close quarters, at least at the usual distance from which you view a model on someone else's layout.

So far I have said little about locomotive chassis construction other than to mention the possibility of adapting proprietary ready-to-run chassis in some cast metal kits. For the out and out beginner this is a safe and reassuring introduction to locomotive kit building. You can concentrate on the bodywork and, provided you make a reasonable job of it and mate it to the chassis in accordance with the manufacturer's instructions you have the confidence of knowing that at the end of the day the model will perform at least as well as the proprietary model from which the chassis came. As previously mentioned, it might even run better due to the added weight of the cast metal body. If you make a mess of the kit you still have the chassis which can be rejoined with its original body if it came with one—the loss of the kit can be put down to experience.

Kit manufacturers have shown great ingenuity in adapting proprietary ready-to-run chassis to different models and they continue to exploit the possibilities whenever new ones become available but, unfortunately, there is a limit to the number of locomotive classes that can be built this way. The main constraint is the length of the wheelbase and the spacing of the driving and coupled wheels. The wheel spacing of locomotives can vary considerably from one class to another and it is inevitable that the range of ready-to-run chassis available is insufficient to provide for every variation of wheel spacing required. Any departure from scale dimensions in the chassis will be transmitted above the running plate which can lead to unacceptable distortion of the body or superstructure. Most affected are likely to be the wheel splashers which may have to be enlarged or displaced to accommodate the incorrectly spaced wheels or it could be that the dimensions of the boiler and firebox have to be adjusted to fit the motor or the cab side sheets realigned relative to the rear coupled wheel. Such dodges are more easily tolerated in N gauge where a greater degree of compromise is accepted partly due to the fact that it is less noticeable in such a small scale but also because the concept of building N gauge chassis is not so well developed as in the larger scales. In 4mm and 7mm scales there are now so many aids to model locomotive chassis construction there is no need to depart from prototype dimensions. Practically all kit manufacturers supply chassis parts where needed either included in the kit or available as separate items. K's who were one of the first to introduce cast whitemetal locomotive kits in this country have always made a feature of supplying everything needed; chassis frames, spacers, wheels, gears, electrical pick-ups and motors, all their own manufacture. Other kit manufacturers may not always supply the wheels, gears and motor but this will be made clear at the point of sale and most retailers will be able to supply the recommended additional items when the kit is purchased.

In view of the wide range of chassis kits and parts now available in 4mm and 7mm scales there is hardly any necessity as there once was to scratch build locomotive chassis from basic raw materials. There is nothing to stop you doing so if you wish but the effort involved is rarely worth the saving in cost unless you are working to a tight budget. At one time the established method of constructing locomotive chassis was to use strip brass for the frames, in 00 gauge ½ inch x 1/16 inch was the size commonly used. Nowadays much thinner material, around 20 thou, is generally preferred in which case it is necessary to insert brass bushes in the axle holes to act as wheel bearings. Such items are available from suppliers. Before turning attention to the chassis frame members it is suggested the coupling rods are made up first out of nickel-silver strip. The spacing of the crank pin holes in the coupling rods can then be used as a template for drilling pilot holes for the axles in the chassis frame members. This will ensure that the axle hole centres will exactly match the crank pin centres which is essential to avoid the coupling rods binding when they revolve. The pilot holes can afterwards be drilled the correct size for the axles or wheel bearings. Accurate pairing of the coupling rods and the chassis frame members will also be achieved if each pair is temporarily soldered together, face to faces before drilling Any other holes needed such as frame spacer bolt holes can also be drilled at the same time. Whether you are constructing a locomotive chassis from scratch or assembling one from a kit it is essential to maintain accurate pairing of the two chassis frame members during the course of construction so that from whatever angle the chassis is viewed – top, bottom, side, front or rear – the axle holes are dead in line and parallel to each other. Lengths of suitable diameter rodding such as some knitting needles, inserted in the axle holes provide a reliable visual aid.

The normal method of assembling the chassis is to bolt or solder the two side frames to a pair of frame spacers, one at each end of the chassis and perhaps a third one amidships on which to locate the electric motor. In 4 mm scale these frame spacers are available from model railway stockists and, since they are relatively cheap, they can be recommended as a worthwhile timesaver. The fore and aft frame spacers can also form fixing points for the body and this should be borne in mind when determining the position of the spacers. The gear wheel should be mounted on the driving axle before the frames are assembled. The placing of the third spacer will be determined by the position of the motor, which in turn will be partly dictated by the position of the driving axle and gear wheel. It is assumed that before they have reached the

Above *The unique LSWR 4–2–4T combined engine and carriage makes a fine model in O gauge.*
Below *Equally full of character is the SR (ex LSWR) Beattie 2–4–0 well tank remarkably well modelled in 3 mm scale by John Bateman.*

(Photos: Peter Parfitt and Geoff Helliwell)

stage of building their own locomotive chassis most modellers will have had some experience of proprietary ready-to-run models. You can learn most of what you need to know from examining these chassis; for example, the positioning of the motor, the gears, the electrical pick-up, body fixing points, cylinders and valve gear, etc. Basically all you are trying to do when making your own chassis is to fabricate the frame out of sheet or strip brass instead of a die-cast metal block as produced by the commercial manufacturers.

The forementioned refers to the construction of a rigid chassis such as used by commercial manufacturers of ready-to-run models and most kit manufacturers. However, this type of chassis no longer commands respect amongst serious modellers who seek means of emanating the characteristics of full sized locomotives whereby the wheels are sprung to overcome irregularities in the track. There is nothing new in the idea of springing model locomotive chassis. John Athern outlined all the arguments currently in vogue in his classic book *Miniature Locomotive Construction* originally published by Percival Marshall & Co Ltd in 1948 but now alas believed to be out of print. What has happened in more recent years is that the introduction of finer scale modelling such as 18.83mm gauge in 4mm scale has spurred the development of flexible sprung chassis out of necessity. It will be readily appreciated that a rigid chassis with unsprung wheels is not the ideal vehicle to traverse trackwork that can in some cases be anything but perfectly flat. Whilst every effort is or ought to be made to ensure the top surfaces of the rails are level there are bound to be places such as at the top and bottom of gradients, at the crossing 'v' of points and turnouts, etc., where this cannot be guaranteed. Any undulation in the track can result in one or more wheels being momentarily suspended above the surface of the rails. With the finer scale flanges now being adopted the flange may lift clear of the rail leading to a derailment. Of even greater significance since it applies to all wheels

whatever standard they are designed to, continuity of the electrical supply through the locomotive wheels will be broken. Most starting and stalling problems are caused by one or more wheels not being in proper contact with the track, particularly so over points and crossings, and the efficiency of an electrically propelled model locomotive which relies on picking up current through the wheels suffers as a consequence. The effects of this can be offset by adding pick-ups to the bogie, pony and tender wheels but this is not an option that can be applied to a 0-6-0 or 0-4-0 tank locomotive. 'Flexible' or sprung chassis will overcome all these problems and it cannot be denied that they are the way to the future. In 4mm scale, 18.83mm gauge, they are essential.

There are two main contenders amongst the various ideas for flexible chassis; sprung chassis whereby each wheel is individually sprung in similar fashion to full size locomotives or, compensated chassis whereby the vertical movement of the wheels and axles within the chassis frame is controlled by a system of pivoted compensating beams. Thankfully, it is not always essential to spring the driving axle, i.e. the axle geared to the motor, since both systems will work satisfactorily with one rigid axle in the chassis frame. However, it is necessary for the coupling rods to be jointed for anything larger than a four-coupled locomotive but this can be effected by pivoting the coupling rods on the crank pins which is easy to accomplish. There is an abundant range of parts available for either system from specialist suppliers. Required reading on the subject of compensated chassis is Mike Sharman's profusely illustrated booklet *Flexichas – A Way to Build Fully Compensated Model Locomotive Chassis* published by the Oakwood Press. As a means of gaining practical experience in building a compensated model locomotive chassis I can well recommend one of the many kits supplied by Perseverance Models. These contain all the parts needed to construct the chassis frame and coupling rods (wheels, gears and motor are supplied separately) for any of the three recognised

4mm scale track gauges; 16.5mm (00), 18.2mm (EM) of 18.83mm (P4/S4). An interesting feature regarding the chassis kits produced by this firm is that some of their kits are designed to replace the chassis in some proprietary ready-to-run models–a complete reversal of the concept of a body kit designed to be fitted to a proprietary ready-to-run chassis!

One piece of advice I would like to mention, born out of painful experience, is to make thoroughly sure whenever you are building a model locomotive, either from scratch or from a kit, that you keep a constant running check throughout every stage of construction that the body fits comfortably on the chassis. Whenever possible, make the chassis first and tailor the body to fit. I would certainly not attempt to make the body first without having the chassis parts available to check it against. One of the easiest mistakes to make is to forget that the boiler is round. You line up a mechanism alongside a scale drawing to check that the motor will fit inside the boiler, forgetting that the square corners of the motor will not fit inside the curvature of the topmost part of the boiler. Allowance must also be made for the brush gear, electrical wiring, TV suppressor, etc., on the motor and for any projections inside the body, such as handrail knobs or split pins. Some locomotive bodies are a very tight fit on the chassis, with limited clearance around the motor, and a cast metal body or metal projections inside a plastic body can easily cause a short circuit by coming into contact with the motor. To avoid this danger it is often a wise move to stick some insulating or self-adhesive tape inside the body at any point where there is the likelihood of contact being made, for it is difficult if not impossible to check thoroughly what is happening when the body is in place on the chassis. One way of finding out is to stick some Plasticine inside the body, fit the body to the chassis, then remove it and note the impression the motor has made on the Plasticine. One of the last features to fit to the body might well be the smokebox front, since it is sometimes pos-

sible to see through the front of the boiler whether or not all is well.

I would also suggest that you concentrate on the main assembly first of all and leave the smaller details such as steps and boiler mountings until last. For one thing they can be knocked off when working on other parts of the model, but with the footplate steps the particular trouble is that they can so easily foul the wheels. The leading bogie or pony wheels are the most troublesome, and on some locomotives where the clearance is particularly tight at these points it may be necessary to reposition the steps or leave them off entirely. The trouble only shows itself as a rule when the locomotive is travelling round a curve, and of course the sharper the curve the worse the trouble is likely to be. Some manufacturers overcome this by fixing the steps to the bogie, but you want to try and avoid these artificial dodges as far as you can. With boiler mountings, chimney, dome and safety valve, it is so essential to have these fittings dead upright and I always leave their assembly as long as possible so that the finished model can be set up and viewed from all angles.

So far I have made no mention of diesel or electric locomotives, and any reference to locomotive building until now has been concerned with steam outline models. I realise that many people find great attraction in the latest forms of motive power and

either combine diesels with their steam loco-motives or else concentrate entirely on diesel or electric locomotives. The writer has had no practical experience of scratch-build-ing a diesel outline model locomotive and there seems little point in introducing the subject since the railway modeller is so well served by the trade. This is particularly the case for British modellers in 00 gauge. There are no significant locomotive classes in British Rail's diesel locomotive fleet, past or present, that are not available either ready-to-run or in kit form, or in most cases both. However, there is considerable scope for the constructive outlet by way of adding varia-tions, improved detail and conversions from one class to another based on ready-to-run models. There have been many articles in all the model railway magazines showing where and how this can be done and there are specialist suppliers who cater for this need by supplying added detail kits, parts and fittings. Perhaps the single most signifi-cant of these is flush-glazed cab windows which can make such striking visual impact on the appearance of a diesel outline model. BR broke out of the mould of their one-time all embracing blue livery some time ago and now, following privatisation, there are even more prototype painting and insignia varia-tions that can be applied to add individu-ality to ready-to-run models. N gauge modellers are not as well off as their 00 brethren but new models are appearing thanks mainly to Graham Farish and there are very few BR diesel locomotives which are not available, either ready-to-run or in kit form. Details will be found in Appendix 5. In O gauge it is understandable there have been few ready-to-run models but it is worth searching for the former Tri-ang 'Big Big Train', later Novo Toys, Class 35 Hymek and the Lima Class 33. Some O gauge diesel locomotive kits are available and their numbers appear to be growing.

Continental and American modellers in N and HO gauges are also very well served with ready-to-run diesel outline locomotive models covering a wide variety of types from most European and American railways. Electric railways working on the overhead catenary system are far more extensive on the Continent than they are in Britain and this is reflected in the catalogues of Continental manufacturers of model railway equipment. I am able to account for no less than 165 different ready-to-run HO gauge models representing over a hundred differ-ent classes of electric locomotives. Truly a staggering figure. Some electric locomotives

The distinctive appearance of the Class 309 EMU's built for the ER Clacton service is well portrayed in these 00 gauge models constructed from MTK kits by Roger Matthews.

London Transport are of course extensive users of EMUs. This 4mm scale model has been made from one of a range of LT tube stock kits produced by Pirate Models.

have endeared themselves to enthusiasts and in some cases to the public at large in much the same way as steam locomotives. The Swiss 'Crocodile' articulated 1-C + C-1 locomotives with their outside coupling rods and jack shafts are perhaps the most famous and on the other side of the Atlantic the stylised Pennsylvania Railroad Class GG1 2-Co + Co-2 became a classic design. Contemporary with the GG1 the German Class E18 (latterly DB Class 118) 1–Do–1 established the same sort of niche in Continental eyes. The DB Class 194 Co-Co is now very much the centre of attention now that the 118s have all been withdrawn. All these designs (all available as commercial models in various gauges from Z to O) show marked variations in outward design, wheel arrangement etc. Nowadays there is greater uniformity in the basic configuration of electric locomotives most being mounted on powered 4-wheel or 6-wheel bogies (Bo-Bo or Co-Co as these are referred to). Notwithstanding this uniformity in basic design there are many subtle variations in style and many more obvious variations in liveries to mark one country's design from

another. A train journey across Continental Europe can provide infinite variety in motive power, all available in model form at least so far as HO gauge is concerned. In contrast to this there are far fewer British overhead catenary electric locomotives to be modelled the principal ones being the Classes 81 – 87 Bo Bo's built for the LMR West Coast main line and the East Coast route Classes 90-91. Details of all BR electric locomotive classes currently modelled in kit or ready-to-run form can be found in Appendix 5. Sadly the one-time Tri-ang ready-to-run 00 gauge model of the Class 76, which was introduced in 1950 for the Manchester to Sheffield route, has been out of production for some time. Models of overhead electric locomotives will, of course, run without an overhead wiring or catenary system but for realism, if for no other reason, a model electric railway would not look authentic without one. I appreciate that not everyone relishes the thought but as with most things connected with the hobby, the trade is there to give support. There are a number of Continental manufacturers of working overhead catenary equipment in

N and HO gauges. Probably the best known since they specialise in the subject are the German firm of Sommerfeldt who produce HO gauge systems representative of the German, Swiss and Italian railways and the French firm JV who produce a catenary system representative of French railways. Yes, even overhead wiring, or more particularly the supporting structures, have recognisably different shapes and styles. Lima also produce a neat and well designed catenary system which can be used either as a scenic accessory or, with the aid of the special Lima pantograph adaptor kit, can be used to carry the electric current to their locomotives.

For many years a high proportion of BR's passenger traffic has been handled by diesel or electric multiple units, referred to as DMUs or EMUs in railway parlance. From the modellers' point of view, these are little more than ordinary carriages with a power bogie at one or both ends. In ready-to-run model form they have never been very prolific. Bearing in mind the need to produce a matching set of trailer coaches, as well as the motor coach, one can understand a certain reluctance on the part of manufacturers to tool up for a model DMU or EMU production run, especially when considering the multiplicity of classes and their sometimes restricted regional alloca-

Jack Browne pays close attention to the catenary on his Spindlebahn Region HO layout using the authentic Swiss version produced by Somerfeldt.

Above *RhB (Rhätische Bahn or Rhaetien Railways) CC electric locomotive No 403 with train of cement wagons on David and Mike Polglaze's Swiss HOm layout Bernhardinbahn. The design of this metre gauge electric locomotive dates back to 1921. The model is by Bemo.*

Below *The French were exponents of diesel railcars, two such being the Nord ADN and Etat Bugatti, both dating from the 1930s and shown here at La Roche. Jouef have recently introduced an HO model of the Bugatti. The typically French buildings forming the backscene are worthy of note.*

Above *The SNCF RGP-1 two-car cross-country DMU's were in the late 'fifties a great advance in comfort. The model at Achaux is a radical rebuild of a very indifferent and dated Lima model.*

(Photo: Andy Hart)

Below *There can be no complaints about Lima's much admired model of GWR railcar No 22, seen at Blaen-Y-Cwm terminus on the 00 gauge layout of Jim Hewlett.*

tion. Nevertheless, the choice of ready-to-run DMUs includes the 'Trans-Pennine' Class 124. 'Calder Valley' set Class 110, Pressed Steel Class 117, Class 142 Pacer, Class 150/2 Sprinter, Class 155 Sprinter, Class 156 Super Sprinter, Class 158 Sprinter Express, Class 159 SWT, all in 00 gauge, and the HST High Speed Train in both N and 00 gauges. The ubiquitous Metro-Cammell Class 101, dropped by Hornby Railways, is now produced in 00 gauge by Lima and N gauge by Graham Farish. Where appropriate, many of these models have appeared with livery and detail variations representative of different periods from the early days of BR's modernisation programme to the present day TOCs. Excepting Hornby Railways' Eurostar and their model of BR's ill-fated APT and Wrenn's 'Brighton Belle', there are no EMUs—the former Hornby-Dublo and Tri-ang suburban EMUs are now collectors' items–but MTK Ltd produce an extensive range of kits. The ever popular GWR diesel railcar is well provided for in both 00 and N gauges in the shape of both ready-to-run models and kits, the latter providing for a number of different versions.

Buses were also used as railcars by a number of Irish railways at one time. They were converted to permanent rail use by the substitution of flanged wheels for the normal road wheels. There are a number of actual prototypes of single unit railcars that once existed in the past to provide the inspiration for an attractive and unusual model for a branch line or light railway layout. Mention must also be made of the steam railcars that once existed on Britain's railways since these make very attractive models, combining in some cases a normal type coach body with a very short stubby locomotive at one end, complete with boiler mountings, outside cylinders and valve gear and all the other paraphernalia of a steam engine. There were also the Sentinal steam railcars of the LNER which were operated in some numbers. In their case the method of propulsion was rather more disguised than the earlier form of steam railcar and outwardly they could only be distinguished by the chimney on the roof. Their colourful green and cream livery makes them attractive subjects. Nu-cast Model Engineering and Langley Miniature Models produce kits in 00 and N gauges respectively .

The final operation with most model building is painting and it is at this point that many otherwise fine models are spoilt. By finding out what not to do you perhaps stand a better chance of avoiding the usual mistakes and thereby achieving some measure of success. There is no doubt the best finished models invariably turn out to have been spray painted—brush painting rarely reaches the same standard. If you intend to take up modelling locomotives and rolling stock seriously, money spent on an airbrush would be a wise investment. The cheapest one on the market, the Modeller's Air Brush by Humbrol Ltd is not at all expensive, costing around £15 excluding the aerosol power pack but you can spend over £100 if you go in for the more expensive equipment and use a compressor as a propellant source. A comprehensive review of airbrush equipment was conducted in the January and February 1978 issues of *Model Railways* by John Talbot-Jones – recommended reading for anyone contemplating branching out into this aspect of the hobby in so far as the technicalities of the subject are concerned though the availability of some of the proprietary equipment will no doubt have changed since the articles were published. Should you be unable to obtain access to these admittedly long dated back numbers it is worth hearing in mind that there are two basic types of air brush: internal mixing and external mixing. It is generally regarded that the internal mixing type gives better results. Needless to say, air brushes using this method are the most expensive but can be acquired from upward of £50. At the time of writing the one-time extensive range of Humbrol authentic railway colours is no longer available but there are other brands offering a wide range of matching railway colours covering most railway liveries. Never fall into the temptation of economising by

Spray painting using a cardboard box as a spray booth.

buying cheap paint brushes. Always buy the dearest and best, generally pure sable, but there are some equally good man-made fibre substitutes which can be obtained from artists materials stockists, if not your model shop. I recommend having at the very least two sizes to work with, one small, say O or 1, and one medium say 3 or 4. For locomotives I prefer smaller brushes since the areas to be painted are not usually very large, but for bigger areas such as the sides and roofs of railway carriages I favour the larger sizes.

The main mistake with painting is to do the job in a hurry. One is invariably told that it is better to put on two thin coats rather than a single thick one. Before the second thin coat can be applied the first thin one needs to dry thoroughly, and this will take time. The more coats of paint the more times the surface is made wet and tacky and liable to attract dust and fluff. These really are enemies to watch and every effort should be made to avoid them: eg by not wearing woollen or fluffy clothes or working in a dusty room and by covering up the model in between painting sessions. One trouble I have often found when applying the second of two coats is that the first coat tends to lift and become mixed with the second. This is annoying since you feel you

might just as well have painted one thick coat in the first place. The only cure so far as I can see is to give the paint longer time to dry or not to work In the second coat too much but to lightly sweep the brush across the surface with a smooth even movement. This sounds all very well but any features in relief on the model, such as a row of rivets or a boiler band, have the effect of dragging extra paint off the brush at one edge and leaving bare metal at the other. You simply have to go back over relief detail such as this and work the brush in both directions.

There is no doubt that some colours are much easier to use and work with than others. For instance, I find black and most greens, particularly GWR green, easy to apply since they cover well and need the minimum number of coats. On the other hand, red, yellow and cream, to say nothing of white, I have found to be very difficult, especially in glossy form. The covering power is increased in matt paint but there is a disadvantage in that it seems to dry up in the tin much quicker and therefore will not keep so long as glossy paint. A possible compromise is to keep stocks of different colour paints in glossy form and mix a flattening agent with them when they are used. Only enough paint to do the job you have in hand needs to be treated on each occasion. I have found storing paints in tins upside-down helps them keep longer, and they then also appear to be easier to mix when they are turned the right way up ready for use. For one thing the sediment in the paint will be found on the lid where it can be easily scraped off and thoroughly mixed in with the rest of the paint. Inverting the tin also forms a seal round the inside of the lid, which helps to keep the air out should the lid not be fitting properly. If the lid is such a bad fit then, of course, the paint will run out, which will be a tell-tale sign that all is not well! It is far better to find out in the early stages than wait until you want to use the tin when you might find that all the paint has dried up. Upside-down storing also helps to avoid the formation of a skin on the surface of the paint. I always try and keep the lid and edge of the tin free of paint before sealing it after use. With paints in bottles this is particularly important, for it is easy to seal up the bottle so that it becomes difficult to unscrew the cap without breaking the glass. I find that paint stored in corked bottles becomes useless after a relatively short while, but happily, few paints appear to be sold that way today.

I assume most modellers will acquire a quantity of thinner and are aware of the necessity of having appropriate thinners for the paints they are using. Whilst most paints are ready for use without thinning, it is necessary eventually as the paint becomes thicker due to evaporation every time the container is opened. On this account it is essential to keep the paint container closed as much as possible, and also to avoid dust and fluff getting into the paint. Thinners are also required for cleaning brushes. I usually keep a separate bottle of dirty thinner which is good enough to use in the early stages of brush cleaning, and clean thinner can be reserved for the final stage. It is an idea to keep a few old empty paint tins or lids in which to pour out small quantities of thinner for brush cleaning. They can also be used when mixing colours or for making up small quantities of matt paint using a matting

agent. It needs to be emphasised that care should be taken when handling paints and thinners and they should only be used in a well ventilated room.

It is essential that the model should be clean and free of grease before and during painting. Most models collect a fair amount of dirt during their construction, as well as swarf, dust from filing and sandpapering and grease from your fingers. What action you take to clean a model will to a certain extent depend on the materials used in its construction. An all-metal model can most likely be safely immersed in warm water containing detergent and scrubbed with a brush. A final rinse in running water will also do it little harm. Greater care needs to be taken with a plastic card structure, however, especially if you have used a water-soluble wood filler. A wipe over with a clean rag or a light brush is probably all you can do in a case such as this.

The first undercoat is important to 'key' the paint to the surface. It will also serve to show up any blemishes in the material or finish of the model, so a rub down with fine sandpaper or flour paper will not only improve the model but it will also help the finish of succeeding coats of paint. Each coat of paint should, in fact, be allowed to dry thoroughly and be rubbed down with flour paper before the next coat is applied. I do not think there is any merit in putting on too many coats of paint since they begin to obscure the detail, however thinly and carefully they may be applied. Such details as the undersides of beading round cab entrances, boiler wash out plugs and boiler bands seem to collect more than their share of paint. I do, however, like to give a coat of varnish. Apart from anything else it preserves any decals or rub-on transfers you may have applied and in some cases helps to preserve the life of bright metal surfaces. I do not like matt varnish since this gives an artificial matt surface which I consider is rarely seen on railway rolling stock. I know they get dirty but the dirt is often accompanied by an oily sheen which is far from a flat matt finish. Certainly high-gloss paint looks

Paul Skinner applying lining with a bow pen. Paperback books either side and slightly higher than the model support the ruler, template and hands.

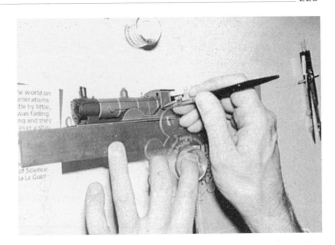

out of place and artificial on a model, but a dead flat matt finish looks just as bad. Somewhere in between, such as a semi-matt or eggshell varnish, is in my opinion to be preferred. For many years I have used Bonds Eggshell Varnish and there is still plenty left after applying it to more than 40 or 50 separate items of rolling stock. Take care when applying this varnish since it will begin to dissolve the paint if it is worked in too thoroughly. It does, however, dry reasonably quickly, which is a great asset.

Lining and lettering locomotives can be a difficult art. Thankfully, there is an impressive range of aids in the form of decals or transfers which cover a wide range of prototype styles. Until recently most transfers produced in the model railway trade have been of the rub-on variety or require varnish or a solution of methylated spirits and water for their application but water slide transfers are now becoming available. I must admit I like the ease of water slide transfers, although I know there are objections to the ring or halo effect that sometimes goes with them. Rub-on transfers are fine except that you have to be careful to position them accurately when making the application as there is little or no room for manoeuvre afterwards like there is with a water slide transfer. Most model railway transfers are very thin, which is commendable from the

appearance point of view but it does make the job of applying them rather critical. Lining and lettering can be applied direct to a model with a bow pen or a brush using ordinary paints if there are no suitable transfers, or alternatively the lining can be painted on to thin cigarette paper which can afterwards be fixed to the model with varnish. Another method is to paint self-adhesive tape which can afterwards be cut into strips and applied to the model. This is particularly suitable for locomotive boiler bands since the thickness of the tape will be just about right for the boiler band itself. I often wonder why we make boiler bands on our models and paint them afterwards only to put transfers on top of the lot. Why not leave the boiler bands off the model until after painting at the end when a strip of painted self-adhesive tape will do the job just as well and make painting much easier?

The difficulty with painting lining is that if you make a mistake and have to remove the lining there is a chance that the base colour will also come away or at the very least be damaged. One way of avoiding this difficulty in the case of a metal locomotive is to paint the base colour with a cellulose paint and do the lining with an oil paint. Unfortunately all the special model railway paints I know of are oil based. It is possible that amongst the very wide range of car touch-up kits and aerosols there may be some colours that approximate to recognised railway liveries in which case you could use these. Aerosol spray cans are not, however terribly easy to control over such small and intricate areas as a model locomotive and you cannot hope to achieve as good a result as you would say with an expensive airbrush. When applying oil paint lining with a bow pen always give the paint a start by drawing on a surface before you apply it to the model. Try and get the job done on one fill of the pen but if you have to reload clean the pen first. It is important not to allow any paint to clog on the surface of the pen. To me, lining with a bow pen is far easier than with a brush but not everyone finds it the same. Lining freehand is not an easy job however and you should not get discouraged if you cannot achieve the same results as the professionals. Two essential aids are good lighting immediately over the work to avoid shadows plus adequate support for the model and for your arms and hands. It is preferable to build up the working surface where your hands are resting to the same height as the model you are painting.

Most model locomotives begin to take on a more natural look after they have been running for a year or more and have been subject to some handling. Whilst you should always be careful not to over-oil the working parts of electric propelled locos there is no harm in running a light smear of oil over the bodywork from time to time. This is very often how the full size locomotives, particularly the steam locomotives, retained their sheen. One enemy of miniature locomotives and rolling stock, and in fact anything connected with model railways, is dust and you will need to give your models a clean up from time to time. An old shaving brush is ideal for this purpose.

Some modellers consider that it adds realism to their layout to dirty up their locomotives a bit. The degree to which you apply such realism depends partly on your taste and possibly also on the type of locomotives and layout you are operating. For instance, most main line express passenger locomo-tives could be seen at one time in reasonably resplendent condition compared to freight locomotives which are generally allowed to become dirty. The standard of cleanliness also varied from one locomotive depot to another and you could at one time almost tell from what depot a locomotive came by the condition it was in. Locomotives operating in predominantly industrial areas will also stand a better chance of getting dirty quicker than other engines which operate in the quieter and more remote country districts. It cannot be assumed that before World War 2 and nationalisation of British railways all locomo-tives looked bright, shiny and brand spank-ing new. Equally it is a mistake to think that after 1939 all locomotives were dirty, rusty and neglected. Even during the war years some locomotives were cleaned and they had to be repainted on occasions so it was by no means impossible to see a shiny, sparkling locomotive. Even those that only received an intermediate overhaul often left the works with a glossy coat of black paint on the smoke box and a bright red buffer beam, which made the whole locomotive look good and new.

One thing that is pretty certain is that all steam locomotives first entered service with a shiny coat of paint—or more likely several coats of paint and coats of varnish to top it off. The larger and more important the loco-motive the greater the attention given to the paint finish. As anyone who runs a car will know, the glossy finish becomes dulled after a while by dust and dirt from the air or by mud thrown up from the road and the move-ment of other passing vehicles. Even the rain is not blameless, as it is either dirty if it falls through a smoke haze for example. or else it makes a solution of the dust and dirt already present and spreads it all over the surface in streaks. Something similar happens with a steam locomotive, but in addition there are the hazards of coal dust, which can be a menace at any time but is particularly trou-blesome when the bunker or tender is refu-elled; soot which blows about from the chim-ney or when the interior of the smokebox is cleaned; ash from the firebox; over-generous

Whether to 'weather' your locomotives or not can perhaps be judged from these illustrations. **Above** *Ex-LNER N7 0–6–2T from the Mid Essex MRC's EM gauge East Anglian branch line Swallows Cross.* **Below** *A grim but nonetheless realistic GWR 0–6–2T No 5664 is put to shame by the polished 'Grange' and 'Britannia' either side on the REC's 00 gauge layout.* (Photo: Peter Parfitt)

lubrication; scuff marks from the feet and hands of the maintenance staff clambering over the engine: and the effects of water, hot or cold, and escaping steam from leaky glands, safety valves and cylinders, etc.

Whilst, as I have said earlier, I prefer not to paint a model initially with a dead matt finish I am the first to admit that with the effects of weathering and all the other hazards mentioned a locomotive that is never cleaned will lose its glossy varnish finish. At the same time, however, it will also lose most of its basic colour. Black will become grey and the pigment in other colours will be considerably toned down. In my opinion, therefore, it is not enough to paint a locomotive with authentic railway colours and simply finish with a dead matt varnish. If you want to show the authentic colours then there should at least be a trace of gloss or semi-gloss finish, otherwise the colours would not be so prominent. A matt finish only comes with dirt, in which case the colour of the dirt itself will show, or the matt finish will come with age, in which case the colour pigments will lose their intensity.

The colour of dirt varies according to what sort it is. Wheels and motion get coated with a rust brown colour, which is a mixture of mud and rust thrown up from the rails and augmented by the filings from the cast metal brake blocks. A similar colour can be detected on passenger coaching stock where it often rises above the waistline and on to the windows. The deposits of coal dust, soot and ash will result in various shades of grey and grey/black and escaping water or steam will often leave whitish/grey streaks as well as rust. Priming via the chimney can also cause whitish stains down the sides of the smokebox as well as on the outside of the chimney itself. Over-lubrication can produce black marks which spread far from the source of the lubrication itself. If it mixes with dirt or dust it will form a heavy shiny sludge, which will collect in pockets wherever there is somewhere for it to lie. There are, of course, plenty of places on a steam locomotive where rust will appear, unless it is kept down by regular cleaning or greasing. There are

parts like buffer heads, coupling hooks, brake blocks, valve gear and connecting rods that lack a protective covering of paint and therefore become subject to rust and cause it to spread to other nearby areas. Other parts that are painted initially lose their protective covering either by wear and tear, such as on footplates, steps and handrails, or by over-heating such as sometimes occurs round the base of badly fitting smokebox doors. Or it could simply be because it is a long time since the locomotive was last painted and the paint is beginning to wear thin!

Steam locomotives used to get pretty dirty at times, but diesel locomotives seem to have reached an all-time low. Even some main line diesels at the head of important passenger trains appear in an unkempt and neglected state. Paint becomes chipped and whole areas are allowed to flake off. The usual muddy rusty brown colour creeps upwards from the wheels, bogies and lower body side panels and, worst of all, apparent over-filling around the fuel tank fillers either causes a creeping black mixture of oil and dirt to spread or else it helps to remove yet more paint from the locomotive. Another oddity is the bluish rainbow effect that can be observed sometimes on the wind-screen glazing.

All these features may be an aid to realism but whether you want to go to this extent is up to you. My own personal view is that unless you are modelling a particular area, period or setting that demands this treatment you might prefer to imagine that the local motive power depot has a full complement of cleaners who are able to do their job prop-erly! I am sure locomotives, whether they be steam, diesel or electric, look better for a spot of cleaning. A natural weathered look will come soon enough after regular handling of the model.

Finally, when it comes to finishing your model locomotives, don't forget to put some coal in the tender or coal bunker. When in service it also helps if there is a crew on the footplate and other little details like lamps or destination boards can all help to give the finishing touch to a model.

CHAPTER 10
Carriages and wagons

If locomotives are one modelling field where plastic is not recognised as a universal construction medium this is not so of carriages and wagons. The vast majority of proprietary ready-to-run wagons and coaches are based on plastic mouldings and it is difficult to imagine what the hobby would be like today without this material. The old tinplate and lithograph models of yesteryear leave a lot to be desired in comparison with today's efforts which, thanks to modern plastic technology, can show in relief every small detail such as strapping, rivets, door handles, hinges, ventilators and planking, and even simulate the wood grain. The light weight of plastic is a virtue when it is applied to wagons since we do not want to increase the weight of the trailing load behind our engines any more than we need to. A certain amount of weight is necessary to give the wagons and coaches stability and such weight should be installed as low down as possible to keep the centre of gravity in the right place. Many manufacturers install a piece of heavy metal between the chassis and the body on their wagon and coach models and this is the ideal place. Metal wheels, insulated of course for 2-rail layouts, can add a little extra weight in an area where it is most wanted although the rolling quality and profile of most of the latest 00 gauge plastic wagon and coach wheels is so good there is not the overriding necessity to replace them with metal wheels that there once was.

It is probably true to say that there are very few model railways that could accommodate every one of the different examples of ready-to-run wagons that are now commercially available in N and 00 gauges and most manufacturers appear to be adding to their ranges all the time. One factor which contributes to the variety is the large number of private owner wagons that once existed on Britain's railways prior to the outbreak of World War 2. The bulk of these were coal wagons owned (or sometimes hired) by coal mining companies and coal merchants, factors and traders. The reason for this was peculiar to Great Britain where at their inception railway companies were not required by statute to supply wagons for coal traffic as they were for other kinds of merchandise. The railways did in fact supply some wagons in certain districts, the Southern Railway in the Kent coalfield, for instance, but in general coal was transported in privately owned wagons of which at one time there were over 600,000 belonging to no less than 5,000 separate owners.

There were other privately owned wagons besides coal wagons as there still are in growing numbers today, but instinctively one thinks of coal wagons when thinking of privately owned wagons. The wagons themselves were made by different wagon builders based on a standard 'Railway Clearing House' specification which laid down standard dimensions for the chassis but

The attraction of pre-WW2 Private Owner wagons can be appreciated in this close up of two Replica Railways (ex-Mainline) 00 gauge 7-plank open minerals. The remarkably fine lettering (every word can be read on the original) and not least the colouring are a testimony to present day production techniques. Imagine trying to do this by hand and, when you have done one side, turning it over and repeating it all on the other!

allowed the body to be built to suit the owner's requirements in such features as the height of the body sides (largely identified by the number of planks used in their construction; 5, 6, 7, or 8 usually) and the number and types of doors, eg end, side or bottom, or a combination of two or more of each. With perhaps the exception of the bottom doors, all these features were readily discernible close to although at a distance the wagons all looked very much alike in overall appearance apart from their varying heights and, of course, their distinctive liveries. Here there was such a tremendous variety, both in the basic body colour and the colour and style of the lettering. Model railway manufacturers have unlimited but legitimate scope for imparting variety to an otherwise undistinguished basic shape of wagon and they have not been slow to appreciate this potential. I do not want to be accused of being a kill-joy but as nice and colourful as all these wagons are, they did have their regional limitations. For instance, wagons owned by coal merchants could find their way almost anywhere since they could be sent to any colliery for loading, but unloading would

normally only take place alongside the coal merchant's yard. Colliery wagons, on the other hand, could be sent to and unloaded almost anywhere although each colliery district had its traditional outlets that were frequently dictated either by the proximity of the customer to the colliery or the existence of a direct railway route and the influence of the adjoining railway company. Long haul coal trains en route from collieries to consumers, or going back empty in the opposite direction, would include a varied selection of wagons, possibly even every one different, but in a country station coal yard the variety is likely to be restricted to those wagons owned by the local coal merchants (or merchant depending on the monopoly situation in the district) or those colliery owned wagons most likely to serve that particular district. In all probability, there would have been more than one wagon from each of an unrestricted range of owners.

Whether or not you stick to such rules is up to you but it is worth considering if your layout is based on any particular region, railway company or, especially in the case of a branch line terminus, one particular town.

Some coal mining companies ranged wider than others. The amalgamation of private collieries that took place before the war resulted in the formation of some very big companies having collieries in more than one coalfield in different parts of the country. One such, and possibly the largest, was Stephenson Clarke & Associated Collieries Ltd who had a very large fleet of wooden bodied wagons attractively finished in grey with 'SC' in large white letters shaded red. They bore the inscription 'Empty to Toton LMSR, Doncaster LNER or Aberdare GWR' which is an indication of their widespread distribution. Personally I am always finding SC wagons popping up in the background of pre-war railway photographs. They are always wooden bodied wagons whenever I see them in photographs yet the only two ready to run models of SC wagons so far produced are based on all-steel prototypes. The excellent Cambrian Models ready-painted 4 mm scale plastic kit is based on a 7-plank 12 ton wagon which is really authentic for the livery chosen and makes this kit a very useful one to build. As I say, whether you concern yourself what

private owner wagons you run, whether you aim at authenticity or simply variety is entirely up to you but it is worth a thought.

As well as the commercially produced ready-to-run wagons in plastic there is a growing range of plastic kits for scale model wagons both in 00 and O gauges and their various parts can also be adapted for conversions into other types of wagon. There are also a fair number of cast metal kits and separate parts such as axle guards, bogie side frames, brake gear and buffers which can be used for scratchbuilding wagons. Mention must also be made at this point of the Peco Wonderful Wagons which have been available in 00 gauge for a number of years. These come in kit form and are probably unique in the world of small scale model railway wagons since they contain so many desirable features. Foremost are the sprung axle boxes and buffers which operate just like they do on the full size wagons. The springs transmit the load of the wagon on to the axle boxes which can move up or down in the axle guard, the spring being deflected in the process. The last

PO wagons also figure prominently in main line freight traffic today. This Lima 00 gauge hopper wagon in ARC yellow livery with grey underframe also features extremely fine lettering and excellent detail in the plastic moulding.

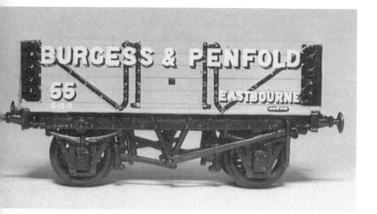

This 5-plank open wagon is one of a number of plastic kits produced by Cambrian Model Products. Care needs to be taken to avoid spoiling the pre-printed sides with adhesive during assembly but otherwise they are delightfully simple to make and are ideal for beginners.

Mk IV series have painted plastic bodies with printed liveries. The Mk III series which had embossed and colour printed card sides and ends overlaid on a die cast metal body has, with limited exceptions been discontinued. The chassis is available separately as a set of parts to enable modellers to construct their own bodies should they so desire. Peco also produce their N gauge Quality Line Wagons in unpainted and easily assembled kit form as well as the fully painted and lettered ready-to-run models.

Scratch-building wagon bodies to be fitted on chassis, using sets of proprietary parts such as the Peco Wonderful Wagons, material taken from other plastic kits or even chassis from commercial ready-to-run models, is simple with plastic card or styrene sheet. Basically a wagon body is nothing more than a box with or without a roof, and the body structure is easily enough assembled. It is only in the detailing that any particular skill is required. For 00 gauge I recommend using 40 thou plastic card to make up the four sides and the base of the 'box' and if you use black plastic card it will save you having to paint the interior. The planking and such features as doors can be represented by scoring the face of the card with a pointed instrument (not too sharp, otherwise it will only cut or scratch the surface). I use the pointed arm of a pair of adjustable dividers, sliding the other arm alongside the edge of the card to act as a

guide. With this tool it is easy to score accurate parallel lines over as long a length of material as you like. I prefer to cut enough material for the two sides and two ends of the body in one strip so that all the planking can be completed in one go. This way the planking will be completely parallel and even around all four sides and there will be no difficulty in matching up the planking where it meets at the corners. For the average 00 gauge wagon a strip of plastic card 8 in long will be enough for all four sides.

When scoring, take care not to dig too deeply with the pointer otherwise you may find the card will bow or, at worst, crack in two. The sides and ends can be assembled round a plastic card floor also similarly scored for planking, and the body cemented to whatever chassis you have chosen. strapping can be cut from 10 thou plastic card and cemented in place using liquid cement such as Mek-pak supplied by Slater's Plastikard Ltd, (The chemical name of the solvent used for cementing plastic card is methylethylketone.) Bolt head detail on the strapping looks very nice and completes the effect, but only if it is done neatly. The bolts can be represented by pressing a blunt pointed instrument such as a knitting needle or a centre punch on the reverse side but this is rather tedious, Unless you make each impression with equal force and dead in line the result will look worse than no rivets or bolt heads at all.

A gear wheel rolled along the back of the strapping so that the teeth leave an impression would be ideal provided you can find an old clock gear wheel with the right spacing of teeth. Another snag with rivet embossing is that it comes out well on large areas but with narrow strips it is difficult to get the plastic card to withstand such treatment. It is probably much better to mark the rivets before you cut out the strapping. Better still, use thin metal foil for the strapping detail which can withstand greater distortion from the embossing tool. Some bracing and strapping on the outside of the wagon bodies takes the form in cross-section of 'L' or 'T' shaped sections which can be built up from strips of plastic card very easily. First the base of the 'L' or the top of the 'T' is cemented in place and then the stem of the 'L' or 'T' can be held on edge with the aid of a pair of tweezers and fixed with a wash of liquid cement.

One point that calls for particular attention when assembling wagons (and indeed all vehicles such as locomotives and tender chassis, coach bogies, etc.) is to ensure that all the wheels sit fairly and squarely on the rails, which will not be the case if you

Wheras the larger manufacturers of ready-to-run models understandably concentrate on the more commonly seen wagons, many of the smaller manufacturers produce kits of less common specialised vehicles. Just such are these GWR Mess and Tool Vans made by Robert Tivendale from a Haye Developments etched brass kit. These vans form part of a breakdown train kept on standby at the larger GWR motive power depots. Notice the rooflights on the Tool Van, the interior of the windowless sides being taken up with racking for tools and stores and the all important workshop to deal with any emergencies.

assemble a wagon with a twist in the chassis! Once completed that way it is difficult to correct. It is a wise precaution to have a dead flat surface such as a piece of plate glass handy when you are assembling wagons and other items of rolling stock to ensure that all the axles are in the same plane and that all the wheels are in contact with the ground. It is just possible that the running surface or tyres of the wheels are true but that one or more of the flanges may be uneven. So, to be thoroughly sure, stand the wagon on a length of track which is itself on the glass. When assembling plastic models in particular it is necessary to check constantly since it is possible for the model to be assembled correctly but to find that the action of the cement drying shrinks, twists or pulls the body and chassis slightly out of shape. You cannot be too careful with this point since a wagon with uneven wheels will be a sure source of derailment. In extreme cases it looks pretty horrible too.

The foregoing assumes that the wagon you are constructing has a rigid four-wheeled chassis which is likely to be the case with the majority of wagon kits, Peco Wonderful Wagons excepted. There is however. a compensated suspension system which can

be adapted to most kits or scratch-built wagons whereby, in its simplest form, one pair of wheels on a four-wheeled vehicle is mounted in the axlebox bearing in the normal way but the second pair of wheels is mounted in a separate wheel bearing unit which is pivoted along the centre line of the vehicle. In essence this gives the wagon a three-point suspension; the rigidly mounted wheels at one end form two of the suspension points and the third is the point along the centre line of the wagon where the wheel bearing unit is pivoted, The principle can be likened to a three-legged stool which adapts itself to an uneven surface far better than a four-legged chair. The wheels in the pivoted wheel bearing unit will rock or tilt on the pivot thereby taking up any undulations in the track as well as any inadvertent twisting of the body or chassis of the wagon This method of compensated suspension can he adapted to all vehicles (four-wheel, six-wheel and bogie stock) and there are a number of proprietary parts available from specialist dealers to aid construction. There are various forms of compensated suspension which are gaining ascendancy in the hobby and, with the finer standards as used by such as

Scalefour and Protofour, it is regarded by many as being absolutely essential if perfect trouble-free running is to be attained.

For those who model railways other than British ones, their needs are well catered for by the wealth of ready-to-run models available. Most enthusiasts could completely stock a Continental or American-style layout 'off the shelf' with no need for kit or scratch building at all. This applies especially to the two most popular gauges, HO and N, but other scales and gauges are commendably well served. It is no small wonder that kits for Continental wagons seem few and far between but this is not the case with American model railroads where there are scores of firms producing complete kits as well as component parts for scratch builders. The kits vary from the 'craftsman' kit in wood and metal up to 'CKD' (completely knocked down) types which can be assembled with screws and cement in as little as 50 minutes. The quality of the latter type is very high indeed and they invariably include body parts ready painted and lettered. The flamboyant liveries and

insignia carried by some American box cars adds to the appeal of these models and brings colour and variety to the American railroad scene. There is also much variety in the design of European rolling stock. Although the majority of Freight wagons are painted in sombre browns, greys and greens, such vehicles as refrigerated wagons, tank wagons and the modern day container legitimately impart colour to a freight train. An added attraction to the modeller is the widespread distribution of European rolling stock whereby wagons from practically every country in Europe can be seen almost anywhere on the Continent, even in the remotest outposts.

Painting wagons needs care, not only for the elaborate colour and lettering schemes that were to be found on some of them (principally the privately owned coal and mineral wagons), but also because of the amount of dirt and rust that all-steel wagons tend to attract. It is not difficult to see why the once extensive BR fleet of 16 ton steel mineral wagons soon lost newness when you consider the treatment they got. To

Varying stages of wear and tear skilfully applied to these loaded PO coal wagons. The Shunter's Truck next to the loco was a very common sight on the GWR.

begin with, they were probably located under a hopper which discharged into the body of the wagon 16 tons of coal in about as many seconds. Unloading could involve the wagon being rotated full circle in a rotary discharger or tilted at one end to discharge through the end door. Alternatively, a mechanical grab may have been employed which, however careful the operator, was bound on occasions to knock against the sides of the wagon. Inevitably paint became chipped and worn and rust formed to take its place—in some cases there appeared to be more rust than paint. Though this may have looked rather drab, if you are striving after realism you will want to consider how to create this dirty neglected effect in miniature. This calls for a little creative artwork which can be applied to all forms of railway modelling—locomotives, coaches, wagons, road vehicles or any painted structure which sees the ravages of wear and tear and wind and rain over a period of time.

Assuming that your model is already painted, the first thing to bear in mind when applying paint to represent rust or weathering is to avoid using a heavy coat which will obliterate the prime colour. Use your paints well thinned and never apply straight from the tin. Keep a pallet or small tin lid handy in which you can play about with your paints and thinners, and perhaps have a spare piece of scrap plastic to experiment with before applying paint to the model. In your tin lid put a dab of black paint, a dab of brick red and a brush full of thinner. Keep adding one or more of these items until you have a weak, watery solution that can be slapped liberally all over the model. If it settles into corners and crevices so much the better, for these are the very places where dirt and rust are likely to congregate. Rust on wagon body sides usually appears in patches, mainly in the centre of large panels where the sides have been dented and the paint has flaked off.

I use an old paint brush that has seen better days, and cut off whatever hairs remain until there is just a stump about $\frac{1}{16}$ in

long. This brush, used end-on, produces a good stipple effect with diluted brick red paint. Dirt can be washed on using dirty thinner—the remains from a bottle which has been used for cleaning paint brushes is ideal. Add a spot of brick red and black if it is not dirty enough. Wash the dirt solution with vertical strokes to represent streaks caused by rain carrying coal dust and grime down the body sides. White lettering can also be toned down using a wash of dirty thinner since it is unusual to see an old rusty wagon with bright white lettering. Another obvious way of adding realism to wagons is to put a few chalk destination markings on the body sides, using a mapping pen and white Indian ink. Parcels vans are particularly prone to this type of decoration and a widely spaced range of destinations, such as Edinburgh, Bournemouth, Cardiff or Liverpool, can often be seen scribbled in chalk on these wagons. It is a wonder the operating staff know which one to take note of.

Wagon loads is a subject in itself since there is so much variety of merchandise and so many different methods of loading. Also, of course, they provide a lot of operating scope since open wagons can be loaded and unloaded just like the real thing. In the majority of cases it is preferable to 'package' the load so that it can be put into the wagon and taken out with the least difficulty. For example, a load of coal for a coal wagon can be represented by a lightweight block of balsa wood with the top shaped and sprinkled with a layer of coal dust or small chippings glued to the wood. Timber loads can be represented by one single block of wood with the planks scored along the top, ends and sides. Many loads such as milk churns, cable drums, containers, barrels and packing eases are available as ready-made accessories from a number of manufacturers and there are many more that can be scratch-built at home from scrap materials. Another source of wagon loads can sometimes be found from within a range of die-cast miniature vehicles such as Lesney's Matchbox series. All too frequently these are not built to recognised model railway scales but some-

Tarpaulin sheeted wagons at Taunton North. Notice also the acid carboys, sacks, barrels and packing cases awaiting collection.

times you can find one that is not too far removed, and there are also some items such as boats and caravans that can be made use of. Military vehicles also make good subjects for wagon loads, especially as the army has always made good use of rail transport.

Mention must also be made of tarpaulins since these were at one time regularly used for sheeting open wagons to protect their contents, the classic example being the Hybar wagon which had a bar that could be swung into place especially to take a tarpaulin. They were also commonly used to drape over a quantity of timber stacked in the

wagon in such a way that it overlapped the edge at one end. Invariably the tip of the timber could be seen poking out from below the tarpaulin. I have found crumpled tissue paper painted with black Indian ink produces an effective miniature tarpaulin They are also available commercially in N and 00 gauges. There is practically no limit to the ingenuity you can put into the subject of wagon loads, both by thinking up new subjects for loads and in the various ways of modelling the loads themselves.

I mentioned in the previous chapter the difficulties that large scale manufacturers

Two 00 gauge coaches first introduced by Airfix, The 'B' Set non-corridor brake composite (top) operated in pairs and has wide appeal due to its widespread route availability. The Centenary Stock 1st/3rd composite (lower) on the other hand was limited to main line running on GWR lines only due to its exceptional width.

must have in trying to produce a range of model locomotives which will satisfy the largest proportion of their customers. It is difficult enough with locomotives and it must be well nigh impossible with railway carriages. The trouble with model railway carriages is that, to a layman, most of them look alike. There are obvious differences such as four-wheel, six-wheel and bogie coaches, non corridor and corridor coaches, first class and second class coaches, and restaurant, buffet and sleeping cars. In reality, however, these are just broad categories and in actual fact, as with locomotives, there are many different styles and designs. At the same time as there were attempts by the various railway companies to produce standard designs of locomotives, every company had a succession of carriages and wagon engineers who had their own ideas on how railway carriages should be built and what they should look like. They all left their mark in various ways and degrees to produce a variety of coaches which, though basically built to a similar pattern, were quite distinguishable in detail. These details are important when it comes to building an authentic model railway, and to create the right atmosphere when modelling a particular railway company you should be as particular about your railway carriages as you are with the locomotives and other items that go to distinguish one company, period or location from another.

To begin at the bottom and work up, all the pre-nationalisation British railway companies had different designs of bogies. The dimensions of the wheelbase differed for a start: the GWR had mostly 9 ft wheelbase bogies, but there were also quite a number of 7 ft bogies, a dimension which was peculiar to the GWR. The LMS standardised on 9 ft and the SR 8 ft. The LNER used 8 ft 6 in bogies but they had a very distinctive appearance since the springing gear was hidden behind the bogie frames which were attractively curved in shape— unlike some outside frame bogies used at one time by the SR which were straight and somewhat ugly in appearance. The shape of the frames also distinguished the GWR 9 ft bogies from the standard LMS bogies which had the same wheelbase. The type of springing also affects the appearance. In the past most bogies have had leaf springs but in recent years BR have used coil springs which markedly change the appearance of a bogie. There is little excuse for running rolling stock with the wrong sort of bogies in 00 gauge, and even in O gauge, where there is a fair selection of bogies or bogie parts.

Bogies are the most noticeable feature of the underframe but there are others that have to be considered, such as the size, shape and position of battery boxes, vacuum brake cylinders, truss rods, buffers, buffer heads (whether round or oval), footboards, etc., and they are all items that sometimes differ from one design to another and which need to be considered when building a particular coach model.

The coach body also has infinite scope for detail variations. To begin with, let's consider the curvature of the body sides, as seen end-on. The majority of designs have sides that curve inwards starting from a point below the waistline so that the overall width of the lower part of the body is less than the middle and top. This is known as 'tumble home' and is a most noticeable feature which must be reproduced correctly if an authentic appearance is to be given to a model. The post-war Bulleid coaches of the SR were unusual in that they had a continuous curvature to the sides, some of them even having curved glass in the windows, whereas the post war Hawksworth coaches of the GWR had nearly straight sides. This is just one example of different thinking by different designers working for separate railway companies

Lima 00 gauge model of the BR Mk 1 BSK (brake second corridor) in Network SouthEast livery.

at the same period in time. Another distinctive and unique feature of the SR Bulleid coaches was the pronounced rounded corners of the window frames. The size and shape of windows and ventilators are themselves distinguishing features which help to make one design different from another.

The roof is a further area where design differences show up. The curved drop ends to the roofs of the Gresley coaches on the LNER were very striking and no model LNER train would really look right without them. At about the time when the LNER broke away from this unique tradition, and started to build their coaches with normal straight tops to the roofs, the GWR inexplicably began building theirs the other way. The positioning of rain strips on the roofs and the type, location and number of ventilators also help to distinguish one coach design from another. At each end of a coach the identifying features can be the number and position of handrails, steps, jumper cables and corridor connections, plus the shape of the end itself and whether it is flat or curved.

With all these individual variations in design it is understandable that manufacturers have a difficult job trying to satisfy everybody. There is also the added complication that, with one or two exceptions, to fulfil the basic needs of modellers, a minimum of two models have to be produced of whatever type of coach is chosen as one at least has to be a brake coach. A brake coach to provide accommodation for the guard must be included in every passenger train. In order to keep tooling costs down to the bare minimum, manufacturers frequently resort to the time honoured expedient of producing one coach as a brake third (or brake second) and the other as a composite, the latter providing accommodation for first class as well as third (or second) class passengers. In reality all-thirds (or latterly all seconds) are probably more common than the composites and there are such things as all-firsts. In the case of pre-nationalisation and early BR coaches this would mean tooling up for two more models if manufacturers were to go to these lengths. The

expense of so doing can arguably be better employed in producing two models of another railway company's design. BR did much to help in this respect since their Mk 3 coaches had a common body shell, the only external distinction between first and second class being the lettering and the yellow line along the cantrail of the first class coach. A much simpler modification to cope with.

Other exceptions are the GWR 'B' set and the autocoach, Only one autocoach is needed for a train since they frequently ran singly although two, or even four, autocoaches with a locomotive sandwiched in between were not unusual. The 'B' set coaches were brake composites and they ran in close coupled pairs with the brake compartments at either end, Airfix were very astute in introducing these models as with only two sets of tooling they could produce two types of coaches capable of forming two types of train. Furthermore, their popularity is assured since they are suited to almost every type of GWR 00 gauge layout down to the smallest terminus-to-fiddle-yard branch line. Should you decide to model a steam age branch line this need not preclude you from running one or two main line corridor coaches since it was not unknown for these to be seen on branch lines. However, Pullman, restaurant, buffet and sleeping cars and TPO (Travelling Post Office) coaches, all of which have been represented by such excellent ready-to-run models, are best kept to the larger main line layouts.

So far I have only referred to British passenger coaches but the variations in design are just as comprehensive in the case of European and American railways. Notwithstanding this variety, a glance through the catalogues of European manufacturers will show there is no shortage of ready-to-run models in HO and N gauge, to mention the two most popular. Whereas at one time European railway carriages were painted in rather drab, uniform colour schemes, dark green being predominant, more and more modern coaches are appearing in every

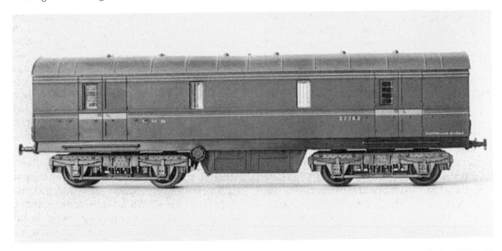

Almost any layout can find room for one or more bogie parcel vans. Shown here are the Lima LMS non-gangwayed GUV (general utility van) and in early BR livery the ex-Mainline LMS 50ft full brake BG (bogie brake van – gangwayed).

conceivable shade of colour. European railway organisations have been even more adventurous with their colour schemes than was at one time the case with BR, all of which adds to the visual attraction of operating a model railway based on Continental practice. Also there are many international carriage or train workings in the European railway timetables which result in carriages from one country being seen in other countries far removed from their home base. For example, the main station in Munich, sees regular workings of Austrian, French, Italian, Yugoslavian, Swiss, and Turkish carriages. Munich is probably far too large a station to contemplate modelling but a much smaller and more compact example which lends itself particularly well to modelling is Luxembourg City station. Here there are regular workings of multiple unit and loco-hauled trains from the railways of Belgium, France and Germany as well as

Luxembourg itself and through carriages from Italy and Switzerland. Hardly any two trains look alike!

British railway modellers looking to the main manufacturers of proprietary ready-to-run models to fulfil their basic coaching stock needs will find a reasonable selection in the two most popular gauges N and 00 although it has to be said that some railway companies are better represented than others. Should you be working in O gauge or you have need to extend the range of available models in N and 00 there are as many aids to constructing railway carriages in the form of kits, spare parts and accessories as there are for locomotives and wagons. It is fortunate that this branch of the railway hobby is as well served as it is since the construction of a model railway carriage is a time consuming business. From my own experience, to make a really good job of scratch building a model railway carriage can take as long as making a model locomotive. Not that it is unduly difficult or anything like that, it is just that there are so many details to attend to. It becomes all the more daunting when you consider the prospect of building a whole train of coaches, three or four possibly being a minimum requirement.

For this reason, coach kits provide a valuable service to modellers in helping to speed up the construction work. There are many types available but the three most popular are moulded plastic, punched aluminium or etched brass or nickel-silver. One of the main advantages of these kits is that the window openings are already produced for you which results in a great saving in time and effort as well as improved accuracy. The plastic and etched metal kits also include all the panelling and relief detail which can be a really laborious job when scratch building from basic raw materials. Most of these kits include all parts necessary to construct a complete model excepting paint and transfers. In some cases, however underframes, bogies and maybe wheels and couplings may have to be purchased separately. A recent

development in 00 gauge is the availability of a wide range of reasonably priced etched brass coach sides which can either be used to overlay a proprietary coach model thus converting it from one type of coach to another, or can be utilised as a basis for a scratch built model. In the latter case the main structure of the coach body, floor, roof, ends, interior partitions, etc., can be built up with plastic card which is a fairly straightforward construction job. Compartment coaches are generally the easiest models to scratch build since the interior compartment partitions add strength and rigidity to the model. The sides almost become cosmetic in so far as the strength of the coach is concerned. Open saloon coaches on the other hand are less well supported internally although many designs do have a partition at some point along the coach, perhaps to separate smoking from non-smoking accommodation or one class from another. The seats themselves will add support to the sides.

It goes almost without saying that you need to furnish the interior with representative seating. The amount of internal detail you are prepared to indulge in is a matter for personal choice. You can go the whole hog fitting luggage racks, pictures and mirrors on the partition walls, etc., but it is very unlikely you are going to see all this detail when the model is finished and put into service unless you also intend fitting interior lighting. In my own opinion, at least so far as 4 mm scale and under is concerned, it is sufficient to paint the seats an overall colour representative of the upholstery (make sure you use matt paint) and the interior partitions and inside of the coach sides brown representative of the wood veneer. Seating is generally supplied in most kits, usually in the form of a moulded strip from which the individual seats are cut. Side corridor partitions are deserving of particular attention since they are clearly visible through the windows. Some railway carriages had corridor partitions finished in contrasting light and dark wood veneers which show up prominently

An exceptionally well-painted, lined and lettered model of a Somerset & Dorset Joint Railway Lavatory Third constructed from a Blacksmith Models 4mm scale etched brass kit. (Photo Cove Models)

in prototype photographs. After painting the main corridor partition a medium or dark shade of brown the light wood panels can be represented by painting with cream paint or by using strips of brown gummed parcel tape which is about the right shade for some of the light wood panels. Another finishing touch which is well worthwhile is to fit antimacassars or headrests to the first class seatbacks. These show up reasonably clearly through the windows however dull the interior. They can be represented by strips of thin white paper cut from gummed paper labels which are ideal for this purpose. Tables also show up well and should be represented if appropriate for the model. Table lamps are almost a sine qua non of Pullman cars and some restaurant cars since they appear so prominently behind the window. You will need to decide during the construction process whether to include passengers in your carriages since it is rarely possible to gain access to the interior of a model railway carriage once it is completed. A few seated passengers (there are many types available) and perhaps one or two standing or

walking along the corridor can be something of an eye-catching feature but whether or not you will tire of the same faces staring at you on every journey, or even worse when the train is standing out of service in the siding, is something you need to decide for yourself. I have found Slater's plastic rodding to be ideal for corridor handrails. These need particular care in fitting since they have to be made individually for each window to avoid the drop light windows in the doors, whereupon it becomes essential to ensure they are all level and at the same height. It is well worthwhile including a few partly or fully opened drop light windows and these can generally be arranged without much difficulty All of this preparatory work which has to be decided upon and carried out before you start the main construction work can take time and patience even when you are working from a kit. You can well see why modelling a railway carriage can take so long. The exterior of a coach is also bounding in detail such as door handles, grab rails, roof ventilators, water tank filler caps, corridor connections, end

This completed and beautifully finished LMS Period 1 Composite was converted from an Airfix/Dapol 60ft Composite, two entirely different body styles, the two-window compartments and the panelling being the most noticeable features.
(Photo: Comet Model)

steps and handrails and all the paraphernalia that goes into the underframe such as truss rods, dynamos, brake rigging, accumulator boxes, etc.

Not least of the problems is the painting and lining. Not everyone can emulate the skilled work of the professional coach builder and should you have doubts about your prowess in this respect it may be as well to avoid some of the more complicated fully lined liveries and choose a period when the liveries were simplified. Lining transfers are an invaluable aid but even these require skill and patience in their application. In all cases it is essential to paint the interior and exterior of coach sides before glazing, at the very least around the window frames. Much will depend on the type of coach kit you are constructing but with some plastic kits it may be possible and possibly easier to fully paint, line and letter the coach sides before assembling the model. With some railway carriages the drop light window frames were left in a varnished wood finish which show up in marked contrast to the main coach body colour. This is particularly pronounced in GWR coaches and is well worth adding to proprietary ready-to-run models which sometimes lack this feature. The varnished wood can be represented by an appropriate shade of brown paint.

With so many coach kits available it is hardly conceivable that you will have need to build a model entirely from scratch. However, this is perfectly possible and was in fact accepted as the norm in the days before coach kits and authentic ready-to-run models were as widespread as they are to day. Various materials can be used but possibly the easiest in so far as the coach sides are concerned is card, either the paper-fibre type or plastic or styrene sheet. Cutting out the window openings is the foremost task. Some modellers have gone to the extent of producing hardened steel punches to make a neat and even job of this but hand cutting with a craft knife will generally suffice. The rounded corners are something of a problem.

One method is to drill holes in the four corners of the opening using a drill which approximates to the radius of the inner curvature, The window is finally cut out with a craft knife from corner to corner. I have never met with much success using this method since I have found it all too easy to misalign the drill holes and finish up with windows at varying heights and sizes. I prefer to cut diagonally across the corners with the craft knife and file out the correct curvature afterwards, using a small round Swiss file. I must confess, however, that I am not terribly happy either way and it is very much easier to cut out windows that have square corners. Luckily plastic card is such wonderful material to work with; should you find that you have gone too far with a craft knife and have cut across a pillar between two separate window openings you can usually repair the damage with a wash of liquid cement.

If you are not unduly deterred with cutting out window openings probably the best method of constructing coach sides using card is the 'sandwich' type of construction whereby three layers of card are used to construct each side. An outer and inner layer with the window openings cut out and a centre layer up to waist height just below the glazing material form the sandwich. The three layers cemented or glued together form a strong side which resists warping and pressure from the fingers when handling the finished model. If the inner layer is made of card just slightly thicker than the glazing material and the glazing material is cut from thin glass microscope slides, the glass can be gently prized out after assembly of the side to facilitate

painting. Plastic glazing can be used instead of glass provided this is smeared with Vaseline to prevent it adhering to the glue or cement during assembly of the sides. Alternatively you can pre-paint the sides around the window openings and permanently fix the glazing in place but there is a risk of the adhesive coming into contact with the glazing marring its appearance. The three layers of card in the lower part of the body make a strong three-ply structure which, if you are using plastic card, can be scraped, filed or sandpapered to produce the correct tumble home to the sides, the separate layers acting as contour lines thus providing a useful visual aid to the accurate and even curvature of the sides.

The remaining parts of the coach body can be made from plastic card as previously briefly mentioned. The roof is probably best made from wood. This is certainly the case with open saloon coaches where there is little internal support though you can use one or more layers of card if you are making a model of a compartment coach wherein the internal compartment partitions,

The LSWR 4-2-4T combined engine and carriage shown on page 214 found little use in SR days except for hauling an ex-SE&CR carriage carrying visitors round Southampton Docks. Justification enough for a recreation in N gauge where the combo is seen en route *to Whittleton Docks on the REC's Recborough & Whittleton exhibition layout.* (Photo: REC)

The well-executed painting and lining and the attention to detail both inside and out make the Hornby Railways Pullman Cars very acceptable and attractive 00 gauge models.

provided they are accurately shaped, act as formers. It is preferable to use a lightweight wood such as balsa rather than some of the hardwood roofs that were at one time specially supplied for coach building since these can be rather heavy and put the weight in the wrong place. It is possible to fill in the grain of whatever wood you are using to produce a perfectly smooth finish but it is worth remembering that some coach roofs were at one time covered with canvas and in these cases a super smooth finish would be inappropriate. Here I suggest covering the roof with a sheet of tissue paper which when painted gives the desired fabric effect. To finish off the roof you will most likely need to fit rain strips which can be cut from thin plastic card. Roof ventilators, buffers, bogies and a number of other parts necessary to complete the model can all be obtained from specialist suppliers. The sum total of such bought-in parts together with the cost of the raw materials you use may show some saving on the price of a kit but if you value your time you may find the saving hardly worthwhile. In the two most popular gauges, N and 00, it is questionable whether you would be able to build a model coach for much less than the cost of a proprietary ready-to-run model which only serves to emphasise the value for money of these items. If only there were more of them.

With all forms of model making using plastic card or wood I cannot emphasise too strongly the necessity to have really sharp tools. Craft knife blades are relatively cheap things to buy and there is no point in struggling on with a blunt blade when it is really time it was changed. The trouble with craft knives is that they are sometimes too useful and you find yourself using them as scrapers and for other purposes for which they are not really intended. I always have at least two knives in use at any one time; one with a new sharp blade which I reserve for the really delicate and precise cutting jobs and another with an older worn blade which is past its prime but is still adequate for the rougher jobs.

Another absolute necessity when it comes to model making, especially accurate cutting, assembly and painting work, is to have really adequate lighting. I speak from experience as I struggled for a long while trying to dodge shadows from a straight edge and wondering why cuts with a craft knife drawn along the straight edge did not always line up properly. I also wondered why model making made me feel so tired after an evening session. I invested in an adjustable studio lamp and it made the world of difference. To have the light immediately over your work and to be able to adjust it so that you can avoid all

Many years separate the production of these two 00 gauge models yet the couplings look very much the same. **Above** *The SR Bogie Utility Van dates back to 1958 when the model was first introduced by Tri-ang. Long since out of production it is a much sought after model at Swapmeets.* **Right** *The BR Railfreight HEA 46 tonnes air-braked mineral hopper is one of the latest to be produced by Replica Railways.*

unwanted shadows is, in my opinion, absolutely essential, not only from the point of view of making worthwhile models but also for the sake of your eyes and your health.

The subject of model locomotives, carriages and wagons would be incomplete without some mention of couplings. Probably more ingenuity has been spent on this subject than almost anything else connected with model railways, and the multiplicity of different designs has perhaps been the cause of more dissatisfaction than anything else. At one time it appeared that no manufacturer would dream of fitting a type of coupling which would enable his

rolling stock to couple up to anyone else's, and it seemed to be a point of honour amongst the different firms that they had to establish themselves by inventing their own coupling. By making them so widely different one assumes that each manufacturer hoped to retain his customer's patronage by making it impossible for him to use any other manufacturer's product. There was probably also a question of copyright and patent rights.

Whatever the reason it was a great inconvenience to modellers who wanted to combine the products of different manufacturers on their layout. Thankfully the situation is nowhere near so bad today as

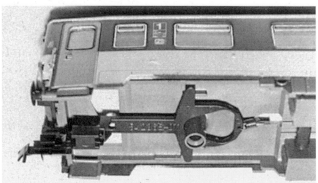

Close coupling of coaches as perfected by Roco. The bogie has been removed to reveal the mechanisms which increases the gap between vehicles when entering curves, thus avoiding buffer locking. Also to be seen is the NEM 362 coupling housing which facilitates the interchange of couplings, This is fast becoming universal with Continental manufacturers.

manufacturers have developed a greater awareness of the needs for compatible couplings and the all round advantage to be gained by adopting common standards. The first realisation dawned with the introduction of TT-3 when British railway modellers accepted the Tri-ang type coupler as standard for the gauge. With the coming of N gauge the process went a stage further whereby an international universal coupling was adopted by all British and Continental manufacturers. The latest of them all, Z gauge, is uncomplicated by the fact that there is at present only one manufacturer producing a complete range of equipment in this gauge.

It is with the older established scales and gauges namely HO and 00 where the coupling problem is most acutely felt there being so many designs to choose from. The majority of HO gauge manufacturers on the Continent use the NEM (European Model Railways Standard) Class A coupling which consists of a hook and a movable bow or loop. The bow pivots upwards to rise over and engage with the hook of the coupling to which it is to be joined. An important exception to the manufacturers using this coupling is Fleischmann whose coupling works on the opposite principle, ie the hook itself is pivoted and the somewhat narrower bow or loop remains in a fixed vertical position. The two types of coupling are incompatible. Yet more different types have been developed in the quest for close coupling but there is a saving grace with these as I will explain in detail later.

The most common coupler used on American HO models is what is usually called the 'horn hook' type sometimes erroneously termed the NMRA type though it has never been sponsored or approved by the body. Airfix used this type in their plastic railway kits. This coupler is very effective for coupling – it has a sideways pressure action – but is less effective when it comes to uncoupling. A simple uncoupler ramp is available but all uncouplers need to be well adjusted, all exactly the same height, and all equally well sprung for the uncoupler ramp to be foolproof. A stiff coupling can result in the vehicle concerned being pushed off the track sideways as the train is pushed over the uncoupler ramp. In practice (and with practice!) it is usually possible to uncouple the 'horn hook' coupler manually using a cocktail stick to force apart the vertical rods of two adjacent couplers. The most desirable American style coupler, though it can be expensive to install, is the Kadee magnetic type. This is a near scale metal knuckle coupler which uncouples automatically from magnetic ramps which are set inconspicuously into the track. A range of different types is available to suit virtually every make or type of rolling stock and locomotive (American prototype, of course), and it can be had in O and N gauge sizes as well as HO; Victors of Islington are the main British Kadee stockists. In America, of course, these couplers are widely sold in hobby shops.

For British outline 00 gauge the Hornby Railways, formerly Tri-ang, tension-lock hook and bar coupling has now gained ascendancy and close variants of it are now used by all manufacturers of ready-to-run locomotives and rolling stock and by a number of kit manufacturers. The coupling works on similar principles to Fleischmann in that the hook pivots upwards to rise over and engage with the loop or bar of the adjoining vehicle There is no denying that the coupling works very well but in its most exaggerated form it is somewhat ugly and obtrusive. Aesthetically more satisfying is the Peco Simplex claw type coupler formerly used by Hornby Dublo and British Trix and latterly included in the Peco Wonderful Wagon kits in the form of the uprated Magni-Simplex Auto Coupler. Whilst it is sometimes possible to engage a hook from the tension-lock coupling on to the claw of a Peco Simplex coupling, for all practical purposes the two types are incompatible. Both types of couplings can be uncoupled remotely; the old Tri-ang type by a ramp between the running rails which lifts the hook and the Peco Simplex by a check rail which guides the coupler to one side. The latest Peco Magni-Simplex Auto Coupler can also be operated by a permanent magnet. The Peco coupler provides for delayed uncoupling whereby a vehicle when pushed over an uncoupling ramp can be positioned on any part of the track without the coupling re-engaging. It also has the advantage that the vehicle can be disengaged from its neighbour and hand lifted from the track without difficulty.

Without an uncoupling ramp, disengaging the tension-lock and similar type couplings can be a troublesome business. Both hooks have to be disengaged simultaneously and I have wrestled many times with an item of rolling stock trying to separate one vehicle from another. The solution is simple. All that is needed is a thin piece of metal, wood or plastic that can be slid under the downward projections of the coupling hooks so that the hooks can be raised and disengaged A thin metal ruler will sometimes do excepting that obstructions such as platforms, boundary fences or a line of wagons on an adjacent siding

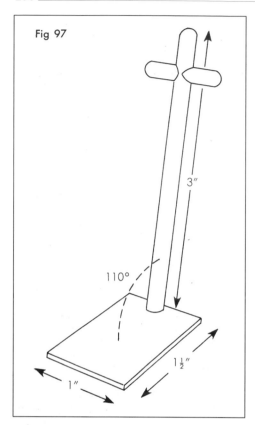

Fig 97 *Uncoupling device for Tri-ang/Hornby Railways' type couplings.*

may prevent access with the ruler. The solution I have hit on is to make a spoon or shovel shaped object as shown in Fig 97. The handle is a piece of plastic sprue left over from a kit. By lucky chance the piece I selected had a small cross piece at one end which I have found useful to hold the handle steady between the thumb and the first and second fingers. The flat plate is an offcut of 20 thou plastic card, 1 in x 1½ in. None of the dimensions is critical except the plastic card which must be thin enough to slide between the tops of the running rails and the downward extension of the pivoting hooks and be wide enough to operate both hooks at the same time. The angle of the

plastic sprue is also not very critical but I have found that the chosen one, 110°, permits the uncoupling device to be manoeuvred between most obstacles including a line of high sided vehicles on an adjacent siding. Such devices are now being offered commercially, but with off-cuts of plastic card and plastic sprue being readily available to most modellers, it costs virtually nothing and is so easy to make.

So far, all the couplings I have mentioned have been the various proprietary type automatic couplings. Their obvious advantage is that they engage with each other automatically when two vehicles are brought together and most of them have the added capability of remote uncoupling. Another feature which they all possess which may not be readily apparent to newcomers to the hobby is that they prevent vehicles coming too close together when being pushed. This is done deliberately to avoid buffer locking. I have already referred to this in Chapter 5 and it must be appreciated that buffer locking is a very serious problem in model railways. It arises mainly due to the sharp radius curves that most modellers are forced by space limitations to use. The sharper the radius of the curve the worse the problem becomes. The length of the vehicle is also a factor to consider. The proprietary type automatic couplings are designed to cater for the extreme conditions found in toy model railways where curves of 1 ft 3 in radius in HO and 00 gauges and 9 in in N gauge are common. In coping with these extreme conditions manufacturers of ready-to-run rolling stock are required to ensure that the buffers of opposing vehicles never meet. The couplings in fact act as buffers. For practical purposes this is fine but from the point of view of realism the wide separation between vehicles leaves a lot to be desired. It also unduly extends the length of a train which on space conscious layouts is a factor to consider. Peco have overcome this problem with their 'Elsie' patented couplings as fitted to the Peco Quality Line N gauge ready-to-run wagons. This coupling which conforms to international standards enables eleven Peco wagons to be coupled together in the same space as ten wagons not fitted with the 'Elsie' coupling.

Roco are one of the leading Continental exponents in the field of close coupling having first patented their design in 1976. Close coupling is particularly desirable in the case of modern day Continental passenger coaches which are designed such that the ends of the bodies overhand the buffers to a very large extent. This results in the gap between coaches being reduced to a bare minimum, the gangway or corridor connection on full size coaches being little more than a length of rubber tubing. The wide gap between vehicles which would follow from using ordinary model railway couplings cannot be disguised by extending the corridor connections such as might have been possible with the old style concertina or bellows type connections and the resultant broad expanse of daylight between coaches looks unsightly and most unrealistic. With the Roco system and others that have followed suit such as the Keen Systems unit referred to in Chapter 5 the coupling is fitted to a special mechanism which has the effect of holding the buffers close together on straight track but increases the separation between vehicles when traversing curves thus reducing the chances of buffer locking even on reverse curves. The Roco close coupling shares the same advantage as the Peco Magni-Simplex in that vehicles can be hand lifted from the track without difficulty and the very latest type of Roco close coupling also provides for remote delayed uncoupling. Fleischmann have also developed a similar system. Marklin have also developed their own close coupling system using conventional Marklin couplings. Needless to say they are all incompatible with each other and the Roco and Fleischmann close couplings are also incompatible with other standard European types. Notwithstanding all this apparent confusion there is hope for the future. Whereas the couplings are incompatible, the shank of the coupling and the coupling housing conform to a standard design referred to as NEM 362

which means that the couplings are freely interchangeable. Without doubt NEM 362 is the way forward and if it is eventually adopted by all manufacturers it could at least mean that changing couplings from one make to another would be simplified. The modeller can then decide which type of coupling he prefers to use and equip all his or her rolling stock accordingly with minimum expense and effort. So far the standard NEM 362 coupler housing is by no means universal amongst Continental manufacturers and has not to my knowledge been adopted in the UK but the advantages are so obvious both from the point of view of the customer and the manufacturer that they cannot be ignored for very much longer.

As an alternative to all the different types of proprietary automatic couplers many British modellers prefer to use the hook and chain, or three-link and screw couplings (as the two types are referred to), as used by all main line standard gauge railways in Europe. Screw couplings are used on all passenger and continuous brake fitted freight stock and on locomotives used for passenger train working. Three-link couplings are only used on wagons without continuous brakes and on locomotives not required for passenger or fitted freight train working. Both types are available in model form down to 4 mm scale but the screw couplings are only representational and do not work like their prototypes. Three-link couplings and miniature screw couplings have been accepted in 00 for many years. Occasionally critics have referred to their overscale appearance, in particular the oversize coupling links, and have pointed out that from the realism point of view the average commercial product is not a lot better than some much maligned automatic couplings. To a large extent such criticism is true and a hard look at the great dangling loops of chain on the end of the average British models fitted with three-link couplings, my own included, will confirm this. Like many things in model railways, the problem looks worse in a photograph than it does in the flesh, but with standards

The Lima version of the tension-lock coupling and the under scale wheels show up rather too readily in this otherwise authentic 00 gauge model of a GWR Paco 'C' Horse Box. The partly-open drop-light window is an unexpected but welcome touch on a ready to run model. Horse boxes are ideal vehicles for fitting dual couplings since they do not look out of place in either goods or passenger trains, though the latter was more usual when they were in service.

improving all the time it was inevitable that someone would point an accusing finger and at the same time come up with a solution. In 4 mm scale, Protofour have produced a fine scale three-link coupling which really looks the part. The links are not only the right size but they are also the right shape and they are the right price as well. A further feature of note is that the links can be lifted by magnetism using a special illuminated shunter's pole which is supplied for the purpose. This overcomes what at first glance might he considered a difficult problem since the links are measurably smaller than the normal commercial 00 gauge 'anchor chains' and might be thought of as being fiddly things to handle. If anything, because of their unique magnetic properties, Protofour three link couplings are easier to use than the other larger types. On all counts, therefore, they are to be recommended, whether or not you are using Protofour standards on the rest of your layout.

Generally speaking loose coupled rolling stock, that is wagons and coaches fitted with three-link couplings or the miniature representation of screw couplings, can only be operated successfully on layouts with curves of 3 ft radius or more. The short wheelbase

four-wheeled wagons can sometimes be propelled over curves of shorter radius but, at the same time, longer wheelbase bogie stock requires curves of even larger radius. Therefore 3 ft is only something of a compromise and even larger radius curves are desirable where possible, to be sure of avoiding buffer locking if three-link or screw couplings are used on all rolling stock, The ideal is perhaps a combination of two different types of coupling; three-link for the smaller four-wheel and shorter wheelbase bogie freight stock and automatic for the longer passenger coaches. In a way this matches prototype British practice to a certain extent, since it is normally only the four-wheel and shorter wheelbase freight vehicles that are not fitted with the continuous vacuum brake and are therefore loose coupled. The difficulty with mixing different types of coupling is that some vehicles and all locomotives, unless they are clearly made for one specific duty, will need to be dual fitted. The vehicles that will need special attention are those that can be seen in both freight and passenger trains, such as passenger luggage and parcel vans, perishable wagons, milk tank wagons and some freight vehicles fitted with vacuum brakes. Dual fitting can be accomplished, however, by having a normal coupling hook on the buffer beam of all vehicles and only fixing the three-link chains to the vehicles without automatic couplings.

Three-link and screw couplings are, of course, non-automatic but for 4 mm scale railway modellers who require an unobtrusive automatic coupling without the disadvantages inherent in most proprietary types I recommend the Alex Jackson coupling. The coupling itself is made out of .011 in diameter (32 gauge) spring steel wire and is therefore very cheap to make. Uncoupling is by electromagnet. The Alex Jackson coupling was fully described in the January 1960 issue of *The Model Railway News* and a revised description giving full constructional and dimensional details was given in the July and August 1977 issues of *Model Railways*. The minimum radius recommended in 4 mm scale is 2 ft 6 in and, bearing in mind my earlier comments about buffer locking, it must be remembered that the Alex Jackson coupling does not fulfil the function of a buffer. When pushing, the vehicle buffers themselves fulfil this role and curves must be laid out to ensure that your longest vehicles will not lock buffers. Something larger than 2 ft 6 in radius may be required depending on the length of your rolling stock. The Alex Jackson coupling is capable of adaption to all gauges from N to O.

Many modellers prefer to assemble their coaching stock into permanently coupled rakes or trains of coaches and there is a lot to be said in favour of this. For one thing it accords with prototype practice since many companies operated their coaching stock in this fashion. The Southern Railway, in particular, even went to the extent of allocating set numbers to each rake of coaches, a set consisting of any number of coaches—two three, four, six or whatever was required to operate a particular service. The advantage in model form is that corridor connections can be made to link up between the coaches and a rigid form of coupling bar can be used which will overcome the problem of buffer locking. The coupling itself can be little

more than a metal bar with a hole drilled at each end, through which it is screwed to the floor of each coach. Normal couplings would, of course, be provided at each end of the rake of coaches for coupling to the locomotive or adding any other items of rolling stock such as extra coaches, parcels vans or express fitted perishable wagons. The one snag with a permanently coupled set of coaches is that units of more than about three coaches can sometimes be awkward things to handle should it be necessary to remove the rake from the layout at any time. Ideally, if you have enough siding space, this need not be necessary and the occasion would only arise infrequently when maintenance is required. If your siding space is limited and you frequently have to resort to hand shunting I recommend that you limit the number of coaches in each set to three.

One obvious candidate for assembly into a permanent rake of coaches is the diesel or electric multiple unit train. Here the more or less permanent connection of the carriages is necessitated by the push pull method of propulsion since with a power bogie at only one end of a unit (it is hardly conceivable that with a model diesel or electric multiple unit you would need more than one power bogie) the train will be operating in 'reverse' for 50 per cent of its time. Coupling the coaches together provides an opportunity to spread the electrical pick-ups throughout the whole length of the train, thereby overcoming any possibility of the relatively short wheelbase power bogie stalling on the dead frogs of point-work.

Rolling stock, whether it be coaches or wagons, has endless variety and one is constantly being tempted to add new items to a layout. Whether the inspiration is the introduction of a new proprietary ready-to-run model, or a new kit, or whether one has just seen a plan in a current issue of one of the monthly magazines, whatever the reason, one is constantly being tempted to buy or construct new items. There comes a time, and it happens all too quickly, when you reach saturation point and the available

An engineer's train such as the one shown here hauled by LMS 1P 0–4–4T No 1407 is an example of a train that could be permanently made up but only run when required.

siding space or station terminal roads will not hold any more wagons or coaches without cluttering up the running lines. This will never do and you have to think about storage facilities off the layout, but at the same time in such a position that they are readily available when required. I do not think it is very satisfactory just to keep spare rolling stock in cardboard boxes. It is too fiddly opening and closing the boxes after each operating session and in any case the average cardboard box will not withstand unlimited handling.

A better way is to construct a series of shallow drawers or trays, just deep enough to cover the height of the rolling stock (in 00 gauge say about 2¼ in) and devise some means of partitioning the interior of the tray so that each item of rolling stock can be kept apart from its neighbour, rather on the lines of a cutlery drawer. There are any number of extensions of the theme beyond

the basic idea. You could, for example, cut grooves in the base of the drawer to take the wheel flanges. A further modification might be to make separate lift-out containers for each item of rolling stock, the containers being designed to fit over the rails and with one open end so that the vehicle it contains can be rolled out directly on the track, along the lines of a re-railing device. Such an elaboration would be particularly useful for bogie rolling stock. Each drawer or magazine could be constructed internally to take the rolling stock for a particular service or train, such as 'newspaper/parcels train', 'milk train' or 'pick-up goods' to mention three examples. Any means you can devise to hold your spare rolling stock and at the same time make easy its transfer to and from the layout will increase enormously the pleasure of operating sessions. Storing rolling stock off the layout under cover will also help to diminish the cleaning problem!

CHAPTER 11
Operating

With the baseboard built, the track laid, the scenery installed and the locomotives, carriages and wagons either bought or built, what do we do now? Well, the whole point of all the foregoing activity, in case you had forgotten, is to provide a layout on which to operate working model trains. Some people tend to lose sight of this object, rather like some motoring enthusiasts who seem to spend all their time peering under the bonnet or clambering underneath the car but who never have any time (or inclination?) to take themselves or their family out in it. Sometimes it is a bit of an anti-climax, after all the feverish activity in building a layout, to find that it is virtually completed. But very rarely is it completely completed (if that is not too much of a contradiction in terms!) as there is always something that can be done, in rather the same way as local authorities are always carrying out road improvements and developers are always pulling down houses and putting up new ones. You may well want to do something similar with your model railway: re-plan a particular track layout, extend a siding, replace a proprietary model goods shed with an exact scale scratch-built model or simply paint a zebra crossing on the road outside the station entrance.

Assuming all the really hard work is over, there is still plenty to keep you occupied when it comes to operating the layout. Exactly what pleasure and fulfilment you obtain will, to a certain extent, depend on your approach to the hobby in the first place. If you merely like to see a locomotive and train on the move then you will find enough pleasure in just that. Watching the motion of the locomotive, the movement of the valve gear, pistons, connecting and coupling rods and the gentle rock of the train as it passes over the points are just some of the things that fascinate the average person who likes to watch the trains go by. On the other hand, if you find the idea of train watching too mild and passive you can add purpose to the operating by running the trains to a timetable, which should embrace a complete service of trains – express passenger, local stopping passenger, goods, empty coaching stock, light engine workings, etc. A specially geared, speeded-up clock can be a useful mechanical aid. It scales down time and enables you to run a full day's service in something like one hour instead of 24, which will also cut out the waiting time between services.

One of the most fascinating operations on a model railway is shunting and the receiving and despatching of goods trains. You can naturally please yourself entirely how to make up your goods trains, and if you want you can do so purely to satisfy aesthetic considerations. For example, one grey wagon, one brown wagon, two white covered vans, one silver oil tanker, one

Many pleasurable hours can be spent shunting a yard such as this one at Eastwell.

green horse box and a dark grey brake van may make a satisfactory goods train in your estimation.

However, it is as well to remember the considerations that dictate the formation of a goods train in real life and to profit from these when you can. The train will consist either of wagons carrying goods from one place to another or it will comprise empty wagons proceeding to a station or loading point to pick up goods. Some wagons (for example, covered parcel vans) will pick up and put down goods all over the system. Others, such as coal wagons, will only carry a load in one direction from coal mine to consumer and for 50 per cent of their time they will run empty.

If you have a goods yard you can add interest to its operation if you try and

imagine a typical day's transit of goods, both inwards and outwards, and arrange the formation of the train accordingly. For instance, you may want to take delivery of two wagon loads of coal, some barrels of mineral oil, a combine harvester and the usual daily supply of sundries and parcels. You may have for forwarding some boxes of fruit and tomatoes, some livestock (say cattle or sheep) and a couple of empty coal wagons that have just been unloaded from a previous day's delivery. To cater for this traffic you will need to send to the yard the two loaded coal wagons, an open wagon containing the mineral oil barrels, a flat truck or Lowmac to carry the combine harvester, a couple of ordinary covered vans for the sundries and parcels and some empty cattle wagons to pick up the livestock. The fruit and tomatoes can probably be despatched in the covered vans after they have deposited the sundries and parcels, but it may be necessary to send in some empty fruit vans specially to pick up this traffic. You must ensure that you have siding space for all these wagons when they arrive, bearing in mind that you have empty wagons already in the yard waiting to be picked up. Also, there must be room to shunt the loaded wagons into the appropriate unloading bays and likewise for the empty wagons to be positioned to pick up their loads.

All this takes a bit of sorting out and if you add further complications, such as limiting the maximum number of wagons that can be hauled by different locomotives, applying weight restrictions which limit the types of locomotive that can enter each siding, plus trying to complete the operation against the clock to meet a timetable, you are likely to find yourself doing a bit of head scratching! To add a little more interest and variety to the

method of determining inwards and outward loads, and to simulate the unpredictable daily fluctuations in traffic that often occur, you can write the description of typical loads on to cards which you can shuffle and deal to yourself. Alternatively, you can use ordinary playing cards and have a list of codes showing what each card represents, eg, Ace of Hearts for one combine harvester, Jack of Clubs for 16 tons of household coal, Nine of Spades for one loaded milk tank wagon, etc. The element of chance and surprise can add a little spice to the operation!

Further interest is added if the layout is fully signalled and interlocked, as in the case of the full size railway, yet very few models ever seem to reach this stage of perfection. Signals are all too often installed more for decoration than for actual control purposes. It is a pity really, as there is no doubt that proper signalling can add considerable interest to the operation. Unfortunately, it is a complex subject in itself and there are a

The era of loose-coupled pick-up goods trains has long since passed but their operation in miniature is just one of the delights of railway modelling. An Adams Radial Tank in early SR livery heads just such a train into Wyndlesham Cove. The Hybar tarpaulin wagon is particularly noteworthy.

A variety of GWR signals can be seen here on Robert Tivendale's Ashley Bridge, all of them based on Ratio components but modified for solenoid operation. The ringed arms are siding signals used for goods lines or yard exits. The platform-mounted bracket signal with two holes in the arm is a backing signal for wrong direction running within station limits.

number of mechanical and electrical problems to solve that the average modeller fears are either beyond his comprehension or his means. Fully operating signalling is certainly an added expense and complication that will delay the completion of a model layout and will not be absolutely essential for its operation. It can, then, if circumstances dictate, be dispensed with and a modeller working to a budget, with limited spare time available, may find the money he would need to spend on signalling more profitably employed on buying a new locomotive or laying a few extra yards of track. Model railways, unlike the full size ones, can operate without working signals and when modellers find this out, as they do very early on, they tend to neglect the subject. However, I do not want to be accused of encouraging this attitude.

One problem with miniature signals, particularly the mechanical semaphore type, is that they can easily be damaged. When it comes to siting signals you must consider

the model railway operator as well as the imaginary driver of the train. Signals at the end of a station platform are a case in point since this is often the place where engines are coupled or uncoupled from a train. If you are using non-automatic couplings you may find the presence of a single post at this particular spot will make it difficult to reach the coupling, or you could even find that the signal becomes damaged because of frequent contact with your hand or arm, or the sleeve of your jacket. Where problems such as this are likely to occur it may be necessary to effect a compromise solution so far as siting is concerned or alternatively you may find a different type of signal, such as a bracket signal, may enable you to position the signal post on the far side of the track out of harm's way. Plastic signals such as Ratio's in 00 gauge are very good, but they are light and will not withstand clumsy or thoughtless handling. Young children find signals particularly fascinating and they love to move the arms up and down.

Unfortunately they are not deterred by the fact that the arms may be linked to, a solenoid or a mechanical lever frame by a relatively fragile piece of wire, and either the wire gets bent or the arm comes off the pivot when they try to move it.

Certainly some practical aspects have to be considered when it comes to the installation of signalling and you may often find that you have to compromise with what is required by railway regulations and what you have room for on your layout. One book which I recommend on the subject, both from the point of view of content and value for money, is 'British Railway Signalling', first published by Ian Allan in 1963 and since revised. The book is a mine of information about different types of signals, their layout at stations and junctions, and the different rules and regulations governing their use and the operating of trains. in fact, it gives all the prototype information the modeller needs to know to enable him to make an authentic installation on his layout.

There is no shortage of proprietary signals, ready-made or in kit form, both for the mechanical semaphore and the colour light variety in all the popular scales and gauges. The extent to which miniaturisation has been extended in the field of working colour light signals is very commendable even down to N gauge. For British prototypes Eckon produce an extensive range of 4 mm scale colour light signal kits in two, three and four aspects in a variety of different combinations and styles such as platform, lineside or wall mounted and ground signals. Built around grain of wheat lamp bulbs the housings are technically oversize but by no means excessively so. Small resistors reduce the normal 12–16 volt AC power supply to prolong the lamp life and avoid the risk of overheating which might otherwise distort the plastic housings. The range of Ratio 4 mm scale plastic kits covering GWR square and tubular posts, LMS upper quadrant, LNWR lower quadrant, LNER latticed posts and a gantry set are now well known. They have also introduced a range

of working semaphore signals based on GWR square post and SR rail-built post prototypes which are a real break through for 4 mm scale modellers requiring a remote control mechanical system. With the GWR signals the post and arms, including the operating wire and the special spring-return mechanism, are supplied ready assembled and painted where necessary and it only remains to fit the ladder, platforms and balance weights to complete the model. A particularly noteworthy feature is that the semaphore arms are fitted with correct colour see-through spectacle lenses. The operating mechanism in the base of the signal is encased in a tube which enables the signal to be installed in a ½ in diameter hole drilled in the baseboard. The signal is operated by a remote control lever which can be similarly installed in a ½ in diameter hole at any point in the baseboard convenient to the operator. The signal and lever

A close up of one of Robert Tivendale's signals showing the operating wires.

Signal posts made out of scrap bull-head rail were a distinctive feature of many SR signals. This 4mm scale 'rail-built' home and distant signal was built by Paul Skinner from a Ratio kit.

are connected below the baseboard by a length of cord passing through small brass eyes at intervals of about 12 in. An adjuster tied into the cord ensures the correct tension. Other manufacturers supply a range of etched brass semaphore arms and signal ladder parts and cast metal brackets to aid home construction using basic raw materials such as metal bars or tubing or even lengths of rail section for the posts. Disc and miniature semaphore ground signals are also available in 4 mm scale.

Throughout I have emphasised the need for cleaning and maintenance. In the chapter on electrical equipment I stressed that rails and wheels should be clean to ensure electrical conductivity between the power source and the motor. A most useful aid to this is Electrolube PL-64X which is available from Peco stockists. Applied to a clean cloth and rubbed well on to rail surfaces and wheel tyres it removes contamination. A further thin coating improves electrical conductivity and reduces the need for frequent cleaning. It is also a mechanical

lubricant ideal for all bearings, gear assemblies, etc., and is particularly suitable for cleaning the brushes and commutators of electric motors. With ordinary lubricating oils, any excess on the gears and wheels can get thrown around on to rail surfaces and electrical pick ups, interfering with the electrical conductivity

Regular cleaning and maintenance of rolling stock wheels and bearings will reduce their drag resistance, thus enabling locomotives to haul longer and heavier loads and improve their performance on starting and on climbing gradients. It will also increase their speed capabilities – but this can be a mixed blessing. Most model railway locomotives are capable of going far faster than their full-size prototypes. It is all too easy to turn the controller to the maximum notch and let the locomotive run away with its train, but the sight of a train lurching into a corner at a scale 150 mph looks utterly ridiculous.

By a simple scaling down you can work out the correct speed for your trains. If you time the train over a measured distance and use the figures in the table below you can calculate its approximate scale speed. For distances less than those quoted in the table the timings would be reduced in proportion, eg, over a distance of 35 feet a 4 mm scale train would take 30 seconds to approximate to a scale speed of 60 mph, or 12 seconds over 14 feet. It is interesting to note that in HO the figures for feet per minute are the same as for miles per hour.

After you have tried a number of runs you will soon get to know where to set the controller to obtain a realistic speed. Periodical timing checks are one way of keeping an eye on the performance of your locomotives and rolling stock. Longer and slower runs may well indicate that the rolling stock is in need of attention either because the rolling resistance is increased or because insufficient power is getting through the circuit to the motor.

Also there are the visual aspects to consider, which brings us to dusting the layout. Many model railway items, especially the smaller lighter scenic accessories, are comparatively fragile, and I find an old shaving brush is an ideal tool for most cleaning purposes. It is small enough to get into most nooks and crannies and to be manageable. Smooth, flat surfaces are the obvious places where dust shows most, and a regular cleaning will make all the difference.

Cleaning also presents the opportunity for inspecting the trackwork and lineside accessories. You should be particularly careful to ensure that there are no loose metal objects such as track pins, nuts or screws lying on or near the tracks. They can very easily cause short circuits across the rails or insulated wheels of locomotives, especially the Triang/Hornby types fitted with Magnadhesion where pins sometimes get attracted to the magnets in the locomotive chassis. These loose objects are a potential source of trouble since they can cause derailment by jamming point switch blades or check rails. Any nuts, bolts or screws should be carefully examined since the odds are they have worked loose and fallen from a passing locomotive or train.

It can be annoying when you start what you hope and expect to be an enjoyable operating session to find things going wrong. Maybe a locomotive refuses to move or stalls on the pointwork, or a wagon or coach keeps derailing or uncoupling itself, or a thousand and one other mishaps. It is the nature of all working things that they do not go on forever, and inevitably something will move out of alignment or bend, break or simply wear out. It is very often the most trivial thing that is the root cause of the problem and it takes far more time finding the source than it does applying the cure. The only course is to approach the problem methodically and eliminate all possible causes one by one.

It is impossible to give a fault finding chart listing all trouble spots and their cure but the two most likely problems are derailments or an interruption or break in the electrical circuit. In the case of electrical troubles, first

	Feet per minute			**Miles per hour**
N Gauge	HO	00/EM Protofour	O Gauge	Scale equivalent
6	10	12	20	10
12	20	23	40	20
18	30	35	60	30
24	40	46	80	40
30	50	58	100	50
36	60	70	120	60
42	70	81	140	70
48	80	93	160	80

of all try another locomotive to see if the fault is with the locomotive or the track. If it is the track, check right through the circuit from the mains plug to the electric motor. If it appears to be the locomotive attach the 12-volt power supply direct to the motor to check whether it is the motor at fault or the electrical pick-up. In the case of derailments this will be due to displacement of either wheels or track. If every item of rolling stock is affected it will most likely be due to the track but if only one item is troublesome it will most likely be the wheels of the offending vehicles. In both cases check for gauge and for any vertical displacement. Wheels sometimes work loose on their axles and some of the lighter plastic items of rolling stock can warp and twist lifting one of the four wheels off the track. Trackwork is very much at the mercy of the baseboard which, if it shrinks, twists or warps, will take the track along with it.

Check this with a straight edge laid along the top of the rails. Premature uncoupling, which is sometimes another source of trouble, is also likely to be caused by uneven track, especially if you find it happens on one particular spot on the layout.

To conclude, I have tried to show in this book that there is a lot more to model railways than may at first meet the eye. It has not been possible to touch exhaustively on every single aspect of the hobby, but the book should give you plenty of ideas on how you can go railway modelling at the present time. To a large extent the hobby is a personal thing. You can get out of it exactly what you want, and although there are certain conventions, rules and guide lines which should normally be followed you can, if you want, flout the lot and you will only have yourself to answer to. How *you* go railway modelling is in the end up to you.

Appendices

1 Model railway and allied clubs

It is not practical in a book of this kind to give accurate details of the several hundred model railway and allied clubs that exist in Great Britain today. The majority of the organising committees of such clubs consist of sparetime volunteers who are elected to their posts and it is inevitable therefore that with changes brought about by Annual General Meetings and with club officers having to resign for private or business reasons, alterations in the names and addresses of club secretaries will arise. Changes also occur in the clubs themselves, particularly in the case of local district clubs as new ones are created and some of the established clubs find for various reasons that they have to close down. A list of such clubs can easily lose its value by becoming out of date.

Readers in Britain who are interested to know whether there is a model railway club in their vicinity are advised to refer to back numbers of the main model railway magazines where club activities are reported regularly each month. The chances are that during the year most clubs will be referred to at one time or another.

Less liable to change are the clubs and societies serving a particular branch or aspect of the hobby which are organised on a national basis. A list showing the scope of such clubs follows. The club titles adequately describe the interests they aim to serve. Such clubs perform a valuable function bringing together modellers with a common interest throughout the country by means of club journals, publications and meetings. Very often these national clubs have their own local branches, autonomous organisations in themselves holding meetings in various centres and circulating their own news sheets to members. If you can identify your interests with any of these national clubs or societies it can very often be to your advantage to apply for membership, since many such organisations offer facilities unobtainable elsewhere. For example, some of the societies who cater for particular scales or gauges produce for their members a range of essential items such as track parts, wheels, or even complete kits for making locomotives and rolling stock not normally available from ordinary trade sources. Demonstrating your interests by joining such a club also helps to establish the potential demand for certain items, and a healthy club acting on behalf of several hundreds or thousands of members can often bring influence to bear on manufacturers to produce the kind of equipment most wanted by members.

The following lists some of the national clubs and societies catering for specialised aspects of the hobby:

Scale and gauges etc

Two Millimetre Scale Association
N Gauge Society
The 009 Society
Three Millimetre Society
British 1:87 Scale Society
Double O Gauge Association
EM Gauge Society
Protofour Society
Scalefour Society
S Gauge Model Railway Society
Gauge O Guild
Association of 16 mm NG Modellers
Gauge 1 Model Railway Association
Hornby Railway Collectors' Association (Gauge O and Dublo)

Prototype interests

Great Western Society Limited
The LMS Society
LNER Study Group
Southern Railways Group
The Broad Gauge Society
Austrian Railways Group
Czech & Slovak Railways Group
German Railway Society
Italian Railway Society
Japanese Railway Society
N.M.R.A. (British Region)
Netherlands Railways Society
Portugese Railways Group
Scandinavian Railways Society
SNCF Society
Swiss Railways Society
Industrial Railway Society
Tramway & Light Railway Society
Historical Model Railway Society
Locomotive Club of Great Britain
Railway Correspondence & Travel Society
Stephenson Locomotive Society

2 Railway books and magazines

There is a vast library of railway books, all of which are potentially interesting to railway modellers depending on the particular project they have chosen. The following titles have been selected either because they have been written and produced with railway modellers in mind or because they contain a wealth of prototype information of general interest to modellers. No guarantee can be given for the up-to-date accuracy of all details Many of the titles may no longer be in print but are listed as copies may be obtainable from specialist second-hand book sellers or on loan from public libraries.

Magazines

British Railway Modelling: Published on the 2nd Thursday of every month. Warners Group Publications plc.
Continental Modeller: Published monthly on the 15th of preceding month. Peco Publications and Publicity Ltd.
Model Railway Enthusiast: Published on the 1st Friday of each month. Link House Magazines Ltd.
Model Railway Journal: Published eight times per year. Wild Swan Publications Ltd.
Model Rail: Published 4 times a year. EMAP Apex Publications Limited.
Model Trains International: Available from leading model railway dealers and specialist railway bookshops or on direct subscription only. Kristall Productions. 4 Surbition Hall Close, Kingston, Surrey. KT1 2JX.
Railway Modeller. Published monthly on the 22nd of preceding month. Peco Publications and Publicity Ltd.
Railmodel Digest: Published 4 times a year. An imprint of Hawkshill Publishing. PO Box 2 Chagford, Devon. TQ13 8TZ.
Rail Miniature Flash and Loco Revue: French language magazines available from Peco Technical Advice Bureau
Model Railroader: Published monthly. Kalmbach Publishing Co, 21027 Cross-Roads Circle. PO Box 1612. Waukesha. W1 53187, U.S.A.
Railroad Model Craftsman: Published monthly. Carstens Publications Inc PO Box 700 Newton, New Jersey 07860 USA.

Practical modelling books

Miniature Building Construction, Miniature Locomotive Construction, Miniature Landscape Modelling, by John H. Ahern, Argus Books Ltd.
Gauge 'O' Guild Handbooks: No 1 Trade Directory, No 2 Standards & Trackwork, No 3 Coach & Wagon Constructlon, No 4 Locomotive Constructlon, No 5 Signal Construction, No 6 Garden Railways in all scales, Modellers' Manual vol 1, Small Layouts, Gauge 'O' Guild.
Wheel Specifications for the modeller, Flexichas— A Way to Build Fully Compensated Model Locomotive Chassis. Gear Fitting for the Small Scale Modeller with No Workshop, by Mike Sharman. The Oakwood Press.
60 Plans for Small Railways, Plans for Larger Layouts, Track Plans, A Home for Your Railway, Starting in Scale 00, Railways in the Garden, by Don Neale. **Period Railway Modelling— Buildings** by Vivien Thompson. **Buckingham Great Central,** by Peter Denny. **Narrow Gauge Adventure,** by P.D. Hancock. **Setrack Planbook-N, Setrack Planbook-HO/00, Lineside & Scenic Features, Texture Modelling.** Peco Publications and Publicity Ltd.
An Introduction to 4mm Finescale Modelling, Building, Laying & Wiring PCB Track, by Tim Shackleton. Railmodel Publications.
PSL Model Railway Guides: 1 Baseboards, Track and Electrification: 2 Layout Planning; 3 Structure Modelling; 4 Scenery; 5 Operating Your Layout; 6 Branch Line Railways; 7 Modern Railways; 8 Narrow Gauge Railways, PSL Complete Guide to Model Railways, Scenic Railway Modelling, all by Michael Andress. **Model Railway Kit Building,** by T. J. Booth. **1001 Model Railway Questions and Answers,**

Model Railway Operation, Model Railway Signalling, The Garden Railway Manual, PSL Book of Model Railway Track Plans, PSL Book of Model Railway Wiring, The Model Railway Design Manual, by C. J. Freezer. Complete Book of Model Railway Electronics, by Roger Amos. Modellers' Guide to the GWR, by T. J. Booth. Professional Approach to Model Railways, by John Wylie. Patrick Stephens Ltd.
Architectural Modelling in 4mm Scale, Industrial & Mechanised Modelling, by David Rowe. Landscape Modelling, by Barry Norman. An Approach to Building Fine Scale Track in 4mm, Model Railway Layout Design, Light Railway Layout Design, Etched Loco Construction, Whitemetal Locos – A Kitbuilder's Guide, Locomotive Kit Chassis Construction in 4mm. Plastic Structure Kits, by Iain Rice. The 4mm Coach: Parts 1, 2, & 3. Great Western Branch Line Modelling: Parts 1, 2 & 3, by Stephen Williams. The 4mm Engine – A Scratchbuilder's Guide, by Guy Williams. Cottage Modelling for Pendon, by Chris Pilton. The Art of Weathering, by Martyn Welch. Carriage Modelling Made Easy, by David Jenkinson, The 4mm Wagon: Parts 1 & 2, by Geoff Kent. 7mm Modelling: Part 1, by Gordon Gravett. Peter Denny's Buckingham Branch Lines: Parts 1 & 2, by Peter Denny. Wild Swan Publications Ltd.

Locomotives

Historic Locomotive Drawings in 4mm Scale, drawn by F.J. Roche. BR Main Line Diesels in 4mm Scale, BR Electric Locomotives in 4mm Scale, Ian Allan Ltd.
GWR Engines, Names, Numbers, Types and Classes (1940 to Preservation), by B. Whitehurst. The Engines of the LMS (Built 1923-51), by J.W.P. Rowledge. The History of Highland Railway Locomotives, by P. Tatlow. A Pictorial Record of Great Western Engines, A Pictorial Record of Great Western Absorbed Engines, A Pictorial Record of Southern Locomotives, by J.H. Russell. An Illustrated History of LMS Locomotives, by Bob Essery & David Jenkinson. An Illustrated History of LNWR Engines, by Edward Talbot, Oxford Publishing Co.
An Illustrated Review of Midland Locomotives from 1883: Vol 1 General Survey, Vol 2 Passenger Tender Classes, Vol 3 Tank Engines, Vol 4 Goods Tender Engines, by R. J. Essery & D. Jenkinson. Midland & South Western Junction Railway: Vol 2 – Locomotives, by Mike Barnsley. Great Western Diesel Railcars, by J. H. Russell. LSWR Locomotives – The Adams Classes, LSWR Locomotives – The Drummond Class, LSWR Locomotives – The Beattie Classes, LSWR Locomotives – The Urie Classes, by D.L. Bradley, Wild Swan Publications Ltd.
Locomotives in Outline, by C. J. Freezer. Peco Publications & Publicity Ltd.
The Locomotives of the GWR, Parts 1-12. Locomotives of the LNER, Parts 1-10 Locomotives of the LB & SCR, Parts 1-3, Locomotives of the LSWR, Parts 1-2, Locomotives of the LC & DR, Locomotives of the SER, Locomotives of the SE & CR Locomotives of the Southern Railway, Parts 1-2, Railway Correspondence & Travel Society.
Locomotives Illustrated. Published bi-monthly by RAS Publishing.
Fowler Locomotives, Stanier Locomotives, Maunsell Locomotives, Bulleid Locomotives, Ivatt & Riddles Locomotives, Gresley Locomotives, Collett & Hawksworth Locomotives, Stroudley Locomotives, Drummond Locomotives, by Brian Haresnape, Churchward Locomotives, by Brian Haresnape & Alec Swain. Robinson Locomotives, by Brian Haresnape & Peter Rowledge. Ian Allan Ltd.

Coaches

Preserved Railway Coaches, Bulleid Coaches in 4mm Scale by S.W. Stevens-Stratten. Rolling Stock Recognition: 1 Coaching Stock, by Colin Marsden. Ian Allan Ltd.
Great Western Railway Coaches 1890–54, Gresley's Coaches, by Michael Harris. David & Charles.
Southern Railway Rolling Stock, Service Stock of the SR, Carriage Stock of Minor Standard Gauge Railways, by R.W. Kidner. Carriage Stock of the SE & CR Maunsell's S.R. Steam Passenger Stock 1923~1939 Bulleid's SR Passenger Stock, by David Gould. Carriage Stock of the LB & SCR, by P.J. Newbury. Isle of Wight Steam Passenger Rolling Stock, by R. J. Maycock & M.J.E. Reed. Oakwood Press. British Raailways Mk.l Coaches, by Keith Parkin. Historical Model Railway Society.
The Coaching Stock of British Railways 1980, by P Mallaband & L. J. Bowles. Railway Correspondence & Travel Society.
British Railway Carriages of the 20th Century, by David Jenkinson. Patrick .Stephens.
LMS Coaches (An Illustrated History) Midland Carriages. An Illustrated Review, by R.J. Essery & D. Jenkinson. Midland Railway Carriages Vol 1 & Vol 2, by R E. Lacey & George Dow. GWR Auto Trailers: Pt.1, by John Lewis. The Midland & South Western Junc. Rly: Vol 3 Carriages & Wagons, by Mike Barnsley. Wild Swan Publications Ltd.
A Pictorial Record of LNWR Coaches, by D. Jenkinson. A Pictorial Record of Great Western Coaches, Vol 1 1838–1913 and Vol 2 1903–1948. Great Western Coaches Appendix Vol 1 & Vol 2, by J.H. Russell, The Illustrated History of LMS Standard Coaching Stock: I & II, by D. Jenkinson & R.J. Essery. Oxford Publishing Co.

Wagons

Historic Wagon Drawings in 4mm Scale, drawn by F.J. Roche. Rolling Stock Recognition: 2 BR & Private Owner Wagons, by Colin Marsden. Ian Allan Ltd.
History of GWR Goods Wagons Vols 1 & 2, by A.G. Atkins, W. Beard, DJ. Hyde & R. Tourret. The LMS Wagon, R.J. Essery & K. Morgan. British Railways Wagons, by Don Rowland. David & Charles.
GWR Iron Minks, by S.H. Lewis, M.E.M. Lloyd, R.G Metcalf & N. Miler. HMRS.
Great Western Wagons Appendix, Great Western Wagons Plan Book, by J.H. Russell. A Pictorial Record of LNER Wagons, by Peter Tatlow. Midland Wagons, Vols I & 2 An Illustrated History of LMS Wagons: Vols I & 2, by R.J. Essery. Private Owner Wagons, Vols I, 2, 3 & 4, by W Hudson. An Illustrated History of Southern Wagons: Vol 1 LSWR & S & DJR, by G. Bixley, A. Blackburn, R. Chorley, M King, J Newton. History of Southern Wagons: Vol 2 LBSCR and Minor Companies, by M. King and J. Newton. An Illustrated History of BR Wagons Vol 1, by P Bartlett, D Larkin, T Mann, R Silsbury, A Ward. Oxford Publishing Co.
The Modeller's Sketchbook of Private Owner

Wagons, Books 1, 2 & 3. Eames (Reading) Ltd.
Wagons of the LNER—North British No.1, by John Hooper. Irwell Press.
Lancashire & Yorkshire Wagons: Vol 1, by Noel Coates. **Official Drawings of LMS Wagons No.1,** by R.J. Essery. Wild Swan Publications Ltd
Modern Private Owners Wagons on British Rail, by D. Ratcliffe. Patrick Stephens Ltd.
Petroleum Rail Tank Wagons of Britain, Tourret Publishing, 5 Bryan Close, Abingdon, Oxon.
BR Standard Freight Wagons, Private Owner Freight Wagons, Pre-nationalisation Freight Wagons, BR General Parcels Rolling Stock, BR Department Rolling Stock, by D. Larkin, D. Bradford Barton Ltd.

General

Historical Model Railway Society Livery Registers: No 1 Caledonian Railway, No 3 LSWR & Southern Railway, LNWR Liveries. Midland Style, by George Dow. **Great Western Way,** by J.N. Dow. **British Railway Signalling,** by G.M. Kichenside & Alan Williams. **Railway Liveries No 1 SR No 2 GWR; No 3 LMS; No 4 LNER,** by Brian Haresnape. **Railway Liveries: BR Steam 1948–68,** by Brian Haresnape & Colin Boocock. **GWR Country Stations Vol 1 & Vol 2, A Railway Modeller's Picture Library – A Sourcebook of Prototype Materials,** by Chris Leigh. **Southern Country Stations: 1 LSWR, 2 SE & CR,** by Robert Antell. Ian Allan Ltd.
Railway Stations – Southern Region, by Nigel Wikeley & John Middleton. Peco Publications & Publicity Ltd.
Modellers' & Enthusiasts' Guide to The Somerset & Dorset Line, by Brian Macdermott. Patrick Stephens Ltd.
An Historical Survey of Great Western Engine Sheds 1947, by E. Lyons. **An Historical Survey of Great Western Engine Sheds 1837–1947** (including amalgamated companies), by E. Lyons & E. Mountford. **An Historical Survey of Southern Sheds 1923–1947,** by C. Hawkins & C, Reeve. Oxford Publishing Co. **LMS Engine Sheds: Vol 1 L&NWR Vol 2 MR; Vol 3 L& YR, Vol 4 Smaller English Constituents; Vol 5 The Caledonian Railway, Great Eastern Railway Engine Sheds Parts One & Two, GWR Engine Sheds London Division, Southern Nouveau,** by Chris Hawkins & George Reeve. Wild Swan Publications Ltd.
A Pictorial Record of Great Western Signailing, by A Vaughan. **A Pictorial Record of LMS Signals,** by G. Warburton. **A Pictorial Record of Southern Signals,** by G Pryer. **A Pictorial Record of LNER Constituent Signalling,** by A A Maclean **A Pictorial Record of LNER Signalling,** by Richard D. Foster. **The Signal Box—Pictorial History & Guide to Designs,** by the Signalling Study Group. Oxford Publishing Co. **Signals for the Railway Modeller,** by Derek L. Mundy, **Road Vehices of the GWR, Great Western Road. Vehicles Appendix,** by Philip J. Kelley Oxford Publishing Co.
A Pictorial Record of Great Western Architecture, by A. Vaughan, **An Historical Survey of Selected Great Western Stations. Vol 1. 2 & 3,** by R. Clark. **Great Western Branch Line Termini, Vols 1 & 2,** by Paul Karau. **A Pictoriai Record of LMS Architecture, A Pictorial History of Midland Railway Architecture Stations & Structures of the Settle & Carlisle Railway,** by V.R. Anderson & G.K. Fox. **An Historical Survey of Selected Southern Stations,** by G.A. Pryer & G.J. Bowring. **An Historical Survey of the Somerset & Dorset Railway** (Track Layout and Illustrations), by C.W. Judge & C. Potts. **North Eastern Branch Line Termini,**

by Ken Hoole. **Bridges for Modellers,** by L. V. Wood. Oxford Publishing Co.
Eric Plans–GWR & LMS Buildings, Downesplans– No.1 Country Buildings, No.2 Railway Buildings, No.3 More Country Buildings, by Allan Downes. **Original Miniature Buildings,** by J.M. Gill, Peco Publications & Publicity Ltd
An Index to Railway Model Drawings, by S.A. Leleux. The Oakwood Press.
MRC Special–7: Model Drawings Reference Book, by Clive S. Carter. Ian Allan Ltd.
19th Century Railway Drawings in 4mm Scale, by Alan Prior. David & Charles.
Track Layout Diagrams of the GWR and BR (WR). A series of publications in several parts, giving detailed diagrams of every station and siding layout. c 1880–1920, with details and dates of alterations up to 1973. Published by R A Cooke. 'Evergreen', School Lane, Harwell, Oxon. OX11 0ES.
An Album of Pre-grouping Signal Boxes, by M. A. King. Turntable Publications.
Along Hornby Lines, by B. Huntingdon, Oxford Publishing Co.
The Bassett Lowle Story, by Roland Fuller. **The Hornby Companion Series: Vol 3 Hornby Dubio Trains,** by Michael Foster. **Vol 5 The Hornby Gauge 0 System,** by C. & J. Graebe. New Cavendish Books.

3 Manufacturers and suppliers

This directory of names and addresses (or countries of origin) of manufacturers and suppliers of model railway equipment available in Great Britain has been compiled from advertisements appearing in the UK model railway periodicals and from firms' catalogues. The brief description of each firm's products is included as an aid to identification and is not intended to be fully comprehensive. The unit size of manufacturers and suppliers in the model railway industry varies considerably from private individuals working in their spare time producing one or two small accessories, to large public companies who manufacture and market a fully comprehensive range of items covering every conceivable aspect of the hobby. Within these two extremes there are, of course, any number of variations, and changes are forever occuring in the industry. Readers are therefore advised to scan the advertisement and editorial pages of the monthly magazines to keep abreast of new manufacturers, new products, new developments and changes in the marketing arrangements of existing firms.

The high quality of goods manufactured in France, Germany, Italy, Austria, Switzerland,

Spain, United States of America and Japan attracts a large number of customers in the UK and there are a number of agencies specialising in the importation of these products. These arrangements alter from time to time as agencies change hands and it is not possible to give a complete picture of this important aspect of the hobby. No responsibility can be accepted for the goods or services provided by the companies listed, nor can we guarantee up-to-date accuracy of all addresses.

AI Models, 111 Anston Avenue, Worksop, Notts.
Diesel Loco kits and conversion parts.
a.b.s. models, 36 Field Barn Drive, Weymouth, Dorset. DT4 OED.
N, 00 and O kits, parts and accessories.
Ace Trains, PO Box 2985, London, W11 2WP.
Gauge O tinplate locos and coaches.
ACME Model Co. PO Box 69, Hampton, Middlesex. TW12 2AX.
Xuron track cutter, pylon kit, wheel quartering jig, etc.
ACME Model Products, The Offices, 52 Station Rd, Rersby, Leics. LE7 4YY.
7mm scale loco, coach & wagon kits.
ADE (Germany).
HO track system and scale length HO DB coaches.
Agenoria Models, 18 St. Peter's Road, Stourbridge, West Midlands. DY9 OTY.
7mm scale loco kits.
AHM—Assoc Hobby Manufacturers Inc (USA).
American HO and HO9 rolling stock and building kits etc.
Albion Models, Preston Wives Farm, Ward Green Lane, Dilworth, Longbridge, Preston. PR3 2ZL.
Etched brass loco kits.
Alco Models (USA)
American HO etched brass locos and rolling stock manufactured in Japan.
Dave Alexander (Models), 37 Glanton Road, Billy Mill, North Shields, Tyne & Wear.
4mm scale cast metal loco kits.
Ian Allan Publishing Ltd, Riverdene Business Park, Molesey Road, Hersham, Surrey KT12 4RG
Model Railway and transport periodicals and books.
All Components. PO Box 94. Hereford. HR2 8YN.
Power controllers and components.
Alphagraphix, 23 Darris Road, Selly Park, Birmingham. B29 7Q7.
4mm & 7mm precision card kits.
AMR Electronics, Hen Efail, Golan, Garndolbenmaen, Gwnedd. LL51 9YU.
Electronic controllers, components and accessories.
Anchoridge (MGS Distributors) Ltd, 712 Attercliffe Rd. Sheffield. S9 3RP.
Anchoridge Motors, gearbox and mounting brackets. 4mm Scale loco kits
Antenna Models, Brandon House, Troon, Ayrshire. KA10 6HX.
Radio control equipment for OO and O gauge locos.
Argus Specialist Publications Ltd. PO. Box 35 Wolsey House, Wolsey Road, Hemel Hempstead, Herts. HP2 4SS.
Wide range of model and model engineering books.
Arnold-N (Germany).
Comprehensive range of N gauge locos, rolling stock and equipment.

Artitec Models (Holland)
N & HO model buildings and boats
Colin Ashby, 7 Lee Lane East. Horsforth, Leeds, Yorks. LS18 5RF.
Plastic injection moulded 4mm Wagon Kits.
Aster Hobby Co. (Japan)
Gauge 1 live steam locos distribtited by Fulgurex SA.
Athearn (USA).
Extensive range of HO diesel locos and rolling stock.
Atlas (USA).
O, HO & N American diesel locomotives and rolling stock.
Graham Avis Details, 151 City Road, London, EC1V 1JH.
1:150 (N) scale accessories.
Bachmann (USA).
American N, HO and G scale gauge locos and rolling stock.
Bachmann Industries Europe Ltd., Moat Way, Barwell, Leicestershire, LE9 8EY.
British outline 00 gauge locos and rolling stock.
Badger Air Brush Co. Ltd., 156 Stanley Green Road. Poole. BH15 3BE
Air brushes, compressors and accessories.
Stephen Barnfield, 3 Caverstede Road, Walton, Peterborough. PE4 6EX.
4mm scale etched loco and coach kits, N.E.R.
Steve Beattie, 9 The Cloisters, King Street, Watford, Herts. WD1 2BG.
7mm scale diesel loco kits.
Beaver Products Co, 36 Field Barn Drive, Weymouth, Dorset. DT4 OED
N loco kits wheels and gears etc.
BEMO (Germany).
HO9 & HO12 German and Swiss narrow gauge rolling stock.
Berliner TT Bahnen (Germany).
Range of TT (1:120 Scale) locos, rolling stock, track and accessories.
BG Railway Replica Models, West Wing, Longdown Hollow, Hindhead Road, Hindhead, Surrey. GU26 6AY.
N & 00 gauge moulded low relief buildings.
Bilteezi, Available from The Engine Shed, 741 High Road, Leytonstone, London. E11.
Card cut-out building sheets.
Blacksmith Models, 119 Lynchford Road, Farnborough, Hants. GU14 6ET
Etched brass loco and coach kits.
Bonds O'Euston Road Ltd, Rumbolds Hill, Midhurst, Sussex. GW29 9NE.
O gauge rail, chairs, sleepers, wheels, castings, motors, etc.
Bowser (USA). American HO loco and rolling stock kits.
Dave Bradwell, South Muirnich Cottage, Gorthleck, Inverness. IV1 2YP.
4mm scale loco, tender and wagon kits.
Branch Lines, PO Box 31, Exeter. EX4 6NA. 4mm scale etched brass rolling stock kits.
Brandbright Ltd. The Old School, Cromer Road, Bodham, Holt, Norfolk. NR25 6QG.
Garden railway specialists
Brassmasters Scale Models, PO Box 1137, Sutton Coldfield, W. Mids. B76 1FU.
4mm scale loco kits.
Bratchell, PO Box 22 Watford. WD1 3WA.
4mm scale kit for Mk3 Driving Van Trailer (D.V.T.)
Brawa (Germany)
N and HO trolley bus, motorway and cable cars, signals, lamposts, traverser, HO locos, etc.
Brekina (Germany).
HO model road vehicles.
S & R Brewster Ltd, 18 Frankfort Gate, Plymouth. PL1 1QD.
S & B Soldering irons & accessories suitable for modellers.

Britains Ltd, Blackhorse La, Walthamstow, London, E17.
1:32 scale models for farm machinery, figures, animals, trees, etc.

B.R. Lines, 97 Park Lane, Guisborough, Redcar & Cleveland. TS14 6PA.
N gauge coach interiors.

D.A. Brown, 15 St Swithins Road, Tankerton, Whitstable, Kent. CT5 2HU.
4mm Scale Loco Kit.

Brumtrarms, 23 Darris Road, Selly Park, Birmingham, West Midlands. B29 7QY.
7mm Scale building and tram kits.

BSL Hobbytime
See under Phoenix Coaches.

BTA Trees, Y Bwthyn, Llwynpiod, Nr. Tregaron, Dyfed.
Tree kits and scenic scatter material.

Busch (Germany).
N and HO gauge building kits, light fittings and scenic materials

Bus Fare, 2 Base Green Avenue, Sheffield, S12 3FA.
4mm scale decals of modern bus fleetnames and logos.

Cambrian Model Products, 1 Sand Street, Milverton, Somerset. TA4 1JN.
Plastic wagon kits, 3-link couplings, 4 mm & 7 mm scale.

Carr's Modelling Products, 528 Kingston Road, Raynes Park, London SW20 8DT.
Solders and miscellaneous materials for modellers.

Cavalier Coaches, 36 Field Barn Drive, Weymouth, Dorset. DT4 0ED
O gauge coach kits and components.

CCH Models—See under Eckon.

CCW Model Manufacturing Co, Unit 11, Craft Workshops, South Place, South Street, Chesterfield, Derbys. S40 1SZ.
Comprehensive range of O gauge kits and parts.

Central Valley (USA).
American freight car kits.

CGW Nameplates, 22 Harold Road, Birchington, Kent. CT7 9NA.
Etched 4mm scale nameplates.

T.R. Chariton, 206 Dower Rd, Four Oaks, Sutton Coldfield, West Midlands. B75 6SZ,
4mm, 7mm and 1 gauge panelled coach parts.

Chatham Kits, Church House Cottage, Trinity Hill, Medstead, Alton, Hants. GU34 5LT.
3, 4 & 7mm wagon and accessory kits.

Cherry Paints, P.O. Box 359, Cheltenham, Glos. GL52 3YN.
Over 120 authentic pre-grouping, grouping and B.R. livery paints.

Chivers Finelines, 49 St Christines Ave, Leyland, Preston, Lancs. PR5 2YS.
N, 009, 4mm and O 16.5 loco and rolling stock kits.

Chowbent Castings, Runcorn Model Centre, 41 Regent Street, Runcorn, Cheshire. WA7 1LJ.
7mm loco kits.

C.J.M. 51 Northwood Road, Tankerton, Whitstable, Kent.
N gauge locos and rolling stock.

Classic Commercials, PO Box 800, West Wratting, Cambridge. CB1 5NB.
1:43 scale vehicle kits.

C & L Finescale, P.O. Box 45, Harold Hill, Essex. RM3 0DW.
4 & 7mm scale track parts.

College Models, 2 College Road, Sutton Coldfield, W. Midlands. G73 5DJ.
7mm scale loco kits.

Comet Models, 105, Mossfield Road, Kings Heath, Birmingham. B14 7JE.
4 & 7mm scale coach kits, coach, loco wagon and architectural items.

Con-cor (USA)
American HO, American passenger car kits, accessories and N gauge model railway system.

Connoisseur Models, 33 Grampian Road, Penfields, Stourbridge. DY8 4UE.
4 and 7mm scale loco and coach kits.

Conrad (Germany)
HO track system, ready ballasted.

Cooper Craft, 17A Barclay Road, London. E11 3DQ.
Series of plastic wagon, lorry and building kits, 4mm scale.

Corgi Classics Ltd, Harcourt Way, Meridian Business Park, Leicester. LE3 2RL.
"Original Omnibus" 1:76 scale public service vehicles.

Cornard Model Co, Holt House, Caswell Bay, Swansea, West Glamorgan.
Wire and polythene tubing for point control systems, signal and point lever frames.

Coupland Models, 56 Rye Walk, Broomfield, Herne Bay, Kent, CT6 7XD.
4mm scale cast resin road vehicles.

Crookes Crafts, 23 Pickmere Road, Sheffield, S. Yorks. S10 1GY.
Card modelling materials and supplies.

Crownline Models Ltd, 8 Rame Terrace, Rame Cross, Penryn, Cornwall. TR10 9DZ.
Loco kits.

Dapol Model Railways Ltd, Lower Dee Exhibition Centre, Llangollen. LL20 8RX.
00 gauge ready-to-run locos, coaches and wagons including ex-Airfix, GMR and railway construction kits.

Dart Castings, 27 Fremantle Road, High Wycombe, Bucks. HP13 7PQ.
4mm cast metal figures, accessories, etc.

D.C. Kits and Models, 111 Norwood Crescent, Stanningly, Leeds. LS28 6NH.
4mm scale modern traction kits.

Dean Sidings, Unit 7, Crucible Way, Mushet Industrial Park, Coleford, Glos. GL16 8BH.
Resin loco bodies.

Decent Models, Hamilton Hobby Horse, 12 Campbell Street, Hamilton, Lanarkshire. ML3 6AS.
Etched brass coach kits and accessories.

D.G. Couplings, 249 Chester Road, Macclesfield, Cheshire. SK11 8RA.
2, 3, 4 and 7mm scale magnetically operated couplings.

DJ.B. Engineering, 17 Meadow Way, Bracknell, Berks.RG42 1UE.
High quality O gauge etched brass loco, carriage and wagon kits.

DJH Models, Grandspot Ltd, Unit 39, No. 1 Industrial Estate, Medomsley Road, Co Durham, DH8 6TW.
4 and 7mm scale cast metal loco kits.

Dornaplas, 1&2 Silverhills Buildings, Decoy Industrial Estate, Newton Abbot, Devon. TQ12 5LZ.
Injection moulded plastic model kits.

Double O Gauge Associaton, PO Box 100, Crawley, W. Sussex. RH10 1SA.
Loco pick up kit, enhancement kit for Lima coaches, etc.

Dragon Models, 9 Kingsey Cose, Sulley, Vale of Glamorgan, CF64 5UW.
2, 4 & 7 mm scale transfers for Welsh wagons.

D & S Models, Acquired by 51L Model Railways.
4mm white metal & etched brass wagon and coach kits, structural accessories.

Duncan Models, 34 Waters Road, Salisbury, Wilts. SP1 3NX.
7mm scale lineside and rural kits and castings.

Dyna-Drive, Formil Model Engineering, 12 Oak Tree Close, Bedale, N. Yorks. DL8 1UG.
Clutched drive system for locos.

Eastfield Models, 1 Dochart Crescent, Polmont, Stirlingshire. FK2 0RE.
4 & 7mm scale loco and wagon kits.

Eckon, CCH Models, 22 Nansen Road, Holland-on-Sea, Essex. CO15 5EU.
4mm Colourlight Signals accessories.

ECM See under AMR Electronics
Electronic controllers, components & accessories.

Edwards Brothers Drawings, MB Products, PO Box 10, Lichfield, Staffs. WS14 0HZ.
Locomotive, rolling stock, structures and trackwork drawings pre-grouping to 1947.

E.F.E., Exclusive first Editions, PO Box 172, Milton Keynes. MK11 3JE.
4mm scale road vehicles.

Efsi Toys (Holland)
Diecast road vehicles.

Egger–Bahn.
H09 narrow gauge rolling stock produced by Jouef, France.

85A Models, 48 Redstone Lane, Stourport-on-Severn, Worcs. DY13 0JB.
7mm scale plastic kit for Hunslet 0–6–0ST.

Eileen's Emporium, PO Box 14753, London SE19 2ZA.
Modelling tools and materials.

Electroten (Spain).
Range of HO gauge items including loco and rolling stock.

Embedded Controls Ltd, Loyal Cottage, Loyal Road, Alyth, Perthshire. PH11 8JG.
N, 00 & O gauge colour light signal systems.

Enthusiasts Kits, 2 Gateways, Epsom Road, Guildford, Surrey. GU1 2LF.
4mm scale narrow boat kits.

Exactoscale, 29 Couchmore Avenue, Esher, Surrey. KT10 9AS.
Components for finescale modellers. Red Arrow infra red control system.

Expo Drills & Tools, Unit 1, Barn Hill Farm, The Ridgeway, Lampuey, Nr. Pembroke. SA71 5PS.
Miniature tools for modellers.

Express Models, 65 Conway Drive, Shepshed, Loughborough, Leics. Le12 9PP.
Electronic coach lighting for 4mm coaches.

Falcon Brass, Clive Thompson, 159 Claphill Rd, Maulden, Beds. MK45 2AF.
Etched brass Loco and Wagon Kits. 4mm scale.

Faller (Germany).
Extensive range of building kits, N and HO.

Festiniog Railway Co, Porthmadog Gwynedd. 009 narrow gauge loco and rolling stock kits.

5IL Model Railways, Unit YO3, Stockton Business Centre, 70 Brunswick Street, Stockton-on-Tees, Cleveland. TS18 1DW.
4mm scale cast metal wagon kits.

Finecast (See South Eastern Finecast).

Martin Finney, 10 Heathfields Way, Shaftesbury, Dorset. SP7 9JZ.
4 & 7mm etched loco kits.

John K. Flack, 1 Meadow Bank, Kilmington, Devon. EX13 7RL.
Supplier of tools and materials for modelmakers.

Fleetline/Skytrex Road 'N' Rail, 32 Fairmont Drive, Loughborough, Leics. LE11 3JR.
N gauge cast metal accessories, coach and loco kits.

Fleischmann (Germany).
Comprehensive range of Continental N and HO locos, coaches and wagons, track and equipment.

Floquil (USA)
Super quality paints.

43 Two I Models, ABS Models, 36 Field Barn Drive, Weymouth, Dorset. DT4 0ED.
O Gauge wagon kits and accessories.

Formil Model Engineering, 12 Oak Tree Close, Bedale, Yorks. DL8 1UC.
4mm etched brass GWR carriage and wagon kits.

Four Most Models, ABS Models, 36 Field Barn Drive, Weymouth, Dorset. DT4 0ED.

Four Track Models, 22 Grange Road, Harrow, Middx. HA1 2AP.
4mm scale DMU body kits and components.

Fox Transfers, 138 Main Street, Markfield, Leics, LE67 9UX.
2, 4 & 7mm scale waterslide transfers.

Freestone Model Accessories, 28 Newland Mill, Witney, Oxon. OX8 6HH.
Card kit specialist.

Freightman, 27 Loynells Road, Rubery, Birmingham. B45 9NS.
7mm scale wagon kits.

Fulgurex (Switzerland).
Craftsman-built brass locos and rolling stock.

Gateneal Ltd, 20 Springfield Drive, Halesowen, West Midlands. B62 8EI.
O & 1 gauge etched brass kits.

Gaugemaster Controls, Gaugemaster House, Ford Road, Arundel, West Sussex. BN18 OBN.
Electronic controllers.

Gee Dee Models Ltd, 19-21 Heathcote Street, Nottingham. NG1 3AF.
4mm scale road vehicle kits.

David Geen, 30 Silverwood Close, Dale Park, Hartlepool, Cleveland. TS27 3QF.
4mm scale wagon kits.

GEM Model Railways – see under Thameshead Models.

Genesis Kits, 224 Walkwood Road, Hunt End, Redditch, Worcs. B97 5NU.
4mm scale diesel loco body kits.

Alan Gibson (Workshop), The Bungalow, Church Road, Lingwood, Norwich, Norfolk. NR13 4TR.
4mm scale wheels, gear sets, 4mm and 7mm loco kits, track components.

Gladiator Models Gun Hill Farm, Lamp Lane, Arley, Coventry. CV7 8FE.
7mm scale brass loco & rolling stock kits.

Golden Arrow Productions, 392 Harold Road, Hastings, E. Sussex. TN35 5HG.
009, 4 & 7mm scale loco kits.

Albert Goodall, 20 Kingswood Road, Dunton Green, Sevenoaks, Kent. TN13 2XE.
S.R. Bulleid nameplates and accessories.

Graham Farish, Romany Works, Holton Heath, Poole, Dorset. BH16 6JL.
Comprehensive range of N British outline ready-to-run locos, rolling stock, track and accessories.

Great Western Scale Models, 7 Castle Drive, Praa Sands, Penzance. TR20 9TF.
Self adhesive loco headboard and coach destination boards.

Greenweld, 27 Park Road, Southampton. SO15 3UQ.
Electronic components.

Gunther (Germany).
HO loco kits and accessories.

Gutzold KG (Germany).
HO ready to run locos and rolling stock. (Formerly marketed under Piko brand).

G.W. Models, 2 Tall Trees, Penstone Park, Lancing, W. Sussex. BN15 9AG.
Boiler roller, gear puller, wheel press, etc.

Hag, (Switzerland).
HO Swiss prototype locos and coaches.
Halcyon Recollection Company, 36 Lavender Close, Thornbury, Glos. BS12 1UL.
Dublo Wrenn Transfers and spares.
Hamo (Germany)
Marklin HO locomotives for 2-rail. Now sold under Trix label.
Harbutt's Plasticine Ltd, Bathampton, Bath, Somerset.
Manufacturers of Plasticine clay.
The Harrow Model Shop, 190-194 Station Road, Harrow, Middx. HA1 2RH.
London Underground kits.
Haywood Railway Wagon & Carriage Co, 29 Lichfiesld Drive, Great Haywood, Staffs. ST18 OSX.
7mm Scale etched brass wagon and coach kits, etc.
Heathcote Electronics, 1 Haydock Close, Cheadle, Staffs. ST10 1VE
Train detection and automatic control devices.
Heki (Germany).
Scenic materials.
Heljan (Denmark).
N, HO and 00 gauge building kits.
Helmsman Electronics Ltd, 31 Faringdon Avenue, South Shore, Blackpool. FY4 9QQ.
Flickering tail lamp, firebox simulator, etc.
Herkat (Germany) N and HO gauge accessories, electrical equipment, etc.
Herpa (Germany).
HO & N Scenic accessories, road vehicles.
Highway Models, PO Box 47, Weston-Super-Mare, Avon. BS24 9SA.
4mm scale lorry kits.
HMRS Transfers, 9 Park Place, Worksop, Notts. S8O 1HL.
Former PC Models "Pressfix" and "Methfix" transfers produced by Historical Model Railway Society.
Hornby Railways, Hornby Railways Ltd, Westwood, Margate, Kent. CT9 4JX
Comprehensive range of 00 British outline ready-to-run locos, rolling stock, track and accessories.
Howard Scenics, Lakeside, 3 Millbrook Close, Blewbury, Oxfordshire.
Embossed 'Brick' card. Shop front signs.
Graham Hughes, 20 MacKelvie Road, Lamlash, Isle of Arran. KA27 8NP.
2mm scale cast white metal loco kits.
Humbrol, Humber Oil Co Ltd, Marfleet, Hull, Humberside.
Manufacturer of enamels, modelling adhesives, craft knives, dopes, thinners, brush cleaners, authentic colours, metallics, poster colours and airbrushes.
Hurst Models, PO Box 373, Manchester, M60 2GH.
4mm scale etched brass kits and accessories.

I.K.B. Models, 36 Field Barn Drive, Weymouth, Dorset. DT4 OED.
4mm scale broad and standard gauge models.
Impetus Models, PO Box 1472, Coggeshall, Colchester. CO6 1UQ.
4mm finescale industrial and O gauge loco kits.

Jackson Exans, 4 Dartmouth Rd, Coventry. CV2 3DQ.
4mm smoke deflectors, pre-cut GWR name and numberplates, locokit, etc.
Jackson Model Products.
Range of 4mm scale wheels now manufactured by Romford Models Ltd.
Javelin Models, Weatherwise, Lucas Lane, Hilton, Derby. DE65 5FL.
7mm scale loco kits.

Jouef (France).
Comprehensive range of French HO model railway equipment and ex-Eggar-Bahn 009.
Joy, Turnbridges Ltd, London. SW17.
Manufactureres of paints, dopes, thinners and model adhesives, etc.
JR Model Supplies, Unit 7, Larchfield Estate, Dowlish Ford, Ilminster, Somerset. TA19 0PF.
Japanese model railway specialist.
JV Catenary (France),
HO overhead catenary system.
Kadee (USA).
N or HO magnetic couplers.
Kato (Japan).
Japanese, American and European outline N gauge locos and rolling stock. Digicon–100 multiple train control.
Kean–Maygib Precision Engineering, Wendover Road, Rackheath Industrial Estate, Norwich, Norfolk. NR13 6LH.
RG4 motor, gearbox, point motor, loco & wagon kits.
Keen Systems, 16 Elm Drive, Market Drayton, Shropshire. TF9 3HE.
Close coupler for British outline coaches.
Kenline Model Products, 1 Gledhill Drive, Main Road, Withern, Alford, Lincs. LN13 OLD.
4mm scale wagon parts, castings and kits.
Charles Kennion, 2 Railway Pl, Hertford, Herts.
Hand tools, materials and sundries for model engineers.
Kent Panel Controls, PO Box 59, Edenbridge, Kent. TN8 7AW.
Quality controllers, electrical accessories, motors, etc.
Kestrel Designs, Unit 9, The Old School, Narbeth, Pembs. SA67 7DU.
N building kits.
Key (USA).
HO brass models made in Japan & Korea.
K's Kits, See under 'Nu-Cast'.
Kibri (UK): No4 Factory Unit, Station Yard, Bala, N Wales.
Z, N, HO & 00 building kits & accessories.
Kirk Coaches, Colin Ashby, The Bijou, 7 Lee Lane East, Horsforth, Leeds. LS18 5RF.
4mm scale plastic coach kits.
Kiss Modelbanen (Switzerland).
Swiss 1:42 scale metre gauge (Om)
Kleinbahn (Austria).
HO equipment, locos and rolling stock.
Krüger (Germany)
TT 12mm gauge flexible track.
Lancaster Model Engineering, 50 Elmwood Road, Hartlepool, Cleveland. TS26 0JS.
4mm scale cast and etched loco kit.
Langley Miniature Models, 166 Three Bridges Road, Crawley, Sussex. RH10 1LE.
00 and N kits and accessories.
Lehmann (Germany).
'LGB' 1:22 1 gauge narrow gauge equipment, locos and rolling stock, etc.
Chris Leigh, 46 Meadow Way, Old Windsor, Berks.
4mm scale cast metal accessories.
Lemaco (Swiss)
Swiss manufacturer of exclusive Swiss, German and Italian etc., locomotives in most scales and gauges.
Life-Like (USA)
N & HO American loco & rolling stock.
Lilliput (Germany).
Extensive range of HO continental locos and rolling stock and HO9 Austrian narrow gauge models.
Lima (Italy).
Extensive range of N, HO, 00 and O locos and rolling stock.

Roy C. Link, 1 Station Cottages, Harling Road, East Harling, Norwich, Norfolk. NR16 2QP.
7mm scale narrow gauge (0.165) Locomotive Kits.
Lionel (USA).
HO and O American locos, rolling stock, track and accessories.
Little Bus Company, 57 Queenswood Avenue, Hutton, Brentwood, Essex. CM13 1HW.
4mm scale bus kits and accessories.
Little Engines, 11 Kings Road, New Milton, Hants. BH25 5AX.
4mm scale loco kits.
Lledo p.l.c., Woodall Road, Enfield, Middx. EN3 4ND.
1:43 scale diecast road vehicles.
Loddon Models, 27 Martin Close, Basingstoke. Hants. RG21 2JY.
4mm scale etched brass loco kits.
London Road Models, 1 The Avenue, Off North Street, Romford, Essex. RM1 4DL.
4mm & 7mm scale etched loco and coach kits.
Mabex Products, 15 Coastguard Square, Barden Rd, Eastbourne, Sussex.
Model bus transfers, cg, fleetnames, destination screens, adverts, numbers, etc.
Mailcoach. see under Cooper Craft.
4mm scale plastic coach kits.
Mainstreet Models, 96 Hall Road, Hull, E. Yorks. HU6 8SB.
2mm & 4mm scale printed card structure kits.
Majestic Models, 15 Kingsway, Braunstone, Leicester. LE3 2JL.
7mm cast whitemetal and etched brass wagon kits.
Mamod Live Steam Models, Adam Leisure, Adam House, Ripon Way, Harrogate, Yorks. HG1 2AU.
ONG live steam loco & rolling stock.
Mantua Metal Products Co (USA).
American HO kits and ready-to-run models sold under the name 'Tyco'.
Marcway, 590 Attercliffe Road, Sheffield, S9 3QS.
Pointwork in all gauges, N to 1.
Markits Model Railway Products, PO Box 40, Watford, Herts, WD2 5TN.
Retail and wholesale suppliers of the Romford/Markits range of products.
Marklin (Germany).
Extensive range of model railway equipment in HO & 1 gauges, also Mini-Club System in Z gauge.
John Marsh Commercial Vehicle Drawings, 'Wychwood', Holcot Road, Walgrave, Northampton. NN6 9QN.
4mm scale road vehicle drawings.
P & D Marsh Model Railways, The Stables, Wakes End Farm, Eversholt, Milton Keynes.
N gauge whitemetal loco and scenic accessory kits.
Masokits, 27 Crotch Crescent, New Marston, Oxford. OX3 0JL.
4mm scale wagon, coach and components kits.
Mastercast, Unit 12/3 Platts Eyot, Lower Sunbury Road, Hampton-on-Thames, Middx, TW12 2HF.
"Down our street collection" detailed 00 figures.
Maygib Componenets, see Kean Maygib Precision Engineering.
McGowan Models, 7 Ringley Park Rd. Reigate, Surrey.
Range of 4mm scale cast metal loco kits.
Mehano (Slovenia)
N & HO American, French & German outline locomotives and rolling stock, trams.
Mendip Models, 29 Catherine Street, Frome, Somerset, BA11 1DB.
4mm scale wagon kits for the modern modeller. 7mm scale loco kits.

Mercian Models, 1A Market Way, Hagley, Stourbridge. DY9 9LT.
Kit manufacturers.
Mercontrol, see under Thameshead Models.
Point control system.
Meridian Models, 124 Blackheatth Hill, London, SE10 8AY .
009 loco .and rolling stock kits.
Merlin Locomotive Works Ltd, Llangyniew, Welshpool, Powys. SV21 0JW.
Live steam narrow gauge.
Merten (Germany).
Wide range of Z N, TT, HO and O figures and lineside accessories.
Metcalf Models & Toys, 1 Carleton Business Park, Carleton New Road, Skipton, N. Yorks. BD23 2AA.
Card kits.
Meteor Models, 62 Church Street, Church Gresley, Swadlincote, Derbys. DE11 9NP.
7mm scale loco and wagon kits.
Metropolitan SA (Switzerland)
HO continental brass locomotives and plastic bodied rolling stock.
Micro-Trains Line (USA).
N & Z gauge American models.
Mike's Models, Holt house, Caswell Bay, Swansea, West Glamorgan.
Range of 4mm, 7mm and 009 cast metal kits and accessories.
Millholme Models & Casting, 5 Silverwood Avenue, Ravenshead, Nottinghamshire, NG15 9BU.
4mm scale cast metal locomotive kits
Minitrix (Germany).
Comprehensive range of British and Continental outline N gauge locos, rolling stock and equipment. Manufactured by Marklin.
Malcolm Mitchell Design, Marsh House, Howard Lane, Stratton, Bude, N. Cornwall. EX23 9TE.
4 & 7mm scale etched loco kits and accessories.
MJT Scale Components, 41 Oak Avenue, Shirley, Croydon, CRO 8EP.
4mm rolling stock fittings.
MKD (France).
French building kits designed by Alain Pras.
Modelex, Incorporating Churchward Models, 36 Apollo Road, Stourbridge, W. Midlands. DY9 8YG.
4mm & 7mm scale loco kit, signal boxes, lattice footbridge, electrical & electronic accessories, tools, etc.
Model-Irish Railways, 35 Kingsway Drive, Portadown, BT62 3DU, Northern Ireland.
4mm scale diesel loco body and wagon kits, transfers, paints and nameplates.
Model Signal Engineering, PO Box 13, Leamington Spa. CV31 1GN.
2, 4 & 7mm scale signalling parts, Sprat & Winkle auto coupler.
Model Spares, 65 Burnley Road, Hapton, Burnley, Lancs. BB11 5QR.
Hornby spare parts and repair specialist.
Model Yard, 16 Helmsley Road, Leeds. LS16 5JA.
4mm scale card building kits.
Modern Motive Power, Trefacwn Fach, Llanrhian, St. Davids, SA62 6DP.
7mm scale steam, diesel and DMU kits.
Modern Outline Kits, 27 Hall Drive, Off Boultham Park Road, Lincoln, LN6 7SW.
4mm and 7mm scale loco kits.
Mod–Roc, Smith & Nephew Ltd., Welwyn Garden City, Herts.
Plaster impregnated bandage used for scenic work in all scales and gauges.

Monty's Model Railways, Ash Lea House, Inghams Road, Tetney, Grimsby, Lincs. DN36 5LW.
4mm scale scenic figures and accessories.

MSC Models, 38B, Searchwood Road, Warlingham, Surrey. CR6 9BA.
O loco brass body and chassis kits. 'Crailcrest motor'.

Roger Murray, 11 Osprey Close, Farlington, Portsmouth, Hants. PO6 1LP.
Controllers, loco lighting, colour light signals etc.

N-Brass Locomotives, 32 Crendon Road, Rowley Regis, Warley, W. Midlands. B65 8LE.
Ready-to-run N gauge locos.

N Gauge Lines, The Old School, Church Street, Stilton, Peterborough. PE7 3RF.
2mm scale loco kit.

Noch (Germany).
Complete formed scenic baseboard for compact layouts, HO, N and Z gauges.

Nonneminstre Models, 46 Hide Gardens, Rustington, W. Sussex. BN16 3NP.
4mm scale industrial diesel loco kits.

Northwest Short Line (USA).
Craftsmen-built American brass locos, HO wheels.

Nu–Cast, Autocom UK Ltd, Unit F, Alexander Bell Centre, West Porthway Industrial Estate, Andover, Hants. SP10 3UR.
Range of 4mm scale cast metal loco and wagon kits.

Oakville Models, PO Box 1723, Selly Oak, Birmingham. B29 6DL.
7mm scale etched brass loco kit.

The Oakwood Press, PO Box 122, Headington, Oxford. OX3 8LU.
Railway and transport books containing prototype material of interest to modellers.

Off-Line Scale Model Products, 1 Anson Drive, Sholing, Southampton, Hants. SO19 8RP.
4mm scale architectural and scenic accessories.

Old Barn Model Craftsmen, Unit 9, Monks Farm Depot, Monks Avenue, Lancing, W. Sussex. B15 077.
Complete model railway design and construction.

Oldbury Models Ltd, Unit 18, Long Lane Trading Estate, Halesowen, W. Midlands. B62 9LT.
7mm scale loco coach and wagon kits.

Omen Miniatures, J.W. Brickett, 22 Shelley Road, Horsham, W. Sussex. RH12 2JH.
7mm scale figures.

On Line Models, 3 Maythorn Avenue, Croft, Cheshire, WA3 7HP.
Ready-to-run O gauge locos at near kit prices.

Orbit Products, The Glen, Kings Street, Combe Martin, N. Devon. EX34 ODB.
Track cleaner fits Lima Class 33 or 73, Supertoller.

Oxford Publishing Co, see under Ian Allan Publishing Ltd.
Publisher of railway books of interest to modellers.

Parkside Dundas, Millie Street, Kirkcaldy, Fife. KY1 2NL.
4mm and 7mm scale wagon kits.

Pearse Locomotives, Woodview, Brockhurst, Church Stretton, Shropshire. SY6 7QY.
Live steam locos for garden railways.

Peco (see Pritchard Patent Products Co Ltd).

Perivale Waggon Works, C.A.S. Croome, 6 Launceston Gardens, Perivale, Greenford, Middx. UB6 7ET.
Exact scale 4mm private owner wagons.

Perseverance Model Railways see under Puffers Model Railway Products.

Peter K (London) Ltd, Hillcroft School, Walnut Tree Manor, Haughley Green, Stowmarket, Suffolk. IP14 3RQ.
Etched brass loco kits and fittings.

Philotrain (Holland).
HO Dutch loco and coach models.

Phoenix Model Developments Ltd, The Square, Earls Barton, Notts. NN6 ONK.
1:43 kits and figures.

Phoenix Paint Co, PO Box 359, Cheltenham, Glos. GL52 3YN.
Authentic railway colour enamels.

Piccolo (Germany).
Comprehensive range of N gauge equipment manufactured by Fleischmann.

Picture Pride Displays, 17 Willow Court, Crystal Drive, Sandwell Business Park, Warley, W. Midlands. B66 1RD.
Display cabinets for models.

Piercy Model Products, 11 Sheringhan Avenue, North Shields, Tyne & Wear. NE29 8HY.
7mm scale loco kits.

Piko (Germany). see under Gutzold Kg.
Range of N and HO locomotives and rolling stock.

Pirate Models, 7 Horsham Lane, Upchurch, Sittingbourne, Kent. ME9 7AL.
4mm and 7mm scale cast metal bus kits.

Pittman (USA).
Electric motors.

Plastruct, EMA Model Supplies Ltd., 58-69 The Centre, Feltham, Middx. TW13 4BH.
Moulded plastic structures, girders and engineering features.

Pola (Germany).
Building kits, 'Pola Maxi' O gauge locos and rolling stock,'Pola-N' N gauge and 'Pola-Quick' 00/HO structure kits.

Portescap (UK) Ltd, Headlands Business Park, Salisbury Road, Ringwood, Hants. BH24 3PB.
Electric motors and gearboxes.

Pow Sides, Poplars Farm, Aythorpe Roding. Nr. Dunmow Essex. CM6 1RY.
4 & 7mm scale private owner wagon transfers and kits.

Praline (Germany).
HO road vehicles.

Preiser (Germany).
Range of figures in Z, N, TT, HO and O.

Pritchard Patent Product Co Ltd, Beer, Seaton, Devon.
Extensive range of kits and parts in all gauges N to O. 'Streamline' track and points. 'Wonderful Wagons', etc. Publisher of 'Railway Modeller' and model railway books.

Prototype Models, May Cottage, Hardigate Road, Cropwell Butler, Notts. NG12 3AH.
Card building kits.

Puffers Model Railway Products, 96 Micklegate, York. YO1 1JX.
Manufacturers of scale model railway equipment.

Q Kits, 50 Hornbeam Way, Leeds, Yorks. LS14 2HP.
Fibreglass moulded diesel loco kits, 4mm scale. Q-driver electronic controller, 4mm scale cast metal loco kits.

Quainton Road Models, Astrope Farm, Watery Lane. Astrope, Tring. HP23 4PJ.
Specialise in manufacturing kits for GCR and Metropolitan Rly. 4 & 7mm scale.

Quaycraft, Harbour Cottage, 2 Quayfield Road, Ilfracombe, Devon. EX34 9EN.
Cast resin boats in various scales 1:60 to 1:128.

Railex (Germany)
Z scale models.

Railmatch Products, 9-10 Broad Street, Oxford. OX1 3AJ.
Authentic railway colour paints: steam, diesel and modern image.

Ratio Plastic Models Ltd, Level 5, Hamlyn House, Mardle Way, Buckfastleigh, Devon. TQ11 0NS.
Plastic loco wagon, coach and signal kits in 4mm scale, 'Emtrack' 4mm scale permanent way.

Ravenscale Model Co, 68 Eastwood Road, South Woodford, London. E18.
O gauge ready-to-run locos and points.

Redcraft, Unit 8 Royal Stuart Workshops, Adelaide Place, Butetown, Cardiff. CF1 6BR.
4mm and 7mm scale brass loco kits. Welsh railways.

Red Dog, 9 Harcourt, Bradwell, Milton Keynes. MK13 9EN.
Baseboards made to order. Specialist fittings by post.

Relco, Rosefair Elecronics, Shakespeare Street, Watford, Herts. WD2 5HD.
HF Generator, track cleaner.

Replica Railways, Unit 46, BSS House, Cheney Manor, Swindon. SN2 2PJ.
00 gauge ready to run locomotives, coaches and wagons.

Riceworks, PO Box 2 Chagford, Devon. TQ13 8TZ.
4mm scale etched loco kits.

Riko International Ltd, 13-15A High Street, Hemel Hempstead, Herts. HP1 3AD.
U.K. Importers of LIMA.

Rising Star Models.
7mm scale loco kits distributed by Slater's (Plasticard) Ltd.

Rivarossi (Italy).
Extensive range of locos, rolling stock and equipment in N, HO and O gauges.

RJH Model Railways Ltd, Unit 19, Wessex Trade Centre, Ringwood Road, Poole, Dorset. BH12 3PF.
Manufacturer of 7mm scale rolling stock kits and models. Post-War prototypes and Cavalier coaches.

Roadscale Models, 57 Queenswood Avenue, Hutton, Brentwood, Essex. CM13 1HU.
Lorry kits and transfers.

Roco (Austria).
Extensive range of N,HO9 & HO locos, rolling stock, track and accessories.

Romford Models Ltd,
Locomotive wheels for TT and 00, and electric motors for TT, 00 and O gauges.

Roskopf Miniature Modelle (Germany).
HO road vehicles.

Roundfield Engineering, 12 High Cote, Riddlesden, Keighley, Yorks.
White-metal wagon kits.

Roundhouse Engineering Co, Unit 6, Churchill Business Park, Churchill Road, Wheatley, Doncaster. DN1 2TF.
Live steam railways for SM/32, S/M45 and G scale.

Roundhouse Products (USA)
Range of American HO loco kits produced by Model Die Casting.

Roxey Mouldings, 58 Dudley Road, Walton-on-Thames, Surrey. KT12 2JU.
4mm and 7mm scale coach kits.

Sachsenmodelle (Germany).
HO continental rolling stock and railcars.

Sagami (Japan).
12V, DC can motors.

Salem Steam Models, Brynglas, Salem, Llandeilo, Dyfed. SA19 7HD.
16mm & G scale items. Specialist in Mamod loco improvements.

Sanspareil, 35 Colville Street, Carlisle, Cumbria. CA2 5HT.
7mm scale etched metal loco kits.

Scalecast, 26 Old Market Court, George Street, Glastonbury, Somerset. BA6 9LS.
4mm scale construction equipment kits.

Scale Link Ltd, Iwerne Minster, Dorset. DT11 8QN.
Etched brass and cast metal acccessories, vintage vehicles.

Scalespeed 9 Andrew Place, Fareham, Hants. PO14 3QA.
Hornby, Dublo, Wrenn and Tri-ang motor repairs

Scale Model Productions (SMP), 1 St. Johns, Warwick. CV34 4NE.
00, EM & D4 flexible track and PCB point kits, "Scaleway".

Scale Timber, Arthur J. North, 11 Lloyd Road, Handsworth Wood, Birmingham. B20 2ND.
Wood and plastic materials to scale sizes.

Scenic Models, 87 Thirlmere Avenue, Tilehurst, Reading, Berks. RG3 6XH.
Model railway layout design and construction.

Scorpio Models, 3 Meads Close, Newport. NP9 0NR.
7mm scale GWR loco, wagon and coach kits.

S & D Models, 13 Oatlands, Crawley, W. Sussex. RH11 8EE.
7mm scale specialist manufacturers for light, industrial and narrow gauge railways and accessories.

SD Mouldings, 96 Sparth Road, Clayton le Moors, Accrington, Lancs. BB5 5QD.
N gauge cast buildings.

Set Scenes, PO Box 63, Crawley, W. Sussex. RH11 8YR.
Landscape modelling specialists.

Seuthe (Germany).
Smoke units for locos.

Sharman Wheels, Hen Efail (Old Smithy), Glan-Henwy, Golan, Garndolbenmaen Gwynedd. LL51 9YU.
4mm fine scale loco bogie and tender wheels.

Shedmaster O gauge models, 10 Victoria Avenue, Hythe, Kent. CT21 6JG.
Ex-Jidenco etched brass loco and wagon kits.

Shinohara (Japan).
Trackwork made to NMRA standards, HO, HO9 and dual gauge.

Shire Scenes, 4 North Cottages, Landscove, Ashburton, Devon. TQ13 7LU.
N & 00 etched accessory kits.

Silver Fox Models, PO Box 248, Ruislip, Middx. HA4 OXE.
N gauge diesel loco kits.

Skinley Prints, c/o P.T. Moore (Models), 56 Archers Court Rd, Whitfield, Dover. CT16 3HS.
Extensive range of scale drawings for railways, tramways and ships.

Slater's (Plastikard) Ltd, Royal Bank Buildings, Temple Rd, Matlock, Bath, Derbyshire. DE4 3PG.
4mm & 7mm scale loco carriage and wagon kits model making materials including Plastikard, Mek-pak, fluid cement, Huminiture figures and many other accessories.

Small World Products Ltd, 3 Well Lane Clare, Suffolk. CO10 8NH.
Remote infra red control and distribution system.

S.M. Models, 46 Barrows Hill Lane, Westwood, Notts, NG16 5HJ.
O gauge loco kits.

D. Smith, Lower Yetson Cottage, Ashprington, Totnes, Devon. TQ9 7EG.
Radio control for Tri-ang/Novo O gauge locos.

Smiths Fittings, see under W & T Models Railway Accessories.
4mm scale wagon tarpaulin sheets and train nameboards.

Sommerfeldt (Germany)
Range of authentic overhead catenary equipment based on German, Swiss and Italian prototypes, N HO & O.

Soundtraxx, The Silver Dollar Railroad, 15 Trimley High Road, Felixstowe, Suffolk. IP11 9QT.
Sound effects for steam and diesel locomotives.

South Eastern Finecast, Glenn House, Hartfield Road, Forest Row, Sussex. RH18 5DZ.
Finecast loco/chassis kits, flush glazed windows, turntable kits, traction engine and car kits.

Southern Pride Models, PO Box 37, Kidderminster Worcs. DY11 6DS.
4mm scale coach kits.
Specialised Products Ltd, Meadow Terrace, Sheffield. S11 8QN.
00 & O gauge, pointwork. Waverley pointwork kits.
Sprat & Winkle, see Model Signal Engineering, 4mm scale etched brass autocouplings.
Springside Models, Units 1 & 2, Silverhills Buildings, Decoy Industrial Estate, Newton Abbot, Devon. TW12 5LZ.
2mm, 4mm & 7mm accessories and loco kits.
Rodney Stenning, 29 Treyford Close, Ifield, Crawley, Sussex. RH10 0JN.
4mm scale loco kits
Stewart Hobbies Inc (USA).
HO 1:87 scale diesel locos
Stonecraft, Wycombe Models, Gomm Road, High Wycombe, Bucks, HP13 7DJ.
Stone scenic building materials suitable for 00 upwards.
Streetscene Series, See ABS Models.
4mm scale road vehicles and accessories.
Studio Scale Models, 'Alhambra', Leopardstown Road, Dublin 18, Eire.
4mm scale Irish wagon, loco and coach kits.
Summerhouse, A.M. Thomas, 19 Bridgewater Park Drive Skellow, Doncaster. DN6 8RL.
4 & 7mm scale quality lineside vehicle kits.
Sundeala Board Co Ltd, Sundeala House, Hanworth Rd. Sunbury-on-Thames, Middx. TW16 5DG.
Baseboard surface material.
Sunset Models (USA).
HO, HO9 limited production locos made in Japan.
Superquick Model Kits, P.E.M.S. Butler Ltd, PO Box 5, Princes Risborough, Bucks. HP27 ORG.
Wide range of printed card 4mm scale building kits.
Swann Morton, Penn Works, Owlerton Green, Sheffield. S6 2BJ.
Craft tools.

Taylor Plastic Models, Unit 235, Stratford Workshops, Burford Road, London. E15 2SP.
N gauge loco kits and accessories.
Tenmille Products, 18 Thorney Road, Capel St. Mary, Ipswich, Suffolk. IP9 2LQ.
Gauge 1 and SM32 narrow gauge rolling stock and accessories.
Tenshodo (Japan).
Brass HO scale locos – "Spud" motor bogies.
Thameshead Models, 101 Harrowden Road, Bedford, MK42 ORT.
N Gauge cast metal loco body kits – GEM model railways.
Peter Thatcher, 4 St Mary's, Gamlingay, Sandy, Beds. SG19 3ET.
7mm scale name and number plates, road signs.
3mm Scale Model Railways, 23 Gilbert Scott Road, Buckingham, Bucks. MK18 1PS.
Catering exlusively for the British TT and 3mm scale modeller.
The Three Millimetre Society.
Range of cast metal and plastic wagon and carriage kits for TT (available for members only).
Tillig (Germany).
TT (1:120) range available from TT International.
Timbercraft Cabinets, Abercorn House, York Farm Business Centre, Watling Street, Towcester, Northants. NN12 8EU.
Display cabinets.
Tiny Signs, Acquired by Gaugemaster Controls.
Replica advertisement posters, N and 00.

Alec Tiranti Ltd, 70 High Street, Theale. Reading, Berks. RG7 5AR.
Silicone rubber and low melt solder.
Tolhurst Model Engineers, 87 Ardgowan Road, Catford, London, SE6 1UY.
Manufacturers of 16mm live steam locos, blowers and accessory kits.
Tomix (Japan).
N Gauge Japanese rolling stock and equipment
Chris C. Topham, 8 Fishponds Drive, Crigglestone, Wakefield. WF4 3PA.
Loco mounted steam sound units.
Tower Models, 44 Cookson Street, Blackpool Lancs. FY1 3EO.
4mm scale plastic tram and bus kits.
Town Scene, available from the Engine Shed, 741 High Road, Leytonstone, London E11.
Scenic backgrounds complementary to the Bilteezi range.
Townstreet, The Old School, Cambee by Anstruther, Fife. KY10 2RU.
House fronts and roof sections moulded in stone powders. 4mm scale.
Tracksetta Templates, Melcam Models, Collett House, 36 New Road, Swindon, Wilts. SN4 OLU.
Templates for laying N & 00 track, straight and curves.
Tractopak Ltd., Mount Pleasant Clapton, Woodbridge, Suffolk. IP13 6QB.
Flexible drive units.
Train Tronics, 335 Holdenhurst Road, Bournemouth. BH8 8BT.
Scale lighting in N, 00 & O.
Tramalan, PO Box 2, Blackpool. FY3 8DZ.
Scale model working overhead tram kits, motors, accessories, street furniture.
Trax Controls, PO Box 419, Norwich, NR1 3BZ.
Train controls and sound effect modules.
Trix Express (Germany).
Continental Trix,
Wide range of locs and rolling stock. Acquired by Marklin in 1997.
TT International, 22 Harold Road, Birchinton, Kent. CT7 9NA.
Tillig Pilz, HOe, HOm and HO track system and kits.
Tillig TT 1:120 locos, coaches and wagons.
Tyco (USA).
Registered trade name for HO kits and ready-to-run models by Mantua Metal Products Co.

Ultima Models, 12 Bartley Close, Olton, Solihull. BS2 7RH.
N gauge coach kits.
Ultrascale Gear Services Ltd, The Wynd East, Letchworth, Herts. SG6 3EL.
4mm and 7mm scale loco, coach and wagon wheels.
Eric Underhill Models, acquired by a.b.s. Models.
7mm scale loco kits.
Union Mills Models, Unit 5, Union Mills Trading Estate, Braddan, Isle of Man. IM14 4AB.
Manufacturers of N gauge ready-to-run locos.

Vau-pe (Germany).
HO building kits and scenic equipment.
Vollmer (UK), No 4 Factory Unit, Station Yard, Bala, N Wales.
N & HO building kis and accessories.
Vulcan Model Engineering, see Eric Underhill Models.
O gauge loco kits.

The Wagon and Carriage Works, Unit F3, Trackside, The Maltings, Station Road, Sawbridgeworth, Herts, CM21 9JX.

O and 1 gauge loco, coach and wagon kits and components.
Colin Waite, 20 Berwick Road London. N22 5QB.
Etched brass van kits and accessories.
Walsall Model Industries, Unit 3, 21-24 Hatherton Street, Walsall, West Midlands. WS4 2LA.
7mm wheels, motors, gearboxes, tools, materials etc. Live steam castings.
Walsworth Models, 34 Tristram Road, Walsworth, Hitchen, Herts, SG4 OBH.
Etched brass loco kits in 00, O and 1 gauges.
Walthers (USA).
HO passenger and freight car kits and accessories.
Waverley, Specialised Products, Meadow Terrace Sheffield. S11 8QN.
7mm scale pointwork kits.
Wayoh Model Railways, 15 Harbour Lane, Edgworth, Bolton. BL7 OPA.
7mm scale coach motor bogies.
Weald Models, see Rodney Stenning,
009 and 00 cast metal loco kits.
Webster's Wagons, see Pritchard Patent Product Co. Ltd.
0 gauge plastic wagon kits.
Westdale Coaches, 46 Beech Tree Road, Holmer Green, High Wycombe, Bucks. HP15 6UT.
O coach body kits.
Westward, see Puffers Model Railway Products.
White-metal loco kits.
Wheeltapper Coaches, PO Box 28(A), Heathfield, E. Sussex. TN21 9ZY.
4mm scale printed side coach kits includes former P.C. Models range.
Wiking (Germany).
N and HO scale road vehicles.
Wild Swan Publications Ltd, 1-3 Hagbourne Road, Didcot, Oxon. OX11 8DP.
Publishers of Model Railway Journal and railway books of interest to railway modellers.
Woodhead Transfers, 1 Evans Grove, St. Albans, Herts. AL4 9PJ.
Woodland Scenics (USA), Bachmann Industries Europe Ltd.
Tree kits and landscaping materials.
G. & R. Wrenn Ltd,
Former manufacturer of ex-Hornby Dublo locos, coaches and wagons in 00 gauge.
Wrightlines Models, see under a.b.s. models.
7mm; ft narrow gauge, on 16.5 loco & coach kits.
W&T Model Railway Accessories Incorporating Smiths, rear of The Talbot Hotel, Iwerne Minster, Dorset. DT11 8EF.
Road vehicle and rolling stock kits and accessories.

X-acto E. Keil & Co Ltd, Russell Gardens, Wick La, Wickford, Essex.
Craft knives and modelling tools.

Zeuke (Germany).
TT and HON-3 locos and rolling stock.
ZTC Systems, PO Box 23, Saffron Walden, Essex. CB10 2XY.
Digital command control system.

4 Stockists

This guide to British railway stockists and model shops has been compiled from advertisements that have appeared in the main British model railway magazines over the past

two-three years, on the assumption that any business prepared to take the trouble of advertising in the specialist model railway press is more likely to take the hobby seriously and therefore provide a satisfactory service to the modeller. Again, no responsibility can be accepted for the goods or services provided by these companies, nor can we guarantee up-to-date accuracy of all addresses.

Bedfordshire

Thameshead, 101 Harrowden Road, Bedford. MK42 ORT.
Model Railway and Miniature Engineering, 'Silverlink', 28 King Street, **Kempston.**
Beatties, 104/106 Cheapside Mall, Arndale Centre, **Luton.** LU1 2TS.

Berkshire

Mydons, 2 Bullbrook Shops, **Bracknell.**
Marlow Donkey Railways, The Old Bank, High Street, **Cookham**, Maidenhead. SL6 9SJ.
Time Machine, model cars and trains, 32 Westborough Road, **Maidenhead.**
Beatties, 25/26 Cheap Street, **Newbury.** RG14 5DB.
Beatties, 51/52 Broad Street Mall Shopping Centre, **Reading.** RG1 7QE.
Beatties, 16 Meadway Shopping Centre, **Tilehurst,** Reading. RG3 4AA.
Beatties, 176 Crockhamwell Road, **Woodley,** Reading. RG5 3JH.

Bristol

Beatties, 17/19 Penn Street, **Bristol.** BS1 3AW.
Modelmania, 13 Clouds Hill Road, St. George, **Bristol.** BS5 7LD.
Trains of Bristol, 20 West Street, Bedminster, **Bristol.** BS3 3LG.

Buckinghamshire

Transport Treasures, 2 London Road, **Aston Clinton.** HP22 5HQ.
Beatties, 13/15 High Street, **Aylesbury.** HP20 1SH
Beatties, 1 The Concourse, Brunel Centre, **Bletchley,** Milton Keynes. MK2 2HK.
Bletchley Railwayana, 21 St Marys Avenue, **Bletchley,** Milton Keynes. MK3 5BR.
Beatties, 27 White Hart Street, **High Wycombe.** HP11 2HL.
Childs Models, 190 Desborough Road, **High Wycombe.** HP11 2QA.
Beatties, 64 Midsoummer Archade, Secklow Gate West, **Central Milton Keynes.** MK9 3ES.
Model World, 3 Weston Road, **Olney.** MK46 5BD.
Garden Railway Specialists, Station Studio, **Princes Risborough.** HP2 9DT.

Cambridgeshire

R&D Models, 17 King Street, **Cambridge.**

The Model Shop. 717 Lincoln Road, **Peterborough.** PE1 3HD
Beatties, Unit 8, Queensgate Centre. **Peterborough.** PE1 1NT.

Channel Islands

The Model Shop (Guernsey), 18 Fountain Street, **Guernsey.**

Cheshire

Arts & Crafts, 15 St Michaels Row, **Chester.**
Wool Station, 9 The Parade, Blacon, **Chester.** CH1 5HN.
Haslington Models, 134 Crewe Road, Haslington, **Crewe.** CW1 5RQ.
Frodsham Toy & Hobby, (Post Office), 80 Main Street, **Frodsham.** WA6 7AR.
Cheshire Models, 37 Sunderland Street, **Macclesfield.**
Trevor Bailey (Macclesfield) Ltd., 4-6 Mill Street, **Macclesfield.**
Macclesfield Model Railway Centre, 41 Sunderland Street, **Macclesfield.** SK11 6JL.
Weaver Models 1994, the Enthusiasts shop, 54 Welsh Row, **Nantwich.** CW5 5EJ.
S&J Models, Indoor Market, Town Centre, **Northwich.**
Station Road Models & Collectors Shop, 62 Station Road **Northwich.**
Runcorn Model Centre, 41 Regent Street, **Runcorn.** WA7 1LJ.
CDS Models, 34 Church Street, **Warrington.** WA1 2SY.
Railway Junction, 187 Orford Lane, **Warrington.** WA2 7BA.
G&I Models, 33 Horsemarket St, **Warrington.** WA1 1TS.

Cleveland

Railway King, 32 Forbes Buildings, Linthorpe Road, **Middlesbrough.**
Redcar Models & Hobbies, 6 Redcar Lane, **Redcar.** TS10 3JF.

Cornwall

The American Railroad Centre, 15 Lower Bore Street, **Bodmin.** PL31 2JR.
World of Model Railways, **Mevagissey.**
Toodees Modesl and Toys, Cliff Road, **Newquay.**
Crownline Models Ltd, 8 Rame Terrace, Rame Cross, Nr. **Penryn.** TR10 9DZ.
Hudsons Scale Models, 65 Causewayhead, **Penzance.**

Cumbria

Townfoot Models, Salvin Cottages, **Alston.**
G & M Models, 1 Crosby Street, **Carlisle.**

Derbyshire

Barry Jones (Models), 15 Chatsworth Road, **Chesterfield.**
The Midlander, 393 Sheffield Road, Whittington Moor, **Chesterfield.** S41 8LS.
Beatties, 115 St. Peter Street, **Derby.** DE1 2AD.

C & B Models, 103 Normanton Road, **Derby.** DE1 2GG.
Train World, 33 Chapel Street, **Ripley.** DE5 3DL.

Devons

Youngs Model Centre, 72 Boutpart Street, **Barnstaple.**
The Model Shop, I5 St David's Hill. **Exeter.** EX4 3RG.
G Bates Models, Shop 5, Market Hall, **Newton Abbot.** TQ12 5RH.
Hobby Horse Model Services, Old Railway Station, Station Road, **Okehampton.** EX20 1EJ.
Mansel's Models, 56/58 Winner Street, **Paignton.**
Platform 1 Models, 48 Church Street, **Paignton.** 7Q3 3AH.
Lawsons of Plymouth, 71 New George Street, **Plymouth.**
Model Rail, **Plymouth** Station. PL4 6BH.
The Vintage Toy & Train Shop, Antiques Centre, All Saints Road, **Sidmouth.**
Tavyside Model Supplies, 11A Mount Tavy Road, **Tavistock.**
Torbay Model Supplies, 59 Victoria Road, Ellacombe **Torquay.**

Dorset

Beatties, 98 Poole Road, Westbourne, **Bournemouth.** BH4 9EG.
Boscombe Models and Collector's Shop, 802C Christchurch Road, Boscombe, **Bournemouth.**
Motor Books, 241 Holdenhurst Road, **Bournemouth.**
Model Railway Centre, 335 Holdenhurst Road, **Bournemouth.**
Railway Mart, 134 Seabourne Road, Southbourne, **Bournemouth.**
Geoff Barlow Models, 28A High Street, **Poole.**

Co. Durham

C & G Model Railways, 95 Parkgate, **Darlington.** DL1 1RZ.

Essex

Braintree Model Railways, 106 South Street, **Braintree.** CM7 6QB.
Beatties, 37 Meadows Shopping Centre, **Chelmsford.** CM2 6FD.
John Dutfield, Wards Yard, 133 Stringfield Park Road, **Chelmsford.** CM2 6EE.
Clacton Models, 67 Meredith Road, **Clacton-on-Sea.**
Beatties, 6 Long Wyre Street, **Colchester.** CO1 1LH.
Mankin (Colchester) Ltd, 213 Shrub End Road, **Colchester.**
Model Magic, Church Elm Walk, **Heathway,** Dagenham. RM10 9QS.
Roneo Models, 32 Roneo Corner, **Hornchurch.** RM12 4TN.
R&R Models, 145 Cranbrook Road, **Ilford.** IG1 4PU.
Beatties, 7/11 High Street, **Romford.** RM1 1JU.
Victoria Model Railways, 1 Old Mill Parade, Victoria Road, **Romford.**
Beatties, Toystation, c/o Keddies Ltd, The High Street **Southend-on-sea.** SS1 1LA.
Rickatrack, (S & D Noyce Studios), 347 Victoria Avenue, **Southend-on-sea.**
"Plus Daughters", 179 St. Mary's Lane, **Upminster.** RM14 3BU.
A.J. Blackwell, (Blackwells of Hawkwell), 733 London Road, **Westciff-on-sea.** SS0 9ST.

Gloucestershire

Bourton Model Railway, Boxbush High Street, **Bourton on the Water.**
Cheltenham Model Centre, 39 High Street, **Cheltenham.** GL50 1DY.
Dean Sidings, Unit 7, Crucible Court, Mushet Ind. Park, **Coleford.** GL16 8BH.
Cotswold Models, 6 Market Parade, **Gloucester.**
Gloucester Model Centre, 120 Barton Street, **Gloucester.**
Model Warehouse Ltd, 38 High Street, **Stonehouse.** GL10 2NA.

Hampshire

Concorde Models, Victoria Road **Aldershot.**
A & M Models, West Street, **Alresford.**
Mainly 'Planes 'N Trains', 6 Ashdown Road, Hiltingbury, **Chandlers Ford.**
Beatties, 20 Chantry Way, **Andover.** SP10 1LX
Beatties, 8 New Market Square, **Basingstoke.** RG21 1JA.
Beatties 8/9 Fryern Arcade, Chandlers Ford, **Eastleigh.** SO5 2DP.
Wicor Models, 110-112 West Street, **Fareham.**
Cove Models, 119 Lynchford Road, **Farnborough.** GU14 6ET.
Milford Models & Hobbies, 48 High Street, **Milford-on-Sea.**
Wicor Models, 2 Castle Street, **Portchester.** PO16 9PP.
Beatties, 28 Arundel Street, **Portsmouth.** PO1 1NL.
Fratton Model Centre Ltd, 171-173 Fratton Road, **Portsmouth.** PO1 5ET.
Tony's Trains & Models, 2A Torrington Road, Hillsea, **Portsmouth.** PO2 OTP.
Portsmouth & Southsea Model Railway Centre, Collector's Corner, 123, New Road, **Portsmouth.**
Beatties, 114 East Street, **Southampton,** SO1 1HD.
Footplate Railway Models, 109 Janson Road, **Southampton.** SO15 5GL.
Greenweld, 27 Park Road, **Southampton.** SO15 3UQ.
Southampton Model Centre, 13 Junction Road, **Totton.** SO40 9HG.
Beatties, 46/47 High Street, **Winchester.** SO23 9BT.

Hereford & Worcester

Kenwater Rail-Ways, Kenwater House, Bridge Street, **Leominster.** HR6 8DX.
Totally Trains, 1 Cantilupe Court. Cantilupe Road, **Ross-on-Wye.** HR9 7AN.

Hertfordshire

Beatties, 203 Marlowes, **Hemel Hempstead,** HP1 1BL.
Junction 20 Models, 51 High Street, **Kings Langley.**
Model Image, 56 Station Road, **Letchworth,**
The Toy Shop, 25 High Street, **Royston.**
Tracks Model Railway Centre, Unit 1, Trackside, The Maltings, Station Road, **Sawbridgeworth.** CM21 9JY.
K.S. Models Ltd, 19 Middle Row, **Stevenage,** SG1 3AW.
Beatties, 70 The Parade, High Street, **Watford,** WD1 2AW.

Isle of Wight

Isle of Wight Model Railways, The Parade, **Cowes.** PO31 7QJ
Isle of Wight Model Centre, c/o Domestic Appliance Spares, **Newport.**

Kent

Bexley Model Centre, 18 Bourne Road, **Bexley.**
Just Trains, 2A, Chatterton Road, **Bromley.** BR2 9QN.
The Hobby Shop, 57 Palace Street, **Canterbury.**
The Hobby Shop, 122 West Street, **Faversham.**
Wheeltappers (Models & Hobbies), 87 Cheriton High Street, **Folkestone.** CT10 4HE.
Chalk Garden Rail, 25 Harmer Street, **Gravesend.** DA12 2AP.
Hythe (Kent) Models, 153A High Street, **Hythe.**
C & T Models, 784 London Road, **Larkfield.**
Exceltech, 187 Petts Wood Road, **Petts Wood.** BR5 1JZ.
Kemco Models 106-108 Delce Road, **Rochester.**
Rons Model Rail, Fagin's Alley, 53 High Street, **Rochester.** ME1 1LN.
The Signal Box Model Railways, 382-386 High Street, **Rochester,** ME1 1DQ.
Kent Garden Railways, 68 High Street, **St Mary Cray.** BR5 3NH.
Ballard's, 54 Grosvenor Road, **Tunbridge Wells.**
Welling Model World, 113 Bellegrove Road, **Welling.**
East Kent Models, 73 High Street, **Whitstable.** CT5 1AY.
The Model Shop, 8 Front Road, **Woodchurch,** Nr. Ashford. TN26 3QE.

Lancashire

Beatties, 19 Houndshill Centre, Victoria Street, **Blackpool.** FY1 4HU.
Palatine Model Railway + The American Connection, 16A Dickson Road, North Shore, **Blackpool.** FY1 2AE.
Tower Models, 44 Cookson Street, **Blackpool.** FY1 3ED.
Modelrail (Burnley), 122-124 Hebrew Road, Duke Bar, **Burnley.** BB10 1LR.
J.H. Models, Park Hill Barn, **Garstang,** Preston. PR3 1HB.
Farnworth Rail & Model Centre, 3 Bolton Road, **Kearsley.**
Charlton & Bagnall Ltd, 3 & 5 Damside Street, **Lancaster.** LA1 1PD.
The Train Shop, 19 Pedder Street, **Morecambe.**
Turntable Models, 42 Station Road, **Padiham.** BB12 8FF
Trains & Transport, 21 Charnley Street, **Preston.**
Transport Models, 6-10 Lawson Street, **Preston.**

Leicestershire

The Signal Box, 1 Albion Street, **Anstey,** LE7 7DD.
Central Models & Hobbies, 2 Winchester Avenue, Off Blaby by Pass, **Blaby.**
Beatties, The Shires, High Street, **Leicester,** LE1 4FR.

Lincolnshire

Beatties, 45 West Street, **Boston.** PE21 8QN.
Caistor Loco, 5A Market Place, **Caistor.**
Loftis, 196 Grimsby Road, **Cleethorpes.**
Grantham Model & Video Centre, Unit 6, Blue Court, Guildhall St. **Grantham.** NG3 6NJ.
D. Hewins Model & Hobbies, 7 East Street, Mary's Gate, **Grimsby.**
B & H Models, 13 Corporation Street, **Lincoln.**
Modelcraft (formerly Mayhew Models), The Forum, Newark Road, North Hykeham, **Lincoln.**
Granary Models & Hobbies, 31 High Street, **Swineshead.**

London

Engine Shed, 745 High Road, **Leytonstone,** London. E11 4QS.
Lewisham Toys & Models, 50 **Lee High Road,** London. SE13.
Beatties, 210 Lewisham High Street, **Lewisham,** London. SE13 6JP.
Engine 'n' Tender, 19 Spring Lane, **Woodside,** London. SE25 8SP.
Norwood Junction Models Ltd, 3 Orton Buildings, Portland Road. **SE25** 4WD.
E.F. Russ, 101 **Battersea Rise,** London. SW11.
Jane's Trains, 35 London Road, Tooting. **SW17** 9JR.
Home of O Gauge, Charles Covey (Models), 528 Kingston Road, **Raynes Park,** London. SW20 8TD.
Beatties, 202 **High Holborn,** London. WC1V 7BD.
Wheels of Steel, Basement of Grays Antique Market, 1-7 Davies Mews. **W1.**
The Booking Hall, 7 **Charlotte Place,** London. W1P 1AQ.
Braley Hobbies Supplies, 141 Little Ealing Lane, **Ealing.** London, W5 4EJ.
Beatties, 72A Broadway, **West Ealing,** London. W13 0SY.
Victors, 166 Pentonville Road, **Islington,** London. Nl 91L.
Beatties, 10 The Broadway, Southgate, London. Nl4 6PN.
The Shunting Yard, 121 Lordship Lane, **Tottenham,** London. N17 6XE.

Greater Manchester

Beatties, 92/94 Stamford New Road, Graftson's Precinct, **Altrincham.** WA14 1DG.
Waltons of Altrincham, 30 Stamford Street, **Altrincham.**
Ashton Models, Old Street, **Ashton-under-Lyme.**
Bolton Model Mart, 124 Bradshawgate, **Bolton.** BL2 1EH.
Farnworth Rail & Model Centre, 3 Bolton Road, **Kearsley,** Nr. Bolton.
Beatties, 4–6 Brown Street, Off Market Street, **Manchester.** M2 1EE.
Railways Unlimited, 22 Corkland Road, Chorlton, **Manchester.** M21 8UT.
The Model Shop, 695 Ripponden Road, **Oldham.**
Norman Wisenden, 95 Chew Valley Road, Greenfield, **Oldham.** OL3 7JJ.
SRA Models, 1 Mersey Square, **Stockport.** SK1 1NLL.
JPL Models, Unit 12, Tyldesley House, Elliott Street, **Tyldesley.** M29 8DS.
G & I Model Railways, 57 Library Street, **Wigan.** WN1 1NU.

Merseyside

Beatties, 36/37 Dawsons Way, St John's Centre, **Liverpool.** L1 1LJ.
City Models, 6 Stanley Street **Liverpool 2.**
Hattons, 180 Smithdown Road, **Liverpool.** L15 3JS.
World of Motion, 277 Wallasey Village, **Wallasey.** L45 3LR.

Middlesex

Jennings Models, 244/248, Hertford Road, **Enfield.** EN3 5BL

E.M.A. Model Supplies, 58-60 The Centre, **Feltham.**
Richardsons of Feltham, 6–7 Rochester Parade, High Street, **Feltham.** TW13 4DX.
The Model Shop, 190-194, Station Road, **Harrow.** HA1 1JU.
Hodgsons Toys & Models Ltd, 44/46 Hounslow Road, **Whitton,** Twickenham. TW2 7EX.

West Midlands

Alton Models. 897 Walsall Road, Great Barr, **Birmingham.**
Beatties, 26 South Mall, The Pallasades, **Birmingham.** B2 4XD.
Model Craft, 61 Spon End, **Coventry.**
Tennent's Trains, Shop 1, No. 130 Hagley Road, Hayley Green, **Halesowen.** B63 1DY.
Modellers Mecca, 450 Albion Street, Wall Heath, **Kingswinford.** DY6 0JP.
Roy's Hobbies & Toys, 155 New Road, **Rubery.** B45 9JW.
Hobbyrail, 55 Riland Road, **Sutton Coldfield.**
Graingers Models & Crafts, 51 George Street, **Walsall.**
A. Oakes. 174/180 Vicarage Road, Oldbury, **Warley.** B68 8JB.
Wolverhampton Models & Hobbies, 1 Meadow Street, Chapel Ash, **Wolverhampton.**

Norfolk

The Great Eastern Railway Company, 199 Plumstead Road, **Norwich.** NRl 4AB.
Langleys, Royal Arcade, **Norwich.** NR2 1NQ.
Trains & Olde Tyme Toys, Aylsham Road, Junction with Woodcock Road, **Norwich.**
G.E. Models, Platform 2, Sheringham Station, North Norfolk Railway, **Sheringham.** NR26 8RA.
Auto-Loco, 44b Station Road, **Sheringham.** NR26 8RG.

Northamptonshire

Beatties, 19-21 Gold Street, Newlands Centre, **Kettering** NN16 8BX.
Beatties, 41 & 43 Princes Walk, Grosvenor Centre, **Northampton,** NNl 2EL.
The Model Shop, 230 Wellinborough Road, **Northampton.**
A. Watts & Sons Ltd, 80 Abington Street, **Northampton.**
T&R Models Etc.., 20 Cannon Street, **Wellingborough.**

Nottinghamshire

R.B.S. Ltd Railway & Barter Shop, 73-75 Main Street, **Long Eaton.**
The Junction, 90 Stockwell Gate, **Mansfield.**
Greenyard Models, Greenyard, Front Street, South Clinton, **Newark.** NG23 7AA.
Beatties, 3 Mount Street, **Nottingham.** NG1 6JW.
Gee Dee Models Ltd, 19/21 Heathcoat Street, Off Goosegate. **Nottingham,** NG1 3AF.
Inter-City Models, 68 Station Road, Sandiacre, **Nottingham.** NG10 5AP.
Sherwood Models, 831 Mansfield Road, Daybrook, **Nottingham.** NG5 3GF.
Harringtons, 51 Outram Street, **Sutton-in-Ashfield.** NG17 4BG.
Geoffrey Allison Railways, 90 Cheapside, **Worksop.** S80 2HY.

Oxfordshire

Geoff Osborn's Railway & Model Shop, 43 Edward Street, **Abingdon.** OX15 1DJ.
Beatties, 28 Bridge Street, The Cherwell Centre, **Banbury.** OX16 8PN.
Tinder Bros Ltd. 2A/4 Broad Street, **Banbury.**
Motor Books, 8 The Roundway, Headington, **Oxford.** OX3 8DH.
Howes Model Shop, 12 Banbury Road, **Kidlington.** OX5 2BT.

Shropshire

Bridgnorth Models, Sydney Cottage Post Office, **Bridgnorth.** WI6 4PP.
Manor Models, 39 Manor Gardens, Dawley, **Telford.** TF4 3LS.
Shrewsbury Model Centre, 15 Mardol Gardens, **Shrewsbury.** SY1 1PR.

Somerset

The Modellers Den Ltd, 2 Lower Borough Walls, **Bath.** BA1 1QR.
Challis Models & Hobbies, 50B High Street, **Shepton Mallet.** BA4 5AS.
Mainly Trains (Dave Cleal), 13 Anchor Street, **Watchet.** TA23 0AZ.
Janet's Hobby, 9 Fore Street, **Wellington.** TA21 8AA.
Modelmasters, 50a Clifton Road, **Weston-Super-Mare.** BS23 1BW.
Trapnells Model Shop, 82 Meadow Street. **Weston-Super-Mare.**
Hendford Halt, 43 West Coker Road, **Yeovil.**

Staffordshire

The Model Shop of the Potteries, Vivian Road, **Fenton,** Stoke-on-Trent. ST4 3JG.
City Centre Models, 44 Piccadilly, **Hanley,** Stoke-on-Trent. ST11 1EG.
The Train Shop, 32 Bird Street, **Lichfield.**
Bagnalls Models, 18 Salter Street, **Stafford.** ST16 2JU.

Suffolk

Beatties, 62 Cornhill, **Bury St. Edmunds.** IP33 1BE.
Model Junction, 10 Whiting Street, **Bury St. Edmunds.** IP33 1BE.
The Train Shed, **Debenham.**
Everybodys Hobbies, 1 Gt Colman Street, **Ipswich.** IP4 2AA.
Eric Bartlett Models, 70 High Street, **Lowestoft.** NR32 1XN.
Parrs, 252 London Road South, **Lowestoft.** NR33 0BE.
Bahnhof for Marklin, Pollards Lane, West Row, Nr. **Mildenhall.** IP28 8RA.

Surrey

Addlestone Models Ltd, 63 Station Road, **Addlestone.**
Roxley Models, Unit 19, Smithbrook Kilns, Horsham Road, **Cranleigh.** QU6 8JJ.
Beatties, 135A North End, **Croydon.** CR0 ITN.
Dorking Model Centre, 13 West Street, **Dorking.**

Masters of Epsom, 29–31 Tattenham Crescent, Tattenham Corner, **Epsom Downs.** KT18 5QJ.
Beatties, 30/32 Eden Street, **Kingston-upon-Thames.** KT1 1EP.
Thames Trains, 29 Walton Road, **East Molesey.** KT8 0DH.

Sussex

The Engine Shed, Gaugemaster House, Ford Road, **Ford,** Nr. Arundel. BN18 0BN.
Trains, 67 London Road, **Bognor Regis.**
Beatties 4/8 Dyke Road, **Brighton.** BN1 3FE.
Valelink Ltd, 26 Queens Road, **Brighton.** BN1 3XA.
Mid Sussex Models,13 Junction Road, **Burgess Hill.** RH15 0HR
Beatties, Unit 75 County Shopping Mall, **Crawley.** RH10 1FD.
Train Times, 37 Seaside, **Eastbourne.** BN22 7NB.
Scale Rail Model Centre, 1 Crown Street, **Eastbourne.** BN21 1NX.
Maintrack Models, 79 Queens Road, **Hastings.** TN34 1RL.
J Morris. 80 Manor Road, **North Lancing.**
Loco-Notion Models, 6 Cliffe Arcade, 34-36 Cliffe High Street, **Lewes.** BN7 2AN.
Railway Roundabout, 5 Avis Parade, Denton Corner, **Newhaven.** BN9 0PL.
The Hobby Box, 8 Framfield Road, **Uckfield.** TN22 5AG.

Tyne & Wear

Beatties, 43/47 Pilgrim Street, **Newcastle-upon-Tyne,** NE1 6QF.
Beatties, 2 High Friars, Eldon Square, **Newcastle,** NE1 7XG.
The Model Shop, 18 Blenheim Street, **Newcastle-upon-Tyne.** NE1 4AZ.
Northumbria Models, 58 Thornton Street (Waterloo Street), **Newcastle-upon-Tyne.**
Rolling Stock, 12 Trevor Terrace, **North Shields.**

Warwickshire

Joto, 7 Lawrence Sherriff Street, **Rugby.**
Model Mayhem, 4 The Minories, Henley Street, **Stratford-upon-Avon.** CV37 6NF.
Much Ado About Toys, 3 Windsor Place, Windsor Street, **Stratford-upon-Avon.** CV37 6NL.
J P Models, 8 High Street, Studley. B80 7HJ.

Wiltshire

Beatties, 25 Bridge Street, **Swindon.** SN1 1BP.
Froude & Hext, 83 Victoria Road, **Swindon.** SN1 3BB.
Spot-On Models, 49 Fleet Street, **Swindon.**

Yorkshire

AK Models, 45 Beacon Road, Wibsey, **Bradford.** BD6 3ET.
Frizinghall Model Railways, 202 Keighley Road, Frizinghall, **Bradford.** BD9 4JZ.
W.B.H. Lord & Sons Ltd, 78 Commercial Street, **Brighouse.**
Evans Models, 65 Silver Street, **Doncaster.**
TAG Models, 4 West Street, **Doncaster.**

Beatties, 24/26 Commercial Street, **Halifax.** HX1 1TA.
Beatties, 47/49 James Street, **Harrogate.** HG1 1SJ.
Starbeck Models, 16 Devonshire Place, **Harrogate.**
Beatties, 28/29 Prospect Shopping Centre, **Hull.** HU2 8PN.
53A Models, 430 Hessle Road, **Hull.**
The Model Shop, 170 Ferensway, **Hull.** HU1 3UA.
Milburn's, 90 Cavendish Street, **Keighley.**
Goodesyard, 74 High Street, **Knaresborough.** HG5 0EA.
Beatties, 16/18 King Charles Street, **Leeds.** LS1 6LT.
Britannia Hobbies, 22 Eastgate, **Leeds.** LS2 7JL.
M.C.L. Models, 15 Chapel Street, Halton, **Leeds.**
LS18 7RN.
John Edmonds, Broading Pharmacy, 26 Otley Road,
Guiseley, **Leeds.** LS20 8AH.
MTFG, 7 Railway Street, **Leyburn.** DL8 5EH.
Puffers of Pickering, 7a Park Street, **Pickering.** YO18 7AJ.
The Train Shop 41 Eastborough, Scarborough.
Beatties, 38 Pinstone Street, **Sheffield.** S1 2HN.
Beatties, 23 High Street, Meadowhall Shopping Centre,
Sheffield. S9 1EN.
Marcway Ltd, 590 Attercliffe Road, **Sheffield.** S9 3QS.
Rail and Road Models, 703 Abbeydale Road, **Sheffield.**
M.G. Sharp Models, 712 Attercliffe Road, **Sheffield.** S9 3RP.
Sheffield Transport Models, 214 London Road, **Sheffield.**
S2 4LW.
Rails, 27/29 Chesterfield Road, **Sheffield.** S8 0RL,
Buffers Coffee Shop, Storiths, Bolton Abbey, **Skipton.**
Craven Model Centre, 4 Mount Pleasant, The High Street,
Skipton.
Wakefield Model Railway Centre, 260 Dewsbury Road,
Wakefield. WF2 9BY.
Monk Bar Model Shop Ltd., 2 Goodramgate, **York.**
Puffers of York, 96 Micklegate, **York.** YO1 1JX.

Ireland

The Model Railway Shop, 18 Monck Place, Phibsboro,
Dublin 7.
'Kavanaghs', 13a Stoneybatter, **Dublin.**
Killarney Model Railway, Beech Road, **Killarney,** Co.
Kerry.

Northern Ireland

Modellers Nook, 15/17 Winetavern Street, **Belfast.**
Elgee Hobbies, 122 Thomas Street, **Portadown,**
Co. Armargh. BT62 3AL.

Isle of Man

Mann Trains Ltd, Tynwald Craft Centre, **St John's.**

Scotland

Beatties, 18/22 Market Street, **Aberdeen.** AB1 2PL.
North East Models, 29 St Andrews Street, **Aberdeen.**
AB25 1JA.
Beatties, 21/25 Newmarket Street, **Ayr,** Strathclyde.
KA7 1LL.
Beatties, 11 Britannia Way, Clyde Regional Centre,
Clydebank, Strathclyde. G81 2RZ.
Beatties, 11C Forth Walk, **Cumbernauld,** Strathclyde.
G67 1BT.
Beatties, 7 Church Place. **Dumfries.** DG1 1BW.
Beatties, 8 Olympia Centre, **East Kilbride,** Strathclyde.
G74 1PG.
Harburn Hobbies Ltd, 67 Elm Row, Leith Walk,

Edinburgh. EH7 4AQ.
Moray's Model Centre, 19a Batchen Street, **Elgin,**
Morayshire. IV30 1BH.
Beatties, 30 St Enoch Square, **Glasgow.** G1 4DF.
D&F Models, 56 Bell Street, **Glasgow.** G1 1LQ.
Glasgow Model Centre, 671 Cathcart Road, **Glasgow.**
G42 8AP.
Pastimes, 126 Maryhill Road, St George's Cross,
Glasgow. G20 7QS.
Mac's Model Railroading, 64a Sinclair Street,
Helensburgh. G84 8JP.
Beatties, 3 & 5 Bank Street, **Kilmarnock,** Strathclyde.
KA1 1HA.
Scoonie Hobbies, 91 St Clair Street, **Kirkcaldy,** Fife.
KY1 2NW.
Mackay Models, Studio 20, Sir James Clark Building,
Abbey Mill Centre, Seedhill, **Paisley,** Strathclyde.
PA1 1TJ.
Beatties, 15 Canal Street, **Perth,** Tay. PH2 8LF.
Model Engineer, 55 Baker Street, **Stirling.**

Wales

Kivoli Centre, 1 Station Yard (Industrial Estate), **Bala,**
Gwynedd. LL23 7NL.
Celt Models, 115 High Street, **Bangor,** Gwynedd.
LL57 1NR.
D.W. Models, 67 Nolton Street, **Bridgend,** Mid
Glamorgan. CF31 3AE.
Beatties, North Gate House, Kingway, **Cardiff.** CF1 4AD.
Lendons of Cardiff, Llanishen Model Shop, 192 Fidlas
Road Llanishen, **Cardiff.** CF4 5LZ.
Bud Morgan, 11 High Street, **Cardiff.**
Terrys Train Shop, 46 Broadway, **Cardiff.**
Clwyd Models & Hobbies, 447 Abergale Road, **Old
Colwyn,** Conwy. LL29 9PR.
Kittle Hobby, 24 Pennard Road, **Kittle,** Gower. SA3 3JS.
Dapol Model Railways Ltd, Lower Dee Exhibition Centre,
Llangollen. LL20 8RX.
Wenallt Models, Wenallt, **Penrhyndeudraeth,**
Gwynedd. LL48 6PW.
Photoworld, 7A Victoria Street, Craig-Y-Don,
Llandudno. LL30 1LQ.
Ffestiniog Model Railway Centre, Harbour Station,
Porthmadog, Gwynedd. LL49 9NF.
Holt Model Railways. Orders & Correspondence: Holt
House, Caswell Bay, **Swansea.** Retail Sales: 100
Bishopston Road, Bishopston, **Swansea,** West
Glamorgan.
Talyllyn Railway, Wharf Station, **Tywyn,** Gwynedd.
LL36 9EY.

5 Locomotive kits and models

The following list of British main-line
company and British Railways locomotives,
showing all known commercially produced
ready-to-run models and construction kits,
was correct at the time of going to press. Also
included are some commercial models which
were at one time readily available but have
now been withdrawn. The supply situation of
models and kits is not, and cannot be, static
as manufacturers reserve the right to with-

draw items from their range. Knowledge of withdrawn models is not without interest, however, as it is sometimes possible to come across samples in out-of-the-way places or to purchase them second-hand from retailers specialising in the sale of such equipment or perhaps a private sale. It is not unknown for manufacturers to re-introduce deleted items, so some models long since withdrawn and elevated to the status of collectors' items may once again appear on the retailers' shelves. I have, however, avoided including limited-run kits and models where it has been made known that the numbers to be produced are such that their availability cannot be guaranteed during the currency of this book. This applies in the main to a number of etched-brass kits and expensive hand-crafted models.

Models in 4 mm scale predominate, as one might expect, and the number of kits and models in the different gauges probably reflects the popularity of each gauge. For the sake of simplicity I have referred to all 4 mm scale kits as '00'. Most 00 gauge kits can be adapted to EM, Scalefour or Protofour standards but some kits can only be converted at the expense of discarding the wheels that come with the kit. The majority of 00 kits are cast white metal but increasing use is being made of etched brass or nickel-silver frets, either for components such as chassis frames, coupling rods and valve gear, or for complete kits. Cast white metal kits are available in O gauge for those who like working in this material but generally sheet metal is preferred. In both 00 and O gauges manufacturers have been quick to adopt new materials such as polyurethane resin which is particularly suitable for casting items such as

boilers, smokeboxes and firebox asemblies and the complex curves of streamlined locomotive casings. Some O gauge kits are fairly basic, consisting of pre-cut sheet metal, rolled boilers and turned or cast metal fittings, requiring the constructor to find his own source of wheels and motor, and calling for a fair degree of skill for assembly and detailed finishing. On the other hand there are some very comprehensive and necessarily more expensive kits in O gauge that include motors, wheels and all the parts needed to assemble a highly detailed model. At the opposite end of the scale, N gauge continues to attract a number of new readyto-run models, thanks largely to Graham Farish whose chassis are also used by a number of other manufacturers producing cast white metal body-line kits for a wide range of British steam and modern motive power locomotives.

The range of currently available kits and ready-to-run models, particularly in 4 mm scale, is now truly remarkable. Whereas in the first edition of this book the check list of representative locomotive types considered to be worthy of modelling showed there to be nearly 60 classes not then covered by commercial manufacturers, the number has now shrunk to 3. These are indicated by a dash –. Certainly there are no serious omissions and in many cases there is more than one kit and/or model of each locomotive class to choose from. The coverage provided by the trade deserves the fullest support from the model railway public.

In the following list (P) indicates that one or more examples of the class have been preserved or set aside for preservation.

Great Western Railway classes

4-6-2	'The Great Bear'		00	Alan Gibson kit
4-6-0	'King' Class	(P)	TT-3	GEM kit
			00	Lima ready-to-run model
			00	Hornby Railways ready-to-run model
			00	South Eastern Finecast kit
			0	Gaterneal etched kit
"	'Castle' Class	(P)	N	Graham Farish ready-to-run model
			00	Hornby Railways ready-to-run model
			00	Wrenn ready-to-run model
			00	South Eastern Finecast kit
			00	Malcolm Mitchell Design kit
			0	Malcolm Mitchell Design kit
"	'Star' Class	(P)	00	South Eastern Finecast kit

4-6-0	'Star' Class (Cont.)	00	Malcom Mitchell Design kit
		0	Malcom Mitchell Design kit
"	'Saint' Class	N	P & D Marsh cast metal body kit
		00	Hornby Railways ready-to-run model
		00	Pro-scale kit
		00	Westward kit
		00	South Eastern Finecast kit
		0	Slater's Plastikard etched and cast resin kit
"	'Hall' Class	(P) N	Graham Farish ready-ro-run model
		00	Hornby Railways ready-to-run model
		00	Bachmann ready-to-run model
		00	DJH kit
		00	Nu-cast kit
		0	Springside Models kit
"	'Grange' Class	N	P & D Marsh body kit
		00	Nu-cast kit
		00	Malcolm Mitchell Design kit
		0	Malcolm Mitchell Design kit
"	'Manor' Class	(P) N	P & D Marsh body kit
		00	Bachmann ready-to-run model
		00	Nu-cast kit
		00	Alan Gibson kit
		0	Springside Models kit
"	'County' Class	N	P & D Marsh cast metal body kt
		00	Hornby Railways ready-to-run model
		00	Nu-cast kit
"	No.36 Outside Frame	00	Alan Gibson kit
2-8-0	28XX Class	(P) N	GEM kit
		00	Hornby Railways ready-to-run model
		00	Nu-cast kit
		00	Martin Finney kit
		0	Slater's Plastikard etched kit
		0	Gatteneal etched kit
"	47XX Class	00	Nu-Cast kit
		0	Martin Finney etched kit
"	ROD 30XX Class	00	Nu-cast kit
		0	Gladiator Models kit
2-6-0	26XX 'Aberdare' Class	00	Nu-cast kit
"	43XX Class	(P) N	P & D Marsh cast metal body kit
		TT-3	GEM kit
		00	Bachmann ready-to-run model
		00	Nu-cast kit
		0	Slater's Plastikard kit
"	93XX Class	(P) N	P & D Marsh cast metal body kit
		00	Bachmann ready-to-run model
		0	CCW kit
4-4-2	De Glehn Compound	00	South Eastern Finecast kit
"	'Scott' Class	00	Westward kit
4-4-0	'Armstrong' Class	00	K's Milestone series kit
"	'City' Class	(P) 00	Dapol ex-Airfix plastic kit
		00	Nu-Cast kit
"	'Flower' Class	00	Nu-Cast kit
"	'Bulldog' Class	00	Nu-cast kit
		0	D.J.B. Engineering kit
"	'Duke' Class	00	Nu-Cast kit
		00	Blacksmith Models kit
"	'Dukedog' 32XX later 99XX Class	(P) 00	Nu-Cast kit
		00	Blacksmith Models etched kit
"	'County'Class	TT-3	GEM kit
		00	Hornby Railways ready-to-run model
		00	South Eastern Finecast kit
"	3521 Class	00	Peter K (London) Ltd kit
2-4-0	Barnum Class	00	Blacksmith Models etched brass kit
"	1334 Class (MSWJR)	00	Nu-Cast kit
4-2-2	3031 'Achilles' Class	00	Hornby Railways ready-to-run (not in production)
		00	K's Milestone Series kit
		00	Alan Gibson kit
"	'Rover' Broad Gauge	4mm scale	K's Milestone series kit
2-2-2	'Firefly' Broad Gauge	4mm scale	Model Railway Services kit
0-6-0	322 'Beyer' Class	00	Nu-Cast kit
"	Armstrong Goods	00	Nu-Cast kit

		(P)	Scale	Description
0-6-0	'Dean' 2301 Class	(P)	TT-3	3mm Society kit
			00	Hornby Railways ready-to-run model
			00	Nu-Cast kit
			0	a.b.s. models kit
			0	DJB Engineering kit
"	'Dean' outside frame		00	Nu-Cast kit
"	2251 Class	(P)	N	Langley Miniature Models body kit
			TT-3	ABS Models & Beaver Products kit
			00	Bachmann ready-to-run model
			00	South Eastern Fincast kit
			0	Springside Models kit
"	Cambrian Rlys Sharp Stewart		00	Peter K (London) Ltd kit
"	'Hercules' Broad Gauge		4mm scale	Model Railway Services kit
2-8-2T	72XX Class	(P)	00	Nu-Cast kit
2-8-0T	42XX Class	(P)	00	Nu-Cast kit
			0	Gladiator Models kit
0-8-2T	Barry Railway Class H		00	Redcraft brass kit
			0	Gateneal etched brass kit
2-6-2T	31XX Class		N	Langley Miniature Models body kit
"	39XX Class		00	Jackson-Evans kit
"	44XX Class		00	Nu-Cast kit
			0	Slater's Plastikard kit
"	45XX Class	(P)	00	Nu-Cast kit
			0	Springside kit
			0	CCW kit
			0	Gateneal Ltd budget etched kit
"	4575 Class	(P)	00	Nu-Cast kit
			00	Lima ready-to-run model
			0	CCW kit
"	61XX Class	(P)	N	Graham Farish ready-to-run model
			00	Dapol-former Airfix plastic kit
			00	South Eastern Finecast kit
0-6-4T	Barry Railway Class L		00	Dean Sidings resin body kit
0-6-2T	56XX Class	(P)	N	Langley Miniature Models body kit
			N	Beaver Products body kit
			TT-3	GEM kit
			00	Dapol ready-to-run model
			00	GEM kit
"	Barry Railway Class K		0	Gaterncal etched brass kit
"	Rhymney Rly R Class		N	Langley miniature Models body kit
			00	Nu-Cast kit
0-6-2PT/ST	Rhymney Rly K Class		0	Gateneal etched brass kit
0-6-2T	TaffVale Rly UI class		00	South Eastern Finecast kit
			0	Gateneal etched brass kit
"	TaffVale Rly A Class		00	Nu-Cast kit
"	TaffVale Rly 04 Class		—	
"	TaffVale Rly 01 Class	(P)	—	
0-6-0T	633 class		00	Alan Gibson kit
0-6-0ST	850 Class (Saddle tank)		00	Alan Gibson kit
0-6-0PT	850 Class (pannier tank)		0	a.b.s. models cast resin kit
"	1076 Class (outside frame)		00	Alan Gibson kit
0-6-0ST	1804		00	South Eastern Finecast kit
0-6-0PT	1854		00	South Eastern Finecast kit
"	2021 Class (pannier tank)		00	Nu-Cast kit
0-6-0ST	2021 Class (saddle tank)		00	Nu-Cast kit
			0	a.b.s. models cast resin kit
0-6-0PT	27XX class		0	Gateneal budget etched brass kit
"	2721 Class		00	Hornby Railway ready-to-run model
0-6-0ST	1361 Class	(P)	00	Nu-Cast kit
			0	Hayward Railway kit
0-6-0PT	1366 Class	(P)	N	Beaver Products Co body kit
			00	DJH kit
			0	Hayward Railway kit
"	15XX Class	(P)	N	Langley Miniature Models body kit
			00	Nu-Cast kit
			0	Oakville Models kit
"	16XX Class	(P)	00	Nu-Cast kit
"	54XX Class Auto		00	Nu-Cast kit
			0	Castle Kits kit
"	57XX Class	(P)	N	Graham Farish ready-to-run model
			TT-3	GEM kit

0-6-0PT	57XX Class	00	Bachmann ready-to-run model
		0	a.b.s. models kit
		0	Vulcan Models ready-to-run
"	64XX Class	(P) 00	Nu-Cast kit
		0	Castle Kits kit
		0	Springside Models kit
		0	On Line Models ready-to-run
"	74XX class	00	Nu-Cast kit
		0	Castle Kits kit
"	8750 Class	(P) N	Graham Farish ready-to-run model
		00	Bachmann ready-to-run model
		00	Hornby Railways ready-to-run model
		00	Nu-Cast
		0	a.b.s. models kit
"	97XX Class Condenser	N	Thameshead Models body kit
		00	K's 'Bodyline' kit (not in production)
"	94XX Class	(P) N	Graham Farish ready-to-run model
		TT-3	a.b.s. models, Beaver Products Co. body kit
		00	Lima ready-to-run model
		00	South Eastern Finecast kit
0-6-0T	Alexandra Docks Nos 666.667	00	Centre Models kit, no longer available
"	Barry Railway Class E	0	Gateneal etched brass kit
0-6-0ST	Barry Railway Class F	0	Gateneal etched brass kit
"	Brecon & Merthyr Class 1	0	Gateneal etched brass kit
"	Rhymney Railway Class J	0	Gateneal etched brass kit
0-6-0T	Rhondda & Swansea Bay	00	Q Kits kit
4-4-4T	M & SWJR	00	D.A. Brown kit
4-4-2T	22XX Class County Tank	00	Alan Gibson kit
"	No 4600	00	Alan Gibson kit
2-4-2T	36XX Class	00	Craftsman kit
"		00	Redcraft kit
"	Barry Railway Class J	0	Gateneal etched brass kit
0-4-2T	48XX later 14XX Class	(P) N	Langley Miniature Models kit (with Autocoach)
		00	Nu-Cast kit
		00	Hornby Railways ready-to-run model
		0	On Line Models ready-to run
		0	Springside Models kit
"	517 Class	00	Blacksmith Models kit
		00	Alan Gibson kit
		00	Malcolm Mitchell Design kit
		00	McGowan Models kit
		0	DJB Engineering kit
		0	Malcolm Mitchell Design kit
2-4-0T	'Metro' tank	00	South Eastern Finecast kit
		0	On Line Models ready-to-run
		0	Castle Kits kit
		0	Gateneal etched brass kit
"	Brecon & Merthyr Class 9	0	Gateneal etched brass kit
"	No 1196 (Cambrian Rlys)	00	GEM kit
0-4-0T	1101 Class	00	Falcon Brass etched brass kit
		0	Gateneal Ltd etched brass kit
"	No 101	00	Hornby Railways ready-to-run model
0-4-0ST	Swansea Harbour Trust	0	a.b.s. models kit
"	TaffVale Rly 'S' Class	00	Nu-Cast kit
Diesel Railcar		(P) N	Graham Farish ready-to-run model
		N	Langley Miniature Models kit
		00	Lima ready-to-run model
		00	MKT Ltd kit
		00	Westward kit
		0	RJH Model Railways, Cavalier Coach kit
Diesel Railcar 'Express Parcels'		N	Langley Miniature Models kit
		00	Lima ready-to-run model
		00	MTK Ltd kit
		00	Westward kit
Diesel Railcar (Twin)		N	Langley Miniature Models kit
		00	MTK Ltd kit
		00	Westward kit
Steam Railmotor		N	Langley Miniature Models kit
		00	Blacksmith Models etched brass kit
		00	Nu-Cast kit
Steam Railmotor		0	Blacksmith Models etched brass kit

A1A-A1A	Brown Boveri Gas Turbine No 18000	(P)	N	Langley Miniature Models body kit
			00	MTK Ltd kit
Co-Co	Metrovick Gas Turbine No 18100		00	Q Kits fibreglass body shell kit
0-4-0	Fowler Diesel Mechanical Shunter		0	a.b.s. models kit

London Midland & Scottish Railway classes

4-6-2	'Princess' Class	(P)	N	D &M body kit
			00	Hornby railways ready-to-run model
			00	Nu-Cast kit
			00	Pro-scale kit
"	'Coronation' Class	(P)	N	Graham Farish ready-to-run model
			N	Langley Miniature Models body kit
			00	Wrenn ready-to-run model
			00	Hornby Railways ready-to-run model
			00	Nu-Cast kit
			00	DJH kit
"	'Coronation' Class Streamlined		N	Langley Miniature Models body kit
			00	Hornby Railways ready-to-run model
			00	Nu-Cast kit
			00	DJH kit
"	Turbomotive		00	Nu-Cast kit
4-6-0	'Royal Scot' Class		TT-3	GEM kit
			HO/00	Rivarossi ready-to-run model
			HO/00	Bachmann ready-to-run model
			00	Wrenn ready-to-run model
			00	South Eastern Finecast kit
"	'Royal Scot' Class Rebuilt	(P)	N	D & M body kit
			00	Bachmann ready-to-run model
			00	McGowan Models kit
"	'Royal Scot' Class 6170 'British Legion'		00	McGowan Models kit
"	'Patriot' Class		N	GEM kit
			00	Hornby Railways ready-to-run model
			00	Millholme Models Ltd kit
			00	Alan Gibson kit
			00	Brassmasters kit
"	'Patriot' Class Rebuilt		00	Bachmann ready-to-run model
"	'Jubilee' Class	(P)	N	Peco ready-to-run model
			00	"Brassmaster cast resin boiler/etched brass kit
			00	Nu-Cast kit
			00	Bachmann ready-to-run model
			00	Alan Gibson kit
			0	CCW kit
"	'Jubilee' Class Rebuilt		N	D & M body kit
			00	McGowan Models kit
			00	Bachmann ready-to-run model
"	Class 5	(P)	N	Graham Farish ready-to-run model
			00	Hornby Railways ready-to-run model
			00	DJH kit
			00	Nu-Cast kit
			00	Alan Gibson kit
			0	CCW kit
"	LNWR 'Claughton'		00	Falcon Brass kit
			00	DJH kit
"	LNWR 'Prince of Wales'		N	Langley Miniature Models body kit
			00	GEM kit
			00	Brassmasters etched brass kit
"	LNWR Whale 19" goods		00	Millholme Models kit
			00	Brassmasters etched brass kit
			0	Gateneal etched brass kit
"	LYR 'Dreadnought'		00	Millholme Models kit
"	CR 'Cardean' Class 903		00	GEM kit
"	CR Class 918		00	DJH Kits Ltd kit
"	CR Pickersgill Class 60		00	DJH Kits Ltd kit
"	CR Class 55 'Oban Bogie'		00	DJH Kits Ltd kit
"	HR Jones Goods	(P)	00	DJH Kits Ltd kit
			00	Falcon Brass etched brass kit
"	HR Cumming Clan Class		00	Falcon Brass etched brass kit
"	HR Cumming Clan Goods Class		00	Falcon Brass etched brass kit
"	HR 'Castle'		00	DJH Kits Ltd kit
"	HR 'Castle'		00	Falcon Brass etched brass kit
4-6-0	G&SWR Manson Class 381		00	DJH Kits Ltd kit

2-8-0	Stanier 8F	(P) N	Graham Farish ready-to-run model
		N	GEM kit
		00	Nu-Cast kit
		00	DJH kit
		00	Hornby Railways ready-to-run model
		00	Wrenn ready-to-run model
		00	Alan Gibson kit
		0	Modern Outline Kits kit
		0	Gateneal etched brass kit
"	S&DJR	(P) N	GEM kit
		00	Nu-Cast kit
		00	DJH kit
		00	Alan Gibson etched brass kit
		0	Alan Gibson kit
		0	JM Model Products etched kit
0-10-0	'Lickey Banker'	00	DJH kit
0-8-0	Fowler 7F	N	GEM kit
		00	Nu-Cast kit
		00	Alan Gibson kit
		N	Graham Hughes body kit
"	LNWR	(P) 00	GEM kit
		00	Brassmasters etched brass kit
		0	Gateneal etched brass kit
"	LYR 7F	00	Nu-Cast kit
"	LYR 6F (small boiler)	00	Nu-Cast kit
2-6-0	Stanier	(P) 00	Nu-Cast kit
		00	Millholme Models Ltd kit
		00	Alan Gibson kit
		0	Chowbent Castings kit
"	Hughes/Fowler 'Crab'	(P) N	Graham Farish ready-to-run model
		00	South Eastern Finecast kit
		00	Lima ready-to-run model
		00	DJH kit
		00	Alan Gibson kit
"	Ivatt 2F	(P) N	Minitrix ready-to-run model
		00	Hornby Railways ready-to-run model
		00	Crownline Models etched and resin boiler kit
"	Ivatt 4F 'Mucky Duck'	(P) 00	Millholme Models Ltd kit
		00	Falcon Brass etched brass kit
"	CR Class 34	00	DJH Kits Ltd kit
4-4-2	LYR Aspinall	00	Millholme Models Ltd kit
4-4-0	Compound 4P Fowler	N	Graham Farish ready-to-run model
		00	Nu-Cast kit
		00	Alan Gibson kit
		0	Chowbent Castings kit
"	Compund 4P Johnson/Deeley	(P) 00	Hornby Railways ready-to-run model
		00	GEM kit
		00	Alan Gibson kit
		0	Slater's Plastikard Ltd kit
"	3P MR Class 700	00	Alan Gibson kit
"	3P MR Class 999	00	GEM kit
		00	Alan Gibson etched brass kit
		0	Alan Gibson kit
"	2P	N	Graham Hughes body kit
		TT-3	ABS Models & Beaver Products Co (EX BEC) kit
		00	Dapol ready-to-run model
		00	Millholme Models Ltd kit
		00	Alan Gibson etched brass kit
		0	JM Model Products etched kit
		0	Alan Gibson etched brass kit
"	2P MR Johnson Rebuilt Fowler	00	Alan Gibson etched brass kit
		00	Millholme Models kit
		0	Alan Gibson etched brass kit
"	2P MR Deeley	00	Maygib etched brass kit
		00	Alan Gibson etched brass kit
		0	Alan Gibson etched brass kit
"	LNWR 'George V'	00	GEM kit
		00	Brassmaster etched brass kit
"	LNWR 'Precursor'	00	GEM kit
		00	Brassmaster etched brass kit
"	CR Pickersgill	00	NU-Cast kit

4-4-0	CR Rebuilt '66'		00	DJH Kits Ltd kit
"	CR '721' or 'Dunalastair 1' Class		00	DJH Kits Ltd kit
"	HR 'Small Ben'		00	Nu-Cast kit
"	HR 'Big Ben'		00	Falcon Brass kit
"	HR 'Loch' Class		00	DJH Kits Ltd kit
"	HR Skye Bogie		00	Falon Brass etched brass kit
2-4-0	LNWR 'Precedent'	(P)	00	GEM kit
"	MR Johnson		00	Falcon Brass etched brass kit
"	MR Kirtley	(P)	00	Millholme Models kit
			00	Falcon Brass etched brass kit
2-2-2-0	LNWR 'Dreadnought' compound		00	Alan Gibson etched brass kit
0-4-2	Liverpool & Manchester Rly 'Lion'	(P)	00	K's Milestone Series kit
0-6-0	MR Kirtley 1F		00	Falcon Brass etched brass kit
"	MR Kirtley 2F		00	Nu-Cast kit
			0	Slater's Plastikard Ltd kit
"	MR Johnson 2F		00	Nu-Cast kit
			00	Alan Gibson etched brass kit
			0	Alan Gibson etched brass kit
"	LNWR 'Special' DX Goods		00	Alan Gibson kit
"	LNWR 17" Coal		00	Alan Gibson kit
"	LNWR 'Cauliflower'		00	GEM kit
"	Fowler 4F	(P)	N	Graham Farish ready-to-run model
			N	D & M body kit
			N	GEM body kit
			TT-3	ABS Models & Beaver Products Co (Ex BEC) kit
			HO	Lima ready-to-run model no longer available
			00	Dapol ready-to-run model
			00	South Eastern Finecast kit
			00	Alan Gibson kit
			0	Lima ready-to-run model
			0	On Line Models ready-to-run
			0	JM Model Products etched kit
			0	Alan Gibson kit
"	Johnson 3F		00	Alan Gibson etched brass kit
			0	Alan Gibson etched brass kit
			0	On Line Models ready-to-run
"	LYR 2F Barton Wright	(P)	00	Falcon Brass etched brass kit
			00	George Norton etched kit
			0	George Norton etched kit
"	LYR 3F Aspinall	(P)	00	Craftsman Models kit
"	LYR 3F Hughes		00	Westward kit
"	FR 3F Pettigrew		00	Millholme Models kit
"	FR Sharp Stewart		00	Peter K (London) Ltd kit
"	CR Drummond 'Jumbo'		00	DJH Kits Ltd kit
"	CR McIntosh 812 Std MT Class	(P)	00	DJH Kits Ltd kit
"	HR 'Barney' Class		00	DJH Kits Ltd kit
			00	Falcon Brass etched brass kit
4-2-2	MR 'Single'	(P)	00	Nu-Cast kit
"	CR 'Single'	(P)	00	Hornby Railways ready-to-run model
2-2-2	LNWR 'Problem' class		00	Former K's kit
"	LNWR 'Cornwall'	(P)	00	Alan Gibson kit
2-6-6-2T	Garratt		N	Skytrex-Railscene kit or r-t-r
			00	Nu-Cast kit
0-8-4T	LNWR 7F		0	Gateneal etched brass kit
0-8-2T	LNWR 6F		00	Falcon Brass etched brass kit
4-6-4T	LYR		00	Millholme Models Ltd kit
4-6-2T	CR Pickersgill		00	DJH Kits Ltd kit
"	LNWR Bowen-Cooke		N	Langley Miniature Models kit
			00	Millholme Models Ltd kit
2-6-4T	Fowler		N	GEM kit
			00	Hornby Railways ready-to-run model
			00	GEM kit
			00	McGowan Models kit
			0	JM Model Products etched kit
"	Stanier 2-cylinder		N	Skytrex-Railscene kit
			00	Nu-Cast kit
			00	Alan Gibson etched and cast pewter kit
"	Stanier 3-cylinder	(P)	00	South Easter Finecast kit
			00	Alan Gibson etched and cast pewter kit
"	Fairburn	(P)	N	N Gauge lines cast and etched kit
			00	DJH Kit

2-6-4T	Fairburn (Cont.)	(P) 0	DJH Kit
2-6-2T	Fowler 3P	00	Nu-Cast kit
		00	Alan Gibson etched brass kit
		0	Chowbent Castings kit
"	Stanier 3P	00	Nu-Cast kit
"	Ivatt 2P	(P) 00	Bachmann ready-to-run model
		00	Nu-Cast kit
		0	DJH kit
0-6-4T	MR 'Flatiron'	N	Beaver Products body kit
		00	South Eastern Finecast kit
		0	Slater's Plastikard Ltd kit
"	HR '39' Class	N	Beaver Products body kit
		00	Nu-Cast kit
0-6-2T	LNWR Webb 'Coal Tank'	N	N-Brass Locomotives ready-to-run
		(P) 00	Nu-Cast kit
		00	Falcon Brass etched brass kit
		0	On Line Models ready-to-run
"	LNWR 'Watford' Tank	00	London Road Models etched kit
"	LYR Kiston Type 5'1"	00	Nu-Cast kit
"	FR 'Cleator' Class L2	00	McGowan Models kit
"	NSR	0	Chowbent Castings etched kit
0-6-0T	Johnson 3F	00	Nu-Cast kit
		00	Alan Gibson etched brass kit
"	Fowler 3F 'Jinty'	(P) N	Graham Farish ready-to-run model
		00	Hornby Railways ready-to-run model
		00	Nu-Cast kit
		00	Alan Gibson kit
		0	Alan Gibson kit
"	CR 3F McIntosh	00	South Eastern Finecast kit
0-6-0ST	LYR 2F Aspinall	(P) N	GEM body kit
		00	Nu-Cast kit
"	LNWR 'Special Tank'	00	GEM kit
		0	a.b.s. models cast resin kit
0-6-0T	2F Dock Tank	(P) N	Minitrix ready-to-run model
		00	Nu-Cast kit
		00	Mercian Models kit
		0	Mercian Models kit
"	NLR 2F	(P) 00	Blacksmith Models etched brass kit
		00	GEM kit
"	MR Johnson 1F	(P) 00	Craftsman Models kit
		0	Slater's Plastikard kit
"	LYR 1F Aspinall	(P) 00	Falcon Brass etched brass kit
4-4-2T	LNWR 'Precursor'	00	GEM kit
		0	CCW kit
"	LTSR	(P) 00	Nu-Cast kit
2-4-2T	LNWR Webb 4'6"	00	GEM kit
"	LNWR Webb 5'6"	00	Alan Gibson kit
"	LYR Aspinall 2P	(P) 00	Nu-Cast kit
"	LYR Hughes 3P	00	Nu-Cast kit
0-4-4WT	MR Kirtley	00	Falcon Brass etched brass kit
0-4-4T	MR Johnson 1P	00	Craftsman kit
		0	Slater's Plastikard Ltd kit
"	CR McIntosh Class 439	(P) 00	DJH Kits Ltd kit
"	HR Drummond	00	Falcon Brass etched brass kit
"	Stanier	00	London Road Models kit
		00	Falcon Brass etched brass kit
4-4-0T	HR Jones	00	Falcon Brass etched brass kit
		00	Alan Gibson kit
"	NLR Rebuilt Class 51	00	Peter K (London) Ltd kit
2-4-0T	LNWR Webb 'Chopper'	00	GEM kit
		00	Riceworks etched kit
0-4-2ST	LNWR Dock Tank	00	Alan Gibson kit
0-4-0ST	Stanier 0F	00	Falcon Brass etched brass kit
		00	Crownline Models kit
"	MR Johnson 0F	00	Nu-Cast kit
		0	a.b.s. models kit
		0	Gateneal Budget etched brass kit
0-4-0T	MR Deeley 0F	00	Millholme Models kit
		0	a.b.s. models kit
0-4-0ST	LYR 'Pug'	(P) 00	Dapol plastic kit
		00	Hornby Railways ready-to-run model

0-4-0ST	LYR 'Pug' (Cont.)	0	Springside Models kit
0-4-0ST	CR Drummond	00	Hornby Railways ready-to-run model
		00	Falcon Brass etched brass kit
		0	Slater's Plastikard Ltd kit
		0	Gateneal Budget etched brass kit
	Steam Railmotor Furness Railway	00	Falcon Brass etched brass kit
	Steam Railmotor LNWR	00	Blacksmith Models etched brass kit
	Steam Railmotor LYR No 10600	N	Langley Miniature Models kit
		00	Falcon Brass etched brass kit
	Co-Co Diesel-electric 10000	00	MTK Ltd kit
		00	Q Kits fibreglass body shell kit
		00	Genesis Kits kit
	Bo-Bo Diesel-electric 10800	00	Q Kits kit
0-6-0	Jackshaft diesel shunter	00	MTK Ltd kit
"	Hunslet diesel shunter No.7051	00	Impetus kit
0-4-0	Fowler diesel shunter	0	a.b.s. models kit
	Karrier Ro. Rail Bus	00	Nu-Cast body kit

London & North Eastern Railway classes

4-6-4	W1 'Hush-Hush'		00	South Eastern Finecast kit
4-6-2	A1 Gresley		00	Hornby Railways ready-to-run model
			00	DJH kit
			00	Proscale etched brass kit
"	A1 Peppercorn		N	Foxhunter cast body kit
			0	DJH kit
			00	Crownline etched/resin boiler kit
"	A2(NER)Raven		00	DJH kit
"	A2 Peppercorn	(P)	00	Crownline etched/resin boiler kit
			00	South Eastern Finecast kit
"	A2/1 Thompson		00	Nu-Cast kit
			00	Crownline etched/resin boiler kit
"	A2/2 Thompson		00	Nu-Cast kit
			00	Millholme Models Ltd kit
"	A2/3 Thompson		00	Millholme Models Ltd kit
"	A3	(P)	N	Graham Farish ready-to-run model
			N	Minitrix ready-to-run model
			N	Langley Miniature Models kit
			00	Lilliput ready-to-run model
			00	Hornby Railways ready-to-run model
			00	Pro-Scale etched brass kit
			00	South Eastern Finecast kit
			00	DJH kit
"	A4	(P)	N	Minitrix ready-to-run model
			N	Langley Miniature Models kit
			TT-3	GEM kit
			00	Bachmann ready-to-run model
			00	Wrenn ready-to-run model
			00	Hornby Railways ready-to-run model
			00	Pro-Scale kit
			00	South Eastern Finecast kit
			0	Martin Finney cast resin and etched kit
2-6-2	V2	(P)	00	Bachmann ready-to-run model
			00	Crownline Models kit
			00	Nu-Cast kit
			0	Impetus etched kit
"	V4 "Bantam Cock"		00	a.b.s. models kit
4-6-0	B1	(P)	N	Langley Miniature Models body kit
			00	Bachmann ready-to-run model
			00	Nu-Cast kit
			00	Pro-Scale etched brass kit
			0	Impetus etched kit
"	B2 GCR "Sir Sam Fay"		00	Nu-Cast kit
			00	Jay Lines etched brass kit
			0	Jay Lines etched brass kit
"	B4 GSR 'Immingham'		00	McGowan Models kit
			0	Gladiator Models brass kit
"	B5 GCR		00	Millholme Models Ltd kit
"	B8 GCR		0	Gladiator Models brass kit
"	B12/1 GER		00	McGowan Models kit
			00	Cooper Craft Ltd etched kit
"	B12/3 GER	(P)	00	Hornby Ralways ready-to-run model, no longer available

4-6-0	B12/3 GER (Cont.)	00	Mc Gowan Models kit
		00	Crownline Models brass kit
"	B16/1	00	DJH kit
		00	Stephen Barnfield etched kit
"	B16/2, B16/3	00	Nu-Cast kit
		00	DJH kit
"	B17/1, B17/4	00	McGowan Models kit
		00	Crownline Models brass kit
"	B17/4 'Football' Class	00	Hornby Railways ready-to-run model
2-6-0	K1 Thompson	(P) 00	Nu-Cast kit
	K2 GNR	00	Nu-Cast kit
		00	London Road Models etched kit
"	K3	00	South Eastern Finecast kit
		00	Anchoridge Steam Heritage kit
		0	CCW etched brass kit
"	K4	(P) N	N-Brass Locomotives ready-to-run
		00	Alexander Models kit
		00	Crownline Models kit
4-4-2	C1 GNR	(P) 00	Nu-Cast kit
		00	DJH kit
"	C2 GNR	(P) 00	DJH kit
"	C4/C5 GCR	00	McGowan Models kit
"	C7 NER	00	DJH Kits Ltd kit
"	C10 NBR	00	GEM kit
4-4-0	D2 GNR	00	Nu-Cast kit
		00	Alan Gibson cast and etched kit
"	D3 GNR	00	Alan Gibson cast and etched kit
"	D6 GCR	00	DJH Kits Ltd kit
"	D9 GCR	00	McGowan Models kit
"	D10 GCR 'Director'	00	ABS Models kit
		00	Little Engines kit
		0	Gladiator Models brass kit
"	D11 GCR 'Director'	(P) N	GEM kit
		00	Little Engines kit
		0	Gladiator Models brass kit
"	D16 GER	00	Blacksmith Models etched brass kit
		00	Little Engines kit
		00	Crownline Models kit (D16/3 Gresley)
		0	Blacksmith Models etched brass kit
"	D17 NER	(P) 00	Stephen Barnfield etched kit
		0	Stephen Barnfield etched kit
"	D20 NER	00	DJH kit
		N	Union Mills Models ready-to-run
"	D21 NER	00	GEM kit
"	D29 NBR 'Scott' Class	00	GEM kit
"	D34 NBR 'Glen' Class	(P) 00	GEM kit
"	D40/D41 GNSR	(P) 00	Nu-Cast kit
"	D49 'Hunt/Shire' Class	(P) 00	Hornby Railways ready-to-run model
		00	McGowan Models kit
2-4-0	E4 GER	(P) 00	Nu-\cast kit
		00	Alan Gibson etched brass kit
		0	Alan Gibson etched brass kit
4-2-2	GNR 'Single'	(P) 00	Millholme Models kit
2-8-2	P2	00	Nu-Cast
		00	Pro-Scale etched brass kit
2-8-0	O1	00	Little Engines kit
"	O2/2, O2/3	00	Nu-Cast kit
"	O4 GCR	(P) 00	Nu-Cast kit
		00	Little Engines kit
		0	Gateneal etched brass kit
		0	Gladiator Models brass kit
"	O7 WD 'Austerity'	N	McGowan Models kit
		00	McGowan Models kit
0-8-0	Q1 GNR 'Long Tom'	00	Nu-Cast kit
"	Q4 GCR	00	Millhome Models Ltd kit
		0	Gladiator Models brass kit
"	Q6 NER	(P) 00	Nu-Cast kit
"	Q7 NER	(P) 00	DJH kit
0-6-0	J3 GNR	00	Nu-Cast kit
"	J6 GNR	00	Nu-Cast kit
"	J9/J10 GCR	00	DJH kit

0-6-0	J11 GCR		N	Langley Miniature Models body kit
			TT-3	ABS Models & Beaver Products Co (Ex BEC) kit
			00	ABS Models & Beaver Products Co (Ex BEC) kit
			00	Little Engines kit
			00	Quainton Road Models kit
			00	Alan Gibson etched brass kit
			0	Gladiator Models brass kit
"	J15 GER	(P)	00	Nu-Cast kit
			00	Alan Gibson kit
			0	Alan Gibson kit
			0	Connoisseur Models etched kit
"	J17 GER	(P)	00	ABS Models & Beaver Products Co (Ex BEC) kit
			00	Crownline Models etched kit
"	J19 GER		00	Crownline Models etched kit
"	J20 GER		00	McGowan Models kit
			00	Crownline Models etched kit
"	J21 NER	(P)	00	Nu-Cast kit
			00	Falcon Brass etched brass kit
"	J24 NER		00	Falcon Brass etched brass kit
"	J25 NER		00	Nu-Cast kit
"	J26/J27 NER	(P)	N	Nu-Cast kit
			00	Nu-Cast kit
			0	Piercy Model Products kit
"	J28 H&BR		00	Millholme Models kit
"	J35 NBR		N	Graham Hughes cast metal body kit
			00	DJH kit
"	J36 NBR	(P)	00	GEM kit
			00	Crownline Models etched kit
"	J37 NBR		00	North British Models kit
			00	Falcon Brass etched brass kit
			0	Gateneal etched brass kit
"	J38		00	South Eastern Finecast kit
"	J39		N	D & M Castings body kit
			N	Union Mills Models ready-to-run
			00	Bachmann ready-to-run model
			00	South Eastern Finecast kit
			0	Connoisseur Models etched brass kit
2-8-8-2T	U1 Garratt		00	Nu-Cast kit
			00	DJH kit
4-6-2T	A5 GCR		N	Graham Hughes kit
			00	Craftsman kit
			00	Nu-Cast klt
"	A6 NER		00	Little Engines kit
"	A7 NER		00	Little Engines kit
"	A8 NER		00	DJH kit
			00	Little Engines kit
2-6-4T	L1		N	Beaver Products body kit
			00	a.b.s. models kit
"	L3 GCR		N	Beaver Products body kit
			N	Langley Miniature Models body kit
2 6-2T	V1/V3		00	Bachmann ready-to-run model
			00	McGowan Models kit
			00	Nu-Cast kit
4-8-0T	T1 NER		00	Nu-Cast kit
			00	Little Engines kit
0-8-4T	S1 GCR		N	Langley Miniature Models body kit
			00	Millholme Models Ltd kit
0-8-0T	Q1 GCR		00	Millhome Models Ltd kit
0-6-2T	N1 GNR		00	WSM kit
			00	Little Engines kit
			00	McGowan Models kit
"	N2 GNR	(P)	N	Langley Miniature Models body kit
			00	Wrenn ready-ro-run model
			00	Dapol ready-ro-run model
			00	Nu-Cast kit
			0	Slater's Plastikard Ltd kit
"	N4/N5 GCR		00	Millholme Models Ltd kit
			00	McGowan Models kit
			00	Quainton Road Models kit
			0	Quainton Road Models kit
"	N7 GER	(P)	N	Langley Miniature Models body kit

0-6-2T	N7 GER (Cont.)	00	South Eastern Finecast kit
		0	Ravenscale etched brass kit
"	N8/9/10 NER	00	Nu-Cast kit
"	N15 NBR	00	North British Models kit
		00	Falcon Brass etched brass kit
		0	Gateneal etched brass kit
4-4-4T	H1 NER	00	DJH Kits Ltd kit
"	H2 Metropolitan Rly	00	Quainton Road Models kit
		0	Quainton Road Models kit
4-4-2T	C12 GNR	00	Craftsman kit
		00	South Eastern Finecast kit
"	C13 GCR	00	Nu-Cast kit
"	C16 NBR	00	Nu-Cast kit
4-4-0T	D51 NBR	00	Riceworks etched brass kit
0-4-4-T	G5 NER	00	Nu-Cast kit
		0	Connoisseur Models etched kit
"	G6 NER	00	Nu-Cast kit
"	G9 NBR	00	Falcon Brass etched brass kit
2-4-2T	F1 GCR	00	Nu-Cast kit
"	F3 GER	00	Cooper Craft etched/cast resin kit
		0	Cooper Craft etched/cast resin kit
"	F4/5 GER	00	Nu-Cast kit
		00	Alan Gibson etched brass kit
		00	Falcon Brass etched brass kit
"	F6/F7 GER	00	Alan Gibson etched brass kit
		00	Falcon Brass etched brass kit
"	F8 GER	00	a.b.s. models kit
		00	Falcon Brass etched brass kit
		0	Slater's Plasikard Ltd kit
0-6-0T	J50	N	N-Brass Locomotives ready-ro-run
		TT-3	ABS Models & Beaver Products Co (Ex Bec) kit
		00	Lima ready-ro-run model
		00	DJH kit
		0	On Line Models ready-to-run
		0	CCW kit
0-6-0ST	J52 GNR	(P) N	Beaver Products body kit
		N	D & M body kit
		00	Hornby Railways ready-to-run model
		00	Walsworth Models etched kit
		0	Walsworth Models etched kit
0-6-0T	J63 GER	N	Beaver Products body kit
"	J65 GER	00	Riceworks etched kit
"	J68 GER	00	Riceworks etched kit
"	J69 GER	(P) N	Graham Farish ready-to-run model withdrawn
		00	South Eastern Finecast kit
		00	Riceworks etched brass kit
"	J70 GER Tram Engine	00	Nu-Cast kit
"	J71 NER	0	Connoisseur Models kit
"	J72 NER	(P) TT-3	ABS Models & Beaver Products Co (Ex Bec) kit
		00	Bachmann ready-to-run model
		00	Nu-Cast kit
		0	Piercy Model Products kit
"	J77 NER	00	Lancaster Model Engineering kit
"	J79 NER	00	Stephen Barnfield etched kit
		0	Connoisseur Models brass kit
"	J83 NBR	00	GEM kit
		00	Hornby Railways ready-to-run model withdrawn 1980
		0	Vulcan Models ready-to-run
"	J88 NBR	00	Falcon Brass etched kit
0-6-0ST	J94 ex-MOS	(P) N	Graham Farish ready-to-run model
		N	P & D Marsh kit
		00	Dapol ready-to-run model
		00	a.b.s. models kit
		00	Former Airfix plastic kit
0-4-0T	Y1/Y3 Sentinel	(P) N	P & D Marsh body-line kit
		00	Nu-Cast kit
0-4-0ST	Y5 GER 'Coffeepot'	(P) 00	Nu-Cast kit
0-4-0T	Y7 NER	(P) 00	Nu-Cast kit
		00	Stephen Barnfield etched kit
		0	Connoisseur Models kit

0-4-0T	Y8 NER	00	Nu-Cast kit
"	Y10 Sentinel	00	Impetus kit
		0	Impetus kit
Sentinel Cammell Steam Railcar		N	Langley Miniature Models kit
		00	Nu-Cast kit

Southern Railway classes

4-6-2	'Merchant Navy' Class	N	Graham Farish ready-to-run model
		00	Millholme Models kit
		00	Crownline Models kit
"	'Merchant Navy' Class rebuilt	(P) N	Graham Farish ready-to-run model
		00	DJH kit
		00	Nu-Cast kit
		00	Crownline Models etched resin boiler kit
"	'West Country'/'Battle of Britain' Classes	(P) N	Graham Farish ready-to-run model
		00	Hornby Railways ready-to-run model
		00	Wrenn ready-to-run model
		00	Former Airfix plastic kit
		00	Anchoridge Steam Heritage kit
		00	Crownline kit
		00	Westward kit
		0	Oakville Models kit
"	'West Country'/ 'Battle of Britain' Classes rebuilt	N	Graham Farish ready-to-run model
		(P) 00	Wrenn ready-to-run model
		00	DJH kit
		00	Crownline Models etched/resin boiler kit
4-6-0	'Lord Nelson' Class	(P) 00	Bachmann ready-to-run model
		00	Craftsman Models kit
		00	Nu-Cast kit
"	'King Arthur' Class	(P) 00	South Eastern Finecast kit
		00	Hornby Railways ready-to-run model – withdrawn 1979
		00	Falcon Brass etched brass kit
		00	Crownline Models kit
"	N15X 'Remembrance'	00	Nu-Cast kit
"	H15 LSWR	00	DJH Kits Ltd kit
"	S15	(P) N	Langley Miniature Models kit
		00	DJH Kits Ltd kit
		00	Crownline Models kit
"	T14 LSWR	00	Nu-Cast kit
		00	Falcon Brass etched kit
2-6-0	N	N	N-Brass Locomotives ready-to-run model
		00	Bachmann ready-to-run model
		(P) 00	Falcon Brass etched brass kit
		00	DJH Kits Ltd kit
"	U	(P) 00	South Eastern Finecast kit
		00	DJH Kits Ltd kit
		00	Falcon Brass etched brass kit
"	U1	00	Falcon Brass etched brass kit
"	K LBSCR	N	Graham Hughes cast body kit
		00	Blacksmith Models etched brass kit
		00	Nu-Cast kit
4-4-2	H1 LBSCR	00	DJH kit
		00	Falcon Brass etched brass kit
"	H2 LBSCR	00	Falcon Brass etched brass kit
4-4-0	'Schools' Class	(P) 00	Dapol Former Airfix plastic kit
		00	Hornby Railways ready-to-run model
		00	South Eastern Finecast kit
"	L1	N	Graham Hughes cast body kit
		00	Tri-ang ready-to-run model – no longer available
"	L SE&CR	N	N-Brass Locomotives ready-to-run
		00	DJH kit
"	T9 LSWR	(P) 00	South Eastern Finecast kit
		00	LSWR Models kit
		00	Westward kit
		00	Falcon Brass etched brass kit
		00	Crownline Models kit
		0	DJB Engineering etched kit
4-4-0	T3 LSWR	(P) 00	Falcon Brass etched brass kit

4-4-0	T6 LSWR	00	Falcon Brass etched brass kit
"	X2 LSWR	00	Falcon Brass etched brass kit
"	X6 LSWR	00	Falcon Brass etched brass kit
"	K10/L11 LSWR	00	Falcon Brass etched brass kit
"	L12 LSWR	00	LSWR Models kit
"	B1 SE&CR	00	Falcon Brass etched brass kit
"	C8 LSWR	00	Falcon Brass etched brass kit
"	D SE&CR	(P) 00	South Eastern Finecast kit
		00	Falcon Brass etched brass kit
"	D1/E1 SE&CR	00	DJH kit
"	D15 LSWR	00	Falcon Brass etched brass kit
		00	Crownline Models kit
"	E SE&CR	00	South Eastern Finecast kit
"	F1 SE&CR	00	Falcon Brass etched brass kit
"	G SE&CR	00	Nu-Cast kit
2-4-0	LSWR 'Falcon' Class	00	Former K's Milestone kit
0-4-2	A12 LSWR	00	Falcon Brass etched brass kit
		00	Nu-Cast kit
"	B1 LB&SCR 'Gladstone'	(P) 00	GEM kit
2-2-2	G LBSCR	00	Peter K (London) Ltd kit
0-6-0	Q	(P) N	Graham Hughes kit
		00	South Eastern Finecast kit
		00	Crownline Models kit
"	Q1	(P) N	Langley Miniature Models body kit
		TT-3	ABS Models & Beaver Products (Ex Bec) kit
		00	Nu-Cast kit
		00	South Eastern Finecast kit
		00	Crownline etched brass kit
"	700 LSWR	00	Westward kit
		00	Falcon Brass etched brass kit
		00	Crownline Models kit
"	0278 LSWR	00	Falcon Brass etched brass kit
"	282 LSWR Ilfracombe Goods	00	Falcon Brass etched brass kit
		00	Branchlines etched and cast kit
		0	Shedmaster etched kit
"	0395 LSWR	00	Falcon Brass etched brass kit
"	C SE&CR	(P) 00	South Eastern Finecast kit
		00	Falcon Brass etched brass kit
"	O SER	00	Branchline kit
"	O1 SE&CR	(P) 00	Falcon Brass etched brass kit
		00	Branchlines kit
"	C2 LB&SCR	00	DJH kit
"	C2X LB&SCR	00	Nu-Cast kit
		00	DJH kit
4-8-0T	G16	00	Millholme Models kit
		00	Falcon Brass etched brass kit
4-6-2T	H16	00	Millhome Models kit
		00	Falcon Brass etched brass kit
4-6-4T	LB&SCR 'Remembrance'	00	Langley Miniature Models kit
2-6-4T	K River Class	00	South Eastern Finecast kit
"	W	00	Falcon Brass etched brass kit
		00	Crownline Models kit
4-4-2T	13 LB&SCR	00	South Eastern Finecast kit
"	0415 LSWR Adams Radial Tank	(P) 00	Nu-Cast kit
		00	Falcon Brass etched brass kit
		00	Peter K (London) Ltd kit
0-8-0T	Z	N	GEM kit
		00	Millholme Models Ltd kit
		00	Falcon Brass etched brass kit
0-6-4T	J SE&CR	00	Chivers Finelines kit
0-6-2T	E1 R	00	South Eastern Finecast kit
		00	Falcon Brass etched brass kit
		00	Gateneal Budget etched brass kit
"	E3 LB&SCR	0	MSC Models etched brass kit
"	E4 LB&SCR	(P) 00	Weald Models kit
		00	Dean Sidings resin body kit
		0	MSC Models kit
"	E5 LB&SCR	N	Langley Miniature Models body kit
		00	South Eastern Finecast kit
0-6-0T	A1 LB&SCR 'Terrier'	(P) 00	Hornby Railways ready-to-run model
		00	Nu-Cast kit

0-6-0T	A1 LB&SCR 'Terrier' (Cont.)	00	Westward kit
		00	Falcon Brass etched brass kit
		0	a.b.s. models kit
"	E1 LB&SCR	(P) 00	South Eastern Finecast kit
		00	Albion Models etched kit
		0	Albion Models etched kit
		0	Meteor Models etched brass kit
		0	Vulcan Models ready-to-run model
"	E2 LB&SCR	N	Langley Miniature Models body kit
		TT-3	ABS Models & Beaver Products Co (Ex Bec) kit
		00	Hornby Railways ready-to-run model
		00	South Eastern Finecast kit
"	G6 LSWR	TT-3	ABS Models & Beaver Products Co (Ex Bec) kit
		00	South Eastern Finecast kit
		00	Falcon Brass etched brass kit
		00	Alan Gibson etched kit
		0	Vulcan Models ready-to-run
		0	Antenna Models ready-to-run radio controlled
		0	Alan Gibson etched kit
		0	Oakville Models Pocket Money etched kit
		0	MSC Models brass body kit
"	P SE&CR	(P) 00	South Eastern Finecast kit
"	R1 SE&CR	00	Wrenn ready-to-run model
"	T LC&DR	00	Q Kits kit
"	USA	(P) N	Chivers Finelines kit
		HO	Hornby-Acho r-t-r-model – no longer available
		00	Q Kits kit
		00	South Eastern Finecast kit
		0	Oakville Models etched brass kit
0-6-0ST	0330 LSWR Beattie	00	Falcon Brass etched brass kit
0-4-4T	D3 LB&SCR	00	Chivers Finelines kit
		0	MSC Models kit
"	H SE&CR	(P) 00	South Eastern Finecast kit
		00	Falcon Brass etched brass kit
		0	Meteor Models Budget kit
"	Q1 SE&CR	00	Falcon Brass etched brass kit
"	R1 SE&CR	00	Q Kits kit
"	M7 LSWR	(P) 00	Hornby Railways ready-to-run model
		00	South Eastern Finecast kit
		00	Falcon Brass etched brass kit
		00	Crownline Models kit
		0	On Line Models ready-to-run
		0	CCW kit
"	O2 LSWR	(P) 00	South Eastern Finecast kit
		00	Alan Gibson etched kit
		00	Falcon Brass etched brass kit
		0	Alan Gibson etched kit
		0	MSC Models brass kit
"	T1 LSWR	00	Craftsman Models kit
		00	Falcon Brass etched brass kit
2-4-0T	0298 LSWR	(P) 00	Westward kit
		00	Falcon Brass etched brass kit
0-4-2T	D1 LB&SCR	00	South Eastern Finecast kit
		00	Albion Models etched kit
		0	Albion Models etched kit
0-4-0T	B4 LSWR	(P) N	Peco kit
		00	McGowan Models kit
		00	Falcon Brass etched brass kit
		0	a.b.s. models kit
0-4-0ST	0458 LSWR 'Ironside'	00	Falcon Brass etched brass kit
4-2-4T	F9 LSWR Inspection Saloon	00	Falcon Brass etched brass kit
Steam Railmotor LSWR		00	Falcon Brass etched brass kit
Co-Co CC1/CC2 Electric		00	MTK Ltd kit
		00	Genesis Kits cast metal kit
Co-Co Diesel-electric Nos 10201/2/3		00	MTK Ltd kit
		00	Q Kits fibreglass body kit
EMU	5 BEL 'Brighton Belle'	(P) 00	Wrenn ready-to-run model
"	4 COR	(P) 00	Branchlines punched aluminium kit
"	4 RES	0	Branchlines punched aluminium kit
"	2 BIL	(P) 00	Ian Kirk plastic kit
"	2 HAL	00	Blacksmith Models etched brass kit

EMU	2 HAL (Cont.)	00	Phoenix/Branchlines kit
"	2 NOL	00	Roxey Mouldings etched kit
"	3 SUB	00	Roxey Mouldings etched kit
"	4 SUB	00	Blacksmith Models etched kit
		00	Phoenix/Branchlines kit

Miscellaneous Locomotives

2-8-0	USA Class S160	(P) —	
4-6-0	English Electric GT3 Gas Turbine	00	Q Kits kit
0-6-2T	Metropolitan Railway 'F' Class	00	GS Models kit
4-4-0T	Metropolitan Railway Beyer Peacock	(P) 00	K's Milestone Series kit
		00	IKB Models cast & etched kit
Bo-Bo	Metropolitan Railway Electric Loco	(P) 00	The Model Shop (Harrow) kit
"	LT Battery Electric Loco	00	The Model Shop (Harrow) kit
0-6-0ST	Bagnall 16"	00	Impetus kit
0-6-0T	Kerr Stuart 'Victory'	00	a.b.s. models kit
		00	Agenoria Models etched kit
0-6-0ST	Hudswell Clarke (Easingwold Railway)	00	Impetus etched brass kit
		0	Impetus etched brass kit
"	Hudswell Clarke (GWR "Hilda")	0	Agenoria Models etched kit
"	Hunslet Standard 16"	00	a.b.s. models kit
"	Hunslet 15"	00	Impetus etched brass kit
		0	Impetus etched brass kit
		0	85A Models plastic kit
"	Manning Wardle Class 1	00	Impetus kit
"	Manning Wardle Class K	0	Peter K (London) kit
		0	Slater's Plastikard kit
0-4-0ST	Andrew Barclay 14"	00	DJH starter kit
		00	Impetus etched brass kit
0-4-0	Andrew Barclay Fireless	0	Eric Underhill Models kit
0-4-0ST	Robert Stephenson & Hawthorns	00	a.b.s. models kit
		00	High Level Kits etched kit
"	Avonside	00	a.b.s.models kit
"	Bagnall 15"	00	Impetus kit
"	Peckett	0	Eric Underhill kit
"	Manning Wardle 'F' Class	0	Slater's Plastikard Ltd kit
4-wheel	Ruston 48DS	00	Impetus kit
"	Muir-Hill Tractor	00	Branchlines cast kit
0-4-0	Sentinel geared steam shunter	00	Impetus cast resin body, etched chasis kit
		0	Impetus cast resin body, etched chasis kit
"	Fowler Diesel Hydraulic	00	Impetus kit
		0	Impetus kit
EMU	L.T. Hammersmith x City Q Stock	00	The Model Shop (Harrow) kit
EMU	L.T. 1920 District F Stock	00	The Model Shop (Harrow) kit
EMU	L.T. 1934 Piccadilly Stock	00	The Model Sho (Harrow) kit
EMU	L.T. Metropolitan 'A' Stock	00	The Model Shop (Harrow) kit
EMU	L.T. 1938 Tube Stock	00	Pirate Models kit
EMU	L.T. 1959/62 Tube Stock	00	Pirate Models kit

British Railways Standard Classes
STEAM

4-6-2	Class 8 "Duke of Gloucester"	(P) 00	DJH kit
"	'Britannia'	(P) N	Minitrix ready-to-run model
		00	Hornby Railways ready-to-run model
		00	DJH kit
"	'Clan'	00	DJH kit
4-6-0	Class 5	(P) TT-3	ABS Models & Beaver Products Co (Ex Bec) kit
		00	DJH kit
		00	Crownline Models kit
		0	DJB Engineering kit
"	Class 4	(P) N	Langley Miniature Models body kit
		00	Bachmann ready-to-run model
		00	DJH kit
2-10-0	Class 9	(P) N	Minitrix ready-to-run model
		00	Dapol Former Airfix plastic kit
		00	Hornby Railways ready-to-run model
		00	DJH kit
2-6-0	Class 4	(P) 00	Dapol Former Airfix plastic kit
		00	DJH kit
2-6-0	Class 3	00	DJH kit

2-6-0	Class 2	(P)	N	Minitrix ready-to-run model
			00	Hornby Railways ready-to-run model, no longer available
			00	DJH kit
			0	DJH kit
2-6-4T	Class 4	(P)	N	Graham Farish ready-to-run model
			TT-3	ABS Models & Beaver Products (Ex Bec) kit
			00	Wrenn ready-to-run model
			00	DJH kit
2-6-2T	Class 3		00	Tri-ang/Hornby ready-to-run model, no longer available
			00	Crownline Models kit
			00	DJH kit
"	Class 2	(P)	N	Minitrix ready-to-run model
			00	Bachmann ready-to-run model
			00	Nu-Cast kit
			00	DJH kit
			0	DJH kit
2-10-0	Austerity ex-MOS	(P)	N	McGowan Models kit
			00	DJH kit
2-8-0	Austerity ex-MOS	(P)	N	McGowan Models kit
			00	Bachmann ready-to-run model
			00	DJH kit
			00	McGowan Models kit
0-6-0T	Austerity ex-MOS	(P)	N	Graham Farish ready-to-run model
			00	Dapol Former Airfix plastic kit – as for LNER J94
			00	Hornby Railways ready-to-run model

Diesel

English. Welsh & Scottish Rly Class 66		–	
BR Class 60 Co-Co		N	Taylor Plastic Models resin body kit
		00	Lima ready-to-run model
		0	RJH Model Railways Ltd etched kit
Foster Yeoman Class 59		00	Lima ready-to-run model
		0	RJH Ltd Cavalier kit
BR Class 58 Co-Co		00	Hornby Railways ready-to-run model
		0	RJH Ltd Cavalier kit
BR Class 56 Co-Co		N	Graham Farish ready-to-run model
		N	Langley Miniature Models body kit
BR Class 56 Co-Co		N	P & D Marsh body line kit
		00	Dapol ready-to-run model
		00	Q Kits fibreglass body shell kit
		00	MTK Ltd kit
		0	RJH Ltd Cavalier kit
'Deltic' Class 55 Co-Co	(P)	N	Graham Farish ready-to-run model
		N	Lima ready-to-run model, withdrawn
		00	Lima ready-to-run model
		00	MTK Ltd kit
		00	Q Kits fibreglass body shell kit
		0	RJH Ltd Cavalier kit
'Western' Class 52 C-C	(P)	N	Graham Farish ready-to-run model
		N	Beaver Products Co kit
		N	Fleetline body kit
		N	MTK Ltd kit
		00	Hornby Railways ready-to-run model
		00	Lima ready-to-run model
		00	Liliput ready-to-run model
		00	MTK Ltd kit
		00	Q Kits fibreglass body shell kit
		0	RJH Ltd Cavalier kit
English Electric Class 50 Co-Co	(P)	N	Graham Farish ready-to-run model
		00	Lima ready-to-run model
		00	MTK Ltd kit
		00	Q Kits fibreglass body shell
		0	RJH Ltd Cavalier Kit
Brush Class 47 Co-Co	(P)	N	Graham Farish ready-to-run model
		N	Minitrix ready-to-run model
		N	P & D Marsh kit
		TT-3	ABS Models & Beaver Products Co (Ex-Bec) kit
		00	Hornby Railways ready-to-run model
		00	Lima ready-to-run model
		00	MTK kit

Brush Class 47 Co-Co (Cont.)		0	RJH Ltd Cavalier kit
'Peak' Classes 45/46 1 Co-Co 1	(P)	N	P & D Marsh body kit
		00	Bachmann ready-to-run model
		00	MTK Ltd kit
		00	Q Kits fibregleass body shell kit
		0	RJH Ltd Cavalier kit
'Warship' Class 42 B-B	(P)	N	Minitrix ready-to-run model
		HO	Fleischman ready-to-run model
		00	Lima ready-to-run model
		00	Bachmann ready-to-run model
		00	MTK Ltd kit
		00	Q Kits fibreglass body shell kit
		0	RJH Ltd Cavalier kit
English Electric Class 40 1 C0-Co 1	(P)	N	Graham Farish ready-to-run model
		00	Jouef ready-to-run model
		00	Lima ready-to-run model
		00	MTK Ltd kit
		00	Q Kits fibreglass body shell kit
		0	RJH Ltd Cavalier kit
English Electric Class 37 Co-Co		N	Graham Farish ready-to-run model
		N	Langley Miniature Models kit
		00	Hornby Railways ready-to-run model
		00	Lima ready-to-run model
		0	RJH Ltd Cavalier kit
'Hymek' Class 35 B-B	(P)	N	Peco kit
		00	Hornby Railways ready-to-run model
		0	Novo Toys Ltd ready-to-run model
Birmingham RC&W Class 33 Bo-Bo	(P)	N	Graham Farish ready-to-run model
		00	Lima ready-to-run model
		00	MTK Ltd kit
		0	Lima ready-to-run model
	(P)	0	RJH Ltd Cavalier kit
Brush Class 31 A1A-A1A	(P)	N	Graham Farish ready-to-run model
		00	Hornby Railways ready-to-run model – withdrawn
		00	Lima ready-to-run model
		0	RJH Ltd Cavalier kit
North British Class 29 Bo-Bo		N	Langley Miniature Models kit
		0	Hornby Railways ready-to-run model
Metro-Vick Class 28 Co-Bo	(P)	00	Hornby Dublo ready-to-run model – no longer available
		00	Peak Model Shop resin moulded body kit
Birmingham RC&W Class 26/27 Bo-Bo	(P)	N	Minitrix ready-to-run model
		N	Silver Fox resin body kit
		00	Lima ready-to-run model
		00	MTK Ltd kit
		0	RJH Ltd Cavalier kit
BR Derby Class 25 Bo-Bo	(P)	N	Graham Farish ready-to-run model
		N	Langley Miniature Models kit
		00	Hornby Railways ready-to-run model
		00	MTK Ltd kit
		00	DJH kit
		0	RJH Ltd Cavalier kit
BR Derby Class 24 Bo-Bo	(P)	N	Langley Miniature Models kit
		N	Silver Fox resin body kit
		00	Silver Fox resin body shell kit
		0	Steve Beattie resin, brass and white metal kit
North British Class 22 B-B		0	Steve Beattie resin, brass and white metal kit
English Electric Class 20 Bo-Bo	(P)	N	Graham Farish ready-to-run model
		00	Wrenn ready-to-run model
		00	Lima ready-to-run model
		00	MTK Ltd kit
		0	RJH Ltd Cavalier kit
Clayton Class 17 Bo-Bo	(P)	00	Dave Alexander kit
		00	MTK Ltd kit
Brisish Thomson-Houston Class 15	(P)	00	Dave Alexander kit
		00	MTK Ltd kit
BR 650hp 0-6-0 Class 14	(P)	00	ConstuctEON Models kit
		00	Alexander Models kit
D600 North British 'Warship' A1A-A1A		00	MTK Ltd kit
		00	Q Kits fibreglass body shell kit
D0260 'Lion' BRC&W Co/Sulzer Co-Co		00	Q Kits fibreglass body shell kit

	D0280 Falcon' Brush-Maybach Co-Co		00	Q Kits fibreglass body shell kit
	DP2 English Electric Co-Co		00	Q Kits fibreglass body shell kit
	HS 4000 'Kestrel' Brush Sulzer Co-Co		00	Q Kits fibreglass body shell kit
Shunter	350hp Class 08	(P)	N	Graham Farish ready-to-run model
			00	Bachmann ready-to-run model
			00	Hornby Railways ready-to-run model
			00	Wrenn ready-to-run model
			00	Modern Outline kit
			0	Oakville Models etched kit
			0	Modern Motive Power etched kit
"	350hp Class 09		00	Lima ready-to-run model
			00	Modern Outline kit
			00	Impetus etched chassis kit
"	Ruston & Hornsby Class 07	(P)	00	Craftsman etched brass kit
			00	MTK Ltd kit
			0	Modern Motive Power resin moulded radiator & bonnet etched kit
"	North British 040/060		00	MTK Ltd kit
"	Andrew Barclay Class 06	(P)	00	Hornby Railways ready-to-run model
			0	MTK Ltd kit
"	Hunslet Class 05	(P)	00	Howe A1-Railmatch etched brass kit
"	204hp Drewry Class 04	(P)	N	Beaver Products body kit
			N	Langley Miniature Models body kit
			00	Bachmann ready-to-run model
			00	Airfix plastic kit, no longer available
			00	Alan Gibson kit
			0	a.b.s. models kit
"	204hp BR Gardner Class 03	(P)	N	Beaver Products body kit
			00	Replica Railways ready-to-run model
			0	Modern Motive Power resin moulded radiator & bonnet etched kit
"	Yorkshire Engine Co Class 02	(P)	00	Craftsman Models kit
			00	DJH Beginners kit
			0	Oakville Models Pocket Money Kit
"	Hudswell Clarke 0-6-0 D2510-19	(P)	00	Impetus etched brass kit
"	Hunslet Class DY1 0-4-0 D2950-2		00	Howe A1-Railmatch etched brass kit
DMU	Class 100 Gloucester Cross Country	(P)	00	MTK aluminium body kit
"	Class 101 Metro-Cammell		N	Graham Farish ready-to-run model
			00	Lima ready-to-run model
			00	Hornby Railways ready-to-run model, no longer available
"	Class 104 Birmingham RCW 3 car set		00	Craftsman Models conversion kit
			00	MTK aluminium body kit
"	Class 105 Cravens 2-car	(P)	00	MTK conversion kit
			00	D. C. Kits plastic kit
"	Class 108 Derby Lightweight	(P)	00	Craftsman etched brass kit
"	Class 110 Birmingham RCW 'Calder Valley' set	(P)	00	Hornby Railways ready-to-run model
"	Class 114 Derby 2-car		00	Craftsman etched brass kit
			00	MTK aluminium body kit
			0	Westdale coaches kit
"	Class 117/2 Pressed Steel Co		00	Lima ready-to-run model
"	Class 119 Gloucester RCW 3-car cross country		00	MTK aluminium body kit
			00	Craftsman Models conversion kit
"	Class 120 Swindon 3-car cross country	(P)	00	Craftsman Models conversion kit
			00	MTK aluminium body kit
"	Class 121 Single car diesel railcar		00	Lima ready-to-run model
			00	Four track models kit
"	Class 122 Gloucester RCW Single unit		00	Craftsman Models conversion kit
"	Class 124 Trans-Pennine 6-car		00	Liliput ready-to-run model
"	Class 127 Parcels	(P)	00	MTK aluminium body kit
"	Class 128 Gloucester parcels van		00	Craftsman Models conversion kit
			0	Westdale coaches kit
	Class 129 Cravens parcels van		00	Craftsman Models conversion kit
			00	D. C Kits plastic kit
"	Class 140 Prototype 2-car railbus		00	MTK aluminium body kit
"	Class 141 2-car		00	MTK aluminium body kit
"	Class 142 'Pacer'		00	Hornby Railways ready-to-run model
			00	MTK cast-whitemetal kit
			0	Modern Motive Power resin body kit

DMU	Class 143 Alexander/Barclay 3-car		00	MTK cast-whitemetal kit
"	Class 144 Andrew Barclay 3-car		00	MTK cast-whitemetal kit
"	Class 150/2		00	Dapol ready-to-run model
			0	Modern Motive Power kit
"	Class 155 Leyland Sprinter		00	Dapol ready-to-run model
"	Class 156 Super Sprinter		00	Lima ready-to-run model
			00	MTK aluminium body kit
			0	Modern Motive Power kit
"	Class 158 Sprinter Express		N	Graham Farish ready-to-run model
			00	Bachmann ready-to-run model
			00	MTK Ltd kit
			0	Modern Motive Power kit
"	Class 159 3-car		N	Graham Farish ready-to-run model
			00	Bachmann ready-to-run model
"	Class 166 'Network Turbo'		00	Bachmann ready-to-run model
"	Classes 201/202/203 Hastings	(P)	00	MTK aluminium body kit
"	Class 205 Hampshire		00	MTK aluminium body kit
"	Class 206 Reading-Tonbridge		00	MTK aluminium body kit
"	Class 207 SR non-electrified lines		00	MTK aluminium body kit
"	Class 253/254 HST High Speed Train		N	Graham Farish ready-to-fun model
			N	MTK Ltd kit
			00	Lima ready-to-run model
			00	Hornby Railways ready-to-run model
4-wheel Railcar AC Cars Ltd		(P)	00	Anbrico kit
"	Park Royal Vehicles Ltd		00	Dapol (ex-Airfix) plastic kit
"	Bristol/ECC		00	MTK cast-whitemetal kit
"	Leyland Railbus LEV3		00	MTK cast-whitemetal kit
"	Waggon und Maschinenbau	(P)	00	MTK cast-whitemetal kit

ELECTRIC

EM2	Co-Co	(P)	00	Tri-ang/Hornby ready-to-run model, no longer available
Class 71	Bo-Bo	(P)	00	MTK Ltd kit
			00	Genesis Kits cast metal kit
Class 73	Electro-diesel		N	A1 Models kit
			00	Lima ready-to-run model
			00	MTK Ltd kit
			0	RJH Ltd Cavalier kit
Class 74	Electro-diesel		N	A1 Models kit
			00	Genesis Kits cast metal kit
Class 76	Bo-Bo	(P)	00	Trix ready-to-run model – no longer available
Class 77	Co-Co		00	Tri-ang Railways ready-to-run – no longer available
			00	D.C Kits kit
Class 81	Bo-Bo	(P)	00	MTK Ltd kit
			0	RJH Ltd Cavalier kit
Class 82	Bo-Bo		00	MTK Ltd kit
Class 83	Bo-Bo		00	Liliput ready-to-run model
			00	MTK Ltd kit
Class 85	Bo-Bo		00	MTK Ltd kit
			0	RJH Ltd Cavalier kit
Class 86	Bo-Bo		N	Lima ready-to-run model – no longer available
			00	Hornby Railways ready-to-run model
			00	MTK Ltd kit
			0	RJH Ltd Cavalier kit
Class 87	Bo-Bo		N	Graham Farish ready-to-run model
			00	Lima ready-to-run model
			0	RJH Ltd Cavalier kit
Class 89	Co-Co		00	MTK Ltd kit
			00	DC Kits kit
			0	RJH Ltd Cavalier kit
Class 90	Bo-Bo		N	Graham Farish ready-to-run model
			00	Hornby Railways ready-to-run model
			0	RJH Ltd Cavalier kit
Class 91	Bo-Bo		N	Graham Farish ready-to-run model
			00	Hornby Railways ready-to-run model
			0	RJH Ltd Cavalier kit
Class 92	Co-Co		00	Hornby Railways ready-to-run model
			00	Lima ready-to-run model
Class 306	Shenfield		00	MTK Ltd aluminium body kit
Class 307	GE Outer Suburban refurbished		00	MTK Ltd aluminium body kit
Class 309	Clacton Set		00	MTK Ltd aluminium body kit

Class 310	Euston–Carlisle and branches		00	MTK Ltd aluminium body kit
Class 312	LMR main line/GE, GN lines		00	MTK Ltd aluminium body kit
Class 313	ER Suburb		00	MTK Ltd aluminium body kit
Class 317/2			00	MTK Ltd aluminium body kit
Class 318			00	MTK Ltd aluminium body kit
Class 319	Thames Link		00	MTK Ltd aluminium body kit
Class 321			00	MTK Ltd aluminium body kit
Class 370	APT	(P)	00	Hornby Railways ready-to-run model
Class 373	'Eurostar'		N	Kato ready-to-run model
			HO	Jouef ready-to-run model
			00	Hornby Railways ready-to-run model
Class 405	4 SUB		00	MTK Ltd aluminium body kit
Class 410	4 BEP		00	MTK Ltd aluminium body kit
Class 411	4 CEP		00	MTK Ltd aluminium body kit
Class 414	2 HAP		00	MTK Ltd aluminium body kit
Class 415	4 EPB		00	Phoenix/Branchlines kit
Class 416	2 EPB		00	Phoenix/Branchlines kit
Class 418	2 HAP		00	Phoenix/Branchlines kit
Class 419	Motor Luggage Van		00	MTK Ltd aluminium body kit
Class 420	4 BIG		00	MTK Ltd aluminium body kit
Class 421	4 CIG		00	MTK Ltd aluminium body kit
			0	Modern Motive Power kit
Class 423	4 VEP		00	MTK Ltd aluminium body kit
			0	Modern Motive Power kit
Class 442	Wessex Electric		00	MTK Ltd aluminium body kit
Class 445			00	MTK Ltd aluminium body kit
Class 466	Networker		00	Hornby Railways ready-to-run model
Class 491	4 TC Trailer Set		00	MTK Ltd aluminium body kit
Class 504	Bury 2-car	(P)	00	MTK Ltd aluminium body kit
Class 506	Glossop 3-car	(P)	00	MTK Ltd aluminium body kit
Class 508	Southern Region 4-car		00	MTK Ltd aluminium body kit

Index

Coogan 1M